CROSSING BORDERS

The Search For Dignity In Palestine

CHRISTA BRUHN

A MEMOIR

Thank you for being part of my journey to peace in Israel and Palestine!
♡ Christa ♡

LITTLE CREEK PRESS®
AND BOOK DESIGN
MINERAL POINT, WISCONSIN

Little Creek Press
5341 Sunny Ridge Road
Mineral Point, WI 53565

ORDERING INFORMATION
Quantity sales. Special discounts are available on quantity purchases by corporations, associations, and others. For details, contact info@littlecreekpress.com

Orders by US trade bookstores and wholesalers.
Please contact Little Creek Press or Ingram for details.

Printed in the United States of America

Cataloging-in-Publication Data
Names: Bruhn, Christa, author
Title: Crossing Borders. The Search for Dignity in Palestine
Description: Mineral Point, WI: Little Creek Press, 2023
Identifiers: LCCN: 2023906605 | ISBN: 978-1-955656-52-8
Subjects: BIOGRAPHY & AUTOBIOGRAPHY / Personal Memoirs

Book design by Mimi Bark and Little Creek Press

Cover art *Life Prevails* (1999) by Ismail Shammout (1930-2006)
Ismail Shammout (1930-2006) was one of Palestine's leading modernist painters who used symbols of Palestinian traditions and culture to construct a visual narrative of Palestinian nationalism. Ismail Shammout was forced at the age of 18 to flee from his birthplace of Lydd and take refuge in the refugee camp of Khan Younis in the Gaza Strip. *Life Prevails* (1999) illustrates the persistence of Palestinian life in spite of the oppressive and ruthless Israeli occupation of Palestine.

To all those, living and dead,
who have kept Palestine alive,
for those yet to return home,
for those yet to be born.

PART III: ROOTEDNESS

50th Commemoration of the Nakba, 1998-1999

PART IV: STEADFASTNESS

Al-Aqsa Intifada and the Collapse of Oslo, 2000-2007

Contents

PART III: ROOTEDNESS

50th Commemoration of the Nakba, 1998-1999

PART IV: STEADFASTNESS

Al-Aqsa Intifada and the Collapse of Oslo, 2000-2007

Contents

PART V: PERSISTENCE

60th Commemoration of the Nakba, 2008-2011

PART VI: PATIENCE

Longing for Palestine, 2012-2017

PART VII: RETURN

70th Commemoration of the Nakba, 2018

Maps and Illustrations

Author's Note

Crossing Borders is a personal narrative of my experience of Palestine based on what I have learned from others, witnessed myself, or imagined as possible. For historical material, I rely on those who have taken the time and have the expertise to delve into historical archives and documents, as well as those who have provided personal testimony to what they lived through. The sources I rely on as trustworthy and most accurate, though not all-encompassing, are listed in my references. They include both Palestinian and Israeli scholars, including the New Historians, who have challenged previous historical narratives of the events leading up to the founding of the State of Israel in 1948—what, for Palestinians, marks the beginning of an ongoing *Nakba*. I also rely on those, like me, who have engaged with the Question of Palestine through their own life journey and can shed light on a part of the world that deserves our immediate attention.

As an American of German ancestry, a specialist of Middle Eastern Studies, and the mother of three Palestinians, I approach the situation in Palestine through those three lenses but, most of all, as a human being trying to understand the humanity of historical and current realities. Note that I refer to places Palestinians hold dear as they would name them, including places that have been destroyed, in order to honor Palestinians' connection to their land and their own understanding of the space of their homeland. Moreover, most transcriptions of Arabic reflect the spoken Arabic dialect I learned in the village of Jalameh unless I am quoting a proverb or verse from the Quran and thus may vary from Modern Standard Arabic in spelling or pronunciation.

I also include a number of maps throughout this memoir to denote particular historical references or realities on the ground that may help the reader appreciate the ways in which borders have factored into my experience of Palestine. That said, it is clear from my decades of traveling there that for Israelis, Palestine is Israel, and for Palestinians, Israel is Palestine. The lines that have been drawn over the last century have only complicated that truth and remain one of the greatest challenges for the future. When two peoples call the same land home, attempting to carve it up only exacerbates historical and ongoing transgressions that stand in the way of either people living a life of dignity.

—Christa Bruhn

What is a homeland? Is it these two chairs that remained in this room for twenty years? The table? Peacock feather? The picture of Jerusalem on the wall? The copper lock? The oak tree? The balcony? What is a homeland? Khaldun? Our illusions about him? Fathers? Their sons? What is a homeland?

—*Return to Haifa,* Ghassan Kanafani

Map 1: Key Places I've Been (Source: United Nations)

PART I

HOMELAND

On the Eve of the First Intifada

1985-1986

1

Homecoming

I am studying in my father's homeland at the Albert-Ludwigs University in Freiburg, Germany, for my junior year abroad when my friends Fabiola and Marwan, both medical students, invite me to a birthday party. It is November 1985, four years before the fall of the Berlin Wall. As we enter the *Dachwohnung*—rooftop apartment, I meet the birthday boy, Salem, a Palestinian like Marwan, whose bright smile softens his towering stature in the dim lights. I extend my hand to him. *Herzlichen Glückwunsch zum Geburtstag!*—Happy Birthday! As we venture farther into the apartment, images of people rooted in the earth as an inseparable part of the land call out to me from paintings on the walls. Salem identifies himself as the artist and offers me a tour of his work. It includes poetry expressing a deep sadness and longing for Palestine. The pastel colors of his paintings fade into each other like the images of his people connected to the soil. His words evoke a consciousness in me of what is wrong with the world and how it could be different.

I already know that Marwan is from a village outside Jerusalem. He is an Israeli citizen, a Palestinian in a Jewish homeland. I learn that Salem, who is studying to become a medical assistant, is from Gaza, his family refugees from the city of Jaffa from which they fled in 1948 during Israel's War of Independence. The mass displacement of Palestinians from the cities and villages of Palestine would come to be called the Nakba—the Catastrophe. I also meet 'Isam, a Palestinian from the city of 'Akka.[1] It is confusing to me why Salem's family had to flee Jaffa, whereas 'Isam and Marwan's families got to stay in their homes in what became Israel. What sticks out in my mind as I listen to Salem's story is that he is stateless in his own homeland. As a student of International Studies, I am studying about war and conflict in the Middle East, but now, Palestine has a face. Salem, Marwan, and 'Isam are in Germany because their opportunities are limited in a Palestine that has become Israel—like Armenia in Turkey, swallowed within its borders but still breathing through the memory of its people.

Marwan plays Arabic music on an acoustic guitar, his face leaning into the footwork of his fingers. The delicate, unfamiliar sound creates tremors in my heart. Salem sits next to Marwan, singing in unison as his broad hands beat rhythmically against a *tableh*, a traditional Palestinian drum made of clay. Salem's intense gaze remains anchored on the floor in front of him as he follows the music with his hands. The fine outline of his jaw moves in sync with words I cannot understand.

Fabiola extends a hand to me, and we dance to the captivating rhythms, laughing into the night, while 'Isam claps his narrow hands to the beat of the drum. The visceral celebration of life in song, paintings, and poetry resonates within me. I have a window into a whole new world. Our circle of friends grows as we meet students from Afghanistan, who came to Germany as refugees to escape the Russian invasion, and from Sudan amidst civil war. Their stories burn a hole in my heart, igniting a passion for peace and justice.

Fabiola's family is from East Germany, so we connect around the deep personal relationships in the East that seem to make up for the lack of material goods that stand in such stark contrast to all the plenty, power, and individualism of the West. After I studied German that spring in Munich at the Goethe Institute, my father, a professor of German and specialist of East German prose, secured me a visa behind the Iron Curtain to visit his friends in East Germany—artists, writers, and musicians—where I also participated in a summer program at the university in Erfurt. There, I was steeped in its Marxist-Leninist worldview. In Berlin, crossing Checkpoint Charlie at Friedrichstraße, I locked my eyes on those of the border guards, wondering what it felt like to have the power to decide who could come and who could go, all the while feeling the privilege of having the right paperwork. Seeing both sides of the Iron Curtain, the affluent West with its bright lights and bold colors and the isolated East adorned with the ruins of World War II, I felt like I was passing between two worlds within the same homeland.

My childhood was marked by moving from place to place as my father climbed the professional ladder of academia. Though I was born in Virginia, where I could have become a Southern belle, we moved to Los Angeles, then New York City, and finally Detroit, where I witnessed the fallout of racism, discrimination, and poverty, so these stories of marginalization and loss feel all too familiar. Even as a child, I was aware of the devastation of the Native American communities of the Great Lakes—the Odawa, Potawatomi, and Ojibwa Nations, who call themselves Anishinabeg, the First People—that I was living on someone else's land.

Here I am at the age of 18 studying in Germany, my father's homeland, but I, too, feel like a foreigner. I pass as a German, but I don't feel German. I simply feel human, yet I live in a world where too many have lost their humanity. The battles of history have left much of the world desperate for dignity. Beyond the deprivation I have personally witnessed, I wonder if I inherited my father's loss of his homeland through the defeat of Nazi Germany, which forced him to build a new life and find a new home. I, too, am searching, wondering where I will ever feel at home.

In my newfound circle of friends, we converse in German, but our connection goes deeper. We are all searching our souls, wondering where we will end up and how we will make our way in this world. Where will our allegiance be? With our whole lives ahead of us, we ask ourselves, isn't humanity enough? As I explore the roots of my own identity in Germany, two seeds begin to sprout within me. How can I make a difference in this world full of division and displacement, struggle and suffering, and where do I belong?

In spring 1986, I travel with my friend Gudrun to Russia, the land of the enemy. Our fathers had studied together in their hometown of Kiel after the war. Now, Gudrun and I are both students in Freiburg in the same Russian class. As a student of Slavic Studies, she hopes to immerse herself in the rich cultural history of Eastern Europe. In contrast, my passion lies in understanding how the powerplay between the superpowers unfolds on the ground. We both have a keen desire to see Russia for ourselves, albeit with different ends in mind. For me, the Cold War is confusing. America claims to symbolize freedom and democracy, and yet the Soviet Union officially supports revolutionary movements around the world for freedom from oppression and imperialism, including the Palestinian struggle for self-determination.

The gap in both contexts between what each superpower says it stands for and how it governs and behaves around the world, feels like hypocrisy. Each wants to control the world, swallow as many countries as it can into its sphere of influence, using whatever means are at its disposal. Military might and economic development are clearly the weapons of this standoff, and yet it is also a war of words and ideology, like East Germany's naming the Berlin Wall the *Antifaschistischer Schutzwall*—Antifascist Protective Wall. Gudrun admires how disheartened I am by the arrogance of American foreign policy that forces other countries into submission, either militarily or economically, and the decades-old arms race intended to bring the Soviet Union to its knees.

Back in Freiburg, Gudrun and I share simple vegetarian meals and sink into our study of Russian. Some weekends, we visit her parents at their eco-friendly home at the edge of the city that is way ahead of its time, complete with solar panels and an organic garden that mirror her father's involvement in the up-and-coming Green Party. Her parents are intrigued by my passion to hold America accountable for its foreign policy as well as my growing interest in Palestine, a place they, until now, have only associated with the Biblical stories of their evangelical upbringing. Other days, the sheer magnitude of the world's problems seems to be more than I can bear, let alone solve.

On April 26, 1986, we are struck with the news of a meltdown at the Chernobyl nuclear facility near Kiev. The food supply across Europe is tainted with radiation such as milk and fresh produce. I can't help myself from eating some red currents from the local market, their bright red translucent glow almost a warning of the contamination. While riding my bike to volleyball, I get caught in the first rain nearly two weeks after the accident, said to be especially dangerous. I play and only later take a shower to wash off the radiation, hoping I have not subject myself to any serious health risks.

My junior year abroad is coming to a close. The May flowers are in full bloom, and I can't imagine returning to the US. Fortunately, I get the opportunity, along with my brother, Dieter, to take part in a year-long internship program through the Deutscher Akademischer Austauschdienst (German Academic Exchange Service) beginning in the fall. Over the summer, Salem invites us to visit him and his family in Gaza. The thrill of getting to see this far-off place races through my body. Dieter's eyes open wide with the excitement of this unexpected travel destination. When we call our parents to discuss the opportunity, my mother's voice is firm with concern. "I'm not sure that's a good idea. Is it safe?"

My father's high-pitched voice carries through the phone with delight at our adventurism. He tells us he has a Jewish colleague at the University of Michigan–Dearborn, whose daughter recently immigrated to Israel with her husband and children. Maybe we can visit them at their home in Jerusalem. This way, Dieter and I would get to spend time with both a Jewish and Palestinian family. Dieter and I look at each other. Just as our father's own professional goals and German identity led him halfway around the world and us as a family from one home to another, now, he is helping us—as a German—find a place to call home in Israel.

It is not long before my father arranges for our visit to the Browns in Jerusalem, where we will spend the first week, then continue to Gaza to visit Salem's family. Through these two families—one Jewish, one Palestinian—I can bypass the overarching facts and figures of the Israeli-Palestinian conflict and enter right into their living rooms. With a total of six weeks to travel, Dieter and I plan to do some exploring on our own. We find a guidebook with a map of Israel at a local bookstore and a basic Arabic language instruction booklet so we can learn a few words of Arabic to connect with Salem's family, and exchange some Deutsche Mark for Israeli shekels.

It is August, the hottest month of the year there, so I pack my bags with an assortment of cotton tops and long skirts. In the midst of all these preparations, I realize the most important thing for me to bring is an open mind and an open heart. What I don't know is that my soul will soon form deep roots in a place I will one day call home.

2

Jerusalem

The bus driver lets us out at the corner of a residential street in Jerusalem. Each carrying our own suitcases, Dieter and I make our way along a narrow sidewalk past bearded men hurrying down the street. I see their tall black hats and long curls dangling from their temples. Women in full-length skirts with their hair covered in simple kerchiefs pass by with young children. Teenage girls and even much younger girls are also wearing long skirts and long sleeves. Boys of all ages are dressed in black slacks and white dress shirts, a black cap secured over crew-cut hair with the same long curls as the men, and tassels hanging from their waists. I later learn the caps are called *yarmulke* or *kippah* and the tassels *tzitzit*, marking the four corners of the small cloak known as *tallit katan*, which remind the wearer of God's commandments.

In one alleyway, a group of boys plays with a ball, running about, their curls swaying away from their heads as they change direction. We approach a woman on the other side of the street to ask for directions, but she quickly turns away from us, shuffling her children ahead. We address two men walking toward us, but they simply bow their heads and lean forward, as if launching themselves for a race. I don't understand why no one will talk to or even look at us. How are we going to find the Browns?

We come to a corner that opens up into yet another world. The men in black hats and women in long skirts are less common. The buzz of cars zooming past in both directions and the subtle hum of conversation drowns out the serenity of the streets behind us. The next man we approach is wideset, his shirt unbuttoned at the top, his pale blue slacks held firm by a brown leather belt. His gentle eyes, almost hidden beneath dark bushy eyebrows, light up when we mention the street. He can hardly speak English but raises his thick arm and points ahead with his hefty hand, leaving us with an encouraging smile. Our pace quickens with the prospect of finding our destination.

My chest softens as I read the street sign and match the number on the piece of paper in my hand to the stone privacy wall before me. Pain shooting through my shoulders from carrying my suitcase dissipates with the promise of having a place to call home, even temporarily. We enter an opening in the wall. As we approach the front steps, a woman with dark curly shoulder-length hair comes out in capris and a fitted white t-shirt, a young boy with strawberry blonde hair hitched to her hip.

"Hey, you made it!" My shoulders relax at the first perfect American English we've heard since we arrived. "You must be Christa and Dieter! I'm Eleanor. This is my youngest, Benjamin. My husband, David, is still at work. He should be here shortly." She laughs when a little girl with soft brown curls creeps up behind her. "This is my big girl, Jessica." Benjamin squirms in his mother's arms when I gently poke his side. My fingers crawl up Jessica's back with one hand, and she twists and giggles, then buries her face in her mother's leg.

Eleanor invites us in. We carry our suitcases up the stone steps. The house looks ancient on the outside with its weathered stone façade and arched windows. I am surprised it is quite modern on the inside, with the living room open to the kitchen and dining area.

Eleanor points to the large wooden dining table. "Go ahead and set your stuff down and have a seat. You must be thirsty. Can I get you something to drink?"

"Sure!" Dieter's enthusiasm makes me forget for a moment how tired I am.

"That'd be great." My tongue is so dry it's sticking to the roof of my mouth.

"I bet you're hungry. How about a snack? Do you guys like hummus?" She pulls a Tupperware container out of the fridge. "I love it. It's like peanut butter in the States but better. We practically live off this stuff."

She sets a bottle of mango juice on the table and goes back to get some glasses. My mouth begins to water in anticipation of our snack. My body is already anchored in the wooden chair, so grateful to have a place to rest.

"So, how was your trip here? Did you have any trouble finding the house?" Dieter and I chuckle, then describe our passage through the neighborhood with the men in tall black hats. She laughs and explains that we must have stumbled upon the Hasidic neighborhood. "They pretty much keep to themselves. You'll find everything here. We love it." Eleanor goes on to tell us how she and her husband are struggling to learn Hebrew. They have a lot of American friends who are recent immigrants.

"Benjamin and Jessica, on the other hand, will grow up learning Hebrew in school. It will become second nature. They won't even have to think about it."

I find myself wondering about this American family who picked up and left the US to become Israelis. What life did they leave behind? What is it like to become someone else?

David arrives home, a slender man with thinning reddish-brown hair, a loose wiry beard and mustache, and wire-framed glasses. David extends his hand to each of us, then walks over to Benjamin in his highchair and kisses him on the cheek. He tousles Jessica's curly brown hair and kisses her on the head. We learn that David has his own frame shop nearby. Eleanor is an English teacher at a private Jewish school in West Jerusalem, the more modern Israeli part of the city. Bubbling like children, they urge us to go to the Old City as soon as we are up to it. It is hard to believe we are in this ancient city for the week, that we can walk out the door, and the Old City is practically at our doorstep. How does such a far-off place become so close?

The next morning, we do just that (see Map 2). Walk out the door, cross the road, and descend the amphitheater-like stairs to Damascus Gate. The arched opening towers over us like a castle, its ancient stone walls extending in both directions. The passageway is at first dark and narrow, like a maze packed tightly with people coming and going, then leads to an open area that slopes downward with tiny shops along the perimeter. Pants, dresses,

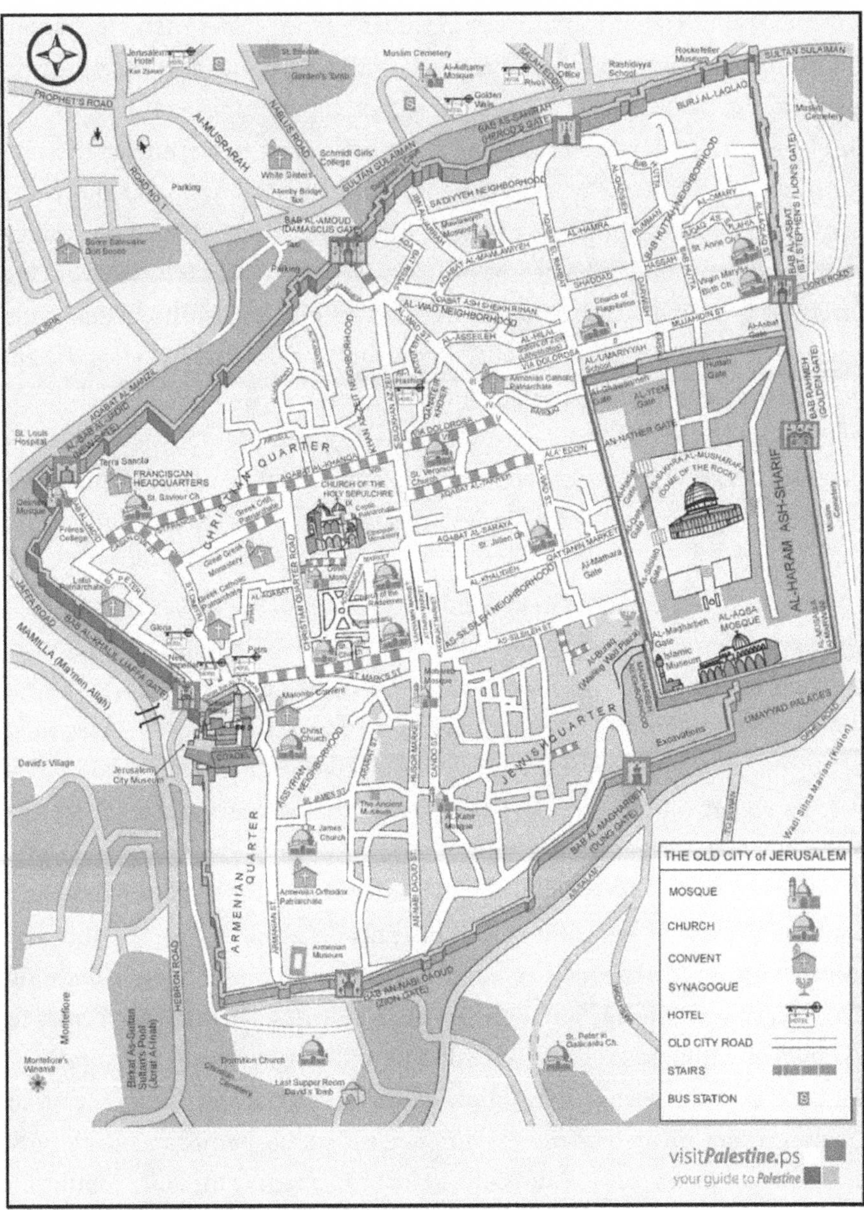

Map 2: The Old City of Jerusalem (Source: Visit Palestine)

scarves, and t-shirts dangle over doorways. Slender countertops display chopped tomatoes, colorful pickled vegetables, and various sauces. Young men scoop falafel into open fryers and shave roasted meat off giant vertical skewers, which I later learn is called shawarma. Arabic music is streaming from a shop filled with solid racks of cassette tapes. Older men are dressed in one-piece robes, their heads covered with long white scarves, others in Western shirts and slacks. Younger men sport tight-fitting jeans and t-shirts or sleek button-down shirts, their short black hair glistening in the late morning sun. Older heavyset women in long, black, embroidered dresses step carefully along the stone pathway, their heads covered in white scarves loosely wrapped under their chins. Younger women move in clusters wearing long Western-style dresses or pants with long-sleeve shirts, their heads covered in colorful scarves wrapped tightly under their chins. Now and then, we pass Western tourists speaking English, French, or German. At the bottom of the slope, two Israeli soldiers are standing against the wall in loose olive-green pants and black boots chatting in Hebrew as they scan the area from behind their dark sunglasses, their hands each gripping an M16 rifle across their chests.

We continue over stone weathered by centuries of footsteps into narrower passageways with tiny shop after tiny shop nestled in cave-like indentations. We step aside as a young boy maneuvers a wooden cart on bicycle wheels past us. Pyramids of fruits and vegetables meticulously arranged on wooden platforms tower above burlap sacks of chickpeas, lentils, rice, and spices. Farther ahead, we find hand-carved, olive wood camels and crèches, and ornately painted ceramic tiles.

Shopkeepers address us in English, competing for us to look at their wares. We want to see some of the historical sites we have read about in our travel guide before we buy anything, so we keep moving. We pass Via Dolorosa at one intersection, where Jesus is said to have carried the cross to his own crucifixion. It seems unreal to be walking by casually as a tourist. Without our map, we wouldn't know when we officially enter the Christian Quarter. There are no borders. The difference is subtle, perhaps more nativity scenes and crosses on display. We head for the Church of the Holy Sepulchre, where the resurrection of Jesus is said to have taken place. The closer we get to the church, the greater the display of olive wood crèches, crosses made out of silver or wood, hand-painted chalices, and rosary beads, along with an abundance of t-shirts, sundresses, and postcards.

I no longer feel like I need to look at the map. "We must be close! Look at all this stuff."

Dieter points to an open area ahead. "There's a bunch of people over there. That must be the entrance."

We reach a plaza scattered with tour groups and enter a large wooden door beneath an arch of stone. Across the threshold, it is so dark I have to blink my eyes until they adjust to the dim light peeking through the narrow, arched windows. It is much cooler inside, but the air is thick with incense. Ornate iron lanterns hang overhead from long chains. The church is like a maze, subdivided according to Armenian, Coptic, Ethiopian, Greek Orthodox, Roman Catholic, and Syriac Orthodox traditions. I feel like I am in a living museum with church caretakers, each sporting their respective attire. I think about how the Old City is also divided into sections, how empires and dynasties have fought over it for centuries, how Christians, Muslims, and Jews all feel a deep religious connection to the same place, and how two peoples call it home.

We step back outside into the blazing sun. I force my eyes open enough to walk into the shade, and then we continue on the main pathway past shops selling menorahs, candles, pendants with Hebrew writing, and dreidels. Hasidic Jews, some with their wives and children, make their way through the passageway. Signs over doorways are written in Hebrew and English. We must be in the Jewish Quarter. We peer down from an opening like a balcony onto the Western Wall, where Jews come to pray and tuck notes to God into the cracks of the only remaining wall of Solomon's Temple. Men in long black coats and black top hats face the wall and bob their heads, their side curls bouncing forward and backward. Other men in Western dress are wearing caps on their heads. I spot a few Hasidic boys dressed like their fathers, bobbing their tiny heads toward the wall. There are a few women in a separate area, some in long dresses with their hair covered in scarves tied behind their necks, some with younger versions of themselves nearby.

We keep walking along the main passageway until we reach another colossal gate of the Old City. We are starving and walk up to a falafel stand and order two sandwiches.

"What would you like on them?" The young man's accent is similar to the airport security guards, only friendlier.

I scan the array of toppings. "I'll have tomatoes, lettuce, and tahini sauce."

Dieter is more adventurous. "You can put everything on mine."

I gaze at the gate behind us, then back at the man as he squishes several pieces of falafel into a loaf of pita bread. "So what gate is this?"

"Jaffa Gate, the entrance to the Jewish Quarter. How do you like our city?" He adds my toppings and hands me my sandwich.

"This is our first day here. It's beautiful, though a bit confusing."

He presses falafel into the next loaf. "It is easy once you spend some time here."

Dieter and I look at each other and laugh, not sure whether to believe him. Dieter watches him bury the falafel in pickles, tomatoes, lettuce, and tahini sauce. "We'll be here all week, so maybe you're right. I guess we'll find out."

"Here you are."

He hands a sandwich to Dieter, who immediately takes a bite. "Thank you! Fantastic!"

I follow suit, savoring the warm falafel and cool vegetables. "This is really delicious!"

The passageway looks darker now that the sun is lower in the sky. Dieter and I look at our map. We have basically cut across the entire Old City. My legs are not sure they want to carry me all the way back, but somehow the way back feels faster. We are anxious to get home before dark. At one of the shops we passed by earlier, Dieter spots a mosaic chess set inlaid with mother-of-pearl in a glass case. He manages to bargain the shopkeeper down to half price. With our package visible, other shopkeepers invite us into their shops, some offering us a cup of tea.

Dusk is setting in. We need to get back to Damascus Gate and head home. I still can't believe we just spent the day in one of the oldest, most contentious cities in the world, wandering around like children in a maze.

Just minutes after we leave the Old City through Damascus Gate, we are back at the familiar stone privacy wall. Eleanor is in the kitchen finishing up dinner. Her face lights up. "Hey! How are you guys?"

"Great, but our feet are tired!" I sigh with relief that we can finally rest.

Dieter chimes in. "Really cool. The best part was bargaining with the shopkeepers." Dieter sets his chess set on the table, opening it so they can examine it. David congratulates Dieter on getting a good price.

Recounting our day, I forget for a moment how tired I am. "We also had falafel sandwiches for lunch over by Jaffa Gate. They were delicious!"

David's eyes brighten. "I love falafel. Two of the best foods here are falafel and hummus. Well, it sounds like you guys are off to a good start."

Eleanor explains that she will be getting off work early the day after tomorrow. "How about I take you guys to the Holocaust Museum in the afternoon. It's really powerful. Then we can wander around West Jerusalem."

I look at Dieter, and we nod our heads. "Sure. That sounds perfect."

The next day, we explore new directions in the Old City until we reach tinier passageways filled only with light and shadow, some with narrow staircases leading up out of sight. We reach the Armenian Quarter, filled with displays of hand-painted ceramics with gorgeous floral patterns outlined in black. I wonder if those who live here are the descendants of survivors of the Armenian genocide slaughtered to make room for a Turkish state. Perhaps Jerusalem is their home away from home. Now, Jews, Christians, and Muslims are all going about their business within these ancient walls, sharing the same space. I wonder what it is like to live in this ancient city. On the surface, it seems so balanced, peaceful, and respectful, as if everyone were welcome. And yet I wonder about the differences that divide people. *Don't we have more in common than what separates us?*

Back at the house, we relay another day's worth of adventures over dinner. David shifts the conversation. "So, you guys are students?"

Dieter starts off. "I actually just graduated from college in International Studies with Econ and German, but Christa and I are both about to start an internship in Germany. I'll be in Bielefeld and Christa in Darmstadt."

I chime in. "I just finished my junior year abroad in Freiburg."

"That's cool. Then you'll go back to the States?" Eleanor wipes her son's face with his bib and hands him a sippy cup, which he grabs with both hands.

"I'm not sure when I'm going back. I have to go back sometime to finish my undergrad."

David turns to me. "So, what are you studying?"

"I'm also doing international studies, but with political science and German. I just took a course in Germany on the civil war in Lebanon."

David's eyes widen. "No kidding. I actually recently served in the war in Lebanon."

"Really?" I gasp, then catch my breath. "What was that like?"

"I had mixed feelings about it at the time, but I realize now we had to get involved. It's really a mess there, but Israel's a small country. We are vulnerable to attack."

I am trying to imagine this small man fighting in a war. It feels so abstract. Lebanon is Israel's neighbor to the north. It's hard to believe what I was studying is happening right here. And that this nice American family is Israeli now. They are directly involved in the war.

"What about right here at home? What about the Palestinians?"

David's face becomes firm, though his eyes are friendly. "It's complicated. We want to live here in peace, but we're always facing a threat, either from the inside or the outside."

I am only a couple of days away from heading to Gaza. I can't help but wonder who is threatening whom.

David's attention also shifts to Gaza. "So, what about your friend? What's he doing in Gaza?"

"He's Palestinian. His family lives there. They are refugees from Jaffa."

David's eyes become glass, his face still. "Oh, I didn't realize you were going to visit a Palestinian."

Eleanor probes further. "Wow, that's unusual. How did you arrange that?"

"We met him in Freiburg. He lives there with his wife, who is German. He's studying to become a radiology technician. He's going to visit his family."

Eleanor is taking in what I'm saying. "Well, that should be an interesting trip. And you're staying there how long?"

"Five weeks, at least that's when we're flying back."

"Well, you guys should come back and see us. You don't need to stay there the whole time. That's a long time to be in Gaza."

David raises his eyebrows. "Yeah, I'm not sure there's a lot to do there."

Dieter sounds encouraged. "Sure, we could come back and see you guys. You're like family now." His comment sets everyone off laughing. We do, after all, share the same last name.

I join in laughing. "You know, 'Bruhn' is actually low German for 'Brown,' so it's not far from the truth." I turn to Eleanor. "And besides, our fathers teach at the same university. So, we have to come back. Then we can tell you all about what it's like in Gaza."

Eleanor gets up from the table. "Well, I have to get the kids to bed, but let's plan on West Jerusalem tomorrow. How about I pick you guys up at noon, and we stop by so you can see David's shop on the way to West Jerusalem?"

David's face softens. "That would be fine."

We help clear the table and retire to our room. Dieter is already dozing off, but my mind is racing. "I can't believe he was in the war. I just wasn't expecting that." I don't know what I was expecting. I guess it makes sense for those who become Israeli. They end up serving in war if they are needed. *But there are Palestinians in Lebanon, refugees from Palestine. Don't they just want to come home? How did everything get so messed up in the first place?* I feel heavy, my body sinking into the sofa bed. Tomorrow, the Holocaust Museum and West Jerusalem.

Dieter and I stay home in the morning to pack for our trip to Gaza. We only have two more days. By the time we have breakfast and get ready to go, Eleanor dashes into the house for some extra diapers, and we all head out the door. We drive a short distance to David's shop. It is on a corner in a newer stone building with large windows. When we enter the shop, a bell on the door jingles. David is working at a large table toward the back of the shop, his eyes focused on his hands. On the wall behind the front counter is a whole collection of frame samples neatly arranged in rows by color and style. I find myself thinking this shop could be anywhere, but it's right here in Jerusalem, one of the oldest cities in the world.

"So, this is my shop." David's eyes move to the worktable. "This is where I do most of my work."

My eyes scan the framed art and photos on the wall. "You've got quite a setup here. It looks like you do just about anything."

David shifts his attention to a customer, who also speaks perfect American English, then rejoins our conversation. "So, you're all off to the Holocaust Museum? I haven't been there in some time. It's pretty amazing."

Eleanor motions us to the door. "I want to drive them by my school, too, to show them where I work. School is not in session now, but we are getting ready for the school year."

"Well, I'll see you all tonight. Enjoy yourselves."

The farther we get from the shop, the wider the roads become. The rough stone buildings and houses with arched windows give way to sleek modern buildings with smooth stone surfaces and squared panes of glass.

Eleanor is our tour guide. "Every building in Jerusalem must be covered with Jerusalem stone. It's the law." Their sleek modern design doesn't have the charming character of the older buildings. I think of how many centuries the older stone has withstood.

"So, this is West Jerusalem. We are coming up on my school right now. It's just up there." Eleanor points to a hill off to the right. Farther ahead, she pulls into a large parking lot. "Here we are." She unloads the stroller and buckles Benjamin in with Jessica by her side.

Eleanor leads the way toward a large cream-colored building covered in Jerusalem stone. The exhibition halls are organized chronologically, beginning well before the Holocaust with archeological evidence of habitation in the area, particularly ancient Israel. The exhibits cover the various conquests until the 20th century. Now, the focus is on building the modern State of Israel with photographs of Theodor Herzl addressing Jews in Europe about the need to settle in the ancient Land of Israel, followed by photos of early Jewish immigrants coming to Palestine to work the land on *kibbutzim* to "make the desert bloom."[2]

We walk past cases with historical documents of support from individuals and governments for Jews to settle in Palestine. A whole area is dedicated to the persecution of Jewish communities in Europe, from the pogroms in Eastern Europe to the culminating central exhibit of Jewish persecution under Nazi Germany. Enormous images of Hitler addressing crowds of Germans, German propaganda posters igniting anti-Semitism, legal measures taken against Jews in Germany, Kristallnacht when Nazi forces smashed the windows of Jewish businesses and synagogues throughout Germany, and Hitler's Final Solution of sending Jews to their deaths in train cars to concentration camps. Haunting images of mass graves found after the war are juxtaposed against desperate attempts of survivors to flee only to find closed borders in other countries.

This vast testimony of Jewish suffering takes a turn with celebratory images of ships carrying Jews from Europe arriving in the port of Jaffa to start a new life. The exhibit culminates in the War of Independence when Jewish militias fight against neighboring Arab armies after Arab nations reject the United Nations' call to divide Palestine into two states. David against Goliath. Jewish militias led by Menachem Begin, leader of Irgun, and David Ben-Gurion, leader of Haganah, manage to secure areas promised to the Jews and declare the State of Israel on May 14, 1948. Overnight, militia leaders become statesmen as the United Nations welcomes them as the leaders of a nation among nations.

I have seen exhibits about the Holocaust in Germany and elsewhere, but these are presented from the perspective of the State of Israel, with Jews telling their own history and making the compelling case for the State of Israel as the one and only safe haven for the Jewish people. The subsequent wars in 1956, 1967, and 1973, as well as conflicts with neighboring Lebanon and Syria, would cast doubt on how safe and secure the State of Israel would be for the Jewish people in the future. And yet Israel manages to win war after war and even make peace with neighboring countries Egypt and Jordan.

As I study the exhibits and trace the history of this young nation, my heart sinks into my stomach at the mention of Palestinians as "Arabs" lumped together into "aggressors," casting a shadow on the future of the State of Israel. I become fixated on the power of words to favor one people over another. It all sounds so noble, so righteous, and yet the entire display leaves out the reality that Palestinians were already living on that land. As Jews established the State of Israel, Palestinians like Salem's family became refugees, and others like 'Isam and Marwan's families became foreigners in their own homeland. As we head through the exit, I realize there may be as many stories about the world as there are people, yet I begin to wonder how and where the Palestinian story is told.

After the museum, Eleanor takes us to the shopping district in West Jerusalem lined with wide sidewalks and one glass-front shop after another like a slideshow of modernity with chic outfits on mannequins and sleek furniture.

I feel worlds away from the narrow passageways of the Old City. We pass a restaurant with tables set out on the sidewalk. Eleanor invites us to have something to drink. We find an empty table next to a group of soldiers sitting with their M16s hanging loosely off their shoulders. Leaning back in their seats, they are laughing like they don't have a care in the world. I can't take my eyes off their rifles and olive-green uniforms, which stand out in complete juxtaposition to their laughter.

Eleanor lifts Jessica onto her lap. "You see, this is totally different than the Old City."

I don't dare ask about the soldiers. "No kidding."

"Definitely, there's not as much character here. It's more like the US. Stuff is quite pricey, too. You can get pretty much anything if you are willing to pay for it."

We finish our drinks and continue down the street, leaving the soldiers behind us. It feels a bit overwhelming, going from ancient stone to modern glitz. Pressure is building in my head trying to put the two worlds together in my mind. After an hour of window shopping, we head home. I can't wait to go to bed and close my eyes, giving my mind a rest from the dichotomies of the day.

It is our last day in Jerusalem. Dieter and I are eager to spend it in the Old City. The narrow passageways, stone walls, and tiny arched doorways feel familiar now. Perhaps if I walk down every nook and cranny, I will carry this ancient city with me even after we leave. As we head back to the Browns, I buy some scarves to wear around my shoulders when I am in Gaza just in case my short-sleeve or sleeveless shirts are inappropriate for the local culture. We also stop at a cart selling logs of sesame, peanuts, and coconut pressed together with honey. We take one for Salem's family and one for the Browns to thank them for being such gracious hosts and welcoming us into their chaotic lives of work, school, and parenthood.

The day is turning to dusk. As we pass through Damascus Gate for the last time, several heavyset women in long, black dresses decorated with embroidery, their heads covered loosely with long, white scarves, are seated just outside the gate selling fresh mint, parsley, and sage arranged neatly on large trays. One calls out to passersby as she points to her bundles. When a man hands her some change, her eyes light up for a moment as she retrieves a pouch from inside her neckline to deposit the change, then tucks it away, switching her attention toward the people leaving the Old City. Maybe she will get a few more customers before dark.

The week feels like a lifetime, with so many new sights, sounds, and scents. We spend a final evening with the Browns, then get to bed early. As I lie in the dark, I reflect on this young American family that has made Israel their home. Tomorrow we are headed to Gaza to a family who lost their home in the making of the State of Israel. My brain struggles to reconcile these entangled histories. My eyes close as I try to anticipate an entirely different world.

3

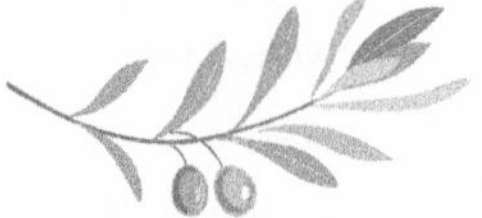

Arrival

Dieter and I walk past the privacy wall around the Browns' house that has become our home in Jerusalem. We cross the main road to the vast parking lot filled with taxis just outside Damascus Gate. We hear a taxi driver call out *Ghazzi!* in the distance. "You want to go to Gaza?" The slant in his eyebrows matches the skepticism in his voice when we approach him.

My eyes meet his in full confidence. "Yes, we are visiting a friend there."

The taxi driver secures our suitcases onto racks on top of the taxi with rope while we climb into the back of the yellow Mercedes limousine with three rows of seats. Others join us, and after a few minutes, the car is full. The other passengers smile at us as if going to Gaza for a visit gives us special status. After all, what foreigners would want to go to Gaza except relief workers? Even though we are going to visit a Palestinian family, I plan to visit the international organization Save the Children while I am there, hoping to better understand the conditions on the ground.

In about an hour, we arrive at the entrance to the Gaza Strip, where a metal gate is blocking the road. The passengers are suddenly quiet when an Israeli soldier walks over to the driver's window and asks to see everyone's ID. When the soldier sees our American passports, he motions for us to get out of the taxi. My stomach tightens at the prospect of having to talk to soldiers. Dieter and I stand there in the morning sun as one of them flips through the pages of our passports, then calls other soldiers over in Hebrew. A flood of questions washes over us. *Why are you going to Gaza? How long will you stay? Who are you visiting? How do you know them? Where are you coming from?* My stomach tightens more as they carry on a muffled exchange in Hebrew, repeatedly looking over in our direction.

I breathe easier when they hand Dieter back his passport until I reach for mine, and one of the soldiers tells me in English, "Just a minute, please." Dieter and I look at each other while the soldier flips through the pages again before launching another round of questions. *What were you doing in East Germany? Why did you go to Russia? Why are you going to Gaza? Is this your first visit to Gaza?* I explain that we are visiting a friend here, that I traveled as a student from Germany to Russia on vacation and to East Germany with my father, who is a professor of German. They discuss my answers amongst themselves in Hebrew. After all, it is the Cold War. What was I doing behind the Iron Curtain? Relief washes over me when the soldier hands me back my passport and opens the gate. The taxi pulls through. Now, we are in Gaza.

The taxi follows a narrow, two-lane road, the area along the road unpaved and sandy. The road is lined with makeshift sheet metal shacks, some lined with stacks of tires with men working on old cars I don't recognize. They are small and mostly white, almost like toy cars that have been played with for many years. Are they French? Russian? Why are they so old? I find out later they are all Subarus, the only car company Israel allowed to import into the Occupied Territories at the time.

Along the way, the taxi driver points out a road that runs parallel to ours. "This only for Jews." He is referring to a Jewish-only road that cuts through the Gaza Strip to provide Jewish settlers direct access to 14 Jewish settlements in the Gaza Strip[3] (see Map 3). *A road only for Jews? Like drinking fountains for "COLORED" and "WHITE" during segregation in the US.* Separate roads and the seizure of Palestinian land for Israeli settlements mean that the overcrowded conditions in the Gaza Strip are only made worse for people who already lost their homeland in Israel's War of Independence in 1948. I find out later that Salem's mother's family is among those whose land Israel seized in order to build the Gush Katif settlements.

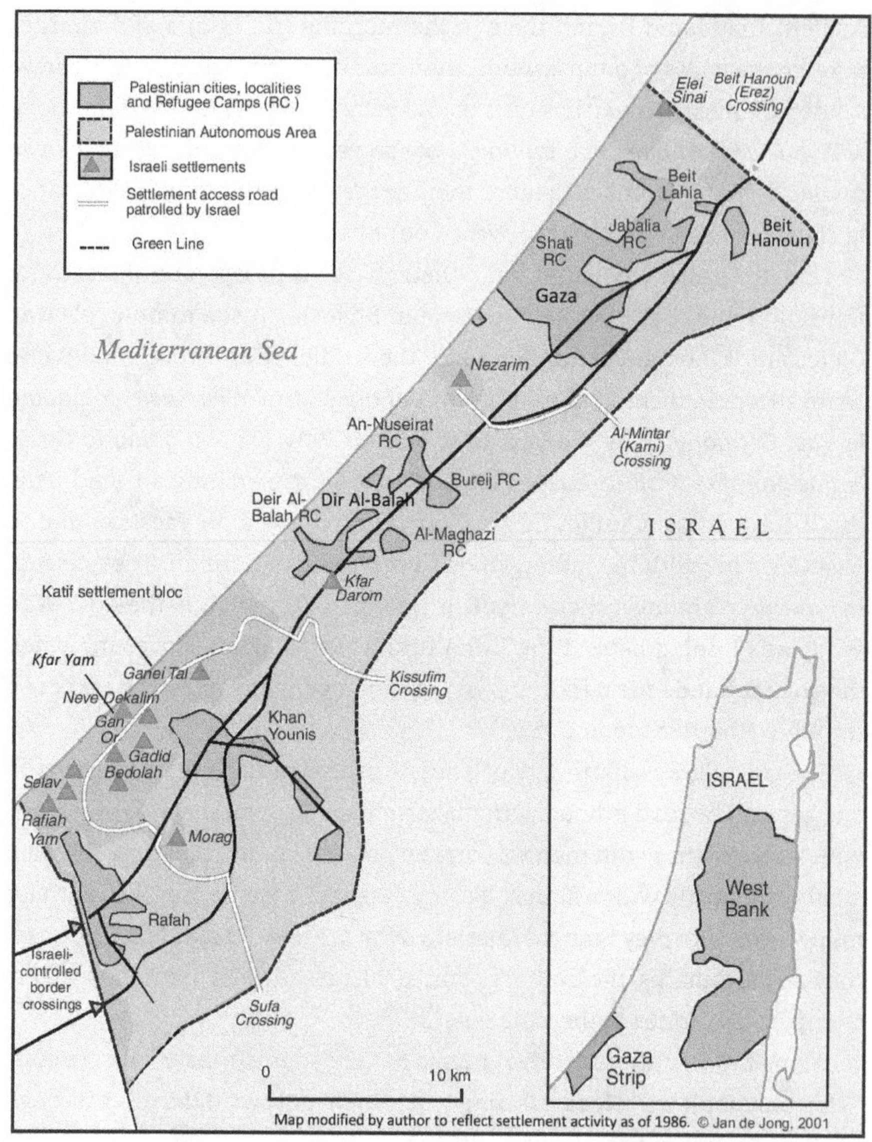

Map 3: Gaza Strip with Existing Settlements, 1986 (Source: PASSIA)

Farther ahead, we approach Gaza City, where wide sidewalks meet square, mostly two-story concrete buildings. The first-floor storefronts are completely open, like larger modern versions of the shops we had seen in the Old City in Jerusalem. Wares are stacked from floor to ceiling, some spilling out onto the sidewalk, painted metal shutters folded to the side. People of all ages are everywhere, walking up and down the sidewalks, even in the street, some carrying bundles of black plastic bags. Most women and girls have their hair covered with a scarf tightly wrapped under their chin. An older woman is wearing a long black dress with red embroidery down the front, a long white scarf trailing down her back as she balances a large metal tub on her head, the contents hidden by cloth. Heavyset, her weight shifts left and right as she walks, one hand steadying her load, the other at her side. Tiny cars are parked along the street and driving in both directions, horns beeping incessantly. The taxis are all yellow Mercedes limousines like ours.

We tell the driver we need to get to the main road—Omar Mukhtar Street—near the hotel close to the Mediterranean Sea. There we will ask for Salem's family by name. We have no address, just a street, a landmark, and a name. The driver pulls up in front of the hotel, though it doesn't look any different than any of the other buildings. I thank him in Arabic with *Shukran* as he sets our suitcases on the sidewalk.

The first few people we approach look puzzled and shrug their shoulders. I can hear the desperation in my voice, scorched with thirst in the afternoon sun. *How will we find Salem's family?* We are relieved when a young man's eyes light up in recognition of the family name, so we follow him into a narrow passageway just off the main road. A solid block of two-story houses extends in both directions, with a trickle of water running down a gutter in the middle of the passageway. Children, thin and mostly barefoot, are playing about.

They peer at us, whispering and laughing, their bright teeth a sea of sparkling smiles. Some of them call out to us in English, giggling. "Hello!" Their warm energy softens the surroundings. The name of the relief organization I plan to visit comes to mind. *Save the Children.*

The young man leads us to a pale-green metal doorway with two concrete steps and knocks. Someone calls out from behind the double doors, and then the right door panel squeaks open. A tall, lanky teenage boy with a square chin leans out. We hesitate. We don't see Salem anywhere. *Are we in the right place?* The boy beckons us to come inside, his eyes wide and friendly, so we step forward, squeezing our suitcases through the narrow opening into a large room with a tile floor open to the sky. In the distance, a lemon tree hangs over a green cinderblock wall.

A sea of eager faces welcomes us. Two women in long dresses step forward, their hair loosely covered with scarves tied at the nape of their necks. They greet us profusely in Arabic, kissing my cheeks, then extending a hand to Dieter. One is a tall pregnant woman with a slender face and sullen eyes, the other an older woman, much shorter and full-figured with a smile as wide as the sea. A number of children surround them. The two women invite us to sit down on large rectangular mats beneath the shade of the lemon tree. We slip off our shoes, and I scrounge for the few words I know in Arabic. I say hello—*Marhaba*. I thank the pregnant woman who offers us a cold drink—*Shukran*. She answers with a soft smile. *Afwan*—You're welcome. The older woman lifts her heavy arms and waves her open hands as she speaks. My self-study of the alphabet is no match for the blur of sounds falling on my ears. Out of words, Dieter and I simply smile and nod our heads.

The bright sun fills the open courtyard. My eyes dash about the interior of the house to find a makeshift chicken coop with several reddish-brown chickens pecking at the floor. Light streams into a tiny room from a narrow window illuminating a single burner over a propane tank. Across from us, next to the kitchen, is a large room with mats on the floor and another in the back corner with a bed in the center, between them a small television on a metal stand. Above us is an overhang with a second floor, but I don't see any stairs. I later learn that another family lives there, and two more on the other side of the wall that cuts the courtyard in two. *One house divided into four.*

I suddenly realize I need to go to the bathroom. The pregnant woman reads my mind as I get to my feet. She leads me to a simple wooden door and points to a pair of black plastic flip-flops on the floor. I slide my bare feet into them, then slowly open the door and peer inside. I don't see a toilet anywhere—just a large hole in the floor. I catch my breath at the stench of raw sewage. It is a tight space with no window, just a dim, naked bulb hanging from the low ceiling. I cringe as I duck my head slightly to step inside. I want to hold my breath but finally am forced to inhale the noxious air. I latch the door.

I examine the room more closely. The hole in the floor has two grooved platforms on either side to place my feet. I briefly consider whether to face the wall or the door. I decide to face the door. I pull up my long, light-blue cotton skirt, gather the fabric in front of me, pull down my underwear, and squat down. I wince when the urine splashes onto my feet as it hits the perimeter. I can hear a gurgling sound echoing below me as the urine finds its way down the hole.

I look around for toilet paper, but all I find is a plastic jug of water. *Am I supposed to wash myself?* I reach my hand into the narrow top, then quickly wipe myself with my wet hand. I don't feel clean, so I reach in again. Shame washes over me that I put my dirty hand into the jug. Later, I realize I should pour the water into my hand to clean myself. I stand up to pull up my underwear, feeling it blot dry my wet body, then let my skirt fall to my sides. I turn around in vain, looking for a handle to push or a cord to pull to flush. I pour the rest of the water down the hole to rinse the area. There is no faucet to refill it, so I simply set it back down.

I am finally done with this peculiar process. I slowly open the door, the bright sun blinding me, relieved to leave the smell of sewage behind. I feel awkward walking out into the courtyard with a dampness between my legs. Eager to wash my hands, I slip off the flip-flops and walk toward a single faucet, the handle like a mini propeller. I grab the bar of soap from a steel dish and rub my hands together vigorously, as if to wash away the memory of the toilet. The water, cool and refreshing, splashes over my hands into the concrete square below. The pregnant woman hands me a towel hanging on a line overhead. When I sit back down, my eyes reconnect with theirs, a sea of smiles between us. I take a deep breath. This is my new home.

4

Beach

It seems like forever until Salem appears in the narrow doorway, filling it completely. He glows like an angel in his white button-down shirt and white cotton pants, the brightness of his clothes in stark contrast to his dark hair. His teeth gleam in the sun as he welcomes us.

I learn that the pregnant woman is his sister Salwa, the tall boy who first opened the door is his brother Salim, the shy girl is his sister Sahar, the boy who speaks with his eyes is Salwa's son Mohammed, and the two younger children are his siblings Miriam and Yusef. Salem has two more sisters, Sana and Sumaya, who are both married. He is the oldest.

It is early afternoon. Salem shows me his parents' room, where I will be staying. I feel shy to take the only room with a bed, but Salem assures me everyone else is fine to sleep on mats in the side room or under the stars in the courtyard. There is a metal locker in the corner with a shelf where I can keep my jewelry and toiletries and a dresser across from the bed. I look out the open window through iron bars—no glass, no screen—framed with lime-green metal shutters, the dazzling blue shimmer of the Mediterranean Sea visible in the distance, like a mirage in the open stretch of sand and concrete.

Back in the courtyard, Salem says something to Salim, who then dashes out the door, returning moments later with a couple of oil-stained brown paper bags steaming with falafel. I bite into one of the crispy reddish-brown balls, sinking my teeth into the moist yellowish-green center. Unlike the falafel sandwiches Dieter and I ate in Jerusalem, this is the first time I eat falafel by itself, and I savor every aromatic bite. Moments later, the bags are empty. I am wishing we had another bag when Salem asks Dieter and me if we'd like to go for a swim. Sitting in the hot August sun, the thought of going swimming sounds delightful.

I close the door to my room to put on my aqua-green string bikini under my cotton skirt and t-shirt. Salem hands us a couple of towels, then picks up a large umbrella and a bulky thermos and heads for the door. We walk into the narrow passageway and around the house past my window toward the sea. The concrete path gives way to sand-covered ground, the grains making their way into the cork footbed of my Birkenstock sandals. Once the glistening blue waves of the sea fill my eyes, I slip off my sandals and let my bare feet sink into the warm sand. My whole body relaxes in anticipation of the sea.

A group of girls in long, dark dresses are wading in the water near the shore, holding onto each other and giggling as the waves crash against their legs. Their dresses, clinging to their sea-soaked legs, swish out to sea and back again with each crashing wave. Their hair peeks out of loose-fitting headscarves blowing in the salty sea air. In the other direction, a group of teenage boys wearing shorts and no shirts chase each other on the beach while other boys play in the water up to their chests, splashing in the waves. Salem sets down the thermos, opens the umbrella, and anchors the pole into the sand. No sooner do we set down our towels than Dieter is taking off his t-shirt and shorts, revealing his Speedo racing suit underneath.

I look at the girls, then turn to Salem, addressing him in German. *Bist du sicher, daß ich meine Kleidung ausziehen kann?*—Are you sure I can take off my clothes?

Sicher—Sure.

Given how the girls are dressed, I am surprised there is no hesitation in his voice. What felt normal in Germany suddenly feels out of place. I override my apprehension and let my skirt fall to the sand, holding my thighs tightly together. Then after glancing around me, I slide my arms out of my thin cotton shirt and place it on my skirt.

Salem turns toward the sea. *Geh mal?*—Shall we?

Also gut—Okay, fine. Dieter and I follow his footsteps. I have never felt so exposed.

We approach the crashing waves, the hot air and bright sun warming my body. Some of the boys call out to us in Arabic, but Salem silences them with a few words and shoos them away. Dieter immediately dives into a wave, then reemerges swimming freestyle. I am surprised when my feet touch the water that the sea is as warm as bath water. I proceed until the water is to my waist, holding myself steady against the choppy waves. I feel so alive with the waves pushing against me and the sun and wind on my face. I let my body melt into the sea, releasing my feet from the firm sand below, leaning my head back until I am floating.

The gentle tug of the waves carries me like a child, my legs stretched out, as if extending for the first time after birth. I brace myself as I plunge underwater and return to the surface, allowing the water to stream off my face before opening my eyes. I embrace the contrast between the soft waves and the stinging salt. Floating freely under the bright Mediterranean sky, the whole world seems at peace. I flip onto my stomach to swim breaststroke, gazing at the wide-open sea as the waves brush against my chin. My eyes close tightly when the saltwater splashes onto my face, seeping into my eyes and mouth. I blink to soothe the burn and run my tongue against my teeth until the intensity of the salt dissipates.

Salem points out a shipwreck in the distance. I peer closely at the sea but see only waves. When I steady my gaze, I notice a dark protrusion coming out of the water at an angle, appearing and disappearing with each wave. Salem tells us the ship crashed during a storm when he was little and has been sinking deeper into the sea ever since. Teenagers love to swim out and dive off the structure. I imagine teenage boys making broad strokes underwater along the ship's sharp edges, then shudder at the thought of them balancing on metal beams amidst the rough water. We swim a while longer, then get out for a drink of water, taking turns tipping the thermos spout over our mouths. The cool water is refreshing. For the first time, I understand the distinction in German between *Salzwasser*—salt water and *Süßwasser*—sweet water.

Closer to shore, a man with graying hair and a loose shirt walks past us carrying a Styrofoam box hanging from a strap around his neck filled with pale-yellow beans called *turmis*. Salem hands him some change and takes a bag. I watch him hold one of the beans between his thumb and forefinger, then pinch gently until the bean slides out of a sheer skin. He pops the bean into his mouth, discarding the skin onto the sand. I take one of the cool beans and press it firmly between my fingers until the bean begins to slide, then quickly bring it to my mouth. It is wet and smooth, slightly salty at first, then almost nutty in flavor. Now, I am thirsty for more water. By the time we finish our snack, we are dry from the warm wind. We take down the umbrella, slip our clothes back on, and head home.

Back at the house, Salem shows me to the tiny kitchen where I can rinse off. There is no sink, only a simple faucet in the wall and a shower head hanging straight from the ceiling over a drain in the floor. I place my clothes at the edge of one of the shelves lined with neatly stacked metal dishes and an assortment of aluminum pots and pans, then turn the knob, and a trickle of water falls to the floor. There is only cold water, but it doesn't matter. It is so hot out that it feels refreshing. I place my body between the trickle of cool water and the shelves, trying not to splash the dishes. When I turn off the water, it disappears into a drain in the floor. I put my clothes back on, careful not to let my skirt touch the wet tile.

After I return to the courtyard, Salem's sister Salwa makes tea and brings out a tray with a teapot, tiny glasses, and a bowl of sugar. She pours a small amount of tea into one glass and swirls it around, then pours it from glass to glass, then back into the teapot to warm the glasses before she fills them so they don't shatter. I realize later she is warming the glasses so they don't shatter. She puts two spoons of sugar in each cup. I watch the sugar swirl around the amber liquid and settle at the bottom until it dissolves and disappears. Yusef wants to drink, but it is too hot, so Salwa pours the tea from one cup to another until it is cool enough to drink.

Later in the evening when I go to the bathroom, I gasp to find dozens of giant beetles scurrying across the walls and floor. I have never seen such enormous beetles. I turn on the light overhead, and they scurry out of sight like magic. Light is my friend at this hour. As long as the light is on, I can go to the bathroom in peace. I shudder as I enter, looking frantically for stragglers. Unfortunately, my shadow is enough to invite some of them out of hiding. I sway my body back and forth to let the light fall beneath my squatting legs to keep the beetles at bay.

It has been a long first day. Salem's brother Salim lies down on one of the mats in the open courtyard. Dieter follows suit. The rest of the family go lie down on mats in the other room. When I go to bed, I lie awake for some time, thoughts of my first day swirling in my mind as a pleasant breeze from the sea comes through my window. Suddenly, I hear scratching sounds coming from the locker, as if something is scurrying about. It sounds bigger than beetles. Then I hear gnawing. I fall asleep, wondering with whom I am sharing this space. In the morning, I find my toothbrush all chewed up at the edges but block out the sounds from the night before. I flinch when I have to brush my teeth, first rinsing off the brush under the cold water, rubbing my fingers over the rough spots. My stomach turns as the rough edges scrape the inside of my cheeks.

Later in the week, Dieter and I wake up to find ourselves alone in the house, wondering where everyone is. The heat of the August sun seems more intense than ever, so we decide to go for a quick swim. We make our way to the wide sandy shoreline, the light breeze offering no relief. We have no umbrella to anchor us, so we set our towels down closer to shore. This time, I don't see any girls wading in the water, but scattered groups of boys are swimming and running about on shore. At first, they don't pay any attention to us. I let my skirt fall to the sand, then slip off my shirt over my head. Dieter and I walk to the edge of the water. The voices of the teenage boys creep closer as I try in vain to decipher what they're saying.

Once my body is immersed in the sea, I feel safe, protected. Only my head is visible. I want to be invisible so I can float in peace. The sound of the boys' voices carries over the sea. The punchy intonation creeps under my wet skin, but the water doesn't wash away the fear. My mind is racing, telling me it is time to go. Dieter seems oblivious to their laughter. The more audible their voices, the more heat builds in my body. The distance between me and my pile of clothes feels like a continent away.

"We need to go." My tone is serious and steady as my ears carefully monitor the language and laughter. I stay close to Dieter as we exit the sea, my shoulders rolled forward, my eyes cast down to the sand. My eyes convey modesty, but my body tells a different tale. The only way to silence it is to get dressed. I dry off quickly as the language and laughter grow louder. Now, even footsteps in the sand are audible. Dieter shares in their laughter for a moment, as if the bond of laughter will convince them we are one of them. My sleeves stick to my still-damp arms as I struggle to get my shirt on. I step into my skirt, trying not to lose my balance on the soft sand, then pull it up over my saltwater hips like a race to home base. The boys' energy swirls around me like a deer surrounded by a pack of wolves. Dieter and I stick close together and manage to slip through their laughter with a polite but nervous smile. My racing heart directs my bare feet back home, where I take a deep breath of relief.

Salem is furious when he gets home and finds out we went to the beach without him. We have shamed his family. I don't fully understand why it was okay for us to be on the beach with him, but not alone, but it doesn't matter. We crossed a cultural line that casts a dark cloud over our visit. The heaviness in the air makes it hard to breathe. That evening, Dieter goes out for fresh air, walking to the beach, the only destination he knows. When he returns, his eyes look like glass, his face lifeless. An Israeli army Jeep had approached him, calling out to him in Hebrew, then Arabic. He raised his arms and called out, "I'm an American. Do you speak English?" The headlights blinded him, but he could make out the outline of their rifles. No passport, only his own voice to vouch for him. Apparently, the beach—lovely by day—is dangerous at night. As a closed military zone, we were lucky no shots were fired. We do not go back to the beach again in Gaza, not even by day.

5

Gaza

The tension of Dieter's scare with the soldiers on the beach dissipates when Salem suggests we head into town the next morning. We walk up and down crowded streets filled with vendors lined up on the sidewalk selling everything from clothes to toiletries arranged neatly on tabletops. It feels chaotic and random, if not desperate, like people are trying to sell anything and everything to anyone. Salem seems oblivious to the chaos. He is right at home and buys some jeans and sunglasses without even trying them on.

Farther in town, he leads us to one of his favorite restaurants to get a break from the heat and the crowds outside. We sit down at a red vinyl booth, and Salem orders us each a large glass of freshly blended mango, one of his favorite treats from childhood. I take a sip, overwhelmed by the pure flavor and thick texture. My body relaxes into the cool vinyl seat. The local charm of this far-off place is growing on me, and I begin to find comfort in its chaos and unpredictability.

We head back out into the bustling street and walk to Salem's father's quilt workshop. We enter a bare concrete room where he is lying on the floor in his *jalabiyeh*—a long shirt-like gown—his bare feet sticking out the end, needle and thread in hand. The concrete floor is spotless, except for a rack of thread off to one side and the two layers of fabric with stuffing in between spread out in front of him. His eyes are laser-focused, his hands steady as he carefully stitches swirling patterns across the soft folds of bright-red fabric.

Moments later, Salem's father's eyes shift to ours. He swings his legs around and gets onto his feet. I am embarrassed to interrupt his deep concentration. His body stiffens as he smooths out his *jalabiyeh*. We greet him with *Marhaba,* and Salem translates how much I admire his work. Salem and his father exchange a few words, their eyes equal in height. I watch his father's mouth move with crisp deliberation to deliver an assortment of sounds I have yet to understand. His father's eyes are soft and serious with a hint of sadness, as if his mind is in some far-off place. I wish there were something I could say besides *Marhaba*—hello, and *Shukran*—thank you. I feel invisible, listening with my eyes. Pressure in my head is mounting at my own frustration. I want to understand what I am hearing. If only I could make sense of these sounds. Salem is my filter through which to know this world.

In town, we find Salem's mother seated on a quilted blanket in the market, selling children's clothes. A young woman walks up and inquires about a dress. Salem's mother's tone is serious and firm as she calls out a price. She is a hard bargainer, her face confident and defiant. Her wide gestures and commanding voice end the negotiating process quickly. She reaches into her dress from the neckline and pulls out a pouch, then tucks it away. *Like the woman sitting outside Damascus Gate in Jerusalem.*

Later at home, she pulls out her breast from her dress to nurse Yusef, just like she pulled out her money pouch at the market. Salem lies down next to her and pretends to nurse. Yusef is outraged and hits him with his tiny fists, then clings to his mother's breast, certain he regained his ground. Salem withdraws and laughs. When Yusef is done, his mother lifts her breast back into her dress and goes on about her business—such a driven, focused woman. I think how there are more than 20 years between Salem and his youngest brother, a lifetime of mothering, a lifetime of motherhood.

I sense frustration in Salem's sister Sana when we visit her at her in-laws, where she lives in a single room with a bed and a dresser. She is only 16, newly married, and her in-laws want her pregnant. All she wants is a house of her own. Her eyes are clenched like a fist, her voice full of defiance. Every conversation is a fight. Her hair is layered and smooth, never covered, and her eyes defined in black eyeliner. She always sits in a chair when she visits her parents, never on the floor. Judging from her short, fitted dresses and rhinestone necklace that says "Paris" in cursive, she wants glamour, but the French double door of her room is the closest she will get to the "City of Light."

That night, a table and chairs appear out of nowhere in the middle of the courtyard. Salem, Salim, and Sana's and Salwa's husbands dump a box of dominoes onto the table and pass some out. I have never played a game of dominoes, only lined them up as a child so I could tap one and watch them all fall down one after the other. Each player takes a turn matching up dominoes with the same number of dots. I shudder as the game gets louder, each player slamming their domino down on the table when it is their turn. Soon, I laugh at their battle of sound.

They invite Dieter and me to play. First, I just set my piece on the table when it's my turn, but little by little, I learn to slam down my domino like them, each of us with our signature slam, our shared language. Salwa sets out dishes of nuts and seeds we nibble on like squirrels while we play. The sky darkens overhead. I feel right at home. I rely on eyes, gestures, and the proximity of whispers. I absorb my surroundings as sights and sounds seep into my soul. I begin to hear a rhythm in the language. Variations in tone clue me into emotions. I am surprised by what I can understand without words.

Not far from Salem's house is the Al-Shati Refugee Camp, where his sister Sumaya lives.[4] It gets its name from its location along the beach, since *shati* means "beach" in Arabic. We step out of the taxi into the blazing sun onto sand-covered streets. Sumaya appears at the doorway of a one-story cinderblock structure in a long, dark dress like her father's *jalabiyeh*, her smile softening the edges of the corrugated sheet-metal roof overhead. Her young daughter clings to her side in her lacy white dress, her feet bare. Her shy, sweet smile melts my heart.

Sumaya invites us to come inside their one-room home. There is a wooden wardrobe closet on one wall and a double bed against the other. A large plastic mat covers the center of the concrete floor. Through the back doorway, I can see a tarp extending over a sandy area with a single faucet.

A solitary burner is suspended in space above a propane tank. *Just like her mother.* We sit down on the concrete floor, where Sumaya offers us juice and a plate of roasted seeds. Her hair hangs loosely around her face, the sparkle of her eyes brightening the gray walls. Her daughter, not older than three, climbs onto Salem's lap. Her smile gives way to giggles when he sings to her. Sumaya's husband sits with us, his movements slow. When Sumaya clears the glasses and seeds, her movements are quick and precise, intent on the next task at hand. I wonder how she ended up here. If only I could talk to her myself, but I simply sit, watch, and listen.

The days pass one into the other with *Alltag*, what Germans call "daily life." It is already the second week into our trip to Gaza, and I have yet to meet with Save the Children. School has started for the children, and the house is quieter during the day. Most mornings, Salwa arrives with vegetables and sometimes meat or yogurt from the market for that day's meal since there is no refrigerator. She and Salem's mother prepare the midday meal over the propane burner. *No oven. No stove.*

We eat gathered on mats arranged around a vinyl tablecloth in the side room across from the lemon tree. I fall in love with eggplant, which is in season, sliced and fried with garlic and served with olives, pickled vegetables, and a lemony garlic sauce called *daqa*. I learn from Salem to first dip my bread in a spicy red paste called *shatta* for an added kick. Occasionally, they make a mound of rice topped with chicken or chunks of meat served with yogurt, which we eat from a large platter with our hands. *No silverware.* I just eat the rice and yogurt since I am a vegetarian.

Even though I am a guest, I don't want to be waited on. I join in to help Salwa and her mother, learning as I go. After all, Salwa is noticeably pregnant and has a house of her own. At first, when I want to help with the dishes, Salwa protests by blocking my hands, staring at me with her intense eyes, but my smile and determination break through her resistance, and soon we work as a team collecting the dishes from the tablecloth and delivering them to the concrete sink, where we wash each dish with a soapy sponge before rinsing them one by one beneath the single faucet, Salwa seated on a wooden stool and me squatting with my skirt tucked between my legs. The dishes, arranged on a large steel tray in the direct sun, dry in no time.

Once we are finished, Salwa retrieves a squeegee from the narrow kitchen to push the water toward a groove by the front doorway that channels the water out into the gutter in the passageway. My throat tightens as my eyes shift to the bathroom door at the front of the house. I wonder if that dirty water also runs into the gutter beneath all those barefoot children. *Where does it end up?*

One afternoon, the side room where we eat transforms into a bakery with white sheets laid out on the mats, hiding circles of flattened dough arranged beneath them. I watch as Salwa places one on the bottom of a deep, round aluminum pan plugged into the wall and closes the lid. After a few minutes, she opens it, flips the dough over, and closes it again, the aroma of freshly baked bread filling the room. The next time she opens it, the dough is a golden balloon. She dumps it onto another sheet to cool, where it deflates like a balloon with a slow leak. She repeats the process again and again into the evening, one loaf at a time until there must be a hundred loaves of pita bread. I help her stack them neatly in a large black plastic bag next to a cylindrical drum of flour they receive through the UN World Food Program, along with cooking oil and sugar. I marvel at the time they spend making one loaf at a time but wonder about the UN food rations. *Are people here dependent on the outside world to survive?*[5]

Later that week, Salwa and her mother fill the courtyard with piles of clothes sorted by color, some soaking in aluminum laundry tubs gleaming in the bright afternoon sun. First, I watch as Salwa and her mother each grip an article of clothing from the soapy water and vigorously scrub the fabric between their knuckles, occasionally dipping the article back into the murky water. I spot one of my shirts in the tub and join in. Salem's mother occasionally sprinkles some laundry soap powder directly on the clothing where she is scrubbing, so I do the same.

I watch how they methodically shift their hands, scrubbing section by section. I start over, working my way from one shoulder across the neckline to the other shoulder, then move down and work my way across again, repeating until I reach the bottom. I grab another shirt, this time one of Salem's white button-down shirts.

We wash all the white clothes, ringing them out piece by piece by folding and twisting, then set them aside in an empty tub until it is full. When Salwa lets the clear water splash onto the clothes at the faucet, they untwist in the water, as if coming to life. As she swishes the clothes back and forth, the water becomes murky again. We twist and rinse the clothes two more times, then move on to the darker clothes and repeat the whole process before hanging them on several clotheslines across the open courtyard. When I rinse my hands under the cool water one last time, I discover I have blisters on my knuckles. Blisters from washing clothes! Salem's white shirts and pants glow in the afternoon sun, surely the whitest clothes I have ever seen. I am surprised by how quickly the clothes dry in the afternoon sun. Within the hour, we take them down, folding and sorting as we work.

As the shadow of the second-floor overhang creeps across the open courtyard, we take a break and eat a simple supper before moving on to the next task. Salwa places a sheet over a blanket on the tile floor and plugs an iron into the wall. We collect the cotton clothes that are stiff and wrinkled. I squat down next to her and spread one of Salem's white shirts out on the sheet. She smiles at me, watching as I transform the stiff, crumbled cloth into a smooth stately shirt. I move on to my full cotton skirt, ironing one section at a time from the hemline to the waistline until I reach the smooth section I already ironed. By the time I finish, night has set in. It feels good to know that another day's work is done, and yet I'm getting restless, wanting to know more, to do more, to discover how I can make a difference beyond these walls.

Salem senses my frustration as he puts one of the cassettes he bought in town into the cassette player. He insists there are more places he wants to take Dieter and me outside of Gaza, assuring me there will be plenty of time to visit Save the Children later in the trip. As rhythm and song fill the room, I feel like I am back at Salem's birthday party when we first met. I return to the moment as Salwa ties a scarf around her hips, just below her belly, then begins to dance. Her movements are graceful, with her pregnant belly, her narrow hips shifting smoothly. Her eyes sparkle, her mouth is taut with concentration, then melts into a smile as the day's work dissipates from her face. Salem joins in. We all laugh as they play off each other's movements. I delight in their silent conversation, shoulders, hips, and hands each moving in isolation like a whole other language with shoulders lifting and dropping rhythmically, hips swaying, then tilting and tugging, hands waving and circling in one constant motion.

Dieter and I clap to the rhythm of the music. Then Salwa takes off her scarf and ties it around my hips. She dances in front of me, and I follow her movements. I loosen my hands so my arms flow like a wave, holding my torso steady as I trace her hips with my own, thrusting my left, then right hip forward or lifting my right hip as I move in a circle around my left foot. My movements are slow and deliberate, then become fluid. I raise my hands to my face like Salwa, then alternate stretching one arm out, then the other in a soft curve. I carefully rise onto the balls of my feet like her as my body succumbs to the rhythm.

We dance toward each other, then move away, glancing back at each other, then turning and dancing past each other. I can feel my body follow the rhythm, mastering the moves, as if I am remembering a long-lost language. Salwa and I have become soul sisters, our smiles swirling in our own solar system, all without uttering a single word.

6

Ein Gedi

After our third week in Gaza, Salem takes Dieter and me on an excursion to a nature reserve called Ein Gedi by the Dead Sea, known as 'Ayn Jedi in Arabic. We get an early start with a simple breakfast of dry biscuits with sesame seeds dipped in tea. We take a taxi to the checkpoint where we first entered the Gaza Strip and cross without incident. From there, we take a 20-minute bus ride to the coastal city of Ashqelon, once the Palestinian town of Al-Majdal Asqalan, then transfer to another bus to Beersheba, or Bi'r As-Saba' in Arabic, what Israel renamed Be'er Sheva.[6]

Within an hour, we arrive in Beersheba, where we board yet another bus to Ein Gedi. As we pass the rocky hillsides, I can't imagine anyone living here. There is no sign of life. Then ahead, I see deep blue water glistening in the desert sun. Pink mountains protrude into the sky in the hazy distance. The road dead-ends at the Dead Sea, the lowest place on Earth, nearly 1,500 feet below sea level. The bus follows along the shoreline until we reach our destination.

I gaze up from the side of the road at a lush green strip that extends up the sloping landscape. I wonder how all these trees and plants can grow here when there is not even a single plant across the road. That is the magic of this place. Where there is water, there is life. We gather our things, walk over to an unobtrusive one-story stone building, pay the park entrance fee, and proceed out the other side. It reminds me of a movie I once saw where people enter a cave from blistering winter winds that opens up to blossoming meadows amidst a summer breeze. We have come from the desert into paradise.

I am wearing a hand-dyed, sleeveless sundress I bought in Germany, the outlines of giant butterflies in off-white and gold fluttering in the breeze. I walk in my brown leather Birkenstocks along a dirt path that becomes a narrow maze of trees and flowering bushes. My ears tune in, as if someone is playing a rainforest track and turning up the volume with each step. The calls of frolicking birds surround us as we come upon a waterway of pools and waterfalls. We walk alongside this magical strip of life, the slope of the land becoming steeper with every step. The sun peeks through, offering speckled patterns of light and shadow. Even though we are protected from the steaming desert sun by the cover of dense foliage, the heat is intense. My dress sticks to my body, dripping with sweat.

The path continues up the slope, but Salem invites Dieter and me into one of the narrow pools. My body springs back to life as the cool water washes away the heat of the blazing sun. As I lower my body into the pool, the water creeps under my dress, at first floating, then sinking below the surface. Salem climbs a short waterfall to the next pool like an underwater staircase. Dieter and I follow him, climbing from one terrace pool to the next. Farther up, we find a larger waterfall with a pool deep enough to swim in. I can see the rocky bottom below, like gazing through a looking glass. My dress floats underwater in slow motion, bringing the butterflies to life. The waterfall is too high to climb, so we continue along the path, my dress dripping onto my feet. At the top, we walk through the fast-moving water, my dress clinging to my body. I peel it off my legs so I can walk through the water rushing past my ankles.

We take our time exploring one pool after another until we reach the top of the falls. The path is one-way, so we have to go down off to the side. Soon, the butterflies on my dress are blowing in the breeze, and I long for the cool relief of the waterfalls. In no time, we are back at the entrance, where we meet one of the employees, a Bedouin named Salim, whom we connect with like family. He insists we stay overnight in the employee dorms so he can take us to his home in the Naqab Desert—what Israel calls the

Negev Desert—then give us a private tour of Masada the next morning. We take him up on the offer and spend a short and uncomfortable night sleeping on the floor of a one-room concrete structure.

In the morning, we take a taxi south toward Masada. We get out on the side of the road and follow Salim across dry, rocky ground. At first the space feels open and random, but upon closer look, I see a path emerge out of the flat rocky landscape, as if my eyes have suddenly come into focus. In the distance is a single cement block building with an open doorway, and to the side, an expansive black tent. Peering out of the doorway is a young girl with black hair, her bangs hanging down slightly over her eyes. When she sees us, she dashes out of sight.

"That's my sister, Salma." Salim invites Salem, Dieter, and me into the cement structure, a one-room house with cutouts for windows but no frames. Even the doorway has no door. As we enter, Salma hides behind her brother. He says something to her in Arabic, and she peeks out from behind him. I smile at her, looking into the depths of her eyes. Her eyes smile back at me, then look down at the ground before she returns to hiding. Salim's eyes move from the open doorway to the windows. "It's not finished yet." He invites us back out and walks toward the tent. He calls out, and a woman appears at one of the corners, her hand resting against a support pole, her eyes wide open. I can see her shift her weight beneath her long black dress. They exchange a few words in Arabic, then Salim introduces us to his mother, who invites us in.

I step inside like I am crossing into yet another universe, my chest swelling with curiosity. I pause for a moment so my eyes adjust to the dim light. Narrow streams of light peek in through cracks like swords. Salim directs his hands toward large rectangular mats. "Please, sit down." His mother disappears behind a black drape. Salma dashes past us into the same opening. A few minutes later, Salim's mother returns with a tiny tulip-shaped cup and a white plastic carafe. The rich aroma of coffee laced with cardamom fills the air as she offers the cup to Salem. He drinks it in one sip and hands it back to her, Arabic flowing between their broad smiles.

She pours another cup and hands it to me. *Shukran*, a single word of thanks, my only offering. My mind struggles to make sense of the sounds dancing in my ears. I listen with my eyes as an entangled string of words leaves her mouth. I take a tiny sip of the aromatic coffee, then finish it off and hand the cup back to her so she can serve Dieter and Salim.

Outside the tent, I hear the rumble of an engine, then the thunk of a car door slamming. It turns out to be one of Salim's brothers. We walk outside to greet him by his blue pickup truck sitting in what appears to be the middle of the desert. Salim motions for us to follow him deeper into the desert. "I want to show you something." I look closely at the rocky, sand-colored ground and realize there is a path of sorts leading off into the distance, where the ground slopes downward into a deep depression carved out of the otherwise flat landscape.

"This is where water flows when the rains come. Now, it's all dried up, but in the winter, it is full." At first, I find it hard to imagine the crevice filled with water, but then my eyes follow the gouged earth, and I can feel the water's movement, even tell which direction it flows. "This time of year, we have to truck in water, but in winter, we have all we need."

I look back at the house and the tent, nothing anywhere around it as far as the eye can see. "You guys are really on your own out here." I can feel the sun baking the top of my head.

"I love it here. We are so free. It feels so different at the university." Salim explains how he is a student at the university in Beersheba. "I always can't wait to come back home."

I ponder his words. "It's like you are living in two worlds. Very different worlds."

"They are different, but I like both."

Salim sparks my curiosity. "What do you think you'll end up doing after you're done at the university?"

"I will probably work in the city, but I'll always come back home."

We walk back to the tent and sit down on the mats, a welcome relief from the direct sun. Salim pours a glass of water from a ceramic jug. He offers it to me, then refills it for Dieter, then Salem. As the sun lowers in the sky, the sides of the tent flap in the wind. Before long, Salim's mother brings out a tray of rice topped with chunks of lamb and almonds. He offers us each a spoon so we can carve out our own quarry. I avoid the meat since I'm a vegetarian, but I can see it fall apart into tender strings when Dieter pokes at it with his spoon. The almonds are roasted to a crunch and full of flavor.

After we eat, I ask Salim about a bathroom, and he directs me to another area off to the side from their compound, where the ground slopes downward. "This is it. Don't worry; we won't be able to see you." I squat down over a deep hole dug into the dry, rocky earth, the breeze blowing in my hair and passing between my legs. As urine flows from my body into the hole, it disappears in an instant. The ground is still so hot and dry that it absorbs every drop and doesn't leave a trace. I don't have water, but I did bring a tissue along. I let it fall into the hole and stand back up. That wasn't so bad. At least there is plenty of fresh air and no giant beetles running around my feet. I turn toward the house and can decipher a path before me. Salim guides me behind the tent, where he offers me a bar of soap and pours water on my hands from a ceramic jug. I dry my hands on a towel hanging over the ledge.

Back in the tent, Salim's mother brings us tea in tiny glasses. I let it cool slightly, then take a sip of the dark golden-brown tea. It is quite sweet, and I can feel the sugar racing through my body. It tastes smooth and flavorful, the perfect finish to a delicious meal. At one point, goosebumps form on my arms. I rub my hands on my forearms.

"Are you cold?" Salim reaches for a blanket on the mat and throws it to me.

"I was just so hot. How can I be cold?"

"Once the sun goes down, it gets pretty cold out here." He rises to his feet. "Come see."

We all follow him out of the tent. I pull the blanket around my shoulders like a shawl. It is pitch black out now. Salim tilts his head back. "Look."

"Wow! Look at all the stars!" The sky is mesmerizing, not a single electric light anywhere. "This is incredible!" A cool breeze sweeps across my face.

"Do you feel that? It's called *nasim*."

Nasim, I repeat, letting the sounds make an imprint on my memory, imagining how it is written in Arabic: نسيم.

"Nasim is the desert wind from the west that comes at night."

"It's really chilly. I still can't believe how cold it gets, just like that." We walk back to the tent, and he offers us more blankets. "You will sleep here. I hope you will be comfortable."

We each claim a mat and tuck ourselves under a blanket. I lie there listening to the silence, my entire body melting into the mat, separating my body from the earth below. In my mind, I can still see the stars overhead.

The air is fresh—the only sound the wind. Our new home for the night. Next thing I know, Salim is softly telling us all to wake up. It is time to leave for Masada.

7

Point of No Return

I pour a trickle of water onto my toothbrush from the ceramic jug cooled by the night air. I spit on the sandy ground, then pour water into my hand to rinse out my mouth. I stare into the stars overhead, still no sign of twilight. Our new Bedouin friend Salim wants to arrive at Masada at sunrise to beat the heat of the day. The cool nasim wind has dissipated to a gentle but chilly breeze. My mind is racing, hyper-alert, my body light and strong, ready for the climb.

We share a simple breakfast of hot tea, sheep cheese, and bread before heading out to the road to catch a bus to Masada. When we arrive some 20 minutes later, the stars are no longer visible. The morning chill has lifted. Before us is a daunting rocky mountain.

Salim points to a ridge on the side. "That's how we're going to get up there." The ground is dry and rocky, the climb at first effortless. Salim explains the history of this island in the desert. "There was a tribe of Jews who came here to get away from the Romans. They held out for some time, but the Romans came after them. When they reached the top, they found everyone had committed suicide. Only a few survivors lived to tell the tale so the others would not die in vain. They opted to die rather than subject themselves to the Romans."

As the incline steepens, my legs ache from the strain of the climb. When the dry ground finds its way under my feet in my open Birkenstock sandals, I kick my foot gently to the side to clear out tiny rocks and dry sand. The higher we climb, the more the surrounding area comes into full view. There is nothing for miles around. The entire landscape is the same color. The moment the sun breaks the horizon, the heat seems to radiate right from the earth. A prickle of sweat forms on my scalp. The nasim breeze has become an illusion. By the time we reach the plateau, the sun is in full view, increasing by the moment in intensity, the Dead Sea visible in the distance. My eyes study the clusters of stone buildings while Salim's words swirl in my mind. I try to imagine people living here on this outpost, cut off from the rest of the world.

Salim shows us the cistern where they stored water, the shade offering a moment of relief, then points out the remains of rooms used for food storage and what is left of the living quarters at the other end. "There were about 80 people living here. Men, women, and children." I think of the adults making the difficult choice to die rather than surrender but wonder about the children, who had no choice in the matter, hostages of their parents' fate. Here they left their bodies on top of the world, surrounded by desert and the relentless heat of the sun. A place of refuge that became a point of no return.

Salim's eyes gaze out into the open desert. "Today people talk about modern Jews having a 'Masada complex.' Israel itself is a kind of outpost, surrounded by Arab countries whom they claim want to drive them into the sea."[7] I think about the geography of Israel—Lebanon to the north, Egypt to the south, Jordan and Syria to the east, and the Mediterranean Sea to the west. No wonder Israelis have fought so hard to keep their neighbors at bay. And yet they live among Palestinians.

I look to Salim for answers. "So, what do you think will happen? I mean with the Israelis and Palestinians?"

Salim's voice is calm, matter of fact. "So far, we're living with the Jews, even though they have taken our land. What are we going to do? We can't leave our homeland." I think of Salim's house out in the desert, an outpost of its own for a single family, but with no protection. They are free to live there, at least for now—a coexistence from a distance.

Salim walks us over to a larger room. "This is where they committed suicide. The Romans found them here." Chills run up my spine. I cannot help but think of the gas chambers in Germany. I wonder who did the killing and what it was like to be waiting to die, to be next. And the children? Were they first? Or did they have to watch their people take their own lives?

We stand under a covered area and drink water. I take a last look around before we head back down. The heat is overbearing, and the sun so bright I squeeze my eyes together, casting them down. The descent is easier on my legs, but I am dripping with sweat. I think of the Romans marching up the ramp to catch their prey with a strange mix of fear, courage, and determination. The Romans ready for a fight. How did they react when they found everyone dead, the only blood shed by their own hands? A story of defiance and sacrifice. Now, this place is a tourist attraction, part of the Israeli national narrative. *Masada complex. Where will it lead?*

When we are back in Gaza, we learn that Salem's grandmother is in the hospital and go visit her. We find her in a large sunny room with multiple beds, hers on the far wall by an open window. Salem calls out to her, and she turns her head. Blurred, bluish lines frame her lips, a tradition that is dying out with this generation. She looks up at Salem, then at Dieter and me with wide-open eyes. Salem introduces me, and her large knobby hand, draped in a sheer covering of skin, reaches out for mine. "Christa." She speaks with steady deliberation, as if trying to remember who I am. She moves her fingers against my hand, reading mine. I gaze at her hand transformed by a lifetime of work. Her body lies motionless beneath a white sheet, the outline of her hip marking the peak of this landscape. My eyes follow the contour of her high cheekbones, her skin dry and tight, her face full of sun and story, each line a long-lost era.

It isn't long after I leave Gaza that she passes away. Salem's father said my name was the last thing she uttered before taking her final breath. The news brought me back into that hospital room, where she was forced to surrender to death, a point of no return. I try to imagine all she witnessed in her lifetime, what she hoped for. Certainly, not to end up destitute in Gaza, never to get to go home. Like a bird in a cage, her homeland before her eyes but out of reach. I wonder if her grandchildren will witness peace in Palestine. *Will they ever get to go back to the homes of their grandparents, or will they forever remain refugees in their own homeland?* I rack my brain to imagine another way forward for future generations.

8

From Jaffa to 'Akka

It is September 12, my 19th birthday. Dieter is not feeling well, so Salem offers to spend the day with me in Jaffa. We take along his little brother Yusef in his umbrella stroller. We travel by taxi from Gaza to Ashqelon, then transfer to a bus to Jaffa. As we walk through the streets, I realize everyone must think I am Salem's wife and Yusef our son, a nice young family out for the day. This adopted status feels like a protective veil over my identity as an American in Gaza and Salem's statelessness in his ancestral town. We are strangers here but feel right at home.

Salem and I find a small park by the sea, where we are surrounded by flowers beneath palm trees dancing in the warm breeze beneath the bright sun. We buy *ka'ak* from a street vendor—round, O-shaped bread covered with sesame seeds, a specialty of Jerusalem. I tear off a piece of the golden crust to reveal a fluffy white center. Salem shows me how to dip it into *za'atar*—a spice mix the man gave us wrapped in a piece of newspaper. My senses come alive as my tongue presses against the tangy spice mix. My heart swells with gratitude to be able to spend my birthday in such a beautiful place.

We walk past another area overlooking the sea with several restaurants surrounded by the stone homes of Palestinians, now refugees. Salem points out one of the restaurants where he used to work as a teenager, recounting how he would spend the evening swimming in the sea after work with his friends before heading back to Gaza. I try to imagine him working in the town his father was forced to leave, an exile that left him a refugee. I try to get my head around the twisted reality that Salem could come there to work but not to live.

As we walk past the shops, Salem tells me more of what became of his family. His father was forced to flee with his family at the age of 11 in April 1948, begging his parents to bring his bicycle with him, but his father—Salem's grandfather—told him no because they would be back in a few days. Not only did they never return to Jaffa, but it would be 22 years before they ever saw Salem's grandmother again. She happened to be visiting relatives in 'Akka when they fled Jaffa and she was unable to return to Gaza. At that time, Gaza fell under Egyptian control, and Palestinians in Israel were under martial law until they were granted citizenship in 1966.

Determined to find his mother, Salem's father traveled to 'Akka without a permit, only to be arrested and put in jail for six months. A few days on the run became a lifetime of living in Gaza as refugees in their homeland, locked away in an outdoor prison, where thousands, over seven decades, have become millions.

The sun is still high above the horizon when we make our way back to Gaza. We pass easily through the checkpoint and arrive at the house before the sun sets. Dieter is sitting on a mat over by the lemon tree with Salem's brother, practicing words in Arabic. *Ana na'san, anta ta'ban*—I am sleepy, you are tired, he says in Arabic, then laughs as Salim smiles with approval. Yusef is tired from the excursion and runs over to his mother, burying his face in her chest as she wraps her arms tightly around him. I think of Salem's father robbed of his mother's arms to hold him until he was a grown man, a bittersweet day seeing the place of Salem's father's birth, his childhood, my mind searching for neural pathways to make sense of Israel's hold on Jaffa, a place we can visit for the day, but from which they are barred for life.

A few days later, we take another day trip, this time to Tel Aviv. Salem wants to show Dieter and me the city and take us to the beach. I bring my aqua-green bikini. I fit right in. The beach is full of people sunning, swimming, and playing volleyball. We could be in the US. Just a bus ride away, and we are in a different world. Since we are all good swimmers, we swim way out to a large boulder protruding from the sea that reminds me of the shipwreck in Gaza. It is sunny and warm, the water soft and soothing. I look back at this Israeli city, full of tall buildings. None of this used to be here. Now, the city completely fills the area as far as the eye can see.

After we rinse off in outdoor showers on the beach and get dressed, Salem takes us to a large restaurant by the sea filled with young people drinking and talking over loud music, as if we are in a pub in Germany, but everyone is speaking Hebrew. We are only 20 miles from Gaza, but we are worlds away, surrounded by people without a care in the world. *Like West Jerusalem*. The atmosphere seeps under my skin. It is too happy, too normal, like a living lie. Life goes on for Israelis and stands still for Palestinians. "I don't want to be here," I tell Salem. "I want to go home to Gaza."

Dieter and I are halfway through our trip when we find out Salem's cousin in 'Akka is getting married. We pack an overnight bag and cross the border of the Gaza Strip, traveling all day from bus to bus up the coast to this Palestinian city that is now in Israel. We arrive at his relatives' house, where we meet a middle-aged couple in a fully furnished home with sleek sofas and armchairs neatly arranged around a coffee table, a full kitchen with appliances, cupboards, and countertops, picture perfect like out of a magazine. Our hostess invites us to sit at a dining room table off the kitchen while she makes hummus in a food processor. She speaks a soft English. I offer to help. "What a lovely home you have."

"Thank you. I am very lucky here." She scoops hummus onto an oval platter, spreads it carefully until an even ridge forms at the edge of the plate, then tops it with olive oil, giving the surface a gleaming green hue. She arranges other salads and spreads on serving plates. The house is quiet and calm, almost surreal.

When we sit down at the table to eat, I realize I feel upright and awkward. Sitting at a table has become a distant memory. I am already so used to the open space of Salem's home that this house begins to feel confining. Both families are Palestinian, relatives, but their lives seem so different.

After lunch, she shows us to our rooms furnished with beds and dressers and the bathroom with its gleaming white tiles from floor to ceiling, large walk-in shower, and flush toilet. Natural light pours in from glass windows. The contrast to Gaza is overwhelming.

The wedding is held at a private outdoor garden full of rows and rows of rectangular tables covered in white tablecloths topped with an array of appetizers, the guests bustling with laughter and conversation. At one point, several men carry the bride and groom seated in chairs on a platform while others gather around singing and dancing in the late afternoon sun, the bride's dress as bright as her smile. Salwa's smile comes to mind when we danced at home in our own private celebration, the next generation taking in the sound and moves from within her belly, a dance of hope.

The following day, we visit Salem's friend, 'Isam, in 'Akka, whom I met in Germany. Like Salem, he is visiting his family, though they are Israeli citizens. I meet his three grown sisters, who all have long narrow faces like their brother, none of them married. They live in their parents' home in the Old City, an ancient stone house handed down from generation to generation.

We enter their home single file through a narrow, stone staircase that opens to high ceilings and dim passageways leading from one room to the next. I wonder what the future holds for 'Isam's family. My few words of Arabic are no match for conversation. I can speak German with 'Isam but can only connect with his sisters through our eyes.

In the afternoon, we wander through the passageways of the Old City, reminding me of the Old City in Jerusalem. I reflect on the successive invasions and conquests as we climb up the Crusader ruins by the sea, the waves crashing against the stone walls. In the distance, local boys dive into the raging waves from cliff-like structures. To think these walls served as a bustling port through the ages. As we sit watching the sunset, I try to make sense of these contested pieces of Palestine I have seen so far.

Back in Gaza, Dieter and I realize we still have some of our things at the Browns in Jerusalem, so we take a day trip with Salem to visit them. Since Salem's family doesn't have a phone, we had no way of letting the Browns know to expect us. We take the short walk to their house from the taxi station and ring the doorbell. Eleanor opens the front door with a bright smile. When her eyes spot Salem towering behind us, her face falls flat, and her eyes turn to glass, as if she is seeing a ghost. I introduce her to Salem, our friend from Gaza, but her face remains unchanged.

Salem sees the fear in her eyes and steps back. *Wir treffen uns später*—I'll meet up with you later, is all he can say before he disappears behind the privacy wall. I don't want him to leave. I feel awkward, like I surrendered to their separation. *Why can't we just all hang out together?*

With Salem out of sight, Eleanor's eyes soften, and she invites us in. "I want to hear all about your trip." *Does she really?*

We sit down at the dining room table. David joins us from the kitchen. My mind is racing. Dieter and I begin to share details of our time in Gaza. How the conditions are so desperate, and at the same time, Palestinians under occupation find a way to carve out beautiful moments of joy and celebration. And yet people are left hanging in unsettled history. Certainly, it doesn't have to be this way. Even if the Browns could not connect with Salem, I want them to care about what is happening in Gaza.

Eleanor and David shift in their seats, growing more uneasy with the complex picture we are painting. David says he used to think there could be peace with the Palestinians, but after he served in Lebanon, he wasn't so sure anymore. It was a terrible war. Israel was forced to retreat. He seems bitter about his military experience there but stands behind the State of Israel. He sounds matter-of-fact when he says Israel is doing what it has to do.

I can't agree, not after what I have seen for myself. Sure, Palestinians are living their lives, making the best of an impossible situation, but at the same time, their lives as refugees are on hold. *What lies ahead for their children?*

As the tension fills the room, I feel a wall go up between us. Their reality doesn't leave much space for thinking about the Palestinians. My heart sinks to the floor. We connected so well as Americans, but somehow my concern about Gaza has created a rift between us. I wonder if they will ever overcome the walls in their minds that only exacerbate the divisions between them as Israelis and the Palestinians. I realize that I'm naïve to think I can have two homes—one in Israel, one in Palestine, and that I can somehow bridge the divide. I fear in that moment I lost my home in Israel.

My heart is heavy as we collect our things. We thank them again for welcoming us into their home, but their enthusiasm from our first week in Jerusalem has waned. When we say goodbye, it feels like forever. We walk over to the taxi area, where Salem is waiting for us. Both our eyes are heavy with the weight of this day. Time to go home to Gaza.

9

Storm

Toward the end of our visit to Gaza, the rainy season starts. The glistening blue sea is dark and roaring, finding its way farther onto shore. The strong winds and crashing waves leave the seaside restaurants damaged in their wake. That first delightful swim at the beach four weeks ago in the afternoon sun feels like a distant memory under these heavy, gray skies. My summer clothes are no match for the chill of the cool, damp air seeping into my bones. The cold kitchen shower feels like torture. Salem says his mother can heat water for us, but Dieter and I tough it out. Hot water seems like too much of a luxury.

The open courtyard is wet and cold. We stay close to home, gathering in the side room with the shutters closed. The mats are lined along the walls, extra mats from the courtyard stacked in one corner. Salem's sister Sahar works silently on her homework, her gaze steady as she copies verses from the Quran into her notebook, using her knee as a desk. Yusef scrambles from Salem's lap to his mother's breast, his body softening as he dozes off in her arms. She lays him on the mat, covering him with one of the quilted blankets his father made.

I listen to their voices, trying to imagine what they are saying. When Yusef wakes up, he wants to return to his mother's breast, but she pushes him away and motions to his sister Salwa, who is prepping for dinner.

Yusef peeks over Salwa's shoulder as she peels and slices garlic, then runs in front of or behind us like an obstacle course. Salem's sister Miriam is sitting quietly hugging her knees, tucking her head in like a turtle whenever Yusef approaches. Salim is leaning against the wall next to Dieter, his hands resting on his lanky legs. Soon Salem's father comes home from work and joins us, lying down on his side propped up on one elbow, his long *jalabiyeh* covering his legs like a sheet. Salem turns on the cassette player, and he and Salwa sing along to one of the current hits, *Miriam T,* lifting the dreariness of the gray afternoon while the cold air seeps through the slats on the green shutters. As evening sets in, Salim flips on the fluorescent light that shines down on us from the wall like a spotlight. Only our bodies warm the room.

In that last week, we visit Salem's sister Sumaya one last time in the refugee camp. After days of heavy rain, we are relieved to get outside. The sun peeks through the clouds dissipating the persistent chill of the last days. A hint of warmth from the fading summer has returned. When we arrive at their one-room house, the bed, the cabinet, and rug are all gone, leaving the floor bare concrete, deep gray with moisture. The rain must have seeped between the sheet metal panels and ruined everything. The area out back is scattered with puddles, reflecting the tarp sagging toward the muddy ground. The mood screams of despair.

Sumaya greets us with a broad smile, but her eyes appear sunken deep into her face. Her daughter appears in the doorway in the same white lacey dress; only now, the brilliant whiteness has faded to a faint gray. Her curls are no longer neatly arranged around her face but rather lay at odd angles across her brow. Her smile is as uplifting as ever as she tilts her chin downward and twists her body by crossing one leg in front of the other. Patches of dried mud decorate her bare legs above her soiled slip-on shoes. I reach out to her, and she untwists her legs and walks toward me. I pick her up and look deep into her eyes, recognizing her mother's cheekbones in her face. Holding her in my arms, I still want to reach out to Save the Children, but somehow the situation here feels beyond the work of a single organization. And yet, I want to find a way to make a difference more than ever.

As the weather turns, so does my stomach. My gut begins to cramp, tugging at my insides. Before I know it, brown water gushes out of my body when I squat down in the bathroom. Dread washes over me like the heaviness of the recent storms. Each day, I feel weaker, my stomach hollowed out. It isn't long before I am lying down much of the time. Salwa offers me a loaf of pita bread and yogurt. I can barely finish a quarter of the loaf.

Even though I am ill, I can't leave Gaza without finally meeting with the director of Save the Children, Chris George. Maybe he can help me make sense of what I have witnessed so far. I pull myself together and meet him in his office in town. My adrenaline is up. In my mind, Save the Children is like UNICEF, vowing to make a difference in the lives of children caught in conflict or poverty, but I quickly realize he is one man facing the insurmountable battle of those forgotten by history.

I tell him I wanted to connect much earlier and that I'd like to volunteer with the organization. He seems grateful—if not relieved—to have a fellow American here who is eager to learn about the challenges Palestinians face in Gaza and my willingness to contribute in some way. Perhaps it is better that I first got to experience life in Gaza for myself. He wants to drive me through the Gaza Strip, all the way to the town of Rafah on the border with Egypt.

I use the bathroom before we go, relieved to see a flush toilet where I can sit instead of squat, given my low energy level from hardly eating and the ongoing diarrhea. Unlike the older cars that fill the streets of Gaza, he has a newer sedan. As we head south on the main road, I look out the window at the Gaza Strip as if watching a movie while he tells me of Israeli settlements—illegal according to international law—and segregated roads for Jews, the dire conditions in refugee camps in the area, and the challenges of getting medical supplies and Israeli approval for development projects to improve the lives of Palestinians here.

When we reach the end of the Gaza Strip, he directs me to get out of the car and explains the town of Rafah is now divided between Egypt and the Gaza Strip with a double fence in between, separating Palestinian family members from each other.

We walk toward the fence, the long dresses of Palestinian women fluttering in the breeze. The idea of placing a fence through the middle of town seems absurd, but witnessing people call out to each other is heartbreaking, their fingers clinging to the fence, pulling their faces forward as if to make their voices more audible to the other side.

On our way back, we stop at an open clearing, the loose sand seeping under my sandals. The director points to a large rectangle of concrete half buried in the sand. "This is a water treatment plant, but the Israelis stopped the project, even though Palestinians have a permit to build it." He points just beyond the area to a dark lake surrounded by a few palm trees with a hint of green foliage along the edges. "That is raw sewage." In the distance, I see neat rows of farms, the bright green of the crops gleaming in the overhead sun. My stomach turns as my eyes shift from the farms to the lake of sewage and back again. Palestinians are farming right next to contaminated water. No wonder I am sick.

Now I know the water running down the narrow passageway in front of Salem's home is raw sewage. Without adequate water treatment facilities, there is nowhere for the wastewater to go, so it collects here, contaminating groundwater. I think of the children in their bare feet, playing in the passageway. My heart aches that Palestinians here have to put up with these conditions. It is my first taste of collective punishment. Israel has the power to block the project and does, leaving Palestinians' hopes for a better life buried in the sand. Israel must be held accountable for this, but how? The director encourages me to contact the main office of Save the Children in the US to see what opportunities there are. I promise him I will send them my information, hoping to cross paths again in the near future.

It is time for Salem, Dieter, and me to leave for the airport, time to say goodbye. I feel like I have lived a completely different life and have a whole new family. Pulling away tugs at my heart. Salem's mother hugs me and kisses me like her own daughter. I promise to come back someday.

Our flight is in the middle of the night, and we have to get to the airport at least three hours early. It is 10:00 p.m. when we leave for the border, where we first entered the Gaza Strip five weeks earlier. The soldiers approach us and ask us where we are going. "We are going to the airport." They say that is impossible. The area is closed.

Ausgangsverbot, Salem tells me in German. Apparently, Gaza has been declared a "closed area," and we can't leave.[8]

I argue with the soldiers. They have to let us out. "We can't go back. We have a flight to catch to Germany." The soldiers consult with each other, then make a call via their walkie-talkie. Finally, they let us through, but when we get to the airport, security at the entrance gate to the airport takes our bags and tells us they have to check them overnight. "Come back tomorrow."

We return to Gaza in defeat. The air is heavy at home. I feel like we have nothing more to give, nothing more to say. We spend one final night in Gaza, then fly out the next day, wondering how the Israelis can simply change our flight. Weaker than ever, I sit collapsed in my seat, my gut cramping the whole way back to Frankfurt. We part and go our separate ways—Salem to Freiburg, Dieter to Bielefeld, and I to Darmstadt. But I do not feel like I'm returning home. I've left it. Palestine has entered my heart, and I am determined to go back, to find a way to make a difference. My life will never be the same.

PART II

RESISTANCE

40th Commemoration of the Nakba

Intifada Through Oslo 1987-1996

10

Sabra and Shatila

After another year in Germany, as my internship is coming to a close, I heed my grandmother's words in her letter to me postmarked from Florida: "I think it's time you came home." The word "home" jumps off the page. Where is home? Germany? The US? My thoughts shift back to Palestine, and my heart warms, then sinks with the thought of going even farther away.

When I arrive in Fort Myers, Florida, in the summer of 1987, my grandmother takes me to her condo in a perfectly manicured retirement subdivision. At first, I do feel somehow right at home among her exquisite antiques and plush furniture I recognize from childhood visits to my grandparents' stately home that overlooked the Blue Ridge Mountains in Blowing Rock, North Carolina. And yet, my mind shifts back to Salem's shared home in Gaza, open to the sky.

My grandmother's home feels almost too comfortable, the wall-to-wall cream carpet covered with Oriental rugs too lavish, the illuminated collection of antique cups in the glass-paneled breakfront frivolous, the hand-painted glass candy jar filled with individually wrapped Andes mint chocolates too perfectly placed. The scent of my grandmother's Sweetheart soap in the guest bathroom outfitted with a tub and shower and flush toilet overwhelms my nostrils as I recall the stench of raw sewage in the squat toilet infested with giant beetles that drains into the passageway in Gaza. The contrast rips at my heart, calling me to even out the inequities of history.

When I tell my grandmother about my travels to Gaza, she is shocked by the hardship Palestinians endure under occupation. She disappears for a moment, then returns with my grandfather's medical instruments as an ear, nose, and throat doctor she had tucked away for safekeeping after he passed away, and wonders if she can donate them to Gaza. Now, even my grandmother cares about Palestine.

The summer goes too fast. I know I need to finish school, but all I can think about is Palestine. I think of Salem's mother, her smile as wide as the sea, Salem's father keeping a steady hand quilting blankets, and their eight children. I think of Salem's older sisters with children of their own, and the younger ones faithfully completing their lessons with such an uncertain future. It has been nearly a year since I visited Save the Children in Gaza. Another year of misery for Salem's family, another year of playing dominoes to pass the time. *What have I done to make a difference there other than longing to go back?* And yet, I begin to wonder if there's some way to make a difference from here. Either that, or I could go back after graduation.

I keep in touch with Salem, expressing my determination to return to his homeland, but he remains focused on building a life for himself in Germany. His family is counting on him to support them from afar. I commit to going back to Palestine as soon as I graduate.

My declared major is international studies with political science and German, and yet I am eager to study Arabic and Russian. Wayne State University in Detroit offers both languages, so I enroll there while finishing up my bachelor's at the University of Michigan–Dearborn. It is a crazy schedule racing from one campus to the other, but this way, I get to take all the classes I want. In my spare time, I read the *New York Times* searching for news on the Palestinian-Israeli conflict, but the reports focus on skirmishes between Israelis and Palestinians, where Israelis are the victims righteously defending themselves from Palestinian violence.

I want others to see the face of the story, but there is still so much to learn. For more in-depth coverage, I turn to the *Christian Science Monitor*, the *Washington Report*, and bulletins I receive in the mail from Amnesty International and Human Rights Watch reporting human rights violations in Israeli prisons, particularly after the Palestinian uprising of the First Intifada breaks out later that year in December 1987, two decades after Israel occupies the West Bank and the Gaza Strip during the Six-Day War and nearly four decades since the Nakba.

I read *Arab and Jew: Wounded Spirits in a Promised Land* by David Shipler, a gift from my sister at Christmas, as well as a collection of Palestinian poetry called *Palestinian Wedding*, both of which keep my head and my heart centered on Palestine. Busy with school, Salem calls me occasionally, his voice my only anchor to Palestine and his family. I write him long letters in German, reflecting on what I hear about the situation there and my frustration over the lack of awareness in the US:

> *No one here can imagine the situation in Gaza. I speak about it often and hope that I can awaken a sense of justice in people. Especially since people here understand the idea of human rights, so they should not tolerate such crimes. They have to see that everyone is affected...Do they understand their money is going to Israel and what comes of it? It's not to plant flowers. People are being killed and treated like dirt. How is it that a state that was born out of the circumstances of history, a people that suffered so much, can inflict such evil on others? Maybe for that very reason! Love cannot come from pain, peace from hate...Peace can only come from love.*

I am in my second week of classes when I hear about two events related to Palestine, both about the 5th Commemoration of the Sabra and Shatila massacre. Over a three-day period in September 1982, at the height of the Lebanese Civil War, the Israeli army gave the green light to Christian Falangists to attack the Sabra and Shatila refugee camps in Lebanon, killing hundreds of Palestinians, including women and children.[9] I decide to go to both events, hoping to learn more about the history of the region. The first is a dinner event at the Beit Hanina Social Club in Dearborn, and the other a campus event at Wayne State University later that week. I enter the one-story building of the social club to find several long lines of tables with a podium at the front and a spread of aluminum foil pans at the back, florescent lights casting a gray shadow across the room. I feel like I am walking into a family gathering with men, women, and children, whole families, some speaking Arabic, some English. My eyes wide open, I scan the room for a place to sit before anyone notices me.

At the end of one table by the entrance, I spot a few empty chairs across from a younger woman with blonde hair. I make my way toward her, say hello, and she invites me to join her. It turns out she is married to a Palestinian. *That is her connection. What is mine?*

I explain how I had traveled to Jerusalem and Gaza the year before. Now, I am studying political science and Arabic and want to learn more about what is going on in Palestine to make sense of what I witnessed with my own eyes. Sitting here on the other side of the world, she and I talk about how we are gathered to commemorate the loss of Palestinian lives. I tell her that being here brings me closer to Palestine, ironically just minutes away from my mother's home in Detroit.

It turns out Beit Hanina is a village in Palestine between Ramallah and Jerusalem. I don't understand why all these Palestinians are here in Dearborn, but I am grateful to be among them to learn more about the massacre, which I only touched on in my studies of the Lebanese Civil War while in Germany.[10] Here I feel the human cost of war. I am among Palestinians, grieving the loss of those forced to flee their homes in 1948 only to end up losing their lives in a massacre sanctioned by Israel. It only adds to my frustration I expressed to Salem—that Americans need to know how American policy plays out on the other side of the world. We are supporting one people at the expense of another.

We eat a simple dinner of *mujadara*—lentils and rice topped with sautéed onions served with a tomato cucumber salad cut into tiny pieces—while someone gives a speech on American policy in the Middle East, the challenges of fighting AIPAC—the American Israel Public Affairs Committee, which is the Israeli lobby in Washington, DC—and the horrors of what happened at the Sabra and Shatila refugee camps in Lebanon only five years earlier. It is a lot of information to digest, of heartache, but I am grateful to be here, to deepen my understanding of history so I can be part of a more just future for Palestine.

Later in the week at Wayne State, I walk up to a tent at the plaza outside the Student Center. It's filled with displays of maps, photos, and information on Palestine. A tall, thin student approaches me, his heavy, reddish-brown mustache more prominent than his short, brown hair. Draped around his neck is a traditional red-and-white Palestinian head scarf called a *kufiyyeh*. He wonders what I know about the situation in Palestine. I explain that I was just there the year before and am following events closely.

A number of Palestinian students are helping out at the event, all young men. I am curious how they came to be students there since Salem had expressed an interest in continuing his studies in the US to become a medical assistant. I learn about student visas, work restrictions, more about the horrors of the Sabra and Shatila massacre, and the plight of the Palestinians. Nasser, the tall student with the kufiyyeh, promises to keep me informed of future events, so I give him my phone number, thank him, and go on my way.

After over two years in Germany, my German is so strong that I take upper-level classes on East German literature with my father as my professor at the University of Michigan–Dearborn. My father recommends I take a history class on the Holocaust from Sidney Bolkowski, one of his colleagues who interviewed over 300 Holocaust survivors, which gives me a deeper understanding of the Zionists' urgency for a Jewish homeland, and philosophy courses from another Jewish professor, Elias Baumgarten, who teaches Medical Ethics and The Ethics of War and Peace. Elias and I become lifelong friends grounded in our shared interest of coming to terms with Nazi Germany and finding peace in Israel and Palestine. I also take a political science class on Sino-Soviet relations and another class with Ronald Stockton on the Israeli-Palestinian conflict, where I have to write a paper predicting what will happen there in 50 years. I imagine that Israel and Palestine will become one state for both peoples. I wonder what will become of my prediction in 2037.

Unfortunately, the following semester another Jewish professor is not as receptive to my interest in Palestine when he assigns us each to do a cultural presentation. He points to his list on the board, which includes

Israel, but I want to present on Palestine. "Why Palestine? I already have Israel." When I challenge him, explaining that Israel and Palestine represent different cultures, he flippantly suggests I do Nazi Germany, which is also not on the list. I ignore this direct attack on my father—his colleague—and my German heritage and insist on Palestine, but my defiance, together with a paper comparing dispossession among Native Americans and Palestinians, lands me a C in the class. I am more sad than angry that this Jewish professor can only see me, my father, and the Palestinians as enemies.

In Arabic class at Wayne State, I meet Annette, who is studying anthropology and also has a strong interest in the Middle East. Nasser faithfully keeps me informed of events on campus, which Annette and I attend together. Palestinian student activism is strong on campus and only increases after the outbreak of the First Intifada in December 1987. Events showcase Palestinian artists such as the cartoonist Naji al-Ali, who was assassinated in August 1987 at the age of 51, just before Nasser and I met. Naji al-Ali created the character Handala to shame leaders of the Arab world in their ineptness in securing justice in Palestine. Exiled at the age of 10 to the Ein al-Hilweh refugee camp in Lebanon, Naji al-Ali mirrors his own loss of Palestine through Handala.

Unfortunately, Handala never got to grow up. He never got to return to his homeland, but in spite of Naji al-Ali's assassination, Handala lives on in the popular culture of Palestinians, waiting for their return.

Nasser, Annette, and I attend films and other events on Palestinian culture and history, such as November 29—the International Day of Solidarity with the Palestinian People,[11] the commemoration of Land Day,[12] and the International Day of Solidarity with Palestinian Political Prisoners, which draws attention to the imprisonment and mounting administrative detention of Palestinians.[13] This practice that Israel adopted from the British Mandate continues to this day, where people can be held without trial for up to six months if they are deemed a security threat and their captivity extended indefinitely. At the height of the intifada, as many as 10,000 Palestinians, mostly young men, were held in a detention camp in the Naqab desert known as Ansar III and subject to torture and the harsh elements of that climate—the blistering heat of summer days and bitter, damp cold of winter nights.

"Handala was born ten years old, and he will remain that way, for I was expelled from Palestine as a ten-year-old, and when I can return to Palestine, he will start growing up."[14]

Handala cartoon from Palestinian artist Naji al-Ali. (Source: Handala.org)

In addition to campus events, we attend local events in the community, such as the annual banquet of ACCESS (Arab Community Center for Economic and Social Services) or the local chapter of the Arab American Anti-Discrimination Committee (ADC), where we hear prominent speakers like Ambassador Clovis Maqsoud or esteemed academic and activist Ibrahim Abu-Lughod.[15]

We also participate in demonstrations against the Israeli occupation and Israeli brutality during the intifada. The chant addressing Israel's prime minister, "Shamir Shamir, you should know, the occupation's got to go!" still rings in my ears. I even learn to dance the traditional Palestinian line dance known as *dabkeh* and participate as a model in a fashion show of traditional handmade Palestinian dresses embroidered with *tatriz*—the cross-stitch of Palestine.[16] *Like the woman at Damascus Gate.* I learn that these dresses are also worn at weddings and on special occasions, their colors and designs distinctive of each region in Palestine. These events, as well as lengthy discussions with Nasser, deepen my cultural and historical understanding of Palestine, Palestinians, and their deep connection to their homeland in their struggle for liberation. And yet, the same questions persist in my mind. *What else can I do to make a difference there? Where do I belong?*

In an attempt to answer these questions, I help organize events under the umbrella of the Palestine Solidarity Committee. I am convinced that if only Americans understood that Palestinians want to live in dignity, they would be supportive of Palestinian self-determination. The more involved I become, the more I want to be part of the solution by learning from the men, women, and children in Palestine, engaged in nonviolent resistance against the Israeli occupation of their homeland.[17]

Some Palestinian students are suspicious of my involvement, assuming

I must be a spy, but Nasser assures them my interest is genuine. My persistence breaks down the wall of mistrust, and soon I have a whole new circle of friends, including from other student groups against apartheid in South Africa, US involvement in Nicaragua, and restrictions on land use among Native Americans right here in the US. We publicize each other's events and sometimes hold joint events. I am honored to meet leaders of the African National Congress (ANC) and make local connections about global struggles.

The more I learn about the hypocrisy of American foreign policy in its thirst for global domination, the more I burn inside. I want to change the world. I want justice. I want to hold political officials accountable for their complicity in ruining people's lives through favoring some nations over others, not because of their leadership in solving world problems and exemplary behavior, but solely because they serve our economic and military interests, our thirst for global hegemony. I want America to practice what it preaches with respect to democracy, liberty, and human rights. What good are our ideals if we close an eye to the transgressions of our friends over our enemies? I start to wonder in my letters to Salem if I am better off trying to make a difference from the US:

> *Maybe I can have more impact from here. It would be nice to simply live and not have to think about all these problems, but I cannot and don't want to as long as everything is so messed up. There are enough people who close their eyes to the truth. Based on what I have already seen, I cannot do that.*

In the spring of 1988, student organizations charter two school buses to Washington, DC, to a massive demonstration down the National Mall in support of self-determination for the Palestinian people. With a black and white kufiyyeh draped around my neck, I join in with others to carry a giant Palestinian flag flat over our heads, the bright sun illuminating red, white, green, and black. We chant in unison. "Hey, hey, ho, ho, the occupation's got to go!" When we reach the White House, speaker after speaker talks about the plight of the Palestinians and America's role in perpetuating their suffering through American policies, including nearly four billion dollars in military aid to Israel, more than to any other country in the world. My voice has joined thousands of others demanding change.

The academic year ends that spring, and I still have one more semester in the fall before I graduate. During that summer, in partial fulfillment of requirements as a student of political science, I secure an internship with Congressman Howard Wolpe from Michigan at his office in Washington, DC. As an intern on Capitol Hill, I can attend congressional hearings on the Middle East. At one hearing on the civil war in Lebanon, I witness American officials scramble for ways to bring stability to the region. Conversations in Hebrew and English echo across the room. *No Arabic. No Arabs.* How are they supposed to find a solution to the crisis in Lebanon if there is no Arab representation?

I attend another hearing on the Israeli army's use of rubber bullets against Palestinians during the intifada in a tiny room with only two members of Congress and no media present to listen to eyewitness testimonies from a delegation that just returned from the area. In comparison, an event I attend hosted by AIPAC is held in a large room set up like an auditorium with hundreds of US representatives present, echoing American support for our friend and ally, Israel. I don't understand how some members of Congress, including Howard Wolpe, can call for sanctions against the apartheid regime in South Africa but are silent on Palestinian rights, clearly intimidated by AIPAC. Some explain that to criticize Israel would ruin their chance for re-election, so they choose to remain silent. I continue to pour my heart out to Salem:

> *Tell me why people are so shameless. Where is people's humanity? This world is so sad—the Earth is treated just as badly as people (and here I mean Palestinians and everyone else, who are treated as subhuman). People have the capacity to be good, but often choose to drown themselves in evil. Some people are so terrified, like some Israelis, who only want power. There is no room left for peace, trust, love, community. People have to defend good as long as they live. All the kids cannot die in vain—we can't do that to them. Never.*

While I am agonizing over American policy, Salem calls me to let me know he has secured a position in a local clinic as a radiology assistant. Finally, he will have income to help support his family. It is clearer to me than ever that I have to do what I can to change American policy. Salem has to focus on making a living so his family can survive.

Evenings, I volunteer at ADC. They are about to launch an ad campaign in the public transportation system in DC to publicize the brutality of the Israeli army given Defense Minister Yitzhak Rabin's "Breaking Bones" policy, which orders soldiers to break wrists and fire rubber bullets and tear gas at Palestinian youth armed with nothing but stones and Molotov cocktails. One night, I plaster the city with posters while rats scurry across the sidewalks. Soon, I see one of the ads in the Metro with the chilling black-and-white photo of an Israeli soldier beating a Palestinian with his baton with the caption "Your Tax Dollars At Work."

I leave DC at the end of the summer completely disillusioned. I hate politics. I don't see how I could ever work for the American government given its policies in the Middle East. Top American officials have sold their souls to be in office. Going into politics is clearly not the answer. I want to get out of the US, find a way to make a difference on the ground in Palestine. I begin to return my focus to organizations like Save the Children, but I have to finish school first. Again, I reach out to Salem:

> *It is hard to focus on my studies when there are more important things going on in the world besides whether I pass my exams or not. Everyone asks me if I am having relationship issues and doesn't believe me when I say I am worrying about the world. That is my love issue—I wish I could love the world! Most people just live their lives either way. We have to keep moving forward, but not just any which way. What will I tell my children?*

More motivated than ever to return to Palestine, I am hired to conduct a study for a local organization interested in interfaith connections between Christians and Muslims in the Arab community in Dearborn, Michigan, where I earn enough for a plane ticket. I graduate in December 1988. Now, I am finally free to go back. Before I leave, I write to Save the Children to volunteer in Gaza, excited to have learned some Arabic and more about the history of Palestine and the struggle for self-determination. I anxiously await their reply, certain they will find a role for me, but when I receive their response, they regret to inform me they are only looking for medical personnel and engineers at this time. Other organizations like Al-Haq, Law in the Service of Man, need lawyers or people with experience in human rights. I have graduated from college and can't find a way to contribute on the ground in this far-off place that has entered my heart.

Despite having nothing lined up, I return to Germany in January 1989 as a stepping stone to Palestine. I get to see Salem, who is grateful to be working as a radiology assistant so he can support his family but admits that he longs to spend time in his homeland, connect with his family, even if it means living life under Israeli occupation. I am energized to make a difference in Palestine, and yet Salem feels his homeland is out of reach.

Rather than return to the US, I secure a five-year work permit thanks to my German ancestry and get a job at a translation firm in a small town near Freiburg, but the workload thins out by summer. In desperation, I work as a server at a local pub, the Warsteiner Keller, to pay my rent. As I wait on people in German, English, or French, it is not long before I ask myself what I am doing in Germany. The whole point was to go back to Palestine, but without a clear idea of what I would do there, Palestine feels out of reach for me, too. All I can do is read the headlines and a few books I brought along, such as Fawaz Turki's *Soul in Exile,* David Grossman's *The Yellow Wind,*[18] and Uri Avnery's *My Friend, the Enemy,*[19] or ones I find in Germany, such as Yoram Binur's *Mein Bruder Mein Feind (My Brother My Enemy)*[20] and an older photography essay of Palestinian refugees I pick up at a secondhand bookstore called *They Are Human Too.*[21]

Meanwhile, pressure is mounting in Eastern Europe, beginning in Poland with the Solidarity movement and sweeping across Eastern Europe until the Soviet Union can no longer maintain its hold on the Eastern Bloc. The Berlin Wall falls. No one is shot. It is November 9, 1989. Border guards simply step aside as East Berliners walk through the checkpoints that only moments before were fortified with a shoot-to-kill policy if anyone dared cross at will.

Young Germans swing sledgehammers at the wall, creating windows through concrete that has separated East and West Berlin for nearly three decades. Germans step through holes in the wall; others climb up to sit on top, their legs dangling like they are on an amusement ride. It is one massive celebration. No one knows what's to come, but everyone is celebrating the end of an era of separation. My eyes pool with tears as I witness the world changing before my eyes. If the global force of the Soviet Union can dissolve like sugar in water, anything is possible.

With no path to Palestine, I go home to Detroit for Christmas in December 1989 to regroup. I am surprised to find that Nasser, who went back to Palestine after graduation, is also in the States, disillusioned by his year back home, where even as a fresh college graduate from an American university, employment opportunities are nonexistent in the midst of the intifada. Nasser explores going back to school to get his master's degree but instead accepts a sales position at a computer networking company, which secures him an H-1B work visa that allows him to stay in the country. I get a job as a German translator at Schlumberger CAD/CAM in Ann Arbor, Michigan, a perfect transition from my translation work in Germany.

Nasser and I go out to dinner at The Rhinoceros, a trendy bistro in the Warehouse District of Detroit, where we spend the evening talking about our hopes and disappointments abroad over the heart-wrenching songs of a female vocalist playing piano. Even though we kept in touch while we were both abroad with occasional letters and phone calls, I am both surprised and delighted when he gives me a framed 3D hand-painted mold of Jerusalem and a pair of gold earrings from Palestine, which lighten the weight of our otherwise heavy conversation.

The intifada is in its second year. The Israeli military administration has closed schools and universities. People can hardly move from one place to another with all the checkpoints and closures. Water and electricity are restricted as a form of collective punishment for resisting the occupation.

I spent a whole year in Germany and never even made it to Palestine. It is as if Nasser and I are both stuck in the US, though our lives are intersecting in ways that have us both feeling like we could have a shared future.

We start our new jobs about the same time, both getting a taste of professional life, the nine-to-five American work schedule, having a paycheck. Working in corporate America is a shift for both of us. Nasser wears a suit and tie to work, and I have a whole new wardrobe of straight polyester dresses or wool-blend suits just below the knee instead of my long, flowing cotton skirts, pantyhose instead of bare legs, and low pumps instead of Birkenstocks.

My life is in order, but the world is in chaos. In spite of Mikhail Gorbachev's efforts at *glasnost* and *perestroika*, the Soviet Union collapses. The West courts Eastern Europe to embrace capitalism and democracy. Countries held together by the Soviet umbrella break apart. Yugoslavia crumbles into a devastating civil war. President George H.W. Bush leads a UN-backed coalition of nations to war against Iraq's invasion of Kuwait. In 2003, his son, President George W. Bush, will again go to war with Iraq on false pretenses of weapons of mass destruction to remove Saddam Hussein from power.

The climate of the Gulf War makes it especially difficult working in a corporate environment where TV monitors are installed in the cafeteria so employees can "watch the war" over lunch or on their breaks and cheer on their American soldiers, as if watching a football game. I do my job and steer clear of the crowd. The 45-minute drive home offers the distance I need from the workday. A calm spreads through my body like a transfusion with each passing mile.

And yet I have hope with the release of Nelson Mandela on February 11, 1990 from prison after 27 years. This historic moment marks the dissolution of the Apartheid regime under President F.W. de Klerk, founded the same year as the establishment of the State of Israel in 1948. Nelson Mandela will go on to become the President of South Africa through democratic elections in 1994.

Just months after his release from prison, I have the privilege of hearing Nelson Mandela speak at Tiger Stadium in Detroit, living proof that the fight for peace, justice, human rights, and dignity can bring about change, that people's fight for freedom was not in vain. It will be 33 years later in

2023 that I get to hear his grandson, Chief Nkosi Zwelivelile Mandela, speak in Milwaukee, Wisconsin, to commemorate the 75th Nakba, carrying his grandfather's support for Palestinian liberation forward. *If it can happen for South Africa, why not Israel and Palestine?*

My connection to Nasser is an island of sanity in a troubled world. Our minds are drawn to each other in a process of mutual sensemaking. We have witnessed America win the Cold War and become the sole superpower calling the shots on the world stage. Countries are either with America or against it. The revolutionary spirit that led to nationalist movements demanding freedom and independence is usurped by the promise of Western democratic institutions and a global economy that pays off friends and starves enemies. It is a New World Order, but one that deliberately bypasses any progress in the Middle East, a reality that promises to plant powerful seeds of resentment across the Arab and Islamic world.

With our minds joined, it only follows that we join our hearts. On Christmas Eve, Nasser and I get engaged. Out of respect for my father, Nasser plays along when my father negotiates in jest over how many camels and chickens he would trade for me, even though he is drawing on the stereotype of the camel jockey of Arabia, which shares no overlap with Nasser's family's farming village culture. On a more serious note, I am aware that Nasser's parents might not be thrilled about the idea of their son marrying an American, so I insist that I will only go through with marriage with their approval. When Nasser relays the message, they are honored that I leave the final decision in their hands and give us their blessing. Our wedding date is set for September 1: 9/1/91.

When the day arrives, the culmination of our first meeting at the Commemoration of the Sabra and Shatila massacre in 1987, Nasser and I are blessed with perfect weather for our wedding ceremony in the Rose Garden at the Henry Ford Mansion in Dearborn, surrounded by my extended family and our college friends. We forego the Islamic ceremony of *katib al-kitab* since neither of us is particularly religious, opting instead to have my parents' Unitarian minister from the First Unitarian-Universalist Church in Detroit guide us through our vows. The intifada has taken its toll on the economic situation in Palestine, so Nasser's family cannot attend except for one of his nephews, who is studying in Dearborn, and another relative he studied with in Canada before coming to Detroit.

The butterflies gather in my stomach as my father walks me down the aisle to the music of a live quartet playing Vivaldi's "Spring." Nasser's best man, Tony, a Palestinian whom he also knows from Canada, and my maid of honor, Annette, whom I met at Wayne State University, read the poem *On Marriage* from the Lebanese poet Gibran Khalil Gibran in Arabic and English, where we promise to:

...stand together yet not too near together:
For the pillars of the temple stand apart,
And the oak tree and the cypress grow
not in each other's shadow.

The entire rite of passage unfolds like clockwork, the sun shining brightly in honor of this day.

The butterflies in my stomach release as we dance the night away beneath spotlights at our *hafleh*—the celebration of our marriage—to the steady rhythm of live Arabic music surrounded by tables of friends and family dining on an Arabic feast. I am reminded of the wedding I attended with Salem in 'Akka when our Palestinian friends parade us around the dance floor on chairs, echoing traditional chants from centuries past, only now, I am the bride. We dance round after round of the traditional line dance dabkeh I had taught my family the night before, as well as the Iraqi version following our Chaldean college friend Wejdan's lead, while her Palestinian husband Nader waves his hand back and forth melodically to the music from the sidelines.

Once my father makes a toast honoring everyone's presence at this celebration and we cut the cake, the festivities come to a close. Nasser and I are husband and wife. My love for Palestine has led me to a lifetime with a Palestinian, though not in Palestine, but in Detroit. I wonder where our future will lead us.

After our honeymoon in the pristine Upper Peninsula of Michigan, one of our favorite destinations for camping trips, and an excursion to Mackinac Island, where we rent a horse and buggy, we are both back at work. I also start my master's program in the Center for Middle Eastern and North African Studies at the University of Michigan in Ann Arbor, taking two classes at a time in an array of disciplines, including political science, history, sociology, and Arabic language and literature.

Fascinated with the mathematical precision of Arabic and its rich linguistic depth, I decide to conduct a sociolinguistic study of Nasser's village dialect for my master's thesis. Perhaps if I focus on the culture and history of Palestine, I will find a better way to have an impact. We plan to visit Palestine the following summer—a perfect opportunity to conduct my fieldwork. In the meantime, I am awarded a Foreign Language and Area Studies (FLAS) fellowship to study Arabic at Middlebury College in Vermont just before we go to Palestine. Unable to take a leave of absence from my job and frustrated with my corporate work environment, I resign so I can take full advantage of these amazing opportunities.

Shifting my focus to learning Arabic and traveling to Palestine, I feel like I am finally back on track. We will spend five weeks there beginning in early August 1992, the same time of year I visited Jerusalem and Gaza six years before. But this time, I am married to a Palestinian and speak Arabic. Nasser's family lives in a small village in the West Bank. His family are farmers, not refugees. I can't imagine what it will be like—and I can't wait to find out.

11

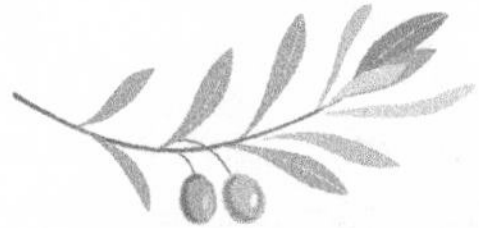

Jalameh

It is afternoon when Nasser and I arrive in his village of Al-Jalameh. The air is hot and still, the sky clear and pale blue, like the cotton jumper dress I am wearing. The butterflies in my stomach from my wedding return when I see a crowd of people gathered in front of a one-story stone house at the end of the road, young children running toward the taxi, peering at us with curiosity. When we get out of the taxi into the bright sun, Nasser's parents, whom I will address as 'Ami and 'Amti as their daughter-in-law, approach us first. 'Ami holds Nasser's shoulders with his wide, strong hands as they exchange kisses on both cheeks.

Ahlan wa sahlan!—Welcome! 'Ami's words, familiar, unlike when I arrived in Gaza six years earlier, filter through my mind and nestle into my soul like a visceral homecoming. His broad smile stands in contrast to his deep sharp voice, which commands the attention of everyone around him. Behind his black plastic-rimmed glasses, his large right eye, magnified by the lens, gives off a friendly sparkle. His left eye, normal in size, offers no particular expression. That must be his glass eye to replace the one he lost at the age of 40 from a metal shard while repairing a tractor. This loss as a young man doesn't seem to interfere with his cheerful and determined spirit. I shift my gaze to his traditional white headdress held in place with a doubled black cord known as *'iqal*. He reaches for my hands and chuckles, his voice softer in English he learned while working under the British Mandate after the fall of the Ottoman Empire in 1922.[22] "Hello, how are you?"

Not expecting 'Ami to speak any English, the butterflies in my stomach float away in the warm breeze over his soft brow and broad smile. "Fine, thank you!"

'Amti reaches her slender hands up to Nasser's face, kissing him repeatedly on both cheeks. A long white scarf wrapped loosely under her chin frames her smooth cheekbones and welcoming eyes and drapes over her long, full, green floral dress with a matching tie around her waist. I lean over to kiss her cheeks as she takes my right hand in hers and puts her other hand around the back of my neck. *Marhaba*—Hello, I offer in Arabic. 'Amti welcomes me repeatedly with the phrase, *Ahlan wa sahlan*, her voice quiet and moved, behind her a sea of eager faces.

Among them is an elderly man who walks toward us, his steps slow, a cane in his right hand. His slender frame is partially hidden by the long white scarf draped down his back, held in place by the same black 'iqal cord 'Ami is wearing. Nasser greets him and shakes his hand. *Ahleen, Sidi Rada!*—Hello, Grandpa Rada! I reach out my hand to him, lean forward, and kiss him on both cheeks. Everyone starts laughing, including the elderly man, whose eyes flutter like a shy schoolboy. Nasser explains that Sidi Rada is the oldest man in the village and that I shouldn't kiss him, but everyone gets a kick out of my lack of cultural knowledge.[23]

One by one, I meet the rest of Nasser's family. His eldest brother Ghazi, who by tradition is called Abu Ahmed, having named his eldest son Ahmed after Nasser's father, greets me in English, as does his wife Amal, the English teacher at the local girls' school across the street. Nasser's brother Jamal is in prison, having been accused of participating in resistance activities, but at least I get to meet his wife Samira and their three young children.

Even though US-led negotiations in Madrid in 1991 between Israel and the Palestinians brought an end to the intifada, many Palestinians remain in prison or under administrative detention. Their youngest child, not more than two, reaches up to Nasser. *Baba!* Nasser explains she thinks he is her father coming home from prison because they look so much alike.

Her mother intervenes. *La, hath 'Amu Nasser habibti. Baba fis-sijin*—No, that's Uncle Nasser, dear. Baba is in prison.

Nasser picks her up and kisses her on the cheek. *Habibti!*—My dear!

She stares at him in disbelief, her narrow chin tucked toward her chest. It has been almost a year since she saw her father. She wants Nasser to be him.

I meet each of Nasser's six sisters, who are all wearing white scarves and long dresses, their hair loosely covered, except for his youngest sister, whose soft, reddish-brown curls gleam in the bright sun. Her children's red hair matches Nasser's mustache. One sister has blonde hair, fair skin, and blue eyes. She looks more German than Palestinian. I feel the absence of his sister Khariyeh when Nasser introduces me to her three children. She passed away when she was seven months pregnant while Nasser was away at college. Nasser feels especially close to them because they are all he has left of her.

I learn that except for Khariyeh—Im Mahmoud—and Huda—Im Mohammed—both of whom married into the extended family in Jalameh, Nasser's sisters live in other towns and villages, having married "outside." Maha—Im Mahmoud—and Nawal—Im Ashraf—are visiting from Saudi Arabia, where their husbands—like many other Palestinians struggling to make ends meet under occupation—work to make enough money to build a life back home. Pressure builds in my head when Nasser explains that his sister Naziha—Im Abdullah—who is visiting from Amman, Jordan, where she lives with her husband, lost her residency following the Six-Day War in 1967.

Israel barred Palestinians, who were out of the country after the Six-Day War of 1967, from coming back to the territories they claimed after the war, including the West Bank, the Gaza Strip, and East Jerusalem, along with the Golan Heights of Syria. Even though Naziha's eldest son was born in Palestine during the Six-Day War, Naziha was living in Saudi Arabia at the time. A few weeks after the war, Naziha went to Jordan to meet up with her husband to travel back to Saudi Arabia. Shortly thereafter, Israel conducted a census in the West Bank and Gaza and declared anyone who wasn't present no longer a resident. Just like that, Naziha's residency was revoked. Now, she needs a visa from Israel to come home, and her sons—like refugees—are barred from visiting. *A visa to visit her homeland.* Only her daughter, who married a man from Jalameh, lives here. Ghazi was studying in Egypt at the time so would have lost his residency as well, except that he happened to be visiting during the census.

We also meet Nasser's two aunts, his father's sisters 'Amti Saymi and 'Amti 'Ayshi. I learn the entire village consists of two extended families, so roughly half the village shares Nasser's family name. My cheeks are aching from smiling, and my heart is filled with gratitude at the warm welcome. Even the youngest children, some held by their mothers, greet me with an outstretched hand or cheek. Though I have studied the Levantine dialect prevalent throughout Palestine, Jordan, Lebanon, and Syria, I mostly speak classical Arabic from my recent study at Middlebury College.[24] I must sound ridiculously formal, though everyone is so thrilled that Nasser's American wife speaks Arabic that they don't seem to care.

Nasser's sister Huda invites us to sit on two of the plastic chairs lined up in front of the house while his sister Suhaila—Im Fayyad—brings out a metal tray with neatly arranged glasses of juice. *Tafaddalou*—Please take one. Nasser and I gladly accept, thirsty from our two-hour drive from the airport. Others from the village come to greet us as the news of our arrival spreads, names and family relationships spinning in my head.

Before long, I have to go to the bathroom. One of his sisters leads me onto the veranda through the off-white double steel doors. *Like the doors of Salem's home in Gaza.* We enter a room with high ceilings and a large window covered with sheer white curtains that extend from the ceiling to the tile floor decorated with a geometric design of brown, green, mustard-yellow, and creamy white triangles. We pass through a room with a low ceiling lined with lime-green Formica cabinets, above them a storage area I later learn is called a *khusheh*, then through the kitchen. Huda shows me a narrow room with a squat toilet like the one in Gaza—though this one has a white porcelain base and a water reservoir positioned below a high window with a cord attached to flush. Beyond it is a larger room with a seated toilet. I thank her and enter the larger bathroom lined with white tile.

On the far wall is a shower head and a faucet below with two handles for hot and cold water above a drain in the floor. To the side is a tiny sink with a tiny mirror and a high window tilted open, flooding the bathroom with natural light. Next to the toilet is a plastic jug, the same type I used in Gaza, with a faucet in the wall to refill it. At least this time, I know how to use it. I close the door. A moment to myself, a moment of silence.

Back in front of the house, Nasser and I continue to greet visitors while

Nasser's sisters serve round after round of sweet Arabic coffee laced with cardamom in tulip-shaped cups, like when I visited the Bedouin family in the Naqab desert, and amber-colored tea with fresh mint in the same glass cups Salem's family used in Gaza. The sun is no longer high in the sky. Before long, dusk sets in. I try in vain to cover my ankles with my cotton dress as mosquitoes come out in full force.

The sky overhead has been dark for some time when we head indoors for the night. Nasser shows me our room, which is actually his parents' room with the same tile floor and high ceilings as the entranceway, a large bed in the center, and a shiny white wardrobe. Floor-to-ceiling sheer curtains frame the front window that faces the street; the other window overlooks an enclosed veranda. Narrow windows over the doorways allow air to circulate even if the doors are closed. Adjacent to this room is another room lined in mats with two large windows.

Nasser shows me the oldest part of the house, a single room with a high, domed ceiling and walls a meter thick called the *'aqid*. The wooden double door used to be the entrance to what was originally a one-room house, where Nasser and his brothers and sisters were all born. The three windowsills are so deep I can imagine sitting there quite comfortably. In the fourth wall is an arched, indented area called a *hamel*, which literally means "carrier," that holds the mats when they are not spread out on the ornate tile floor that frames the room like a giant rug. Nasser points out photographs hanging on the wall of his grandfather wearing the same traditional white headdress with 'iqal—a photograph of his father as a younger man wearing a suit and tie without a headdress, a temporary flirtation with modernity under the British Mandate, and a photo of his mother when she was younger with a simple white scarf tied under her chin revealing her dark hair parted in the middle.

Off the veranda at the front of the house is the formal living room called a *diwan*, the walls lined with a brown plush sofa set and a matching Formica coffee table in the center with smaller versions off to the sides. A double set of steel doors leads to the back of the house. Each room has a single fluorescent bulb on one wall, reminiscent of Gaza.

I will come to learn that this house is the center of Nasser's extended family, the gathering point for all the children and grandchildren. It is simple and spacious, bare of furnishings but filled with family, a space full of life. As I drift off to sleep that night, all the friendly faces of Nasser's family swirl in my head. I have a home in Palestine, while Palestinians in Gaza still long to return home.

We awake to the faint glow of dawn and the sound of roosters crowing flowing in with the cool breeze from the open window of our bedroom. Nasser's brother Ghazi and his oldest son arrive with several black buckets and a metal pole outfitted with a metal cup at one end. Jamal's wife Samira is waiting outside with her three children, their bright, friendly eyes eager with anticipation. *Sabah al-khair!*—Good morning! I respond in kind. *Sabah an-nur!* I feel wide awake, excited for our early morning adventure while the rest of the village sleeps.

We head to the *wa'ra*—the rocky hills just outside the village—to pick *saber*—cactus pears. I can't wait to try this unique fruit I have neither seen nor tasted. It is August, the hottest month of the year, when the saber are ready to harvest.

We walk through the village along one- and two-story concrete houses, an occasional scrawny, stray cat scattering out of sight. It is not only the hottest time of year, but also the driest. It has already been months since it rained, and it will be some months more before the scorched earth finds relief. The narrow road is paved, but not along the houses, so our feet stir up dust as we walk. My ears tune in to Nasser and Ghazi's animated exchange in the village dialect, the children prancing along through the quiet, empty streets while Samira and I exchange an occasional smile when our eyes meet.

We pass between the last houses of the village where the pavement ends, then continue on a dirt road between dry fields until we reach a wide path up the rocky hillside. We pass between two giant clumps of cactus that glisten bright green in the early morning sun until we reach an open clearing scattered with olive trees. Sprawling dried brush peeks out from uneven boulders, the thorns of one bush forming a perfect hexagon known as *shantoul*. My ankles catch on the thirsty vegetation as we navigate the uneven terrain. Nasser explains that saber survives only on rainfall and serves as a natural fence to demarcate people's share of the wa'ra. It is only later I learn that saber is a symbol of resilience for Palestinians because it is all that is left in the villages Israel destroyed in 1948, an eyewitness to where they once lived.

The sun already feels scorching against my bare neck, exposed by my high ponytail, when Nasser announces we have arrived at his family's section of the wa'ra. We pause in front of a broad cluster of saber. My eyes follow the interconnected green leaves speckled with sizable thorns. Closer to the ground, the uniform leaves fuse together to become the grayish-brown bark of its sturdy trunk. Nasser positions himself with his feet apart, raises both arms, and extends the pole toward the upper crust of one of the cactus leaves to the oval-shaped cactus pears that line the top edge of each leaf like a crown. The pale-green saber appear smooth with evenly spaced brown specks. The riper ones have a soft peachy hue, as if an artist added a splash of color with a soft brush.

Ghazi cautions us to stand upwind since the saber are covered with tiny, nearly invisible thorns that can easily get lodged in our skin or eyes. Gripping the pole with both hands, Nasser positions the cup end over one of the ripe pears, and with a quick rotation of his wrist, he snaps the cactus pear into the cup, lowers it to the ground, and dumps it onto the dry earth. Each saber sparks a wave of jubilation.

I am eager to try my hand at the technique, but the tool feels heavy and awkward in my grip. The first couple of saber fall to the ground with a thud, landing out of reach between the thorny leaves. Shame warms my face to have wasted the fruit, but Ghazi smiles encouragingly, delighted at my determination. Finally, I catch one in the cup and lower it to the ground, then hand the tool back to Nasser to carry on. He and Ghazi take turns picking this unusual fruit one by one, moving along the mass of thorns in search of other prime specimens until the sun is high overhead.

As the mounds of saber form on the dry earth, Samira gathers a bunch of one of the brush plants called *shtella* that grows wild among the boulders, breaking them off at the stem to make a hand broom she brushes back and forth against the cactus pears. I marvel at this technique to remove the fine thorns from the thick peel, all part of the local knowledge to harvest this intimidating fruit. The children are still too young to either pick or clean the saber, but they watch attentively, just as their parents must have watched when they were children.

Once Samira has brushed the saber thoroughly, Ghazi carefully transfers them into the black buckets. It is only after we have filled three buckets that we are invited to sit in the shade of an olive tree and taste this unique fruit. We gather around Ghazi as the eldest among us and watch him cut off one end of the thick peel with a pocketknife, then the other, exposing a light-green flesh that glistens in the sun. He makes a clean cut into the leathery peel from end to end, then pulls it back from both sides until the egg-shaped inner fruit is exposed like a jewel on a platter.

"Try it!" His small, friendly eyes eagerly await my reaction.

I look to Nasser for direction.

"Go ahead. You'll like it."

I reach for the glistening fruit, tugging gently since it is still attached to the peel. I cup my hand around the wet fruit so it doesn't slip through my fingers and take my first bite—so juicy and sweet! The flesh, still cool from the night air, has a soft crunch like watermelon but denser. My taste buds struggle to associate this fresh taste with fruit I know, but I can't place it. With my second bite, I discover buried within this fruit are sizable seeds. My sudden pause and wide eyes give me away.

Nasser laughs. "Just swallow them!"

I override my hesitation and allow what seem like cherry pits to pass into my throat by only partially chewing to keep them buried in the flesh. Success! Ghazi and Samira smile approvingly, as if I have just engaged in a rite of passage. Ghazi cuts open another saber and offers it to Samira. Then the children each get one, and finally, Nasser and Ghazi indulge.

We share another round or two of this intimate ritual before making our way back to the village. Nasser explains that the fruit itself is like the life of the Palestinians, surrounded by the thorns of Israeli occupation. Palestinians must have a thick skin to survive the denial of their identity and right to live in their homeland, but on the inside, they are full of life and carry on, drawing from their deep connection to the land that sustains them.

Nasser and Ghazi each carry one of the buckets packed with freshly picked saber. Ghazi's son takes the pole, balancing it on his shoulders with his long, slender arms. Samira carries the third bucket. When I try to take it from her, she refuses with a click of her tongue, as if I have insulted her, then smiles with gratitude that I want to carry back the harvest. Rather than surrender the handle completely, she allows me to place my hand next to hers so we carry the load together, sharing both the burden and the bounty. Nothing could make me feel more welcome.

The sun nearly overhead is almost unbearable, with not a cloud in the sky. Hours have passed since we left the house. Already the refreshing saber gives way to an undeniable thirst as we follow the dirt road back into the village, now bustling with activity. Children scatter as small dusty cars drive by. Men gather here and there, chatting amongst themselves, and groups of women coming and going pause to admire our harvest. Samira and Ghazi each take a bucket home. Nasser's parents' eyes open wide at the sight of our treasure. Nasser cuts open several saber for them, an unwavering gift from their land, then dumps the rest into the lower drawer of the refrigerator to keep cool for another time. Nothing more beautiful than sharing the fruits of our labor!

In the afternoon, Nasser's sisters make what becomes my favorite dish, *kusa mahshi*, which is stuffed baby squash in a tangy yogurt soup over rice. They serve the soup in large bowls next to a platter of rice sprinkled with parsley and roasted almonds topped with chunks of lamb. 'Amti makes her best attempt to be exempt from her children's generosity of spooning heaps of rice into a flat-rimmed soup bowl by clicking her tongue, then calling out in her distinctive village dialect laden with *chaf*, the affricated version of the Arabic letter *kaf* (ك).[25] *Mish chithir*—Not too much.

But it is too late. 'Amti's bowl is already piled with rice topped with a large chunk of lamb and almonds. They offer me a separate bowl of yogurt soup with extra almonds since I don't eat meat. As the sauce seeps into the rice, I add more, delighting in my first experience eating yogurt warm. Dinner is followed by hot tea with fresh mint, then a platter of green grapes from the grapevine on the side of the house.

We all laugh as 'Amti tells a story about how when Nasser was little, he went missing. They looked through the whole house and outside, asked the neighbors, but he was nowhere to be found, only to discover him lying on his back under the bed next to a large platter of grapes she picked earlier that day, clasping a bunch of grapes in each hand, his cheeks bulging. My heart swells with the image of Nasser tucked away in his own paradise. I am not surprised since nothing makes him happier than fresh, delicious food. Growing up surrounded by the richest soil in the world, it is no wonder Nasser carries this deep appreciation for the bounty of the harvest throughout his life. Now I, too, am sharing in the harvest.

The next day, we are invited to Nasser's brother Faisal's house for the midday meal, *al-ghada*. Nasser's sister Kifah—Im Fadi—who is visiting from Nablus with her six children, comes with us, along with along with 'Ami and 'Amti. It is mid-afternoon when Faisal's eldest son summons us to their house they recently built with money Faisal earned in Saudi Arabia. We pass through a set of steel double doors into a center stairwell. The rest of the ground floor is still unfinished with no walls, only concrete columns supporting the second floor where they live.

At the top of the stairs, Faisal, whose eldest son is also named Fadi, giving him the traditional name Abu Fadi, is standing in the threshold, welcoming us with his smile and his words. *Ahlan wa sahlan!*

We take off our shoes, and he invites us to sit down on mats arranged around an impressive spread of stuffed baby squash cooked in tomato soup and stuffed grape leaves known as *dawali*, which will become our family's favorite dish. Feriyal points out small bowls of yogurt scattered across the tablecloth to eat with the dawali.

I hope my broad smile conveys more than my words. *Shukran*—Thank you.

Feriyal serves herself, then invites us to begin with *Tafaddalou*.

A chorus of *Bismillah ir-rahman ir-rahim*—In the name of God, the Almighty and Merciful—crosses the room.

Nasser says a shortened version, *Bismillah*—In the name of God, then starts eating.

The rice stuffing soaked in olive oil and lemon offers a rich and tangy taste as the tender leaves melt in my mouth. The tomato-soaked rice inside the baby squash complements this delicacy perfectly! When Feriyal sees how much I enjoy the grape leaves, she refills my plate, reminding me not to forget the yogurt. I put up my hand to interrupt her generosity, but it's no use. When I cannot finish my plate, her face beams that her guest is well fed.

After dinner, we walk down the road in front of their house called *Tariq Burqin*—Burqin Road—which leads all the way to the village of Burqin, where both Feriyal's and Nasser's mothers were born. I learn that 'Amti was brought on horseback at the age of 13 from Burqin to Jalameh via Tariq Burqin on her wedding day. That was the first time Nasser's parents saw each other. 'Amti giggles when 'Ami proudly declares that his mother couldn't have picked him a better wife!

We continue to their greenhouse made of PVC pipe and plastic sheeting shaped like a semi-cylinder they call *hamamot*—Hebrew for greenhouses since it is Israel who manufactures them. They are cultivating *khiyar*—cucumbers—on a plot of 'Ami's land. We enter through a wood-framed door covered in plastic, the moist heat enveloping my face. I breathe in the damp earth and fresh greenery towering over us in neat rows, each plant adorned with brilliant yellow flowers at the end of each cucumber. Feriyal, wearing a long burgundy *dishdasheh*—a traditional straight dress with loose sleeves embroidered in tatriz—snaps one of the cucumbers off the vine and hands it to me. *Dukki*—Try it. I remove the flower with my thumb and bite off the end, the sweet flavor and soft crunch delighting my senses. I take another bite.

Feriyal's smile awaits my response. *Zaki?*—Delicious?

Ah, zaki kithir!—Yes, very delicious!

Hathola baladi—These are local.

Nasser explains they are native to the land, the most prized cucumbers among Palestinians. I can see the pride in Faisal's and Feriyal's eyes as they show us their bountiful harvest they will sell at the market in Jenin. While I take the last few bites of my cucumber, Faisal calls out to the children to get buckets so we can all pick these perfectly formed cucumbers that fit neatly in our hands. The buckets fill quickly with a beautiful display of green adorned with yellow flowers. Now and then, we hear a crunch through the vines as their children sample the delicious bounty. It is not long before we fill all three buckets. Faisal gives us one bucket to take home, our share of the harvest.

We also visit Nasser's brother Jamal's greenhouse, where Samira is growing *pandoura*—tomatoes—on the land his father gave him to build a house someday. Boxes of tomatoes are already lined up to take to market. It is high season for tomatoes and cucumbers, so the prices are on the low side. Samira gives us a black bucket that we fill with the brightest red tomatoes off vines that cling to vertical strings in neat rows, those not yet ripe blending into the glowing green leaves. She insists we take home our bucket, though we do so with hesitation, especially while Jamal is in prison and doesn't have the income from his accounting business. I can't help but think of the desperation I witnessed in Gaza. No wonder, since refugees lost their land, and land is livelihood.

It is late afternoon when Nasser and I walk to the northernmost point in the village, where 'Ami owns land covered with olive and almond trees. Many of Nasser's young nieces and nephews follow along in the late afternoon sun. It is still hot, but a breeze picking up from the West provides some relief. Once we pass the last house, the road is no longer paved. Just ahead, we reach the land. There are no borders, no gates. Nasser simply knows we are there. Just beyond us is the Jalameh checkpoint, the gateway across the Green Line—the 1949 Armistice line—where a group of Israeli soldiers stand in the sun, their M16 rifles pointing toward the open sky.

The land slopes down farther north, offering a breathtaking view of the two neighboring Palestinian villages of Muqeibileh and Sandala, both of which now lie on the other side of the Green Line. Nasser points out tall, narrow pine trees called *surou* that mark the southern border of his father's land. The ground is dry and rocky. We walk over to one of many almond trees, where Nasser pulls off whole almonds in the shell with his hands. The trunk of the almond trees is smoother and leaner than that of the olive trees, the branches extending up and out like long arms, giving them an upright posture. Nasser lays a pile of almonds on the rocky ground, then returns to one of the trees to pick more. After he has gathered a small mound, he places an almond on a large flat rock, then takes a small rock with a flat edge and hits the almond with it repeatedly until the shell cracks open to reveal a reddish-brown almond, perfectly intact. He offers it to me. I carefully pull the almond out of its shell and pop it into my mouth, savoring the delightful crunch and sweet, sun-roasted flavor.

Nasser's nieces and nephews all gather their own mounds of almonds, the older ones helping the younger ones. Soon the *tak* of stones hitting almond shells fills the area. Some of the almonds come out in twos, carefully molded into each other like a yin-yang symbol. I crack open a few of my own, careful to hit just hard enough to crack the shell without smashing the almond.

The warm glow of the setting sun signals it is time to summon the children to head home. We reluctantly abandon our stations littered with cracked shells. Some of the children have folded up the bottom of their shirts to create a sack to take home their harvest. I take a final glance at the villages across the Green Line. Their white stone houses nestled between trees appear illuminated on the soft hillside. A single minaret towers over the village mosque to carry the voice of the *muezzin* to call Muslims to prayer five times a day. These towers have become the telltale signs of Palestinian villages, like a hand waving in the distance, calling out, "I am still here."

The rooftops of the Israeli settlement Gan Ner explode in fiery red above the line of neat white boxes below them. Their uniformity and starkness look severe in contrast to the nearby Palestinian villages that seem to grow right out of the soft curves of the landscape. I cannot help but cast a final glimpse on 'Ami's land across the Green Line. These borders that separate communities remind me of the fence in Rafah, blocking access of family members to each other, present but out of reach. The borders feel arbitrary and disruptive. I want Palestinians to be able to cross through them to restore access to their land. As I am learning in Nasser's village, the land is not only people's livelihood but also the cornerstone of Palestinian identity.

12

Jenin

One evening, Nasser and I are taking a walk through Jalameh when we see flares flying through the sky in the distance. I stand dumbfounded as the sky lights up over the city.

Nasser's face tightens. "They are looking for someone."

Barely does the sky begin to darken when another set of flares shoots into the sky like fireworks. *This is how the Israeli army hunts Palestinians.* By morning, news travels to the village that the Israeli army killed a young man the night before accused of engaging in resistance activities. Palestine's freedom fighters willing to sacrifice themselves for Palestine are known as *fida'iyin*. Those who die for Palestine are known generally as *shahid*—martyrs. It is customary to visit the martyr's family to show respect for their loss.

Jenin has been known as a hotbed of resistance dating back to the 1930s when Palestinian fighters under the leadership of Syrian-born Sheikh Izz ad-Din al-Qassam held out in the hills near the village of Ya'bid until the British assassinated him in 1935, igniting the Arab Revolt of 1936. This wave of Palestinian resistance came to a head with a significant rise in Jewish immigration to Palestine, which had doubled prior to the revolt. The traditional farming community of the *fellahin*, which made up the bulk of Palestinian society, felt particularly threatened by land sales of wealthy landowners to Jewish immigrants or the Jewish National Fund. Britain crushed this Palestinian uprising in collaboration with Zionist forces, resulting in the death of thousands and tens of thousands injured or imprisoned, including the Palestinian leadership, which greatly undermined their capacity to demand national representation, not to mention their ability to advocate for Palestine when Israel declared statehood in 1948.[26]

For Palestinians, the loss of their land with the establishment of the State of Israel in 1948 and the experience of living under Israeli occupation since 1967 were only exacerbated by the building of hundreds of Israeli settlements in the West Bank and Gaza, two of which were established near Jenin in 1983, namely the settlement of Ganim, named after Jenin, and Qadim, which means "ancient" in both Arabic and Hebrew. It is Palestinian resistance, particularly in Jenin and Gaza, that ultimately leads to the dismantling of these and other settlements in 2005, even though former residents vow to reestablish them to this day.

When we arrive at the martyr's family home in Jenin, we see two rooms, one filled with men, the other packed with women and children. All eyes turn toward us. When they realize I am a foreigner, they show us the house from the outside and explain how the Israeli army surrounded the house before opening fire. Some of the paint is blown off of the front steel double doors, decorated with black iron in the shape of a heart on each narrow door, where more than a dozen bullets pierced through. At one window, nearly 20 shots were fired, leaving gaping holes in the concrete exterior. In another area, the soot of black smoke carries up from the window, marking where the soldiers attempted to firebomb the house to force him out before his final escape to the roof, where they shot him dead.

Back inside, Nasser motions for me to enter a room with the women so he can go pay his respects to the men. I walk over to a line of women sitting on chairs, offering my hand to each. One of the women summons me to the far corner of the room, where a group of women are sitting on mats on the floor. She points to a young woman. *Hay maratu*—This is his wife. I lean over, take her hands in mine, and kiss her on both cheeks, her eyes sunk into her tense brow beneath the black scarf wrapped closely around her face. My stomach turns, knowing that Palestinians are being hunted like animals while Americans finance the killing.

I sit near her and listen to their silence. Now and then, they whimper, placing their hands to their foreheads. I feel the heat of their bodies and their pain dampen my clothes with sweat. When Nasser appears at the doorway, I rise to my feet to join him. He is holding a postcard of the young man standing under an olive tree with a cluster of saber around him, symbolizing rootedness and resilience, like the cactus pears Nasser and I picked on our first morning after arriving in Palestine. The young man is smiling, holding a rifle upright, wearing an olive-green shirt and pants and black boots. I look once more at the smattering of bullet holes in the front steel doors before we leave. I wonder if our presence softens their pain, but it doesn't feel like enough. There must be something we can do to stop all this senseless killing. I can't help but think of Israel's historical representation of self as David overcoming the colossal Goliath of the Arab armies threatening to push the Jews into the sea back in 1948, when in reality, it is the Palestinians who are facing a Goliath in Israel determined to crush Palestinian resistance in defense of their homeland.

We call for a car to take us to the center of town so Nasser can show me the city. It is a small, old car like the cars in Gaza. We get into the tight back seat and close the door, the dust of the dry summer thick on the dashboard and floor mats at our feet. There are only official taxis for greater distances between cities like Jenin, Nablus, or Ramallah, so private cars serve as taxis. For a few shekels, we get a ride from the house to the center of Jenin.

The driver drops us off in front of a bakery at the edge of the Old City. We get out quickly so as not to hold up traffic. There are no walls here like in Jerusalem, but I spot a large mosque ahead with a pale-green painted dome. Nasser points across the street to what would be a passageway to the oldest part of the city, completely blocked with oil barrels stacked several rows high. "The Israelis did that to control people's movement in the center of town."

We walk farther ahead past a man at the corner selling cassette tapes from a tall, flat cabinet, Arabic music blasting from a boom box into the street. Beneath the deep, forceful lyrics, I hear the distinctive, rhythmic patterns of the traditional tableh drum switching from deep *dum* tones to short *tak* clicks. I picture two hands alternating between the center and edge of a sheepskin drumhead attached to a ceramic base like the tableh Nasser and I have from his brother Jamal's wedding on display at our house in Detroit.

The beat is quick and catchy, and my eyes and ears are drawn to the music like a spell. Unlike when I first met Salem in Germany, the music no longer feels foreign to my ears.

We pass someone on the sidewalk selling giant laminated photos of Jerusalem with the Dome of the Rock prominent in the center. When we decide to buy one, the vendor rolls it up and puts a rubber band around it. We cross the street to a line of two-story buildings with storefronts under a covered walkway, some stores packed with household items, others with clothes on display out front and hanging overhead. Still others sell packaged food neatly stacked on shelves or grains in large burlap sacks on the sidewalk, reminiscent of the Old City in Jerusalem.

At the next corner, Nasser's steps quicken. "You have to try this." He walks over to a street vendor in front of a wooden cart with two plastic dispensers, each filled with a single block of ice, one with a yellow liquid, the other brown. *Ithneen tamar*—Two tamarinds. The man dispenses the brown liquid into two plastic cups, and Nasser hands him some change. "This is *tamar hindi*. Try it." My mouth comes alive with the nutty sweetness of this refreshing drink. "They grow on trees, then they soak them in water and add sugar."

Down a side street, I see more carts stacked with pyramids of cucumbers and tomatoes, wondering if they are from Nasser's brothers' farms. Several boys are pushing empty carts, offering to carry our things for five shekels. *'Arabai?*—Need a cart?

La, shukran, habibi—No, thanks, dear. Nasser smiles and continues down the sidewalk.

The main road is a boulevard lined with parked cars along the crowded sidewalks and cars driving bumper to bumper, beeping in vain to get the traffic moving with people walking around and in between them, reminiscent of Gaza. A young man is standing on the narrow median selling black buckets of saber just like we picked on our first morning in Jalameh. We cross the road between parked cars and a traffic jam creeping along at a snail's pace to a shop with a crowd of people standing in front of a counter. "This is the best place for hummus. It's all they make." Nasser orders a plate, which we enjoy with a basket of warm pita bread and sides of brightly colored pickled vegetables. The hummus is so tangy and creamy. "They still make it by hand—no machines." I try to imagine smashing such a large quantity of chickpeas by hand with a giant mortar and pestle.

We cross back over and continue down the main road. Around one corner, I see a stone monument with a pyramid-shaped top surrounded by a black metal fence with writing in German: *FLIEGER-ABTEILUNG 303*—Aviation Department 303—and a list of names of those missing or dead with dates listed below. Then, on another side, the word *JAGDSTAFFEL 1*—Hunting Division 1—is prominently written at the top with a plane propeller below mounted on the monument.

"What is that doing here?"

Nasser explains that a German warplane crash-landed here during WWI, so they made a monument honoring the crew. At that time, Palestine was under the Ottoman Empire, and Germany sent reinforcements known as the Asia Corps to back them against the British, a reminder of how contested this space was then and remains to this day.

Moments later, we hear gunshots and stop in our tracks. Just ahead, several Israeli soldiers are standing in the middle of the road aiming their M16 rifles in several directions. People scatter to safety. My eyes scan the area, only to find smoke from the gunfire dissipating from the second floor of a building across the street. Nasser takes my hand, and we cut through a side street to the other end of town. Clearly, Palestinians are hunted day and night, a terrifying game of cat and mouse, where Palestinians resist the occupation and Israelis crack down on those who dare defy their power.

We catch our breath at a money-changing shop, where Nasser knows the owner. The shots are still ringing in my ears when the shop owner greets us. *Ahleen, ya Nasser! Shou, hay maratak?*—Hello, Nasser! Is this your wife?

Nasser introduces me, and I shake his hand, trying to put the shots out of my mind. *Sharafna*—Glad to meet you.

Btakhki 'arabi!—She speaks Arabic! They briefly talk about the gunshots in Arabic. Before we leave, Nasser changes a hundred-dollar bill into Israeli shekels. His friend waves to both of us. *Ma'a salameh*—Go with peace.

Nasser answers in kind, *Allah yisalmak*—May God bless you.

I notice there is an appropriate phrase and response for all sorts of occasions in Arabic. *How long will it take me to learn what to say and when?* Still unsettled from the gunshots, I review the words they exchanged as we leave, wishing I had a notebook to write them down. Fortunately, we pass a shop with office supplies, where I pick out several notebooks. The shelves are full floor to ceiling since school will be starting soon. We wait in line while mothers pile stacks of notebooks, lesson books, and other school supplies onto the counter, my few notebooks sparse in comparison. Now, I will be able to write down the Arabic sayings as I hear them.

On our way back to the bakery, we pass a shop with 21-karat gold earrings, necklaces, and bracelets hanging neatly on racks in the window, gleaming under the bright spotlights. I have never seen so much gold packed so tightly in one space. Nasser sees me eyeing the jewelry. "The best place to buy gold is in Nablus. There's a whole gold market there. Let's look when we visit my sister, Kifah."

Brides in Palestine are adorned with gold at their wedding, which doubles as security in marriage. Because we got married in the US, we did not follow this tradition, though at least I have the gold earrings Nasser brought me from Palestine when we first reconnected after our time abroad, along with a gold necklace with a map of Palestine as a pendant we had custom-made after we got married. A diamond in the center marks Jerusalem.

In the same area where we drank tamar hindi, we find a street vendor selling fresh figs. Nasser's eyes open wide with delight. *Kilo tin ballah*—One kilo of figs, please. The man places several handfuls of greenish-purple figs in a plastic bag on one side of a scale, then sets metal disks on the other side until they are even. Nasser hands him some shekels and takes the bag.

Soon, we are back where we started. "Let's get some bread for the house." We walk into the bakery with neatly arranged plastic bags of pita bread on display, some with one stack of bread, others with two. In the back, several men are busy baking and bagging more bread. The rich aroma makes me hungry all over again. Nasser takes a single stack with 10 loaves, then waves down a car to head home. Nasser puts the bread, figs, and poster in the trunk while I get a closer look at the steel barrels stacked to block the entrance to the Old City. It seems absurd to block it off when the city is so crowded. *Aren't people just going about their business?* I get into the car, relieved to sit down after a full day of exploring. Time to go home.

13

Johnny

It is our second week in Jalameh when Nasser's friend Johnny arrives from Canada. They know each other from when Nasser first went to Ottawa, Canada, at the age of 18 to complete the required 13th year of high school there in order to be eligible to enroll in a local college.[27] Johnny is a Palestinian whose family was driven out of the city of Ramleh by the Israeli army—when Israel was less than two months old—and never allowed to return.[28] The neighboring city of Lydd—renamed Lod by Israel, where the Ben Gurion Airport now stands—met the same fate, even though both towns were located within areas designated for a Palestinian state by the 1947 UN Partition Plan that called for the partition of Palestine into a Jewish and Arab state.[29]

Johnny's father emigrated to Canada, hoping for a better life for his children, so Johnny was born in Canada. He traveled to Palestine with his family only once back in 1967, the same year Israel took control of the West Bank and Gaza from Jordan and Egypt, respectively, and the Golan Heights of Syria during the Six-Day War.[30]

At that time, Johnny's family visited some of his mother's relatives who managed to stay in Jaffa after Israel became a state in 1948, only a year after they became Israeli citizens. This change shifted their status from stateless subjects under martial law to second-class citizens of the Jewish state. Some five decades later, the State of Israel will demand proof of ownership of their family home in Jaffa, where Johnny's grandfather was born. When Johnny's uncle cannot produce the proper paperwork, the state promptly seizes the house and forces the family to pay rent. *Pay rent to live in their own home.*

It is 25 years after that visit in 1967 that Johnny travels to Israel as a Canadian tourist so he can see Palestine. He wants to experience his homeland with Nasser and me and visit his remaining relatives in Jaffa. Johnny arrives in a rental car from Jerusalem with yellow Israeli license plates with his cousin Tony from Jaffa. A car with Israeli plates offers access to the whole country, so Johnny, with his Canadian citizenship and no residency as a Palestinian, can travel freely within Israel and to Nasser's village in the West Bank.[31]

He rolls up in front of the house in a compact gray car. His straight, jet-black hair is reflecting the sun, but nothing is brighter in that moment than his gentle smile. His mannerisms are all Western, his language as English Canadian as you can get, down to "Eh?" after each utterance, but I get the sense that his heart has found its way home.

Tony steps forward, his movements slow and deliberate. His shoulders soften when he sinks into a brief exchange with Nasser in Arabic. Johnny was too young to recall much from his childhood visit to Palestine. He is bubbling with excitement. "I can't believe I'm here!" Now, he is standing on Palestinian soil, reconnecting with a fellow Palestinian who had the privilege of being born and raised in his own village. Nasser's parents and siblings gather around Johnny, eager to meet one of Nasser's Palestinian friends from Canada.

Nasser's sister Suhaila brings out a tray of juice and holds it in front of Johnny. *Tafaddal*—Please, take one.

Shukran!—Thank you! Johnny greets them all in Arabic, but beyond these simple expressions, the words fail him. What he cannot say in words pours out of his eyes until a whole sea of gratitude washes over them. I detect no boundaries between this exiled Christian Palestinian boy from Ramleh and the largely Muslim community of Jalameh. Like a long-lost gift from afar, all the handshakes and kisses envelop him, ground him in this place that is no longer simply a word on his tongue. Palestine is this village. Palestine is these people. He is one of them.

"Hey, are you guys ready to go?" Johnny is determined to make full use of the time he will have a rental car. While we get our bags from inside the house, Johnny and Tony accept a tiny cup of Arabic coffee. Nasser's sisters insist they stay for the midday meal and leave first thing in the morning.

Nasser clicks his tongue. *Khalih yokil samak min il-buhayra!*—Let him eat fish from the sea! Nasser will be our tour guide and suggests we first head north to the city of Tabariya—the Arabic name for Tiberias on the Sea of Galilee, where Jesus is said to have walked on water. Nasser's sister Huda insists we take a pot of *malfouf*—stuffed cabbage—with us wrapped in a blanket to eat later in the day.

Johnny waves goodbye to Nasser's family, eager to start our tour of Palestine. "Take me everywhere!"

We pass through the Jalameh checkpoint into what Palestinians refer to as *Montiqat thamanyeh wa arba'in*—literally "Area '48"—or *juwa*, meaning "inside," a reference to 1948 Palestine, which includes the Palestinian lands on the other side of the Green Line that were lost to Israel leading up to and following its founding in 1948. The checkpoint is a simple, open-air structure to the side of the road to give the Israeli soldiers some shade. We have to jog around a few makeshift concrete barriers staggered in the road, but no one asks us to stop. The soldiers, talking amongst themselves, offer only a brief glance in our direction as we pass through. Our yellow Israeli plates give us free passage.

"See that building right there?" Nasser points to the side of the road as we pass the checkpoint where a single square stone building no larger than a house stands among a cluster of tall trees. Its deep, rectangular windows stare into the distance like eye sockets, the open doorway exposed like a gaping mouth. The vegetation around it has grown wild. "That used to be the school for our village and those two villages there. That's Sandala, and over there is Muqeibileh." Just across the checkpoint, Nasser points off to the far right. "And over there, that's my father's land. The Israelis took it in 1949, even the watermelon he had planted."

Johnny slows down as the sparkle in his eyes dims. "Right there? That's so messed up."

"And see those red rooftops over there?" Nasser points past his father's land to the east to a cluster of box-like homes in neat rows topped with the distinctive red Spanish tile rooftops. "That's the settlement Gan Ner. They farm his land now. It is part of Marj ibn 'Amer—the fertile plains that lie between the Jordan Valley and the Mediterranean Sea, the breadbasket of Palestine."

I wonder at the pain Nasser's father must carry of never being able to cultivate his land again. I wonder what the Israelis are growing there now. I wonder if it is native to the soil of Palestine.

Nasser's gaze follows from the settlement back toward Sandala. "See those mountains in the distance? That's Haifa, where my father went to pick up a brand-new tractor from the port in 1948, the first in the village. It was an *Internash*." Nasser explains *Internash* stands for International, an American tractor company.[32]

"He managed to get it back to the village but then lost much of his land the same year."

Johnny's eyes turn to Nasser, wide open, taking in his words.

Nasser points in the distance. "Haifa is less than an hour from here. Just past that mountain is the Mediterranean Sea."

Johnny speeds up again as Nasser directs him north through flat farmland past the Israeli town of Afula. The road begins to climb until we reach Nazareth, which still has a significant Palestinian population.[33]

We drive to the center of town by the main church, the Basilica of the Annunciation, its massive stone walls and geometric dome-like structure towering over the Old City. We briefly go inside and walk up to the altar area flooded with light from the dome, then enter the Old City from a narrow opening across from the church. Other stone passageways lead us past tiny shops with kitchenware and olive wood crafts. Nasser and I buy a royal-blue three-piece enamel Arabic coffee pot set painted with colorful peacocks along with a stainless-steel teapot. Johnny is more interested in the crafts and buys an olive wood crèche.

We continue our journey northeast toward Tabariya. The sun is high in the sky, not a cloud in sight. Nasser and Johnny catch up on news from Toronto and reminisce about their student days together there. Within an hour, we enter the city from the west. Nasser spots a side street and signals to Johnny to pull in. "Let's park along here and walk into town and to the sea. Then we can come back and find a restaurant." We pass a prominent-looking house across the street with a triple-arched overhang built of black stone, the archways and windows outlined in white stone.

Nasser's voice is full of conviction. "That's a Palestinian house." As we approach the front of the house, we realize the glass in the windows is broken, and there are huge cracks in the foundation. We peer inside to what must have been the kitchen, a single porcelain sink still connected to the wall, above it ceramic tiles but no faucet, only a single black leather woman's shoe on the counter covered in dust. From another window, we can see through a large archway to the back of the house, where the top part of a wood-framed window is hanging down, and the rest swung open into the house. There is no glass. The floor is covered with debris, the paint on the walls discolored and peeling, exposing some of the stone walls beneath. In cities like 'Akka, Beisan, Haifa, Jaffa, Safad, Tiberias, and West Jerusalem, Israel leased Palestinian homes to new Jewish immigrants after residents were forced out in 1948.[34]

What happened with this house? I wonder who the original owners were, where they are now, how they would feel to know their house is left to degenerate.

The house next door, also from the same era, has a palm tree full of dates hanging down from beneath the expansive palm leaves. Nasser looks up at the tree. "We should pick some. They are our dates anyway." Johnny and Tony's eyes widen with the prospect of picking some of "our" dates and follow Nasser to the tree. Nasser calls out to them. "Lift me up."

Johnny interlaces his hands. "Step here." Johnny and Tony steady Nasser by grabbing onto his legs while he reaches for the dates.

Nasser pulls off a cluster. "Here, try some." Squinting in the bright sun, we each bite into one of the golden dates with their distinctive soft crunch. They taste a bit dry, but the nutty flavor is delicious. Farther ahead, we approach a shopping district with a pedestrian zone that opens up to a plaza with a mosque prominently situated in the center built with the same black stones as the house we just saw, proof of a Palestinian past.[35]

We walk over to the front to admire its magnificent triple-arched entranceway with three domed rooftops positioned overhead. Around the minaret reaching for the sky is a covered platform encircled in a black iron fence, from where the muezzin once called Muslims to prayer.

My throat tightens when we walk up the stairs to the center archway to find the steel double front doors chained shut. Above them is an Arabic inscription carved in stone framed in decorative blue ceramic tiles. I can barely swallow when we walk around the outside to discover the exterior stone façade is crumbling at the corners, now home to plants growing between the discolored blocks of stone. We peer through the iron bars and dust-covered windows only to find wooden furniture piled against them. *Are there no Palestinians left here to tend to the mosque?*[36]

Nasser reads my mind. "Most Palestinians were forced out of Tabariya in 1948."[37] I take one final look into the sky at the minaret towering overhead like a last outpost of a Palestinian past. As we continue walking toward the sea, I wonder how much longer this mosque will be standing here and where the people who used to live here are now.

Soon, we reach a road that runs along the lake. I try to imagine Jesus walking across the deep blue, choppy water. Nasser is combing the buildings with his eyes, looking out for a restaurant until he spots one along the water. "This looks like a nice place." Nasser turns to Johnny. "You have to eat fish here." A waiter greets us in Hebrew. Nasser asks in English for a table by the water. The waiter seats us at a square metal table under an overhang on the back side of the restaurant with an open view of the sea. There are several kinds of fish on the menu, all fresh caught from the Sea of Galilee. Johnny asks the waiter which one was Jesus' favorite, and we all laugh. The waiter recommends *mishit*, also known as St. Peter's fish. Nasser also takes an order of *mishit* pan-fried, and I try it grilled.

The breeze along the water, coupled with the shade of the overhang, offers some relief from the hot sun overhead. We start out with a plate of hummus and pickled vegetables and some pita bread which is gone in no time. Soon after, the fish comes out on oval plates with heads and tails intact and a mound of French fries for us to share. We each carefully pull the delicate fish from its bones.

"Delicious!" Johnny's eyes sparkle with delight. We manage to each eat a whole fish, only the heads and tails remaining on our plates connected by their bare skeletons.

We head back to the car and follow the road around the Sea of Galilee into the mountainous landscape of the Golan Heights through an Israeli checkpoint with a chain-link fence extending in either direction topped with barbed wire.[38] The ground is dry and dusty, its pale camel color reflecting the unforgiving sun. Johnny slows down to a stop and rolls down his window. When we hear the soldiers speaking Arabic, Nasser explains they must be Druze. "They are the only Palestinians who are allowed to serve in the Israeli army."[39]

Nasser leans over to Johnny's window and greets them in Arabic. With our Israeli plates and American and Canadian passports, we have no trouble entering the area. I am wondering who cannot enter here. Perhaps it is the Syrians of the Golan Heights who cannot leave the area.

It is not long before we arrive at Al-Hamm As-Souriya—what Israel calls Hamat Gader—ancient hot springs in the Yarmouk River valley dating back to Roman times. We place a blanket and Huda's pot of *malfouf*—still wrapped in a blanket to keep warm—on a grassy hill in the shade overlooking the large pool of dark water. We walk past an area of semi-private enclosures to get changed. We take turns lowering ourselves into the pool at a ladder at the edge, then make our way to the curved edge on the other side, where the water cascades over like a waterfall. It is eerie to swim in such dark water, but the warm water and open sky overhead are soothing.

Nasser and Johnny stay at the edge, but I venture out into the middle of the pool and float on my back, closing my eyes beneath the bright sun. Swimming reawakens our appetites, so we get dressed and return to our hilltop post to indulge in the finger-sized stuffed cabbage laced with whole cloves of garlic that is miraculously still warm! What a lovely treat!

Over the next hour, we follow the road as it climbs up the mountain in twists and turns past Druze villages nestled in the mountains, then turn off onto another winding road to the Banyas waterfalls. The air along the path toward the waterfall is crisp and clear, the earth moist and dark like chocolate fudge. The sound of the water cascading over rocks begins to drown out our conversation.

We follow the water uphill along its left bank. I am glowing in my white cotton dress and white tennis shoes, my hair in a high ponytail with a matching white cotton scrunchy. We follow along the cool, rushing water under a canopy of lush trees, the water at times skimming over flat boulders. I feel like a young girl in a fairytale prancing through the forest. When we reach the larger pools and falls at the top, it is time to turn around and follow the same majestic path back down.

We wind our way back to the main road, then continue north through the remote village of Majdal Shams,[40] a Syrian Druze village, with prominent plazas and men walking along the side of the road in traditional *sirwal* pants of black silk that balloon out below the waist and tailored neatly at the calf with silk bands. White, flat-topped hats adorn their heads. In the center of the village is a bronze statue with several figures, one holding a sword up toward the sky.[41]

Nasser explains how the area is known for its large crispy apples. Up here, even in the direct sun, the air is cool—such a contrast to the relentless heat at the base of the mountain. The chilly mountain air is energizing. My mind feels clearer, my feet lighter as I take in every detail.

From Majdal Shams, we cut across the north along the Lebanese border down to the city of Safad, a Palestinian town and center of Jewish mysticism which was completely emptied of its Palestinian inhabitants in 1948.[42] Walking through town, we find a large art gallery. The street signs are all in Hebrew.

At the end of the road, we see an old, abandoned house, the windows gaping holes. I peer inside one of the open windows and realize I can see the sky through a massive shelling hole on the second floor. I feel the stark absence of Palestinians as we wander the streets that now house mostly religious Jews and venture into nearby galleries that were once the homes of Palestinians.[43]

I wonder who lived in that house, what it was like to be driven out of their home by force, and where they are today. Israelis have successfully reclaimed a lost treasure of religious significance, but for those who call Safad home and are forbidden to return, it is a place of mourning.

We need an hour to reach Ra's An-Naqura, what Israel refers to as Rosh HaNikra, the northernmost point on the Mediterranean coast, which marks the border with Lebanon. On our way, we briefly stop in the village of Kufr Bir'im, not far from Safad, where Jewish militias drove out all the villagers and the family of Nasser's best man from our wedding, Tony, in 1948.[44] All we find is an isolated stone church. We spend a few minutes there in silence.

I think of Tony's family, having to leave this lush, green place, Tony growing up in Lebanon, and never being able to see his homeland. I think of his three children growing up in Canada, forced to become residents of other places. This is the fate of so many Palestinians whose descendants remain scattered across the globe, while any Jew anywhere in the world can come to Israel and become an Israeli citizen through the Law of Return.[45]

I cannot see how this law, these restrictions, this outcome of history can ever be considered fair. People don't forget who they are. They remember and share their memories with their children and their children's children. The bitter taste of injustice never dissipates.

It is with heavy hearts that we leave Tony's village and head along the Lebanese border to Ra's An-Naqura. I don't know then that all Palestinian villages along this route were systematically destroyed in 1948, the entire area cleansed of its people, swept away to rid the border areas of Palestinians. *What must it be like to play God and redraw entire areas of a people's homeland, decide who shall remain and who shall go? How strokes of a pen translate into military campaigns that change people's lives for generations. And where was the rest of the world when these lines were being drawn?* Of course, France and Britain are guilty of drawing lines of their own when they carved up the Middle East during World War I with the Sykes-Picot Agreement.[46] But the Zionists carved out their place in the Holy Land as they went after their vision of the Land of Israel with fervor, a determination that pulled the rug out from under Palestinian villagers and city dwellers alike, far and wide.

When we travel as far west as we can go, we enter an observation platform that overlooks the Mediterranean Sea. At the edge of the platform, steel bars extend off the mountainside, marking the border with Lebanon. I gaze out at the sparkling sea, then down at the coastline, watching the water crash against large boulders. Nasser points down along the coast. "See those train tracks? They're from the British Mandate" (see Map 4). My eyes follow them into the distance heading south along the coast. I trace the tracks back north only to find they come to an abrupt halt. The days are long gone when one could travel freely to Lebanon and Syria. The blue-and-white Israeli flag with the blue Star of David flutters in the wind high up on the rocky hillside. Below is what looks like a military outpost overlooking the area with several Israeli soldiers patrolling with M16s in hand.

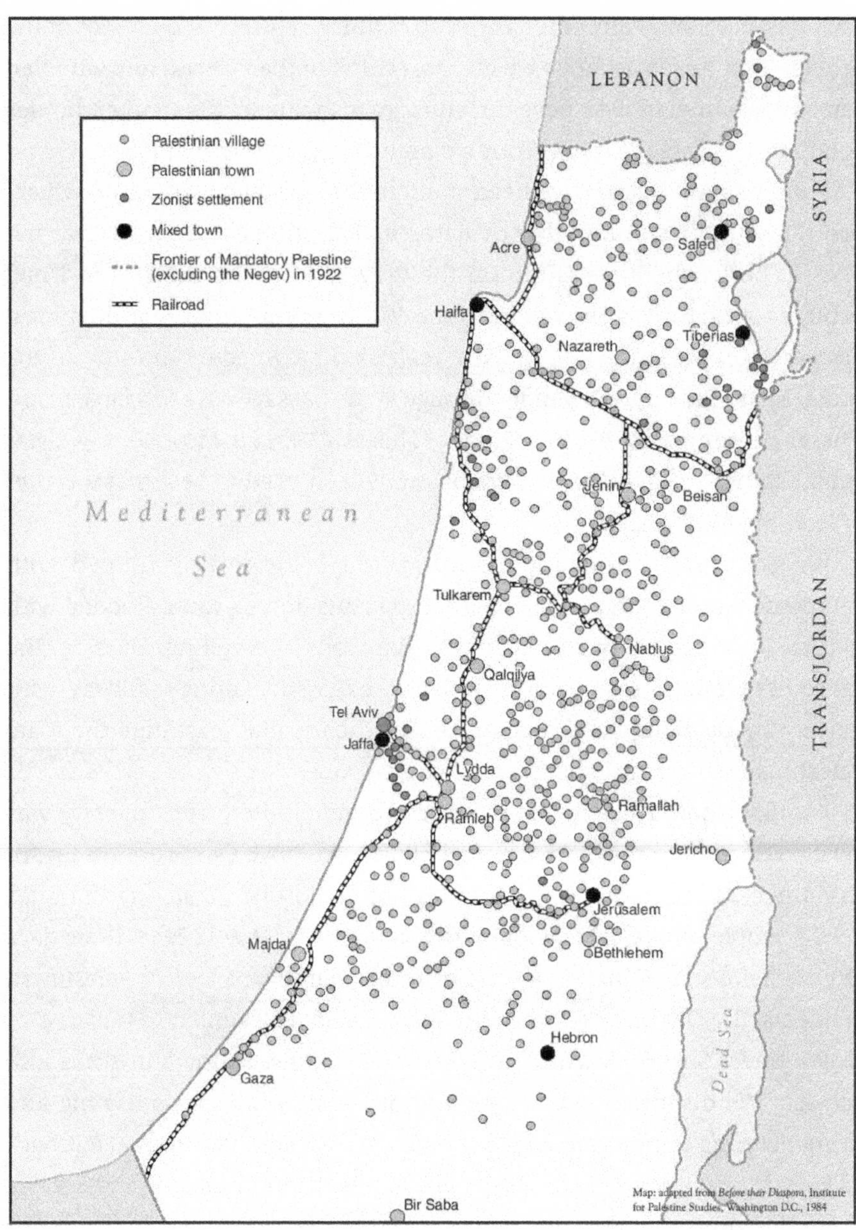

Map 4: British Mandate Palestine, 1922 (Source: PASSIA)

Nasser turns to Johnny. "My father used to drive his truck to sell his cauliflower in Damascus!" Today those hundred miles he used to travel may as well be a million miles away. "Now, if you have an Israeli stamp in your passport, you can't enter any Arab country." Johnny and I wince at the thought that this is as far as we can go. I think of the Palestinians who fled across this border in 1948, never to return, many with the keys to their homes still in hand. Nasser's friend Tony's parents were among them.

From Ra's An-Naqura, we head south to the coastal city of 'Akka, which, like Nazareth, is still heavily populated by Palestinians. We park near the ancient port, where we climb on the very same ruins Dieter and I had explored with Salem six years earlier. We watch in amazement as local boys dive off the ruins into the sea, their skin browned by the sun. In the center of the Old City, we wander through stone passageways to a large plaza. Nasser continues as our tour guide. "This is Al-Jazzar Mosque. My sister Huda's father-in-law studied here before 1948. It used to be a major center of learning for the area."

We enter the prominent mosque through a doorway framed with geometric patterns of inlaid stone to a spacious domed room flooded with natural light and more stonework on the walls and ceiling. Outside, the mosque compound is surrounded by an expansive stone walkway with narrow shops along its perimeter. Unlike Tabariya, at least here there are Palestinians to care for and frequent the mosque.

I wonder how Palestinians managed to remain here after the city was swallowed up into the State of Israel on May 14, 1948. Only later do I learn that three-quarters of the Palestinian population of 'Akka—as many as 17,000 people—were driven out by Israeli forces on May 17, 1948, three days after Israel declared statehood. Despite this significant loss of Palestinian residents, the Old City of 'Akka remains majority Palestinian to this day.

We travel farther down the Mediterranean coast as the sun sinks into the sea. We decide to bypass the city of Haifa, which feels too big and overwhelming to navigate so late in the day. We still have to make it back to Johnny's relatives in Jaffa. We make a quick stop in Caesarea to see the Byzantine ruins that glow from the spotlights.[47]

As we walk across a vast stone area toward the Mediterranean Sea, my eyes lock onto what appears to be a mosque. On the wall beneath a beautifully illuminated minaret reads in large black letters, "CHARLEY'S RESTAURANT." My eyes follow the lights back up the side of the building to the minaret overhead, glowing in the dark sky. Nasser's steps are measured, his posture firm and upright as he approaches it.

Johnny's head shakes as his bright eyes scan the site before us. "Are you serious? That's a mosque!"

I cannot take my eyes off the sign. "I can't believe this." Then I spot a prominent arched doorway. "I have to go inside."

People are going in and coming out. We step inside and are met by the host, who addresses us in Hebrew. Nasser responds in English. "We don't want to eat. We would just like to see the mosque."

The host's eyes narrow as he looks Nasser in the eye. "I'm sorry, we can only seat you for dinner." My chest tightens as my eyes creep past him to get a glimpse of the dining room beyond. What was once the main prayer room is full of square tables arranged between stone columns that support a series of domed ceilings. I can hear the chatter of conversation. My mind is racing. *Don't these people realize this building is a mosque?*

The host shifts his weight and steps out from behind his podium. "Is there anything else I can help you with?" He is blocking my view now into the dining area.

"*Yallah,* Let's go."[48] Nasser looks at us, his chin held high, his shoulders square, and turns toward the main door. Johnny and I exchange glances and follow Nasser and Tony out of the mosque. As we walk back to the car, we all turn around to take a final look. I cannot wrap my head around what I am seeing. I cannot take my eyes off the restaurant sign. The longer I stare, the more I can feel it brand itself into my memory.

I turn to Nasser in disbelief. "I really can't believe it. How can they do that?"

Shaking his head, I can feel Nasser's body tighten with anger and frustration. "They do whatever they want."

It's been a long, full day. My light footsteps along the waterfall in the Golan Heights now feel heavy with the weight of history seeping into my soul.[49] We make a beeline to the car. I sit quietly in the back seat, looking out at the streetlights as we head farther south to Johnny's relatives in Jaffa. My head is spinning with the details of the day. Ancient history of the Romans, the recent history of the British, and now, under Israel, history in the making right before my eyes.

14

Next Generation

It is late by the time Johnny, Tony, Nasser, and I reach Jaffa. Johnny's relatives welcome us into their modest apartment. We are all tired, so after we debrief them on our adventures of the day, they show Nasser and me to a modest bedroom. I'm relieved to rest my mind from the day's events.

That first night at Johnny's relatives, I suddenly feel sick to my stomach. By morning, I am throwing up what little is left in my stomach from the day before. Initially, I think it is from something I ate on our packed all-day tour. But then, a surge bolts through my brain. I look down at my abdomen and wonder if I am carrying a child. I am convinced I must be. I have never felt quite this way before, as if my whole body were on high alert.

My confusion over what to make of my nausea quickly shifts to a whirlwind of thrill and excitement. I immediately go find Nasser. "I don't feel well. I just threw up, and I still feel sick to my stomach." My face is long and pale. "I actually think I might be pregnant." For a moment, we are both quiet. I am wondering how I will handle the rest of our travels with Johnny. At the same time, the thought of a child is racing through my body like wildfire. I have always wanted children. Now, I will have a child of my own. *A Palestinian child.*

We sit down for a moment, hoping I will feel better, when we hear

Johnny's voice from the hallway. "Hey, guys, breakfast is ready." Nasser and I look at each other and laugh.

Nasser turns to me. "Do you think you can eat anything?"

I take a deep breath as I assess whether I am more hungry than nauseous. "I don't know, but I'll come sit with you guys and see how I feel. I'd better try to eat something."

"She thinks she might be pregnant."

Johnny's eyes open wide, his jaw drops, then he holds out his arms like Santa Claus welcoming children to his lap. "Wow, that's great!"

Nasser puts his arm around my waist and leads me out to the family. I nibble on some pita bread, cheese, and a few grapes. My stomach is settling, but I don't want to push my luck, so I stop there. Nasser and Johnny are discussing the agenda for the day, but I am not listening. The thought that I am carrying a child does not leave my mind. *I am going to be a mother.* Here I am in Palestine, where thousands of Palestinians were driven out of this very place, and now, I am carrying new life, a Palestinian child. I think of Golda Meir's unforgettable statement from 1969: "There were no such thing as Palestinians."[50] *No, Golda Meir, you are wrong. They have been here all along, and they are not going away. In fact, I am carrying one inside of me.*

After breakfast, Johnny, Tony, Nasser, and I venture out to what remains of the Palestinian city of Ramleh, just a few miles from the Mediterranean Sea. Nasser points out the signature White Tower in the center of town. Here we are in the very place where Johnny's family did not get to live, a place that became only a memory passed down from one generation to the next. The sparkle has left Johnny's eyes, at least for this moment. I leave him in silence.

Nearby in Lydd, Nasser shows us a white building on a corner that is an admirable display of religious coexistence, where the local mosque and church are actually part of the same building.[51] The minaret appears to have been restored, as there are bright creamy-white stones mixed in toward the top beneath an iron railing that encircles the tower in contrast to the weathered grayish stones of the base.

We enter the door at the corner and can either turn left to go to the church or right to the mosque. First, we enter the mosque area. There we find an open courtyard of stone benches with faucets along the wall where an elderly man is carrying out the ritual washing before prayer, known as *wudu'*. We continue into the mosque, where natural light pours in from arched windows underneath towering archways around the perimeter suspended by stone columns that support a balcony overhead. A wide ribbon of blue tiles with inscriptions from the Quran lines the walls above the lower windows and over the archways. The walls are inlaid with shiny peach, cream, and black marble blocks in geometric patterns.

We walk back toward the entrance and enter the church, where the sun streams through arched, stained-glass windows at the altar, evenly spaced between large square columns that support the ceiling. Wooden pews are neatly arranged in rows on the stone floor facing the altar. The walls and ceiling are stark white, but the ceiling has an elaborate crown molding that runs around the entirety of the oval-shaped ceiling. Being in this multi-religion space reminds me of how Palestinians proudly claim that Muslims, Christians, and Jews all lived together peacefully prior to the Zionist movement that declared Palestine should become a Jewish homeland. *Were Palestinians simply part of the landscape as romanticized by early European travelers to the Orient so eloquently described by Edward Said in his groundbreaking work* Orientalism?[52] My heart is heavy with the power of narrative to become truth in the minds of those who believe it, a truth that negates the very existence of those who were already here.

From Lydd Nasser, Johnny, Tony, and I head toward the Mediterranean Sea to the city of Jaffa to explore the Old City. We park Johnny's rental car on a side street and walk toward the sea. We pass a few restaurants with tables set out in the open, then enter a narrow, stone stairwell that continues into a series of passageways with galleries and antique shops filled with ancient relics of the past. I peer into the spotless storefront windows displaying illuminated artifacts in their deep stone ledges. I realize I am looking into the living rooms of Palestinians who once lived in this city. My stomach turns as I try to see past the items on display that erase their presence here. We make our way through the maze, occasionally climbing up and then downstairs, the sea finally coming into full view.

My steps quicken as I spot a minaret in the distance. "Hey, there's a mosque! Let's go see."[53]

The closer we get, the more the minaret comes into view. My eyes follow it down from the narrow tower of the muezzin. I stop in my tracks when the top of the building comes into view. I can see right through to the sea. The upper windows have no glass, and parts of the interior walls are hanging down. Out front, it is cordoned off with barriers.

"They probably want it to fall down." As he speaks, Johnny's eyes are dark and narrow in the bright sun. My stomach turns from the sight of this neglect. A beautiful mosque by the sea closed, silent, even though there are Palestinians living here. I see it anchored there, empty, gazing at the sea while the city that was once famous for its Jaffa oranges is transformed into a Jewish town.[54]

My thoughts jump from Tabariya to Caesarea to here. I cannot seem to shake off the pattern of neglect, disrespect, and dispossession crawling under my skin. As I cast a final glance through the gaping windows, my heart sinks a little deeper into the sea.

We have a late lunch back where we started at one of the restaurants overlooking the sea, probably not far from where Salem's family once lived before they were forced to leave in 1948. It is a beautiful setting, but the weight of our morning and the history of this place dampen our spirits. Our waitress is hip and friendly with sleek red streaks in her black hair. "Where are you from?" Her heavy Israeli accent feels sharp compared to her smooth movements and sultry eyes. She refills our water glasses.

"Ramleh, but I live in Canada." The waitress smiles. I cannot tell if she fully appreciates the significance of Johnny having no Arabic accent, that his family was not allowed to stay here and raise their son in his homeland.

"I am from Jenin." Nasser's heavy Arabic accent catches her attention as the flow of water from her pitcher thins to a trickle.

She continues pouring. "Jenin? That is a long way for you. What are you doing here?" I am wondering why Canada is not farther. After all, Jenin is only 40 miles away.

"We want to see Jaffa." Nasser is looking her in the eye now as if to remind her that we are not exactly tourists. Nasser turns to Johnny. "He hasn't been here in 25 years."

We are all sharing the weight of this place and its history. Clearly, the waitress is not used to having visitors from Jenin, or from Ramleh, who don't live here anymore. "Welcome." Now, she is moving in what feels like slow motion. Somehow amidst the strange tension, we manage to order our lunch. "I will be right back with your food." The waitress checks on a few other tables before she disappears into the kitchen.

We glance at each other and smile. I feel like we are honored guests, though self-invited. My stomach relaxes a bit, knowing that our rare presence here will not go completely unnoticed. This young Israeli woman got to serve a Palestinian from Ramleh, *who does not live here anymore*, and a Palestinian from Jenin, *where other Palestinians still live.* I realize history is not only in the past. It is right here, right now, unfolding on this sunny day at this seaside restaurant in Jaffa.

As we walk to our car, we see several young Palestinian men smoking behind the restaurant. *Maybe this is where Salem worked before he left to study in Germany.* Nasser addresses them in Arabic. Their eyes light up, and their faces soften, as if they are long-lost cousins catching up after years of separation.

On the road back to Johnny's relatives, Nasser tells us that the young men at the restaurant like working at the restaurant, that the owner is a good man. Besides, it's better than being a janitor or doing back-breaking work in construction. *What else are they going to do?* The question echoes in my mind. I can't help but think there must be more to life for these Palestinians.

In the evening at Johnny's relatives, we learn that most Palestinian youth here lurk in the shadows and work as unskilled laborers. When I ask them about going to college, the parents cast their eyes to the floor. Their children simply laugh in unison. There is no point. There are no real jobs for Palestinians in Israel, no promising opportunities. Many turn to drugs. I am shocked to hear them say "Israel." I want to lift their spirits. "Why do you say Israel? You are Palestinian. Isn't this Palestine?" They look surprised, even shy, as if I have said a bad word. It hasn't been that long since, even in the West Bank, a Palestinian could be arrested for wearing the colors of the Palestinian flag.[55] *What about in Israel? Who am I kidding?*

The children's shoulders roll forward like caged birds with broken wings. I think of Nasser's nieces and nephews in Jalameh, who are so full of energy and confidence. They grew up calling their homeland Palestine, taking pride in the colors of their flag, but here everyone's spirit seems broken, as if Palestine is long gone, too painful to remember, as if being Palestinian is a curse, a secret that must be kept at all costs. *How different life is here for these Palestinians, who grew up in Israel's shadow, a completely different world on the same soil. Is it the schools that only teach Israeli history? The predominance of the Hebrew language? The subjugation of Palestinians in the West Bank and Gaza that makes silence feel safer?* Here they are virtually invisible, even to themselves. But I see them.

The next morning, we bid Johnny's relatives farewell and make the hour-long drive inland to Jerusalem. On the way, Johnny laughs. "I want to visit all three holy sites there!" referring to the Church of the Holy Sepulchre, the Dome of the Rock, and the Western Wall. "I'm going to be a Christian, a Muslim, and a Jew all in the same day!" He says he will call himself *John* at the church, *Hasan* at the mosque, and *Khasan* at the Western Wall, alluding to how Israelis would pronounce *Hasan*.

Nasser and I laugh at his determination to personify all three religions. Nasser suggests we enter the Old City via *Bab al-'Amud*, known as Damascus Gate in English, the same gate Dieter and I entered years before during our visit to the Browns. The passageways feel familiar and unchanged, as if time has stood still. Tiny shops are overflowing with goods in front of adjacent storefronts. The city is bustling with activity.

On the way to the Christian Quarter, Nasser insists we stop at Jafar Sweets to have a piece of *knafeh*, a delicious, warm desert of wheat-string pastry filled with local cheese from the Palestinian city of Nablus, topped with a bright orange spice and sugar syrup. When we enter the shop, we see ornate round metal trays of knafeh being kept warm over flaming pedestals. Several men are taking orders from a crowd of customers, calling out the number of servings ordered in Arabic.

Nasser places our order. *Thalatheh knafeh, ballah*—Three knafeh, please. They promptly cut into the knafeh with steel spatulas and slide each square onto a plate. They have other sweets on display made from filo dough, but everyone seems to be ordering knafeh. We sit down at a two-person table against the wall lined with gray and black marble and mirrors.

Yallah?—Let's start? Nasser cuts easily into his piece of knafeh and takes a bite. I follow suit, the combination of syrup-soaked pastry and warm cheese melting in my mouth. I am worried it will be too rich for my stomach, but after my first few bites, I feel fine, so I continue until my plate is bare. It is so filling—like a meal in and of itself! Nasser says this place makes the best knafeh in Palestine. I am thrilled to have experienced the gold standard. We each rinse our mouths with water at a sink and return to the narrow passageway. Farther ahead, we enter the Christian Quarter and easily find the Church of the Holy Sepulchre, the dark, cool interior a welcome relief from the hot August sun. We meander past tour groups to a chapel, where Johnny enters and offers a brief prayer at the altar, then work our way back through the crowds into the bright sun to find the Dome of the Rock.

We enter the compound through a massive wooden double doorway and cross the open plaza to one of the broad staircases framed with a stone archway, the gold dome gleaming in the distance. As we ascend the stairs, the rest of the hexagon-shaped building comes into view, complete with its brilliant blue tile façade lined with Arabic inscriptions from the Quran. We slip off our shoes and wander through the ornate, carpeted interior to the center to touch the boulder, where Mohammed is said to have ascended to heaven on horseback, then gaze up at the breathtaking domed ceiling.

Off to the side, Johnny, or Hasan as he reminds us, laughing, has Nasser instruct him in prayer, so they both get on their knees and bow forward as Nasser recites verses from the Quran.

Once outside, we cross the compound to the Al-Aqsa Mosque, taking off our shoes at the door. Toward the back of the mosque is a plexiglass box partially filled with rubber bullets, rifle shells, and tear gas canisters. I cringe when I read a sign indicating they were all fired into the mosque by the Israeli army during the days of the intifada, a chilling reminder that the area has not always been so peaceful. I imagine shots being fired into this sacred space, people running from tear gas, others losing their lives. I wonder if any more shots will be fired, if that plexiglass box will fill up or become a relic of the past.

We continue to the Western Wall, where Johnny picks up a loaner *kippah* to place on his head so he can walk up to this sacred space of prayer. Nasser and I watch from a distance while Johnny, or Khasan, faces the Wall while others pray. His mission is complete to visit all three sites holy to Christians, Muslims, and Jews.

Nearby, we discover an area where we can climb up onto the walls of the Old City, giving us a perfect view of ancient domed rooftops amidst clotheslines and TV antennae. We reach a staircase where our only choice is to descend into the narrow passageways. We find our way back to Damascus Gate, eating falafel and shawarma sandwiches on the way. Our visit to the Old City has come to an end.

Our tour with Johnny has also come to an end. It is time to head back to Nasser's family. Through Johnny, we relived the Palestine lost to him his entire life. Growing up in Canada, he only knew this place in stories. I can only hope my children will come to know Palestine as their homeland.

Back in Jalameh, as we walk through the village, I notice wrappers and plastic bottles caught in the dried weeds along the side of the road, in narrow walkways between houses, or behind homes on bare patches of land. Shock races through my veins when I see one of Nasser's nieces throw her candy wrapper toward the hibiscus bush off the veranda out front. My eyes dart from the candy wrapper back to her. *Lesh? Mish hun*—Why? Not here.

She looks at her cousins, and they all laugh. One of them stops laughing and turns to her. *Hutti 'a zabaleh*—Put it in the garbage.

I look around me and point to other garbage in the street. *Mish helu*—Not beautiful. Their startled eyes follow mine to the garbage. Some shrug their shoulders.

Bithutu zabaleh heik fil-beit?—Do you throw garbage in your house like that? Some of the children laugh, then their faces become still.

La—No.

Shou al-farq?—What's the difference? I sweep my arms across the landscape. *Hathi Falastin. Khaliha halwa.*—This is Palestine. Keep it beautiful.

When one of Nasser's nephews finishes his candy, he looks at me, then at the others, and dashes inside his grandparents' house to throw it away. When he comes back, I thank him. *Shater*—Good job. *Heik lazem*—This is how it should be. My language is simple, but they get the message.

Not long after, Nasser and I visit the mayor of the village, Abu Samir, who happens to be our next-door neighbor. An older woman in a long white dress with a wide silk band around her waist leads us upstairs, her white curly hair peeking out of her smooth white scarf wrapped loosely around her head. We follow her to a room with big windows on all sides, where Abu Samir is sitting on a built-in bench. He quickly stands up, towering over us with his broad shoulders, his forehead visible under his white headscarf held in place by the black 'iqal cord, like 'Ami wears. His plastic, wide-framed glasses make his eyes appear larger.

The woman introduces us, and Abu Samir welcomes us in a loud and deep voice, his tone friendly. He outstretches his hand to Nasser, then to me. His handshake is long and firm. Nasser also extends his hand to a woman sitting in a chair whom he calls Hajji, her mouth hanging open, her eyes heavy on her face as they move slowly to meet Nasser's, then mine. I lean over to kiss her on both cheeks.

Soon, two of Abu Samir's sons join us. One of them, who studied in India, explains to me in English that Hajji is his father's first wife. "She didn't have children, so he married a second wife. That's Mama." Hajji helped raise them and is part of the family to this day. "He didn't want to divorce her just because she could not have children."

I wonder about the pressure to have children, how it can be a curse if a woman cannot bear children. At least this woman got to stay in the household. At the time of Mohammed, many men were killed in war, so there was a surplus of women. Some say this practice may have evolved out of necessity so that women would have the protection of a man and his family. According to Islamic law, a Muslim man can marry up to four wives if he can treat them equally.[56] I wonder if any man can treat two or more women the same.

Mama brings us Arabic coffee in tulip-shaped cups. Abu Samir asks me how I like Palestine and how life is in America. *Helu, al-ithneen helwin*—Beautiful, both are beautiful.

Mama smiles but probes further. *Shou ahsan, hun wala Amrika?*—What's better, here or America?

Falastin ahsan—Palestine is better. They all laugh as Mama rocks forward and back with delight, her eyes gleaming with pride.

I listen as Abu Samir discusses the news of the village, his mind sharp, his language quick and complex. My ears tighten to break down the sounds streaming from above his broad chin. He looks in my direction repeatedly as if his gaze alone could help me understand what he is saying.

Now and then, Nasser translates so I can join in, though I quickly lose track of the conversation. Still, I listen closely as his eyes shift from person to person. There is something about his commanding presence that makes me hang on every word.

When I delight in finding out he is also a poet, he recites some lines from one of his poems and gives me a copy of a collection he published. My ears have been adjusting to the village dialect, but now, I hear the classical Arabic I studied at the university. The contrast is stark with its precision of short and long vowels that give formal Arabic a metered quality, as if reading to a metronome. I can only make out some of the words, but the sound is intriguing, so smooth and integrated in its rhyme and rhythm.

The intimacy of Abu Samir's poetry gives me the courage to bring up the garbage in the village. After all, he is the mayor. Maybe he could do something about it. I seize the opportunity. *Shahadtu kithir zabaleh fish-shari'*—I saw a lot of garbage in the street. He is calm now, listening with his whole body.

His sons explain the challenges of managing garbage in a village under occupation since there is no central government for Palestinians, only the Israeli Civil Administration, which is run by the military. I point out that Palestinians have many challenges under occupation, but it doesn't force anyone to throw garbage in the streets. Shouldn't we be role models for our children? Abu Samir is quiet and still, his eyes steady. He ponders for a moment, then agrees that the village could use some garbage cans. I joke that maybe what the village needs is a clean-up day. *Yom tanthif*—Day of cleaning. Everyone laughs.

Later that week, I hear that Abu Samir has ordered just that, a *yom tanthif* for the entire village. The next time we take a walk, the street is clean and clear of all the garbage that lined the streets, as if overnight someone had waved a magic wand. Green plastic garbage bins hang from light posts. A simple observation, one conversation, immediate results. I am honored that Abu Samir took my words to heart to honor the village. *Is it really that easy to make a difference?*

15

Nablus

Once Nasser and I have visited all his relatives in the village, we head to Nablus to visit his youngest sister Kifah. We take a taxi south along the main road through Palestinian villages nestled along the road and in the hillsides. The farther south we travel, the hillier it gets, and the more Israeli settlements tower over Palestinian villages from the hilltops.[57] Steep access roads lead to fenced and well-fortified perimeters. Nasser explains that all Israeli settlers are armed and trained to use their weapons. The only place the settlers and the local villagers cross paths is on the main road.

Nearly an hour has passed when we approach Nablus where the road curves along the side of a steep mountain at the edge of a deep valley. There is no railing along the side of the two-lane road, so traffic is careful and slow. Just ahead of us is an army Jeep full of Israeli soldiers, some peering out the back. I feel uneasy watching their helmet-framed faces through the rear opening, talking amongst themselves, laughing, as if they are on a road trip. *Armed soldiers with the right to kill.* I want to look away but cannot take my eyes off them.

The narrow road finally opens to a four-lane road that leads to Kifah's house. We go up to the third floor of the apartment building and ring the bell. Kifah opens the door, her high round cheeks especially pronounced with her broad smile, her wavy reddish-brown hair hanging loosely around her face. *Ahleen, Nasser! Ahleen, Christa! Tafaddalou!*—Hello, Nasser! Hello, Christa! Please come in!

Kifah is in the middle of cooking, so she has us follow her through the living room furnished with ornate upholstered sofas, built-in shelves filled with a wall of books and a television, then the dining room with an oval wooden table, and on to the kitchen lined in cabinets on one wall. A vast veranda offers an open view of the main road below.

I notice a bowl of whole tomatoes and cucumbers with a few sprigs of parsley on the counter and offer to make the salad. She apologizes for not having the meal ready but promises it won't take long. Nasser reminds her we want to go to the Gold Market before they close. She peeks into the pot of rice on the stove. *Mestawi*—Done. She scoops it onto a large round platter and tops it with golden almonds and roasted chicken from the oven.

Once I finish dicing tomatoes and cucumbers, I chop the parsley while Kifah squeezes fresh lemon juice onto the salad, then adds salt, pepper, and olive oil. She stirs the salad and distributes it into smaller glass bowls. She calls out to her daughters to get plates and spoons while we carry the food out to the dining room table. Just then, her husband Abu Fadi arrives, named after his first son. He looks like the famous Syrian comedian Duraid Lahham, known as Ghawar, though Abu Fadi is no comedian. He is starting a factory for packaged Arabic food, like falafel mix.

One by one, Kifah's six children emerge, eager to see their uncle and his American wife. By our next trip to Palestine, Kifah—Im Fadi—will give birth to twins. Even now, there are not enough chairs for everyone, so the smaller children sit two to a chair. Kifah scoops rice into each bowl and tops it with almonds and a piece of chicken, piling extra almonds on my plate instead of chicken. After we eat, I help clear the bowls to the kitchen, but Kifah stops me. She excuses herself to get dressed so we can all go to the *suq*, the old market in the *qazbah*.

Kifah returns in a long dress with a matching scarf loosely tied around her head. We wave down a car to get to the center of town. As we pass three- and four-story buildings along the way, Nasser points to a low building surrounded by barbed wire. "That's the prison. It houses political prisoners accused of resisting the occupation." Farther ahead, the street is lined with perfectly manicured trees with dense, dark-green foliage, their trunks painted white up to the branches. The city is bustling with shoppers but feels more orderly than Jenin.

The car lets us out near the Old City. We walk to an area that is one gold shop after the other, the front windows filled with racks of delicate earrings, thick bracelets, and chunky necklaces gleaming under bright spotlights. I look more closely and spot two thin, gold bracelets with a diamond-shaped pattern etched along the outer edges. Nasser sees my eyes lock on them and suggests we go inside. The man behind the counter carefully removes them off the rack and hands them to me. Once I slide them over my wrist, they dangle freely.

Kifah examines them more closely and frowns. *Mish khafif?*—Aren't they too light?

Most Palestinian women wear heavy gold bracelets they received as wedding presents. I assure her I want them *khafif,* finding the heavy ones too chunky. After all, I want them to wear as jewelry, not as financial security in my marriage. The salesman sets them on a small scale and punches in some numbers on a calculator since gold is sold by the gram. Nasser is pleased with the price and says we'll take them. The man offers me a bag, but I tell him I want to wear them. Nasser turns to me and smiles. *Mabrouk!*—Congratulations! It is just before our first wedding anniversary. Now, I feel like a true Palestinian bride.

Years later, I realize Kifah was right. My two gold bangle bracelets were too *khafif* and got bent and disfigured in no time. Nasser trades them in for a single, thicker filigree bracelet. Unfortunately, the delicate design deteriorates and catches on my clothes, so on a later trip we go to a gold shop in Jenin to trade it in for a sturdier one to mark our fifth wedding anniversary in 1996. My eyes scan the rack of traditional 21-karat gold bracelets until a single bracelet off to the side catches my eye. It is made of gold coins with the face of a woman framed in filigree. The shopkeeper places it around my wrist and slides a gold rod through a set of three tiny cylinders to lock it.

I am admiring the bracelet when the shopkeeper brings out a matching necklace made of the same gold coins linked together in a "V" with one additional coin suspended from the center as a pendant. Nasser places it around my neck. I can't help but ask if there are matching earrings. Sure enough, the shopkeeper finds matching gold wire earrings. My heart is racing with delight. I feel like a queen. I can't believe even pieces with such fine detail are sold by weight. I surrender my bangle bracelet, which gives us a hefty discount. My heart is racing with excitement to find such a treasure right here in Jenin. I feel like a bride all over again!

On the way home from Nablus after that first visit to Kifah's, we pass by the village of Sanur. It is long past the winter rains when the farmers normally plant their crops, but the village fields are still flooded with rainwater, creating a shallow lake. Aside from seasonal waterways that swell during the rainy season, there are no natural bodies of water in the West Bank. The local children's smiles and laughter sail across the sparkling water reflecting in their eyes as they splash about along the shoreline. The rows of neatly cultivated fields dead-end at the water's edge. Even though the lake is magical, my heart sinks when I think of the farmers who could not cultivate their land beneath the water. After all, it is their livelihood. They will have to wait until the next season for it to evaporate. Sometimes, water can be both a blessing and a curse.

16

Megiddo

With Nasser's brother Jamal in prison, his wife Samira invites us to eat at their house next door. Like Nasser's brother Faisal's house, they live on the second floor with the first floor unfinished to have greater access to the pleasant western wind that blows in from the Mediterranean Sea. Samira welcomes us into her home, where we find a large platter that almost looks like it has a torte in the center called *maqloubeh*. Nasser explains maqloubeh means "upside down" since you dump this layered dish of rice, chicken, eggplant, and cauliflower over to serve it. Small bowls of Arabic salad and yogurt are spaced out in front of the mats on a vinyl tablecloth.

Samira's eyes are heavy when she speaks of her husband Jamal, who is being held in the Megiddo Prison less than an hour from Jenin across the Green Line. I don't know then that Megiddo is a kibbutz originally established by Holocaust survivors in 1949 after Israeli forces drove out the residents of the Palestinian village of Lajjun and destroyed it on May 30, 1948, just two weeks after Israel's declaration of statehood. The kibbutz was moved to a nearby hill a few years later, the exact location Christian prophecy deems the battle of Armageddon will take place. Historic battles were fought there, and an ancient church was discovered below the prison where Jamal is being held.

Samira sends Jamal letters in jail and visits him as often as she can. At least with a prison sentence, Jamal is charged with a specific crime and a defined prison sentence, unlike the thousands of Palestinians held in administrative detention who have no formal charges against them, nor do they know when they will ever be free since their detention can be renewed indefinitely. Either way, both are subject to grueling conditions and torture.

Samira's eyes tear up as she describes how they smash Jamal's wrists repeatedly with a baton, making them swell up like balloons. I feel the weight of Jamal's imprisonment on Samira—her movements slow, her eyes still, her voice subdued and defeated. She is left to raise their three young children on her own until he is released. Because she is alone, all eyes in the village are on her. Each morning, her three children appear in the street, freshly bathed in crisp, clean outfits, their hair still wet, slickly combed back. They play more quietly than the other children, more reserved. Their eyes hang low, and their movements are measured, controlled. Their long faces brighten when they see Nasser, giving them a hopeful distraction from their longing for their father.

Nasser vows to visit Jamal in prison. Jamal's youngest daughter, still not convinced Nasser is not her father, makes her way over to him and sits on his lap after she is done eating. She keeps touching his face, looking into his eyes.

Hath 'Amu Nasser—That's Uncle Nasser, her mother reminds her.

We end the meal with a cup of hot black tea with fresh mint. A little later, Samira offers us a plate of fresh figs and sliced cucumbers, then Arabic coffee before we go. How I wish Jamal could have been here to enjoy this meal with us!

The next day, we hire a taxi to take us to Megiddo Prison. We cross through the Jalameh checkpoint and head toward Haifa. When we arrive at the prison, there are a few women and men of all ages gathered in an open gravel area outside the prison, standing in the hot August sun, waiting to see their sons, brothers, or husbands. One group of women is anticipating the imminent release of their relative, as they have a large cardboard box filled with green grapes and other fresh food from the land.

We cross the gravel area and walk through an opening in a one-story building to a bulletproof window, an Israeli soldier glaring at us from the other side. Nasser tells him we are here to visit his brother Jamal. He looks at Nasser, then at me as he flips through our IDs. He tells us only Nasser can see him, not me. We insist he let us both in, but he remains firm that I have to wait outside. I stand in the open area, the sharp gravel poking through my brown leather flats, now covered in dust.

I am burning inside that they will not let me enter the prison. This is my only chance to see Jamal. I stand there in the hot sun, my arms folded in defiance. I can feel the sweat trickle down my back beneath my silk blouse, soaking the waistband of my straight brown skirt, my thighs stuck together.

I want to assert my will some other way, so I ask the soldiers for water. They peer at each other and chuckle, then look back at me. My face is firm, my mouth tight. When they don't respond, I repeat my request, looking them straight in the eyes. They say they don't have any water. I insist they must have water. After all, don't they need to drink water, too? They can't expect me to stand out in the hot sun with no water.

One of them gets up and walks deeper into the prison, disappearing into a doorway. A few minutes later, he comes back, opens a locked security gate, beckons me to come through, then locks it behind me. I am in, hopeful I will see something of the prison this way, but all he does is lead me down an open hallway toward the back of the prison to a drinking fountain. He motions for me to drink, then lets me out the back and locks the gate.

I realize I am completely outside the prison now, no one in sight. *How will Nasser find me?* I walk along the building until I find my way back to the large gravel courtyard, the heat radiating from the stones like a furnace. I make a beeline by the gate to the bulletproof window. It has been at least an hour, maybe longer, and no sign of Nasser. People are withering from the heat, many sitting along the concrete perimeter waiting, just waiting. I remain standing, arms folded, facing the soldiers, hoping they feel the absurdity of all this waiting. The hot, dry air is thick with dust, clinging to my moist face. I feel it get trapped in my nostrils with each breath.

I peer beyond the soldiers. No one goes in. No one comes out. I check in with one of the soldiers, who assures me I am in the right place. I shift my weight from my right foot to my left and back again, trying to give my feet some relief. Finally, two hours later, Nasser appears from behind the soldiers. I am so relieved to see him that I forget the heat for a moment.

"Did you get to see him? How is he? Is he okay?"

"Yes, he's fine. He says hello to you."

My throat tightens. I wish I could see him, even for a minute. He is right there, somewhere behind these walls and locked gates, but out of reach. I try to imagine his cell. Is he with others? I ask about his wrists, if they have healed. Is he in pain? Can he move his hands? I have so many questions, but Nasser is eager to get away from the prison and return to Jalameh.

"He's okay. *Yallah*—Let's go."

It will be months before Jamal is released from prison. In the meantime, letters from his wife and rare visits are his only contact with the outside world. Jamal's wrists heal, but nothing can remove the memory of being held prisoner in his own homeland. Even if he were "guilty as charged," who wouldn't resist the occupation and renaming of one's homeland? What son wouldn't challenge the seizure of his father's land? Who wouldn't be outraged at the theft of their property, homes, and businesses, the destruction of their villages? *Why are Palestinians the criminals? Is there no one to hold Israel accountable?*

17

Burqin

Nasser and I spend the whole day with his parents visiting relatives from 'Amti's side of the family in the village of Burqin just west of Jenin. As we enter the village, the streets wind around ancient olive trees, some of them so old that the trunks are more than three feet wide. The homes we pass are nestled deep between the trees, with only a narrow driveway to reach them. The setting looks mystical, as if the trees are gathering to rehash the changing times. Each one has a slightly different character in the way they lean or in the bumpy patterns of their trunks, their branches as winding as the roads. Planted generations ago, they are like living ancestors cared for by each subsequent generation.

Farther ahead, the winding road opens into the center of the village, where stone houses are situated right next to each other. Off the main road, the streets are so narrow we can hardly pass through by car. First, we visit Nasser's uncle Khali Khaled, one of 'Amti's brothers. Khali Khaled and his wife greet us at the door. I see the resemblance to 'Amti in his slender face and narrow chin. His hair is thin and graying though still blonde, his eyes blue. 'Amti's side of the family is known for being lighter in complexion and hair color. When a baby is born blonde, the first response among family members is *Burqini*, noting their resemblance to their ancestors in the village of Burqin. It reminds me of people's general distinction on whether a child is *ashkar* or *asmar*—blonde or black, meaning light or dark in complexion. Similarly, Khali Khaled's wife has striking blue eyes and a long thin face. Her straight dark-blonde hair peeks out of the white scarf loosely wrapped around her head.

Khali Khaled leads us through the concrete house to a shed, where he is drying tobacco he grew himself to sell on the local market as an affordable alternative to Western brands of cigarettes. Back inside, we sit in the recently constructed diwan on slender, wood-framed armchairs with smooth upholstered seats. His wife offers us juice on a steel platter. *Tafaddalou*—Please take one. Her eyes light up the dim concrete room.

Just then, Nasser's other uncle, Khali Mahmoud, walks in, and we move to the family room, also new, where we sit on mats arranged against unpainted concrete walls. 'Amti and her brother Khali Khaled lie down, their heads meeting at the corner of the room. Their laughter makes them seem like two teenagers still living under one roof.

I think about how 'Amti left Burqin at 13 on horseback to marry 'Ami in Jalameh. Her brothers, on the other hand, stayed in the village, married, and raised their families here. Now, they are all in their 60s. There is a youthfulness about them behind their graying hair and weathered faces. Maybe we are all children, even in old age. We change on the outside, but some core of our child selves remains.

Nasser rises to his feet, reminding his uncles that we still have to visit his aunt Mart Khali Isma'ayn. Khali Khaled's wife insists we stay for the midday meal, but we stick to our program and head for the door.

When we arrive at Mart Khali Isma'ayn's, she is sitting on the floor in the kitchen with her daughter-in-law—*chintha*—making a traditional dish called *musakhan*. Mart Khali Isma'ayn is a heavyset woman with the kindest eyes I have ever seen. Her wavy, graying, black hair peeks out of her long white scarf wrapped loosely around her head. Her dress is the same style as 'Amti's, long and flowing with a matching sash around her waist. We meet her eldest son and his wife and children, a boy and a girl, both blonde—*Burqini* through and through.

I lean over to kiss Mart Khali Isma'ayn on both cheeks, then watch her make *musakhan*, traditionally made after the olive harvest in October given the large amount of olive oil used to create this delicacy. She lays out large loaves of flat bread baked in the traditional *taboun* oven. She soaks them in olive oil, then piles each one with a generous amount of sautéed chopped onions, a reddish spice called sumac, and roasted almonds. Her daughter-in-law carries the platter stacked with loaves into the other room, where we all sit down on mats arranged around a vinyl tablecloth on the floor. Then she brings out a round aluminum pan of roasted chicken. Mart Khali Isma'ayn leans forward, lowers herself to the floor, then rests back on the mat, stretching her legs out in front of her, covered by the long flowing skirt of her dress, then pulls a sheet over her feet since it is considered rude to let someone see the bottom of your feet.

Mart Khali Isma'ayn holds out her hands. *Hatti as-saniyeh*—Give me the platter. She leans over and tears the top loaf in half, then tears it again and piles the quartered pieces on a soup plate topped with roasted chicken. She offers it to Nasser, her hands glistening with olive oil. When she prepares my plate, she insists on giving me a piece of chicken, her eyes pleading, but I repeatedly decline, so she places an extra quarter loaf of *musakhan* on my plate instead, along with the usual substitute, a generous amount of roasted almonds. I tear off bite-sized pieces of the olive oil-soaked bread, carefully scooping up a generous pile of roasted onions with each bite. The crunch of the roasted almonds offers a delicious contrast to the olive oil-soaked bread, which melts in my mouth. I understand why this dish is traditional in a place where olive trees far outnumber houses.

After dinner, Mart Khali Isma'ayn's daughters come by and join us for tea. Nasser and I brought along our wedding video to watch with them. Their faces light up with excitement to see us wander through the Henry Ford Mansion Gardens as newlyweds, admiring how romantically our day unfolds. They clap along with excitement as we dance at our wedding party later that evening to live Arabic music and traditional wedding songs, as if they were there, no longer so many miles between us.

18

Rummaneh

Another afternoon, Nasser and I take a taxi with 'Ami and 'Amti through Jenin to *Shari' Haifa*—Haifa Street—until we reach the village of Rummaneh to visit his sister Suhaila for the midday meal. Like Jalameh, Rummaneh is located just inside the Green Line. The village is named after *rumman*—pomegranate. Sure enough, the village is filled with pomegranate trees that flourish in the higher elevation.

We enter their house quickly to get out of the narrow street. I kiss Suhaila on both cheeks several times, then shake her husband Riyadh's hand and say hello to their six children, who welcome us with broad smiles and bright eyes. Suhaila invites us into the living room of their one-story house, where her children arrange mats in a square for the midday meal around a vinyl tablecloth. I follow her into the narrow kitchen, where she arranges glass bowls of Arabic salad and olives on a steel tray. I help distribute them around the tablecloth, along with plates of hummus drizzled in olive oil and a platter of hand-cut fries. Suhaila is right behind me, carrying a platter piled with whole fried fish.

Mish btokli samak?—Don't you eat fish? Suhaila's wide smile tells me she knows that I do. I wonder how they get fish here with the sea out of reach.

With Nasser's parents, there are 12 of us. We all gather around on the mats to enjoy this delicious meal, some of the children sitting on their knees so we all fit. Suhaila keeps offering me more fish and pushing plates of hummus and salad closer to make sure I can reach everything. I thank her profusely, followed by *Alhamdillah*, to let her know I am full. I think of the German expression people say after eating fish, *Der fisch muß schwimmen!*—The fish must swim!—meaning that if you eat fish, you need to drink water after. Suhaila offers me a glass, then says *Hani'an*—May you be gratified. I learn the response to this expression is *Allah yahanik*—May God gratify you. Another expression to record in my notebook.

After dinner, I help wash the dishes in the kitchen while she consolidates the leftovers and sets a teapot on a two-burner stovetop, then joins me at the sink, shoulder to shoulder, to wash the dishes. We return to the living room with tea, the mats now arranged against the wall, the late afternoon sun streaming through the wide western window.

I listen while Nasser, Suhaila, and Riyadh discuss how a young man in the village was recently killed by the Israeli army. Like in Jenin, we visit the martyr's family. The father is standing outside in a white long-sleeved shirt and loose pants when we arrive, his face long and subdued as he welcomes us into their home. A black machine gun pointing toward the sky is spray-painted on the concrete privacy wall. Just inside the entrance is a framed photo of their son squatting down outside, smiling, his elbow resting on his knee. We join the martyr's mother in the living room, where she is sitting upright, her shoulders squared, her eyes a tapestry of pride and despair, a black-and-white kufiyyeh draped around her shoulders like a shawl of honor.

The room is set up like a shrine with various photos of their son displayed around the room holding a rifle, one decorated with flowers and a kufiyyeh draped behind it with a Palestinian flag hanging from the bottom, others on posterboards, including one with the Palestinian flag drawn in each corner and a poem in the center written by his father. His mother hands me a postcard of her son wearing jeans and a gray shirt, pointing a rifle off to the side, as if aiming to shoot. Tucked under his brown leather belt is a smaller handgun. I try to make sense of all these images of their son with guns when all I have ever seen are Palestinian youth throwing stones at soldiers. I wonder how he has access to them.

A little boy enters the room, the martyr's younger brother. His mother pulls up his shirt to reveal where one of the soldiers scraped his side and stomach when they took his brother. I don't know what his older brother did to warrant being gunned down, but I do wonder, as I look into his brother's eyes, what mark the Israeli soldier left on his mind. His mother's anger is evident as she runs her hand across her son's defaced body. Her anger shifts to pride as her shoulders rise with the tone of her voice as she recounts her older son's courage to stand up to the Israeli army, even if it cost him his life. Israel shows no hesitation in crushing any resistance to the theft and occupation of Palestinian land. I think about how Palestinians are protected under International Law and the Fourth Geneva Convention of 1949, to which Israel is a signatory.[58] It feels like a catch-22, where resistance results in Israeli violence, but "compliance" results in humiliation and the further loss of land. *What recourse do Palestinians have? What difficult choices will my own children have to make?*

Nasser explains that the village of Rummaneh has been particularly active in resisting the Israeli occupation. Many young men here have been killed at the hands of the Israeli army, particularly those affiliated with the Black Panthers. I have only heard of the Black Panthers in the US as part of the Civil Rights Movement. Here we are in Palestine with a whole generation of youth fighting for their dignity and right to self-determination.

Israel cracks down on any form of resistance, having recently deported Mubarak Awad, who founded the Palestinian Center for Nonviolent Resistance in Ramallah. Often violent and nonviolent resistance go hand in hand, as with the Civil Rights Movement, but I wonder if spilling blood is the price people have to pay for their freedom. *Shouldn't respect for human rights be enough? Don't we live in a world where people, organizations, and countries can hold others accountable for their actions? Why is Israel somehow exempt from the laws of democratic nations?* All these questions are spinning in my head as we head back to Suhaila's house.

The children are on the concrete staircase off the kitchen, cracking almonds and leaving the stairs covered with almond shells. The older children are each hitting a stone against the almond shells, just as we did on Nasser's family's land with the olive and almond trees. The younger ones wait anxiously for their share in the bounty. I think of the children in Gaza, refugees with no access to the trees of their ancestors. And yet all these children deserve freedom. I realize Save the Children is not the answer. Just as Nasser and I chanted during demonstrations in college, "The occupation's got to go." Suhaila asks them to clean up the shells so she can make us homemade knaffeh—the wheat-string pastry with cheese Nasser and I ate with Johnny in Jerusalem.

I follow Suhaila to the kitchen, where she gathers some ingredients onto a large round aluminum pan, then sets them on the floor in the concrete stairwell. She lights a simple steel oven connected to a propane tank under the stairwell that looks like a box on four legs made from a single piece of sheet metal with two steel doors that open like shutters. There is no temperature gauge, just a dial to increase or lower the flame.

Suhaila squats down and spreads string pastry onto a large pan, distributes the famous Nablus cheese over it, which has been soaking in water to remove the salt, then spreads another layer of string pastry over it before sprinkling a reddish-orange powder that gives knaffeh its signature bright color. Her face glows orange like the top of the knaffeh when she opens the steel double doors of the simple oven and slides in the pan, the flames dancing beneath it. When it is done, she pours a simple syrup over it and adds the final touch of ground pistachios.

All eyes are on Suhaila as she cuts into the knaffeh. The crisp pastry, coupled with the warm cheese and sweet syrup, are a winning combination. Once the sun sets, the evening breeze pours through the western window, the hill outside dotted with lights from people's homes. Nasser wants to head home, but Suhaila insists on making Arabic coffee first since no guest may leave until *qahweh* has been served. She invites us to sit on the rooftop beneath a spread of grape vines. Riyadh shows me how he trained one vine to climb up the side of the house and creep across the metal lattice overhead. Here among the grape vines, I don't feel like a guest. I feel right at home.

19

Nakba and Naksa

The weeks have come and gone, and I have yet to interview Nasser's parents for my master's thesis.[59] Spoken Arabic varies not only from country to country across the Middle East but even from village to village, so I need to record them speaking so I can conduct a phonemic analysis of the dialect of Jalameh. One of the topics I decide to focus on is the loss of Palestine in 1948, the Nakba. After all, 'Ami was 27 years old and 'Amti 20 when the United Nations voted to partition Palestine. I will also ask them about their experience in 1967 during the Six-Day War, the Naksa, Arabic for Setback. I want to hear about these key moments in history from those who witnessed them, survived them, and are still here to talk about them.

It is midafternoon when Nasser and I join his parents in the domed ceiling 'aqid. The sounds of children playing outside, cars and trucks occasionally driving by, and chickens cackling in the distance float into my ears through the open window. 'Ami is sitting cross-legged on one of the mats against the far wall, his white scarf draped over his shoulders beneath the black 'iqal cord. 'Amti is sitting next to him, her delicate hands resting on her legs extending out in front of her. I can see the outline of her knees beneath the folds of her deep green dress. Nasser and I drag one of the mats toward the center of the room so we can sit right across from them. I have a microcassette recorder and want to be sure their voices are audible.

'Amti explains how in 1948, she, nearly eight months pregnant, and 'Ami, along with their two daughters, Khariyeh and Naziha, who were only toddlers, fled with the whole village at night when Jewish forces ran them out of their homes. That would have been on June 1 or 2, two weeks after Israel declared statehood, when Jewish forces overran the villages of Jalameh, Sandala, Muqeibileh, and 'Arana with the intention of capturing the city of Jenin after they attacked and destroyed the villages of Zir'in, Nuris, and Al-Mazar on May 28–30, 1948.

'Amti recalls, *Baka 'anna kheil u baka 'anna sayyara wa lamma rehalna, rahalna biha, u kul il-balad hazdatna*—We had horses, and we had a car, and when we fled, we fled in it, and the whole town envied us.

Nasser's parents fled south through the village of 'Arraneh to 'Arrabeh, then farther south to the village of 'Ajja. I try to imagine 'Amti fleeing for her life at night with two toddlers when she was about to deliver their third child.

When I ask how long they stayed away from the village, 'Ami continues: *Kanat hudna thamanyeh u 'ashrin yom 'imlat-ha hayit al-umum ba'ad ma khalasat il-hudna hajamna*—There was a ceasefire for 28 days called for by the United Nations.[60] After the ceasefire ended, we dashed back to the village.[61]

The ceasefire 'Ami refers to, which came to be known as the First Truce, was from June 11 to July 9, 1948. It was then that 'Ami, along with other men from the village, returned to fight alongside the Iraqi army, which had entered the area following Israel's declaration of independence, while Nasser's mother stayed behind in 'Ajja.[62]

'Ami's eyes dart around the room as he continues the shattering story of 1948. Occasionally, he lifts his arms as if they alone could assert his memory of that year the people from the villages in the Jenin area almost lost their homes. He shakes his head as he continues. *Il-yehud kanu hun fid-dar u kanu huna fil-kam u kanu fil-balad*—The Jews were here in the house, and here in the camp, and in town.

By the time the United Nations called the next ceasefire, or Second Truce, on July 18, 'Amti had already given birth to her eldest son Ghazi the day before in a cave, earning her the traditional name *Im Ghazi*—Mother of Ghazi, and 'Ami *Abu Ghazi*—Father of Ghazi. I can't imagine 'Amti having to deliver her son in a cave and then caring for a newborn and two toddlers on the road.

The time in between the two truces is what historians refer to as the Ten Days, a period of intense fighting, though neither ceasefire brought an end to the hostilities. It was then that local Palestinians, along with the support of the Iraqi army, were able to drive Jewish forces out of Jenin and surrounding villages, including Nasser's village of Jalameh.

'Ami lifts his chest, his eyes now still and focused, as he tells how the villagers and the Iraqi army managed to force the Jewish militias to retreat north of the village, enabling residents to return to their homes. In fact, it was only after the Second Truce that 'Amti returned to the village. The city of Jenin and the villages of Jalameh, Sandala, and Muqeibileh were saved. Villages farther north were not so lucky.[63]

I cannot turn back the clock now, but I wish I had known more then about the intricacies of the history of this place I came to call home. Reflecting back, my mind is flooded with questions I never knew to ask 'Ami and 'Amti about these critical events while they were still alive. When exactly did they find out that the UN formally recommended the partition of Palestine on November 29, 1947?[64] How did they find out that the Arab League and Arab Higher Committee rejected giving over half of Palestine to a new Jewish state? What was their reaction when they knew that Britain decided to terminate the mandate in Palestine, set to expire on May 14, 1948, at midnight, essentially leaving a power vacuum in Palestine that would put Palestinians at a significant disadvantage to negotiate their fate?

When 'Ami and 'Amti fled in that spring of 1948, did they know that already during the previous winter, the Jewish militia groups Haganah and Irgun had already begun attacking Palestinian villages and Bedouin camps along the coast of the Mediterranean Sea north of Tel Aviv?[65] Did Palestinians know that during that winter, Haganah had arranged to get weapons from Czechoslovakia?[66]

Given its secrecy, I doubt any of them knew that Haganah had developed a formal plan—Plan Dalet—to systematically conquer cities, towns, and villages designated for the Jewish state by clearing the Palestinian populations from them—area by area—either through intimidation or by force.[67] Certainly, they didn't know that Plan Dalet intended to conquer territory and expel Palestinians within and beyond what the Jewish state was promised through the UN (see Map 5 and 6).

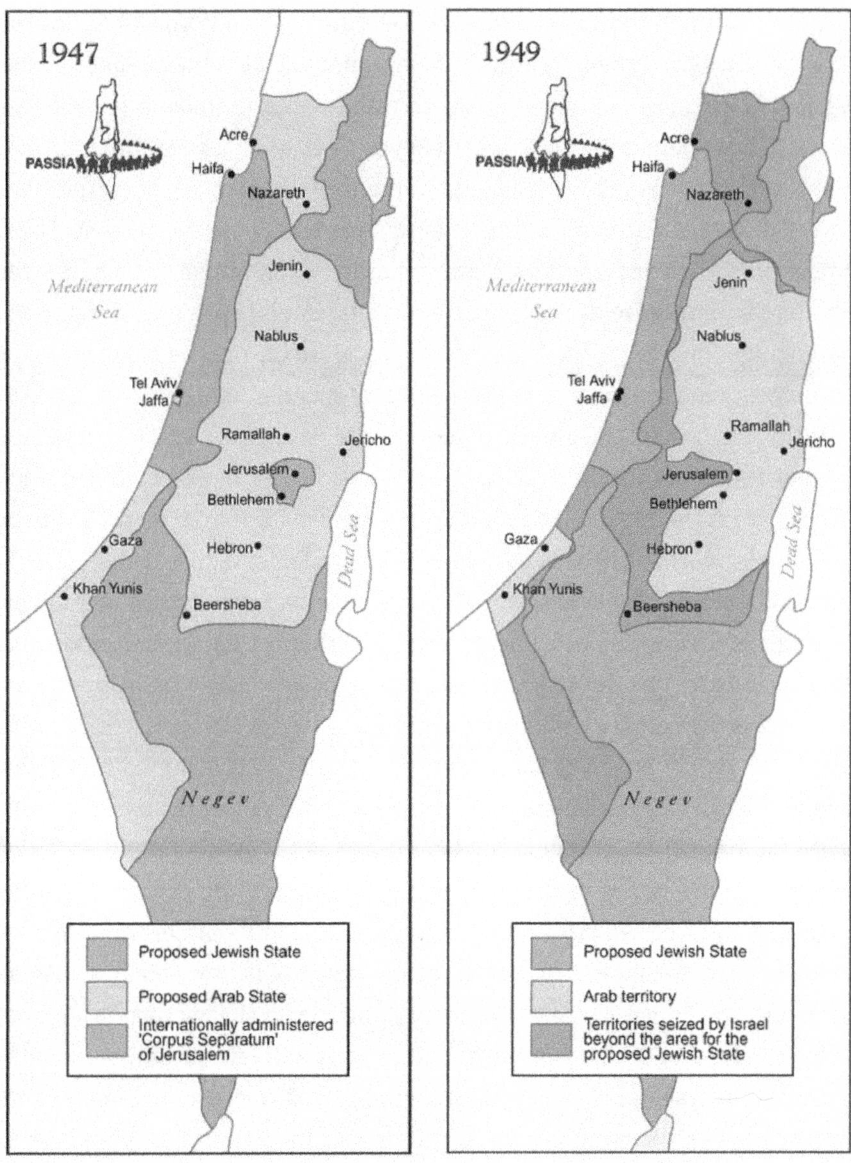

Map 5: United Nations Partition Plan, 1947, and Rhodes Armistice Lines, 1949 (Source: PASSIA)

That spring of 1948, when Irgun and the Stern Gang massacred hundreds of Palestinians in their homes in the village of Deir Yassin near Jerusalem on April 9, news of the massacre spread like wildfire.[68] My friend Suad in Madison, Wisconsin, shared with me how her family fled the Old City of Jerusalem in 1948 when she was 12, taking with them only enough to get by for a week until the war was over and they could return home. She recalled how the news of women and children being shot dead in their homes in the village of Deir Yassin outside Jerusalem was enough to make everyone run for their lives. Her family ended up in Egypt. That week turned into months, years, a lifetime. She never saw her home in Jerusalem again, barred like other Palestinians from returning after the war was over and Israel declared statehood. On one of my trips, I found her house in Jerusalem, which still had the same massive front wooden door she remembered from childhood. I encouraged her to go see it for herself since, as an American citizen, she could go as a tourist, but she could not bear seeing her homeland occupied.[69]

When did 'Ami and 'Amti hear about the massacre in Deir Yassin? When did they learn about Jewish militias occupying villages and capturing the city of Tiberias on the Sea of Galilee less than 40 miles from their own village on April 17–18, 1948, the first of 12 Palestinian cities to fall into the hands of Jewish forces? Did they know that it was British forces who evacuated Palestinians from the city? When did they hear that Haganah, only days later, conducted shelling and ground offensives in Haifa, driving out the Palestinian population there and demolishing Palestinian villages along the Tel Aviv–Jerusalem Road? That Haganah was attacking Palestinians in Jerusalem and taking control of the neighborhoods of West Jerusalem, emptying it of its Palestinian inhabitants later that month?[70] When did they hear of the fall of Beisan and then Jaffa, beginning with Irgun's massive shelling campaign of the city, followed by Haganah's clearing of surrounding villages? And all this under the watch of and with the assistance of the British before the establishment of the State of Israel on May 14, 1948, to which President Truman had already secretly agreed.

Even after the declaration of the State of Israel, Jewish militias, which became the Israeli army, continued their clearing operations. They seized the city of 'Akka, driving out three-quarters of the Palestinian population. At what point did 'Ami and 'Amti learn that Nazareth, due to its large Christian population, was the only city in what became Israel to be spared this onslaught?

Did 'Ami and 'Amti have any idea that during the Ten Days—July 9 to 18, between the First and Second Truce while 'Ami was defending the village and 'Amti was delivering their eldest son—Jewish forces were working on multiple fronts, clearing Palestinian villages in the Lower Galilee and the south Hebron Hills, while driving the 50,000 to 70,000 Palestinian residents out of Lydd and Ramleh and surrounding villages, including Johnny's family, forcing them to walk in the summer heat during the Islamic holy fasting month of Ramadan, causing hundreds of Palestinians to die on the way? *A Palestinian Trail of Tears.*[71]

And once 'Ami and 'Amti were back home in Jalameh, did they get word of the clearing of Bedouin villages in the Naqab Desert? Then after the Second Truce ended on October 5, 1948, what did they know of Jewish forces clearing the villages of the Upper Galilee into mid-November, along with those located in the Jerusalem corridor and along the Lebanese border, including Nasser's best man Tony's family's village of Kufr Bir'im? Were they aware of the seizure of the cities of Beersheba, Isdud, and Majdal, all cities with large Palestinian populations?

And then, with more than half the Palestinians having become refugees, did 'Ami and 'Amti hear how the newly established state quickly solidified its control over Palestinian communities it had conquered by placing those who managed to remain in areas declared the State of Israel under martial law, forcing some into labor camps or fenced-in areas that required permits to leave for work?

Did 'Ami and 'Amti know what laws Israel put in place that led to the "legal" confiscation of Palestinian land and property for Palestinians who fled or were internally displaced during the war? Laws such as the Abandoned Areas Ordinance of 1948, the Uncultivated Land Law of 1949, the Absentee Property Law of 1950, and the Land Acquisition Law of 1953 that designated Palestinian land or property as abandoned or uncultivated wastelands—since Palestinians were barred from returning to their homes—laws that led to the confiscation of hundreds of villages and adjacent fruit groves, as well as dwellings, buildings, and personal property in villages and cities alike, all of which would be subsequently seized by the state? Did 'Ami and 'Amti hear how in cities like 'Akka, Beisan, Haifa, Jaffa, Safad, Tiberias, and West Jerusalem, Palestinian homes were made available to new Jewish immigrants, often complete with the furnishings of Palestinians?[72] What about when the state seized the majority of Muslim-held religious properties—land, mosques, and cemeteries? I never got to ask them any of these questions while they were still alive.

As we sit there in the 'aqid, 'Ami explains that during the winter of 1948–1949, Palestinians were still in control of much of Marj ibn 'Amer, the fertile plains that extend north of the village. There was no border between the three villages that historically shared the same school. In fact, these areas had been designated for a Palestinian state under the UN Partition Plan of 1947. However, in the spring of 1949, during the Armistice Agreements between Israel and Egypt, Jordan, Lebanon, and Syria, King Abdullah of Jordan made a secret agreement with Israel that moved the Green Line farther south and east than originally planned. It is this agreement that results in the Green Line cutting the villages of Sandala and Muqeibileh off from Jalameh.[73] It also leads to the loss of village lands north of the village, including much of Nasser's father's land.

'Ami's voice is loud and angry. *Il-malak 'Abdullah salamhum iyaha*—King Abdullah gave it to them. 'Amti recalls it was winter since they had planted watermelon. 'Ami elaborates how the Israelis took their land. *Zara'na il-batikh hunaka bil-marj wakhathu uzara'na simsim wakhathu*—We planted watermelon there in the Marj, and they took it, and we planted sesame, and they took it. 'Ami explains how the Israelis let him harvest the sesame because they didn't know how to harvest it, but they kept the watermelon for themselves. That is the last time he planted his land he lost that year.

It is hard for me to get my head around the fact that in less than a year from the time the UN proposed to partition Palestine in November 1947, Jewish militias successfully took over 12 cities and cleansed vast areas of Palestine of its people in order to secure a Jewish majority for the Jewish state[74] (see Map 6). Not only did they dispossess people from their homes, but they destroyed the very fabric of Palestinian society. Palestine would never be the same.

These Palestinians, who became refugees—some 750,000—ended up in refugee camps in the West Bank and the Gaza Strip and in neighboring Lebanon, Syria, and Jordan. Roughly half of these people became refugees before Israel even declared statehood under the watchful eye of the British Mandate.[75] To this day, they have not been allowed to return to their homes[76] (see Map 7). And for those who remained, their lives would never be the same.

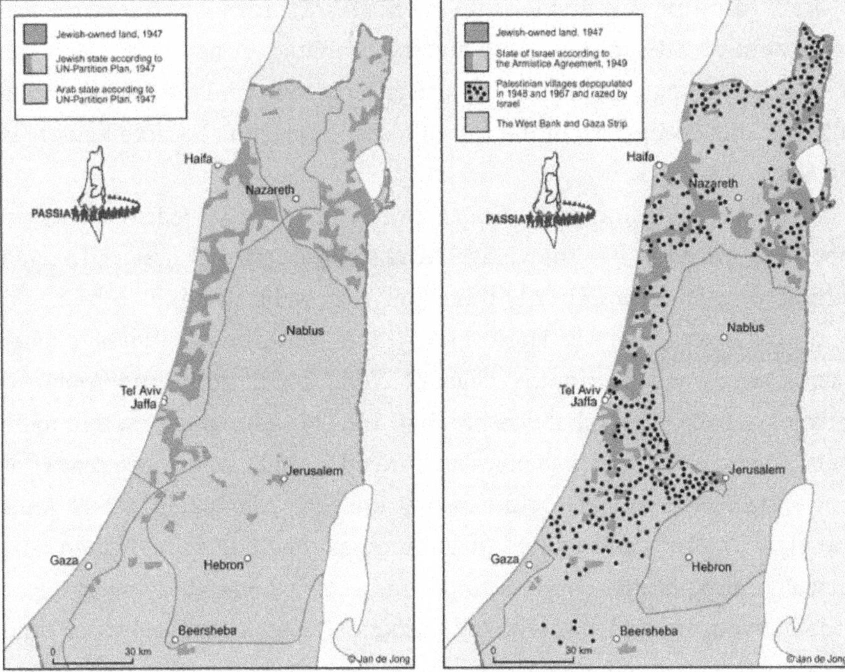

Map 6: Jewish Land Ownership in Palestine with UN Partition Plan, 1947, Compared to Palestinian Villages Depopulated and Destroyed by Israel, 1947–1948 and 1967, with 1949 Armistice Lines (Source: PASSIA)

More than seven decades later, that number has grown to more than six million registered Palestinian refugees, more than half of the total number of Palestinians worldwide.[77] By 1949, Jewish forces had occupied and bulldozed or blown up homes in over 500 Palestinians villages in what became the State of Israel so that there was nothing for Palestinians to return to but rubble.[78] Palestinians who managed to sneak back to their villages to at least harvest their land were shot dead. Though Israel established Israeli colonies or parks on or near some of the destroyed villages, most of the village sites still stand vacant to this day, laced with unattended fruit trees, grape vines, and clusters of saber marking the borders between their land.

Nasser's family and the other residents of Jalameh are lucky that they managed to recover their village and stay in their homes, unlike Salem's family and so many others whom the newly established State of Israel barred from returning to their homes. Staying, however, meant they were living in a part of Palestine that first fell into the hands of Jordan with the Armistice Agreement of 1949, then became an Israeli military zone in 1967 after the Six-Day War along with the Gaza Strip, East Jerusalem, and the Golan Heights of Syria. This occupation of the rest of historic Palestine became known as the *Naksa*—Setback.

When I ask 'Ami and 'Amti about the war in 1967, I learn that again they were forced to flee the village. 'Ami was reluctant at first and stayed behind, only to follow shortly thereafter with radio in hand so he could follow the news of the war. Not knowing there would be war, Nasser's sister Naziha, who was nine months pregnant, came to visit from Saudi Arabia to deliver her baby. After all, it was her first, and she wanted her mother to be there. Only a week later, Israeli forces entered Jenin. It was only a matter of time—perhaps moments—before they would enter Jalameh. 'Ami and 'Amti and eight of their children fled to 'Arraneh as they had in 1948, then Deir Ghazaleh, then farther south onto Jalqamus. Ghazi was studying in Egypt and Khariyeh, married, fled with her husband. Nasser's youngest sister, little Zahara—*Allah yirhamha*—had already passed away earlier that year. It was in Jalqamus that Naziha delivered her son Abdullah in a cave and became *Im Abdullah*—Mother of Abdullah. *Like mother, like daughter. Both gave birth to their eldest sons in a cave in the midst of war, one in 1948, one in 1967.*

Two weeks later, Nasser's family returned to Jalameh. 'Amti describes how the village had been ransacked by Jewish forces. *Ilkin il-qamih mekhthina il-yehud*—We found the wheat taken by the Jews. She raises her hands over her head and lets them fall toward the tile floor as she tells us how Jewish forces had dumped the sugar and other foodstuff onto the tile floor in the hallway. Her eyes roll back to the ceiling, then sink to the floor in front of her, as if she can still see the sugar. She is grieving the loss of the sugar, the wheat, but all I can think is that at least Nasser's family did not lose their home, their village, not in 1948 or 1967. Again, other villages were not so lucky. In 1967, another 500,000 Palestinians had become refugees.

While Salem's entire family has spent their lives as refugees, Nasser's parents have spent the rest of their lives living under Israeli occupation. Their children, grandchildren, and great-grandchildren have never known anything else. They all grew up in their village and raised their children in

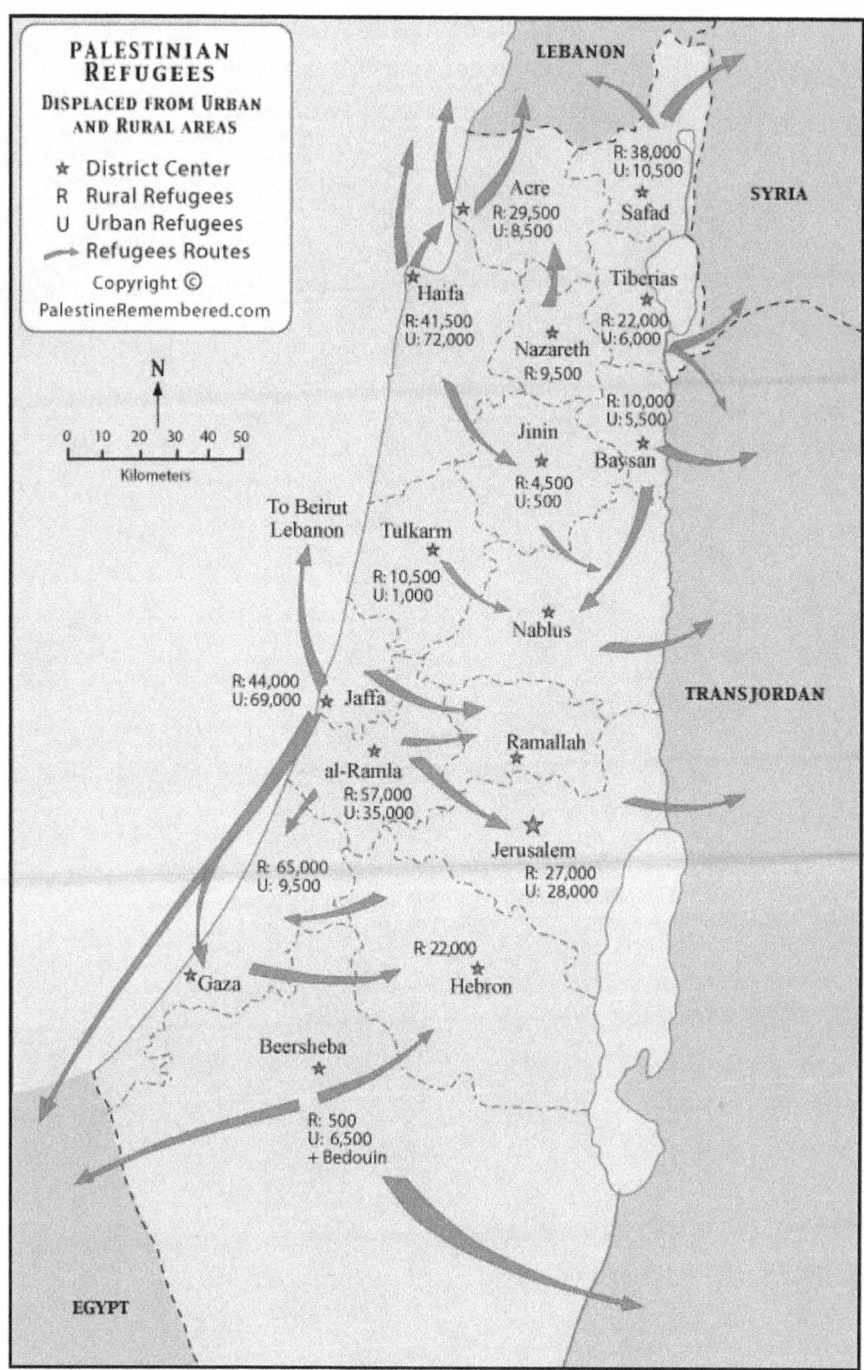

Map 7: Palestinian Refugee Expulsion Routes, 1948 (Source: Palestine Remembered)

their homeland but have lived their entire lives under occupation. Palestine remains before their eyes and under their feet but is still absent from the world map, and they remain subject to this day to the State of Israel.

20

Canaan (كنعان)

Shortly after Nasser and I return to Madison from Palestine, I confirm what I already know. We are going to have our first child. *I am going to be a mother.* I study my baby's development, tracking the weekly milestones while finishing up my coursework for my master's degree at the University of Michigan. Through my class with Palestinian author Anton Shammas, I get to travel across the Middle East and North Africa in my mind with one of the assigned readings, *Leo Africanus* by Amin Maalouf. Anton delights in the anticipation of our first child since he has recently had a son. The complex identity of his son through his marriage to a Jewish Israeli—Palestinian, Jewish, Israeli—gives me hope that someday Israelis and Palestinians will live together on the same land.

I am visiting my grandmother in Fort Myers, Florida, for Christmas when someone backs into our car in a parking lot, and I am rushed to the hospital to make sure the baby is okay. I am five months pregnant.

No taking chances. The nurse smiles as she conducts the ultrasound. "Do you want to know what you are having?"

At five months, I know that my baby's ears have developed enough to hear my voice. "Can you tell?"

Nasser and I always said that we did not want to know what we were having unless we happened to find out. I guess this is one of those situations, so I tell her it's okay to tell me.

"It's a boy."

A boy. I am having a son. Nasser is delighted with the news. Now, we can refer to "him" and name him Canaan (كنعان). Palestinians refer to Palestine as *Ard Kana'an*—The Land of Canaan—as the grandfather of all Palestinians, to the ancient ancestors of Palestine. Nasser and I will be called *Abu Canaan* and *Im Canaan*—Father and Mother of Canaan—after our first son. Palestinians will say *Inshallah bi 'aris Kana'an*—At Canaan's wedding, God willing. People in Palestine are always thinking of the future generations.

I spend the next four months finishing my coursework and master's thesis, driving between my classes at the University of Michigan in Ann Arbor and Wayne State University in Detroit, where I am also brushing up on my high school French. It reminds me of my college days when I would drive between the University of Michigan–Dearborn and Wayne State University when I first met Nasser, listening to cassette tapes Nasser gave me of the heartfelt revolutionary songs of Sabreen (Palestinian) and George Kirmiz (Palestinian).[79]

I feel lucky to have our son at a birthing center with the support of midwives. I trust in the age-old natural process of giving birth. Nasser, my mother, and my dear friend Annette are all present when I finally deliver. Tears of joy stream down my face as Nasser says with a wide smile and a trembling voice, "It's Canaan." He announces him as if he has just walked into the room, into our lives. With his long, dark hair and mature face, we have given birth to an old soul. He is indeed like the grandfather his name implies.

It is May 14, 1993, exactly 45 years since Israel became a state, almost to the minute.[80] My first child, a Palestinian, born on the day Palestine was erased from the map. The synchronicity feels larger than life itself. First, I suspected I was pregnant while visiting Johnny's relatives in Jaffa, which was emptied of most of its Palestinian inhabitants in 1948, and then I deliver on the Nakba. In that moment, the weight of this difficult history feels lighter with the joy of our newborn son. All I can hope is that there is a future for him in Palestine. And yet I worry about what the future holds. Living here in the US, how do I make sure he has a home there and doesn't become another Palestinian in exile?

When the midwives place him on my chest, I gaze into his dark eyes, wide open, staring into mine. Such curiosity in this little man's face, as if to say, "I have been wondering all this time what you look like, Mama." Neither Nasser nor I can take our eyes off him. Nasser calls his parents in Palestine to share the news. It is almost 11:00 p.m. there with the seven-hour time difference. Nasser's eyes light up when they answer the phone. His voice fills with pride as he announces, *Aja Kana'an!*—Canaan has arrived! When we return home later that evening, I realize we left as two and came home as three.

I awaken to light streaming in from the window. Panic jolts through my body as I turn toward Canaan. *Maybe the whole experience was a dream.* But there he is, eyes wide open. "Nasser, Canaan is awake. It's morning."

After I nurse Canaan, Nasser cradles him in his arms, Canaan's big dark eyes staring back at him. Then he sings to him. *Kana'an, ya Kana'an, fil hub shou fanan!*—Canaan, oh Canaan, such an artist in love! I listen carefully so I can commit the words and melody to memory.

After the first week, I venture outdoors in the warm, late-spring weather, carrying Canaan in a striped cotton pouch my father brought me from Germany. At home, I dance with him to the music of Lebanese musician Marcel Khalife (Lebanese) playing the delicate strings of the *'oud* accompanied by an orchestra or listen to the treasured songs of Lebanese singer Fairuz (Lebanese). At two weeks, we have a party at our house and roast a whole lamb on a skewer for family and friends. As Canaan grows, I walk with him in the park in his stroller. He kicks his feet happily as he watches the leaves dance overhead. They are green and dense all summer, then turn golden orange and red come fall.

By November, the leaves have fallen when I am accepted to the PhD program in Near Eastern Studies at the University of Michigan in Ann Arbor for the fall of 1994. Despite this exciting opportunity and having friends and family close by, gunshots at night plant the seed in our heads to leave Detroit behind. We move to Fort Myers, Florida, before the end of the year to start an almond-roasting business after meeting the man who makes *frisch gebrannte Mandeln*—German roasted almonds—at Noel Night in Detroit, an outdoor winter celebration of the arts.

I like the idea of getting to spend time with my grandmother, now 84 years old. She finds us a comfortable apartment with lots of windows and a screened-in porch. We feel like we are on vacation. While our friends in Detroit are shivering through another winter, we are roasting almonds in a rented storefront and delivering them to shops around town and on Sanibel and Captiva Islands, even as far south as Naples and Marco Island. At art fairs and festivals, Nasser roasts almonds in our copper kettle and packages them between batches while I hold Canaan in my arms and hand out bags of roasted almonds to customers.

After we celebrate Canaan's first birthday in May, we buy an RV and head north to escape Florida's summer heat and humidity to tour New England and the Midwest, booking shows in Connecticut, New Hampshire, Massachusetts, Michigan, and Wisconsin, listening to cassette tapes of the old-time Egyptian masters Um Kalthoum (Egyptian), Mohammed Abdel Wahab (Egyptian), and Abdel Halim Hafez (Egyptian) or Iraqi singer Sa'doun Jaber (Iraq) on the way. We fall in love with Madison, Wisconsin, which in 1995 had just been voted the best place to live in America. It even has a great university in case I ever want to go back to school for my doctorate. My grandmother is surprised that we are already thinking of moving again, but Canaan is asking about school, and we can't imagine settling for good in Florida. Besides, we miss the seasons. Our mind is made up.

The following spring, we head to Naples for our last show before we leave Florida once and for all and move to Wisconsin. The weather is perfect, warm and sunny, as the patrons meander by to sample our German roasted almonds. It is that last spring in Florida that my grandmother learns she has stomach cancer. Within two weeks of her diagnosis, she is no longer with us. My mother, brother, and sisters all come to Florida to mourn her passing. It is at this family gathering that I announce I am pregnant with our second child. Virtually everyone in the room—my mother, her brother, and their children and grandchildren—would not be there if it weren't for my grandmother. And now, I am adding one more being to the family. *One more Palestinian child.*

21

Back to Jalameh

It is August 1995. This time when Nasser and I travel to Palestine, I am a mother—*Im Kana'an* (ام كنعان)—Mother of Canaan—and I am five months pregnant with our second child. Canaan is thrilled about the plane ride. Except for a nap here and there, he is busy entertaining himself with storybooks, toy dinosaurs, and other animal figures along with a notebook and markers. Now and then, we take a walk up and down the aisles of the dim cabin past sleeping heads.

It is mid-afternoon when we arrive at the airport in Tel Aviv. This time, we will stay at Nasser's brother Faisal's house since his oldest brother Ghazi, his wife, and their five children are temporarily living with his parents. They were living in an apartment building in Jenin their father built, but he sold it once most tenants were unable to pay their rent during the intifada. Even though, as their daughter-in-law, I address Nasser's parents as 'Ami and 'Amti, for Canaan, they are *Sidi* and *Sitti*—Arabic for Grandpa and Grandma. Sidi is elated when Nasser offers him cassette tapes of Mohammed Abdel Wahab and Abdel Halim Hafez's music and a cassette player so he can listen to this treasured music anytime.

It doesn't take long for the extended family to hear of our arrival. Finally, I get to meet Nasser's brother Jamal, who has been released from prison. I kiss his wife, Samira, on both cheeks and admire how their children have grown.

I see why his youngest daughter thought Nasser was her father. Everyone is thrilled to meet Canaan, who is now two years old, filling his face with kisses. He is too shy to leave my side at first, but soon he gives in to his cousins' invitation to play in the street. After dusk, Nasser's sister Huda invites us to eat supper on the veranda, where she has arranged mats around a tray with fried eggs, fresh-cut fries, cheese, olives, and sliced tomatoes. She hands us each a loaf of warm pita bread.

It is late evening by the time we head back to Faisal's house. Faisal's wife, Feriyal, leads us into a narrow hallway past a sink and small tiled room with a squat toilet. Farther down the hall is another tiled room with a window, where a showerhead hangs over a drain in the floor. At the end of the hallway is their master bedroom. *Hay ghurfitkum*—This is your room. Feriyal's eyes glow with generosity. I am worried where they will sleep, but she assures me they will be fine. The room is furnished with their wedding set that includes a large platform bed with an ornate white wooden frame, a matching vanity with a three-way mirror, and a wardrobe closet that fills an entire wall. *Darna darkum*—Our house is your house. I feel right at home.

A cool evening breeze blows in from the west as I learn the names of their five children, which all start with "F" like their parents. It reminds me of Salem's older siblings that all start with "S." Feriyal says we should leave the fan on at night to keep the mosquitos away. I can't sleep with the hum of the fan, so I turn it off in the middle of the night, and just like she said, it gives the mosquitos the green light to feast on us while we are asleep. Poor Canaan wakes up with red bumps all over his face and arms.

After a simple breakfast of strained yogurt called *lebneh*, olive oil, and za'atar, along with olives, sliced cucumbers, and tomatoes, we take a walk down the road to see their plastic hamamot greenhouse, where they are growing cucumbers like on our last trip. There are more hamamot than on our last visit since, with the high price of water, the greenhouses prevent the water from evaporating in the hot sun. Feriyal picks several cucumbers off the vine and hands them to each of us. Canaan eats his cucumber like candy and is already helping himself to another cucumber from one of the boxes.

His cousins grab him a few extra as we head back out into the cool morning air. Canaan has taken part in the harvest.

Nasser's aunt 'Amti Saymi, 'Ami's sister, invites us to dinner, but we insist on *fatour*—breakfast—instead. They grow most of their own food, bake traditional *taboun* bread, and make traditional *jibneh* cheese from their herd of goats, so breakfast is a real treat. 'Amti Saymi's daughters show up at our door to let us know they are ready to receive us, the morning sun already high in the open blue sky. They escort us with 'Ami and 'Amti to their house, as if we are royalty.

We arrive at their two-story house and walk through a gate in the privacy wall, where a number of children from the household peer at us from the courtyard and stairwell overhead. All three of 'Amti Saymi's sons live in this compound with their wives and children, along with the two unmarried daughters, who brought us to the house. Adjacent to the house is a one-story slaughterhouse for chickens, where one of the sons is burning off feathers with a blow torch while the customer patiently waits. I recognize *miramiyeh* and *na'na'*—sage and mint—thriving along the privacy wall, but my eyes open wide when I spot a mature bush of basil among the flowering bushes. The two sisters look at me with skepticism when I tell them Italians use *rihan* all the time in cooking. They insist they only planted it for its fragrant scent.

'Amti Saymi is sitting on a sofa on the veranda by the front door. She calls out to us as we approach her, raising both arms above her head. Her twinkling eyes sparkle above her wide grin. *Ahlan wa sahlan Abu Kana'an wa Im Kana'an!* She welcomes us as the father and mother of Canaan as we each lean over to take her hands and kiss her on both cheeks. Canaan stays close by me, a little intimidated by all the people around us. She pulls him toward her and kisses him on both cheeks. *Kif halak, ya Kana'an?*—How are you, Canaan? I tell him to say *mabsout*—good.

'Amti Saymi is a delightful woman with sharp eyes and a quick mind. Unlike Sitti, who never had the opportunity to go to school, 'Amti Saymi can read and write and has strong ideas about everything. She is clearly a resilient woman both in mind and body. She is both well liked and highly respected—the solid core of this extended family. Her husband is tall and slender and wears the traditional headdress like Sidi. He is a quiet, slow-moving man, who tends to the goats, an unmistakable contrast to his outspoken wife.

After we greet the extended family, we are invited into a living room with a TV on a wheeled cart and a glass case with tiny coffee cups. 'Amti Saymi's daughters guide us to sit down on mats along the back wall, where an especially large vinyl tablecloth is spread out on the floor. Canaan is nervous and wants to nurse, tugging at the buttons of my dress. 'Amti Saymi wants him to wait and eat food, not nurse. *Khalli yokel*—Let him eat! They tell me he should stop nursing since he is two and I am five months pregnant but also admire that an American woman would nurse her son for two years. They show their approval by quoting a verse from the Quran advising a gestation and weaning period of 30 months.[81] To ease their concern for the baby, I assure them I eat enough for two.

The daughters make runs to the kitchen, and a feast appears before our eyes. Squares of jibneh, some fried to a golden crisp, bowls of falafel piled high, and a platter of fresh-cut fries along with several smaller plates of hummus, baba ghanouj, lebneh, and za'atar, sliced tomatoes and cucumbers, and plenty of pickled vegetables and olives. They also bring out large plates of *'ajjeh*, an egg dish packed with onions and parsley. And last but not least, freshly baked taboun bread with its soft and crusty texture covered with bubbles of air pockets, some soft and golden, some crispy brown. 'Amti Saymi proudly holds up her piece. *Fish ahsan min khubiz taboun!*—Nothing better than taboun bread! I can't agree more, steamy loaf in hand.

Bismillah—In the name of God—falls from the lips of most everyone in the room as we begin to eat. The choices are endless, and they are eager for us to try everything, pushing tiny plates closer so we can reach. I particularly like the *'ajjeh* packed with parsley and drenched in olive oil. I find I like to dip the flaky falafel in the hummus for the perfect mix of crunch and tanginess. I savor the deep smoky flavor of baba ghanouj made with eggplant roasted in the taboun oven mixed with tahini, lemon, and a distinct bite of garlic. The refreshing cucumber offsets the salty cheese. I find I prefer the crispy texture of the fried version. I immerse bread in the olive oil before scooping up some lebneh, then dip it in za'atar for a flavorful finish. It is truly a feast! I divert their complaints that Canaan didn't eat enough by thanking them profusely for such a delicious meal. *Yislamu ideikum! Ahsan min al-ghada!*—Bless your hands! Better than the midday meal!

After we have hot tea with fresh mint, I take Canaan to see the goats out back. The other children gather the kittens one by one once they realize he is more interested in kittens than goats. Canaan is especially fond of one of the kittens, which the family has named Foufou. My heart swells with joy to see Canaan delight in village life. I, too, can't think of any place I'd rather be.

As a young mother, who is nursing one child and five months pregnant with another, I see that everyone is eager to celebrate our growing family. We are invited to Nasser's brothers' and sisters' houses for one midday meal after another—*al-ghada*. Jamal is especially eager to formally honor us as his guests since he was in jail the last time we visited. His wife, Samira, makes my favorite dish—*kusa mahshi*—stuffed squash in yogurt soup. We gather on mats around a tablecloth on the floor to take part in this delicious feast. Canaan enjoys this dish as much as I do, savoring the tangy yogurt soup over rice topped with roasted almonds.

Later that evening, Nasser's sisters and sisters-in-law come over to Jamal's to make *ma'moul*—special cookies made with semolina flour and stuffed with nuts and spices or date paste. How lucky I am to be there to witness the process. We gather on the stairwell to the rooftop, where their propane-powered steel oven is located. There I watch them carefully press the semolina dough into ornate round or oval-shaped wooden blocks. They add some chopped nuts or date paste before pressing a thin layer of dough to seal it, then knock the wooden form against the edge of the stairs to release the newly formed cookies, which they arrange on a baking tray.

Samira opens the steel doors of the oven with a rag and slides the tray onto the rack. Her face glows as the flames reach up to the tray to transform these carefully assembled delicacies into crunchy delights. The rich aroma of roasted nuts and spices fills the stairwell. Periodically, Samira turns the trays or switches the upper and lower trays so they brown evenly until she declares, *Mastawi*—Done! She slides the first batch onto a steel tray and hands me one of the cookies. *Dukki*—Try one. The cookie crumbles in my mouth to reveal the roasted nuts inside.

Zaki, yislamu ideiki!—Delicious, thank you! I take another bite, delighting in the delicate flavors and texture. She hands me another one filled with dates, which is moist and sweeter, also quite delicious. The process seems complicated, so I simply watch and listen to them compare notes on how they make the stuffing for the cookies, each with their own variation in the proportions of ingredients. The warm glow of the sun coming through the stairwell window fades to dark just as Samira takes the last batch out of the oven. Inside the kitchen, we carefully arrange the cooled cookies on platters so Samira can dust powdered sugar across them like fresh snow on mountaintops. We enjoy a sampling of ma'moul cookies with Arabic coffee, the cardamom melding perfectly with the spices. Then Samira arranges a mix of both varieties on several soup plates for us each to take home. How fortunate am I to take part in this delicacy!

The next morning, Nasser, Canaan, and I head over to the family home to find his sister Maha at the stove over a pot. Her face widens with her smile when she sees us. She is making *bahti*—rice pudding. When it is ready, she pours it into soup plates and has her children deliver each one to her brothers' houses and Nasser's sister Huda's house. She makes several plates for us to enjoy warm. Its creamy texture and touch of sweetness with a hint of rose water make for a delicious treat. Canaan is hooked, already looking for the next bite. Maha tells me how to make it—rice, milk, sugar, and cornstarch, adding rose water at the end. I will definitely add this dessert to my repertoire!

Nasser's sister Huda invites us over for the midday meal. We arrive to a generous spread of roasted chicken as well as a round platter of rice topped with roasted almonds, along with a baking dish of *beitinjan bi tahini*, one of Nasser's favorite dishes made with eggplant baked in tahini sauce, and *bamiyeh*, which is whole okra baked in fresh tomatoes. Scattered across the tablecloth are tiny glass bowls of finely chopped tomato and cucumber salad and larger bowls of yogurt. After dinner, we sit on their rooftop terrace, the cool air soothing after such a delicious meal. Huda brings out a Bundt cake pan filled with crème caramel and spoons some of the creamy custard into bowls, drizzling the caramel sauce over each serving. Canaan is an instant fan. Huda tells me it is so easy. Simply mix eggs, milk, sugar, and vanilla and pour it into the pan lined with burnt sugar. Another dessert to add to my collection!

Another afternoon at Nasser's family home, Suhaila sets out a spread of roasted chicken over a platter of rice topped with roasted almonds and bowls of *imlukhiyeh,* which are local leaves harvested in summer prepared finely chopped into a soup. When I take a bite of rice topped with this deep green soup, I am surprised by its slightly slimy texture, though the flavor grows on me. As the soup seeps into the rice, Suhaila insists on adding more soup. It is fun to discover a dish I didn't even know existed. Years later, I get to help Suhaila pull the leaves off the long stalks of *imlukhiyeh* on the rooftop of their home so she can freeze them to enjoy throughout the year.

In the evening, I find Suhaila and Maha grinding black seeds they call *kizha* in a food processor to make into dessert bars. I watch the process closely. First, they roast the seeds in a pan, then grind them into a powder. They dump the black powder into a large steel bowl, add semolina and wheat flour, a cup with yeast bubbling in warm water, and a little sugar, and blend it all together with their bare hands until it forms a stiff dough that they press onto a cookie sheet until smooth. Then they cut lines into the dough to form diamond-shaped pieces.

Maha boils almonds in water, then one by one, we press the almonds between our fingers until the dark skin slips off, revealing the creamy white almonds within. The process reminds me of pealing *turmis* beans on the beach in Gaza. At first, the almond flies out onto the tile floor, but I finally get the hang of it. Maha is impressed. *Shatreh!*—Great job! Suhaila and I press one almond in the center of each piece before baking it while Maha boils water and sugar and a touch of lemon to make *qatr*—sugar syrup.

Soon, the house is filled with a nutty aroma. As soon as Suhaila takes the tray out of the oven, she pours the sugar syrup evenly over the black diamond-shaped bars, which immediately soaks in and disappears. She recuts the same lines with a knife, then offers me a plate with several pieces. *Tafaddali*—Enjoy! I bite off one of the pointy ends, my taste buds taking in the spicy and nutty flavor laced with sweetness. When Canaan takes a bite, he immediately makes a face and shakes his head. Suhaila laughs. *Mish zaki, habibi?*—Not delicious, my dear? I finish his piece and eat another, thanking them for such a delicious treat. Her response, *'ala qulbik*—On your heart!

I later learn that the dessert known as *kizha* is made from black seed, which is highly nutritious and heals all kinds of illnesses. I can't help but think while Americans are eating donuts and Danishes, Palestinian food is like medicine, down to the desserts! I am honored to share in these traditions, eat food that is both nourishing and delicious. Something about this ancient culture not only lives on but is thriving right here in this small village in Palestine. Just as Palestinian food nourishes Palestinians, perhaps it is these rich, time-tested traditions that keep Palestine alive even if the political future remains in question.

In the morning, Feriyal mentions she wants to do laundry—*ghasil*—and wonders if I have anything to wash. I sort our clothes and follow her into the large bathroom. She fills water into one side of a simple steel frame with two compartments, the other side a cylinder like a *Schleuder*—a spinner I have seen in Germany to wring out clothes. *Hathi ghasali qadim, min al-arba'inat, bas temshi*—This washing machine is old, from the 1940s, but it works.

I can hardly believe it is 1995, and they are using an electric washing machine from the 1940s. At least they have a washing machine. Feriyal adds some powdered laundry soap, flips a switch, and the soap swirls downward. She instructs me to give her the white clothes first, which sink into the fresh water. After about 15 minutes, we put them in the other compartment and turn on the spinner. Feriyal sprays them with a hose until the water coming out of the drainage hose on the floor runs clear into the drain.

We set the freshly washed clothes aside, then add the next darker load into the murky water. We continue this process until we have washed all the loads, then hang them on clotheslines on the rooftop in the direct August sun. Within an hour, they are dry, now much lighter when we bring them down to the family room to sort and fold. Washing clothes in this old machine is messy and tedious, but it's easier than washing clothes by hand as I had done in Gaza, though I am not sure they are quite as clean!

In the afternoon, Nasser and I take a walk with Canaan and some of his cousins to the olive and almond groves on the north end of the village by the Green Line, where we picked almonds with Nasser's nieces and nephews on our first trip in 1992. I hold Canaan up to one of the trees so he can pick some almonds. His cousins show him how to break them open with a rock. Canaan sets up his own workstation and tries to hit the almond with a rock, but it flies off to the side. One of his cousins retrieves it off the stony ground and hands it to Canaan to try again. Canaan manages to crack the shell but can't get the almond out. He surrenders his rock to his cousin, who smashes the shell, pulls out the almond, and hands it to Canaan. He pops it into his mouth and chews with rock in hand to open the next shell. Now, all of Canaan's cousins are cracking open almonds and handing him one after another. What a treat to eat from the land, to witness Sidi's grandchildren nourishing themselves with such delight.

While the children continue to crack almonds in the late afternoon sun, Nasser's eyes scan the landscape from the tall, narrow *surou* pine trees to the east toward the villages of Sandala and Muqeibileh to the north. "This is where I want to build a house." We approach the *surou* trees, trying to imagine a spot for our future home as we take in the gorgeous view of the Marj ibn 'Amr fields that include Sidi's land across the Green Line. We don't see borders, only the possibility of our life on the land.

Back at the house, we join Nasser's parents out on the veranda to enjoy a huge platter of watermelon cut into cubes served with squares of jibneh. Sidi especially likes the salty cheese paired with the sweet and juicy watermelon. As dusk sets in, we move inside to the domed ceiling 'aqid to have tea. Sidi removes his headdress as he enters the 'aqid and hangs it on a hook on the wall. I place two cups of tea on the tile floor in front of Nasser's parents. Sidi takes a sip right away, as he is well known for drinking his tea piping hot.

When Canaan reaches for his cup, I warn him it's still too hot. Nasser asks me for an empty cup. *Lazem adayirha*—I have to cool it. He slowly pours Canaan's tea into the empty glass, then back again. *Like Salem's sister Salwa had done for her brother Yusef in Gaza*. Canaan's eyes are fixed on the stream of tea as it fills one cup, then the other. One last time and Nasser hands the cup to Canaan, who eagerly takes a sip.

Nasser takes a sip of tea, then turns to his father and announces we want to build a house on the land where we had cracked almonds earlier that day. In an instant, this lighthearted man with a wide smile stiffens, takes his last sip of tea, and sets the cup in front of him, the chink on the tile floor echoing beneath the domed ceiling. His good eye beneath the thick lens of his black glasses is fixed on the patterned tiles, then darts up toward Nasser and me, his broad shoulders now square and upright.

I feel my own body stiffen as Sidi begins to speak, his voice loud and sharp. *Al-harb mish imkhallas!*—The war is not over! He raises his arms in front of him, his eyes severe, his mouth tight. *La, ma tibna'u hunak*—No, you can't build there. He waves his index finger at us. *Hath al-hadoud*—That's the border. *Bit-tukhu al-yehud awal 'aleikum*—You'll be the first ones the Jews shoot at. He shakes his head, then slumps forward as if robbed of his last energy.

Canaan cannot understand Sidi's words, but his tone and gestures are enough. He climbs into my lap and pulls at my blouse to nurse. Nasser and I look at each other, secretly thinking we can defy his father's words, that he is living in the past, that in the not-too-distant future, there is room to have a house so close to the Green Line. Perhaps one day, the Green Line will be a relic of the past. Perhaps one day, there will be no borders.

It is toward the end of our trip that Nasser and I take Canaan in the two-hour shared taxi to Ramallah to visit our friend Farah, a Palestinian we know from our student days at Wayne State University in Detroit. He has become a pharmacist like his father and is working in the family business. He has just added a second level to his parents' home, so he has the entire floor to himself, outfitted with sleek fixtures and modern furniture with clean lines and panoramic windows that offer a beautiful view of the city. I think of all the sons and daughters of refugees who are barred generation after generation from returning to their homeland, to the homes of their parents or grandparents, their land or family businesses all swept away with the Nakba, now in Jewish hands.

Farah takes us to visit the Palestinian Cultural Center, where the El-Funoun Palestinian Popular Dance Troupe rehearses traditional dabkeh performances.[82] It is powerful to see the colorful murals and practice space where they transform stories of life, struggle, and resistance into song and dance by interviewing older generations who knew life before the Nakba and personally experienced the loss of land and livelihood. Nasser and I had seen them perform in Dearborn while we were students. I recall scenes of collecting water at the well, celebrating the harvest, mourning the loss of life and land, expressing resilience by resisting occupation, and demanding the Right of Return. I feel hopeful that one day there will be justice for Palestinians, and yet that burning question remains. *How can I make a difference?*

22

Karmel (كرمل)

Back in the States, the crisp fall air joins Canaan as he starts preschool and I prepare for the birth of our second child. My father, who Canaan calls Opa, German for Grandpa, has been living in Germany since he retired from the university. He comes to visit us in Madison, Wisconsin, with a beautiful collection of gender-neutral German baby clothes since we don't know what we are having. If we have a boy, we will name him Karmel (كرمل) after Mount Carmel—*Jebl Karmel* (جبل كرمل)—in Haifa on the Mediterranean Sea, a city that remains deep in the hearts of Palestinians. If we have a girl, we will name her Jenin (جنين) after the closest city to Nasser's village.

It is just two days before Christmas when I go into labor. I have the flu with a fever, so my lungs are heavy and inflamed with bouts of coughing, my head filled with pressure, my energy dragging. We rush to the birthing center at the hospital, but because of my fever, my body is slow to progress into active labor. When hours go by, the midwives give me Tylenol, the fever drops, and my body kicks in to deliver our second child.

Opa takes Canaan out into the waiting room, and before I know it, a beautiful boy is held up before me, his back resting on the midwives' hands under a warming light. His hair is streaming with light, and his skin is glowing, a stunning sight.

Nasser's cheeks are wide with joy. "It's Karmel!"

Karmel's hairline and round face immediately remind me of Nasser's uncle. "He looks just like Khali Mahmoud!"

Nasser and I both blurt out *Burqini* at almost the same moment and laugh at our reference to his light features so characteristic of Sitti's village of Burqin. With his blonde hair and fair skin, he also takes after my father's family typical of northern Germany.

Another little man has entered our lives. Opa and Canaan come back into the room. Nasser calls out to Canaan. "Come say hello to Karmel." Canaan peers at his small, glowing face. "This is your baby brother." Canaan, now two-and-a-half years old, suddenly looks so big next to Karmel.

Opa's eyes melt into pure endearment as he looks down at little Karmel, gently pressing his hand on his grandson's shoulder. "Ah, look at that. What a sweet boy."

Sidi and Sitti are delighted when Nasser calls to deliver the news. *Aja Karmel!*—Karmel has arrived! Like in so many cultures around the world, sons are particularly celebrated in Palestine. Now, I have borne two. *Two more Palestinians to walk the Earth.*

We call my mother in Detroit, who can't wait to see her new grandson. Canaan climbs into bed with me, tired from the long day, while the midwives place Karmel on the other side of me. I feel a beautiful sense of balance framed by my two sons. I spend one night in the hospital to regain my strength while Nasser takes Opa and Canaan home for the night. The next morning, I am rested and strong, ready to go home. *Now, we are a family of four.*

It is Christmas Eve. Nasser prepares a delicious spread of appetizers in our family room by the fire, like my father's traditional *Abendbrot* I enjoyed growing up. It feels good to be home, wonderful to have nowhere anyone needs to go. Canaan can hardly wait until Christmas, only a day away.

Santa Claus manages to come, so Christmas morning is even more thrilling. Canaan opens his stocking and helps go through Karmel's stocking, too—double the fun. Karmel is calm and quiet, completely content in his new life. Canaan spends the morning building castles and skyscrapers from beautiful wooden block sets Opa brought from Germany. Karmel is tucked in my arms, quietly taking in his new surroundings.

All seems well with the world, and yet Palestine is still up for negotiation. The Oslo Accords—sealed by the infamous handshake in 1993 between Prime Minister Yitzhak Rabin and PLO Chairman Yasser Arafat at the White House with President Clinton towering over them—have superseded Palestinians represented at the Madrid Conference of 1992. Instead of empowering the leadership that grew out of the intifada, Arafat was resurrected as the father of the Palestinian struggle and brought from exile in Tunisia to Ramallah in exchange for recognizing Israel's right to exist.

Subsequently, with the Oslo II Accords in 1995, what is left of Palestine is carved up into Areas A, B, and C, the ultimate fate of Palestinians left to "final status negotiations" that have yet to materialize (see Map 8). *How will Palestine be anchored in my sons' hearts if it is reduced to mere crumbs of a homeland? How do I secure their future as Palestinians? What can I do as their mother?* At least for now, our growing family and show circuit as food vendors take center stage.

After the new year, we spend one last winter in Florida in our RV to participate in our lineup of shows through April. Spending the winter in Florida with a newborn is delightful. No need to bundle Karmel up in snowsuits. Instead, we all enjoy the warm weather and sunshine. Most weekends, we head to another city for a show, then come back to Fort Myers during the week, where we spend time with my aunt and uncle, who marvel at our adventurous life. How I wish my grandmother were still alive so she could see Karmel!

When we return to Madison, Canaan is thrilled to start Montessori school. For our summer lineup of shows, Nasser and I expand our setup to include Arabic food under the name Mediterranean Healthy Delights. Now, we will serve chicken kabobs and falafel sandwiches with a smear of hummus, lettuce and tomatoes, and tahini sauce, in addition to our German roasted almonds setup with an expanded menu that includes crêpes, iced cappuccino, and fresh fruit smoothies. We double our booth to 20 feet and hire several people to work with us. The Arabic food is such a success that we have inquiry after inquiry. "Where is your restaurant?" It is only a matter of time before we succumb to the pressure to open our very own Middle Eastern restaurant. But first, we are off to Palestine again.

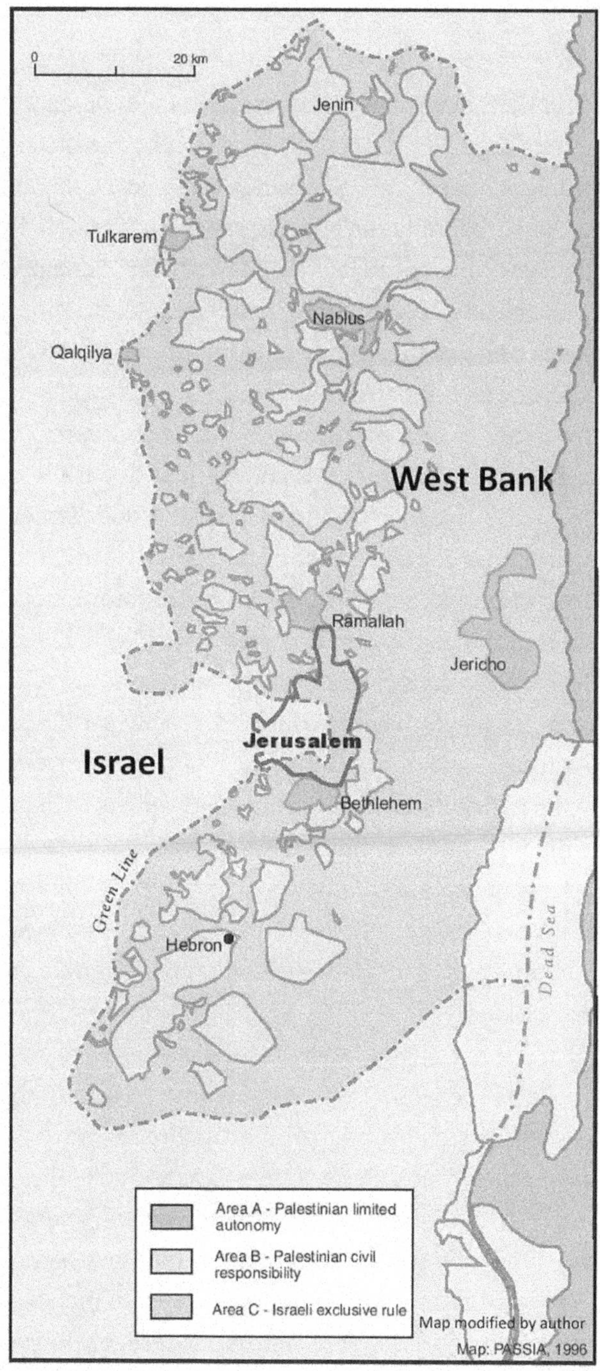

Map 8: Areas A, B, and C in the West Bank according to the Oslo II Accords, 1995 (Source: PASSIA)

Both Canaan and Karmel were in Palestine when I was pregnant with them. Now, they are here together, Karmel's first trip and Canaan's second trip to their homeland. It is August 1996. Canaan is three years old, and Karmel is seven months. Nasser's family can't wait to see them. Karmel's face is round, his thin blonde hair draped neatly across his forehead. Canaan is tall for his age and thin. An onslaught of pressure to get him to eat more awaits me, but he is so eager to play with his cousins from morning until night that any attempts at fattening him up are of no use.

This time, we stay in Nasser's family home with Nasser's parents. His brother Ghazi has since built his own house just down the road next to his brother Faisal's house, each on the plot of land their father gave them. Nasser's family home is full of visitors from the extended family, including all of Canaan and Karmel's cousins. Sometimes, the commotion is too much for Sidi, and he commands his grandchildren to go play outside in his stern, loud voice. Instead of obeying, the children laugh and carry on until Sitti shoos them away to give him some peace. Inevitably, the cousins come by when we are eating. Canaan takes his last bite and dashes out the door, where he delights in finding trinkets in the dusty streets to play with, much like his father did when he was his age.

Karmel is shy and protests if anyone wants to hold him but Nasser or me, except for his cousin Ayk, who is blonde like him, *Burqiniyeh*. She takes him easily into her arms. *Ta'al 'andi*—Come to me. Karmel's cousins circle around them like planets.

The summer heat has already scorched the earth. When we do dishes, I discover Sitti collects the water from the sink in a bucket on the other side of the wall to water the guava tree behind the house. Water is a precious resource here, and she doesn't waste a drop. Canaan and I follow her outside and watch the dry earth around the tree turn rich brown. I help Canaan onto one of the lower branches and watch him climb into the shade of the bright green leaves. He grabs onto the smooth bark of two branches and steadies himself on a third, the sun dappling across his face. Sitti's eyes lock on a ripe guava suspended among the foliage. *Jawafa!* Canaan tugs at it until it releases into his hand. Sitti directs him to others until we end up with several pale-yellow guavas. Nasser is thrilled with our find and promptly cuts them open into narrow wedges to reveal white flesh with large seeds in the center like saber. It is my first time eating this unique fruit. The soft flesh is sweet, almost nutty. Nasser's mother's eyes sparkle as Canaan eagerly takes another wedge. Now, I see why she is so attentive to this tree with its precious fruit.

Later in the afternoon, we walk down the road to the *bayara*, what used to be the orchard filled with orange trees of all types, but there are no trees, not anymore, only a metal gate by the side of the road marking the original entrance. Orange trees need a lot of water, so once Israel took control of this area in 1967 after the Six-Day War, it also seized the groundwater, selling it back to the Palestinians at three times the rate it charges Israelis. No one could afford to buy water for their trees, so they could only produce small dry oranges that were no good to eat and, certainly, no good to sell. Over time, all the families cut down their orange trees until not a single orchard remains, the land replaced with plastic hamamot greenhouses, where farmers mostly grow cucumbers and tomatoes this time of year. Farmers have to sign up to irrigate their crops, often forced to take shifts late into the night, which can take hours.

On our first trip to Jalameh in 1992, there was still one orchard left in the village owned by a family who had a large water reservoir. I got to peek in once, years later, behind the high walls around their home, the reservoir like a deep, dark swimming pool in the courtyard. The high walls around the house gave the family privacy so their daughters could swim in it without being seen by the neighbors. Only this family could afford to water their trees, though ultimately, even they surrendered their trees, and the land became bare. Little did I know then that one day the family would move away, and Nasser would grab the opportunity to buy the house and the adjacent land to serve as a community center for the village.

The loss of access to water has changed the landscape in the village, as well as what crops farmers cultivate. Now, instead of being surrounded by the lush green of orange trees full of songbirds, rows of white plastic hamamot greenhouses fill those spaces. Farmers are still farming but have had to make difficult choices about what to grow. Changes force them to find new ways to make a living. Resilient as they are, the farmers adapt to these new conditions imposed on them by their occupiers. As Nasser would say years later, farmers insist on life. That is how they survive and thrive even under occupation.

A week into our visit, Karmel gets his first two teeth. Sitti is delighted to witness this milestone in her newest grandson's life. Nasser taps Karmel's bottom lip. *Wen sinnu?*—Where's his tooth? Then he presses gently on his bottom gums. *Hayo!*—There it is! Karmel giggles as they repeat this little game again and again.

Nasser's sisters do the same when they come by the house, bubbling with excitement. *Lazem na'mal snouniyeh!*—We have to do *snouniyeh!*

Nasser responds to my puzzled face. "When a baby gets its first tooth, you make this dish from wheat and candied almonds and chickpeas and pass it out to all the neighbors."

Sitti gets right to it. She gives one of her grandsons some change to go to the local shop in the village. *Khuth, ya Sitti, ruh ishtari kilo qamih, kilo mulebbis loz, u nus kilo mulebbis iqdami*—Here, take this, go buy me a kilo of wheat, a kilo of candied almonds, and half a kilo of candied chickpeas.[83] He takes the change and dashes out the door.

He is back from the shop in no time with three clear plastic bags. He hands her the change. *Tafaddali, ya Sitti*—Here you are, Sitti.

Allah yifathlak—May God bless you.

Nasser's sisters dump the wheat into a pot, add water, and set it on the stove. Ayk is back with Karmel, who is hungry and sleepy from all the activity. As I nurse him in the 'aqid, his head becomes heavier on my arm and his eyes close. *Naym*—He's asleep, I whisper. I take him to the bedroom, cover him with a light blanket, and close the door.

When the wheat is done cooking, Suhaila sets the big pot on the tile floor in the front hallway. Maha is close behind with a tall stack of soup plates. Sitti opens the two plastic bags of candied almonds and chickpeas. We all sit on the tile floor, and the assembly begins. I join in as Maha puts a spoonful of the steaming wheat into each of the dishes while Suhaila sprinkles a handful of candied almonds on top, and Huda adds a few candied chickpeas. At the end, we sprinkle some sugar on top.

One of Nasser's nephews turns toward the bedroom door. *Karmel sahi*—Karmel's awake.

I can hear Karmel crying. I open the door, and he turns his head toward me. "We made you *snouniyeh!* Come see!" I whisk him out into the hallway and face the array of dishes on the floor in front of him. Karmel is all smiles now and reaches for the bowls topped with colorful pink, blue, and white almonds and chickpeas, but he is too little to try it.

Sitti calls on her older grandchildren to get their cousins to help deliver *snouniyeh* to the neighboring houses, designating where each plate should be taken as she hands them out until all the close relatives and neighbors are covered. We keep a couple of plates for us to enjoy. I take a spoonful. The wheat is still warm, moist, and hearty in contrast to the sweet crunch of the almonds and chickpeas.

Maha looks on eagerly as I sample this traditional treat. *Zaki?*—Do you like it?

Ah, zaki!—Yes, delicious!

I feel so lucky to be able to experience this age-old tradition of celebrating little Karmel's first teeth. I love the way Nasser's family honors this occasion and how they include all the relatives and neighbors in the celebration. And what a treat, and all grown here on the land! I wish I had known about this tradition for Canaan when he got his first tooth, but we were in the US, where my family is spread out across the whole country and where we don't even know most of our neighbors. What a privilege to be in a place where everyone knows everyone, where news is shared far and wide, where all generations take part in such celebrations, a sense of community I have longed for my whole life.

One afternoon toward the end of our trip, Sitti announces she wants to make *maftoul*. Nasser explains that it is like couscous, but it is made by hand. I watch her prepare this traditional food by spreading flour in the bottom of a laundry tub next to a smaller bowl of finely ground bulgur wheat. She stuffs a bundle of twigs into the spout of a plastic pitcher to sprinkle the water onto her hand, then takes a handful of the bulgur and a little flour and rubs her hands gently together. The flour and water coat the wheat into little balls. When they are smooth and even, she dumps them into another bowl and starts the process over again. I watch her for a few rounds, then join in. I can feel the tiny grains of wheat become smooth as the flour sticks to them. Some of the balls are larger than others, so I rub my hands more methodically. The little balls of dough-covered wheat look more even this time like tiny pearls. Just then, Huda arrives with a round pan of chicken legs, potatoes, and carrots, which she places in the oven, then comes over to admire our work.

Shou, 'amiltu maftoul? Wallah shatreh—So you made maftoul? Nice job. *Atbukh-hin, yama?*—Shall I cook them, Mama?[84]

Sitti answers in the village dialect with its signature *chaf. Ah, ma yichun*—Yes, sure.

Huda boils the maftoul in a pot of water on low fire. It's done in no time.

When we sit down to eat, I fish out potatoes and carrots to eat with the maftoul since I am still a vegetarian. The maftoul is so tender and chewy. I am amazed by the process shared among the women of each generation, ensuring these wholesome delicacies thrive to nourish future generations. I have eaten couscous in Moroccan restaurants in France, which is much smaller in diameter and more delicate. Maftoul is heartier and pleasant to chew.

Akh, ya thahri![85]—Oh, my back! Sitti places her hand on her lower back, then lies down in the 'aqid to rest. I am happy that she and Sidi will be coming to the US with us at the end of our trip. Finally, she will get to travel and have a break from all the hard work at home. I am eager to have her back checked in the US. I don't want her to be in pain. We will also have Sidi's eye checked since he is suffering from glaucoma from the strain on his remaining eye. I can't wait for them to get a glimpse of our life in the US.

23

Amrika

Sidi and Sitti travel back with us to the US at the tail end of that summer of 1996. The shift from the dry heat of summer in Palestine to the lush green weather of Wisconsin, with its sporadic rainfall, thunderstorms, and spectacular cloud formations, is dramatic, followed by the crisp autumn air and brilliant fall foliage. We show them Madison, including the University of Wisconsin and State Street, as well as the four lakes in the area, what the indigenous Ho-Chunk Nation calls *Dejope*. We take a day trip to two of our favorite camping spots, including Devil's Lake, known as Spirit Lake among the indigenous people of the area, and Wyalusing State Park, where the burial mounds of the Munsee-Delaware nations are still visible on the bluffs overlooking the Wisconsin and Mississippi Rivers. Both their lands have become state parks, like many of the destroyed village sites in Palestine. At least the US and Canada have begun to acknowledge their ruthless past of uprooting indigenous peoples from their lands. *When will Israel acknowledge the Nakba?*

Opa comes to visit from Germany, so Canaan and Karmel get to spend time with three of their four grandparents, all from overseas. Sidi tries to retrieve his English from the days of the British Mandate to speak to my father, but it has been too long, so Nasser and I translate. We go to the farmers' market around the Capitol Square, where Sidi and Sitti gaze upon the last of the season's local tomatoes and berries and numerous varieties of squash for the fall harvest. It is beautiful to see Nasser's parents—lifelong farmers—connect with the local farmers of Wisconsin. *The meeting of two worlds.*

Sidi is delighted to hear venison is available at the market. The days of hunting deer in Palestine are long over since Israel prohibits Palestinians from bearing arms, except the emerging police and security apparatus of the Palestinian Authority born out of the Oslo Accords. It is difficult for Nasser's parents to get their heads around all the varieties of cheese when in Palestine, there is basically one type of cheese made locally into flat, two-inch square blocks preserved in salt water.

Sitti is exhausted from all the walking and standing, so we sit down on the grass and let Canaan find a tree to climb while Karmel crawls happily through the lush green grass. Canaan peers down at us through the dancing leaves. I pick Karmel up and point up at Canaan, who disappears under the canopy, then braces himself to look out into the distance, as if on a pirate ship, scanning the horizon from the center mast. "*Yallah*, Canaan! Come down! We need to go. Sidi and Sitti are getting tired." Canaan scrambles across to another cluster of branches, then makes his way down with a final jump to the earth.

We apply for green cards for Nasser's parents, which entitle them to medical care. This way we can get Sitti's back checked. After a lifetime of cooking, cleaning, washing clothes, baking bread, delivering 12 children, and working in the fields, no wonder her back hurts! We take her to an ophthalmologist since she complains she can no longer thread a needle. Her brow softens, and her mouth widens to a delightful smile when the technician places a delicate pair of wire-framed glasses on her face, careful to tuck the arms underneath her scarf. We also get her a dainty golden watch so she knows when it is time to pray. I am grateful she is reclaiming her health, her eyesight, and the knowledge of time. We have Sidi's eyes checked, but unfortunately, there is no way to improve his vision in his remaining eye. He will have to depend on Sitti to be his eyes.

During their visit, we drive to Detroit so Nasser's parents can meet my mother, whom Canaan and Karmel call Grandma. Sidi and Sitti also get to see their grandson, Nawal's son Ashraf, who lived with us while he was in college when we were first married. We drive up north in our RV, taking the long way through Wisconsin into the Upper Peninsula of Michigan to show them the Porcupine Mountains on Lake Superior so they can witness the sea of trees and the lake that seems as big as the Mediterranean Sea. We treat ourselves to local delicacies of smoked fish and Cornish pasties, then cross the Mackinaw Bridge and make a beeline south to Detroit.

Nasser and I show Sidi and Sitti Dearborn, which has so many Arabic shops and businesses, being the largest concentration of Arabs outside the Middle East. We buy an assortment of pastries from Shatila Bakery to enjoy at Grandma's, including *halawat ij-jibin*, a Syrian specialty of rich cream called *kushta* wrapped in a delicate dough made of cheese, topped with crushed pistachios and rose water syrup. Sidi hasn't had this dessert since he drove his truck to the market in Damascus to sell melons and cauliflower—the borders closed to such activity since the establishment of the State of Israel in 1948.

Nasser and I also show Sidi and Sitti the skyscrapers in downtown Detroit and point out Canada just across the Detroit River. We all have dinner at one of our favorite Arabic restaurants, La Shish, the inspiration for our own restaurant, where we order fresh carrot juice and a sampler platter with all kinds of grilled meat and chicken kabobs, dawali, hummus, baba ghanouj, tabouleh, fattoush salad with toasted pita chips, and rice, as if we were in Palestine. It is a truly a feast.

Back in Madison, Sidi and Sitti are not prepared for the blistering cold of the Wisconsin winter. In Palestine, the temperature rarely drops below freezing, even during the coldest months of winter's rainy season. There is only rarely snowfall in the higher elevations of Ramallah and Bethlehem. Sidi wraps his head in a black-and-white kufiyyeh to keep warm. Confined indoors, we take up baking our own pita bread with whole wheat flour, like in the old days in Palestine. Thanks to my KitchenAid mixer, we don't have to knead the dough by hand. The first time we bake bread, Canaan and Karmel already have their pajamas on. Their faces are all smiles when I give them each a ball of dough to play with while we work.

Sitti wrinkles her brow when Canaan and Karmel get flour all over their arms and faces while they "make bread" by pressing and shaping their dough. *Lesh 'itihum 'ajin?*—Why are you giving them dough? I try to reassure her.

Khallihum imbasat—Let them have fun. She shakes her head, shifting her attention to forming the dough into balls, then rolling them flat. Four circles of dough fit on a baking sheet. I think back to baking pita bread in Gaza one loaf at a time in that electric, hand-held oven for such a large family.

The delicious smell of bread fills the house when I peek into the oven. The flat disks inflate, as if they are each taking a breath. When I pull the tray out of the oven, they collapse with steam. Nasser pours some olive oil into a bowl with a sprinkle of salt. We each tear off a piece of the bread and dip it into the deep green oil, letting it saturate the bread. The moist bread bursts with flavor and melts on my tongue. I dip another piece for Karmel. Canaan is already eagerly dipping his own piece into the oil. Once the loaves are cool, I put them in Ziploc bags in the freezer to keep them fresh so we can reheat what we need at mealtime.

Sitti takes a bite and gives her stamp of approval. *Wallah zachi*—It's really delicious. When I think of how much bread she has baked in her life, I am lucky to learn from a master.

Because Nasser and I converse in Arabic with Sidi and Sitti, we end up speaking in Arabic to Canaan and Karmel. One day, I notice Canaan speaking Arabic to Karmel. If he wants something from him, he demands, *'Atini*—Give me. Or if he doesn't want Karmel to do something, he says, *La!*—No! When he wants him to come, he calls out, *Ta'al*—Come. I realize that Canaan thinks Karmel only understands Arabic. It is only later, after Nasser's parents leave, that Canaan notices that Karmel understands English and reverts back. At least the seed of Arabic is planted.

The days ahead are filled with planning for our restaurant, the Shish Café. As a vegetarian, I make sure we have an array of vegetarian appetizers and entrées. We start with traditional fare of falafel, hummus, baba ghanouj, and tabouleh. Nasser's father insists on *shoribut addas,* a traditional crushed lentil soup. We find a supplier for pickled grape leaves from California so we can make dawali. Sitti suggests we include a baked dish of homemade whole wheat noodles layered with brown lentils in a yogurt sauce called *rashta*. Entrées include *shish tawouk* and *shish kabob* made with chicken and beef or lamb on skewers, grilled oval-shaped ground spiced meat called *kafta*, and ground meat and pine nuts surrounded by a bulgur wheat crust known as *kibbeh*.

We order two vertical skewer grills for chicken and beef shawarma. And like La Shish, we offer a Shish Feast, as well as a Vegetarian Feast. We have pita bread shipped from Yasmeen Bakery in Dearborn for sandwiches. I make two desserts I learned from Nasser's sisters: crème caramel and the rice pudding called *bahti* as well as chocolate mousse for variety. We order an assortment of *baklawa* filo pastries from Shatila Bakery in Dearborn and have our favorite mango and pistachio ice cream shipped directly from the Lebanese company Sweet Dreams in California.

It is wonderful, after all the planning and preparation, to have Sidi and Sitti there for our grand opening in December, just before Karmel's first birthday. They sit in the dining room while we work and order from the menu. Canaan, in his red apron and paper chef's hat, mixes his own concoctions at the soda machine while I take on one-handed tasks with baby Karmel, like setting the tables with the tablecloths I made out of gorgeous red, green, and gold upholstery fabric using my grandmother's sewing machine. During Karmel's naps, I roll a pot of grape leaves or make yogurt and desserts.

As much as Nasser's parents enjoy getting to know our life in the US and meeting my parents, they are relieved after four months to go home to Jalameh, where they have the whole village at their fingertips. Meanwhile, we build up a loyal clientele of customers after receiving a strong review commending us on the freshness and attractive presentation of our food in a warm and welcoming setting decorated with our personal Palestinian décor. We become good friends with one of our waitstaff, Huda, whose husband is doing his post-doc at the university.

One evening at dinner, one of the customer's ears perk up when he hears Huda's Arabic accent. "Where are you from?" He speaks with a heavy Israeli accent.

Huda hesitates, then smiles. "Beirut."

"Oh, really!" He breaks into laughter. "I have seen Beirut at night."

Huda freezes. "Excuse me, please." She pulls away from the table and confides in me in the kitchen. "I'm so sorry. I cannot wait on that table."

"Of course. Don't worry about it. I will take care of him."

I return to the table. "So, I hear you've been to Beirut." My smile dissipates when the man explains that he was an Israeli pilot during the war in Lebanon and conducted bombing raids at night on Beirut. *No apologies. No regrets.*

I force myself to respond. "People live there, you know." He is silent. I am relieved when he has finished his meal. "I will get your check."

The simple interaction has spun me completely around. That night, I don't sleep. How can we just go on with our lives when history is so unsettled? Here we are running an Arabic restaurant in Madison, Wisconsin. I love sharing Palestinian food with our customers and even forego being a vegetarian so that I am not serving something I don't eat myself, but it doesn't feel like we are doing enough to make a difference on the ground in Palestine. *How will our children feel at home in Palestine if all we do is visit our occupied homeland and then carry on with our lives in the US?*

The following summer, the phone rings. It is Nasser's uncle from Jordan, 'Ami Othman. I watch Nasser's face turn to stone. His eyes pool with tears. Sidi was having a cup of tea with Sitti in front of the house in Palestine—a day like any other day—when he fell forward to the ground. Sitti called out for help, but it was too late. No breath, no heartbeat. Sidi's body, warm but still, lay on the concrete, where only the sky could bear witness to this life taken in an instant.

My heart sinks to the floor. My throat tightens as my own tears distort the image of Nasser's face. His father, who witnessed the loss of Palestine, is no more. *What about his land?* Now, the burden of recovering the loss of his land falls on his sons, perhaps even their sons.

Because Islamic tradition calls for the body to be buried within 24 hours, Nasser cannot get home in time and foregoes his father's funeral. I cannot help but think of this closure of a life born in the wake of the Ottoman Empire, a life that served the British as the next "protectorate" of his homeland, only to live the rest of his life under Israeli occupation. A farmer who never recovered the land he lost in 1948, who could only leave his children and grandchildren the stories of what once was. From now on, as tradition calls for, when I and others mention his name, we will say, *Allah yirhamu*—May God bless his soul.

My throat softens as I recall how Sidi always found a way to laugh and enjoy his life in the village he fervently defended so many years ago. *A bittersweet ending*. I feel a renewed sense of urgency that his struggle to defend his homeland cannot end with his passing. Just as he shared his memories of the loss of his land with me, I must pass that memory onto our children, the next generation. These are their Sidi's stories that will remind them of what came before, who they are, and serve as their guide for the future. These stories, coupled with what I have witnessed myself are, after all, what guide me in my own life and continue to inspire me to make a difference in Palestine, even if I have yet to fully understand how.

PART III

ROOTEDNESS

50th Commemoration of the Nakba

1998-1999

24

Rooted

It is 1998, 50 years since Israel declared statehood in Palestine and five years into the Oslo Accords. Nasser's mother is excited about how the agreement has brought new roads to Jenin, and others celebrate how unemployment is offset with the quasi-state apparatus of the newly established Palestinian Authority—what Palestinians refer to as the *Sulta*—under the leadership of Arafat, even though it comes without the full privileges of statehood. In fact, Palestinians now manage their own occupation while Israeli settlers in their midst have the backing of the Israeli government and army to establish new outposts, expand settlements, seizing more Palestinian land. My stomach turns at the façade of statehood in the streets of Jenin, Nablus, and Ramallah, where thousands of armed Palestinian police officers—the *Shurta*—stand guard in crisp uniforms on behalf of the Israeli army and Shin Bet intelligence services to conduct the day-to-day policing of Palestinians in the streets.

It is September of that year when I bring Canaan and Karmel to their homeland for an extended stay, so they may come to know Palestine as their own. They will go to a newly opened bilingual school affiliated with a new university planned in the Jenin area. Nasser stays in Madison to run our restaurant and manage our show business, which we have expanded to include art shows in the Midwest. I want our sons to spend time in their homeland, hear the language, and see their extended family. I want them to feel the warmth of the sun and the western wind that sails in from the Mediterranean Sea. I want to make sure Palestine finds its way into their soul as it has mine.

Nasser has a Ford Taurus shipped to Haifa from the US for us to use while we are in Palestine, but it hasn't arrived yet, so we travel the two-hour car ride by taxi from the Ben Gurion Airport to Jalameh. When we pull up at Nasser's family home, Sidi and Sitti come out to greet us. Nasser's brother Jamal, who lives next door, is sitting on his veranda with his wife Samira and calls out to us. *Al-hamdillah 'as-silameh, Im Canaan*—Glad you arrived safely, Mother of Canaan! They come down from the veranda to greet us.

I welcome them in kind, acknowledging the name of their eldest son. *Ahleen, Im Osama! Ahleen, Abu Osama!* Jamal shakes my hand vigorously. Samira approaches me, and we kiss each other on both cheeks several times. My heart is soaring with delight. We made it! We are back in Palestine.

The late-summer heat permeates the landscape, so the village is dry and dusty. It will be several months before the winter rains begin. Jamal carries our luggage inside to the extra bedroom. Just then, Nasser's nephew appears, whom we affectionately call *Mahmoud, ibn Khariyeh* in honor of his mother who is no longer with us. He is recently back from India, where he was studying. "How are you, Canaan? Hi, Karmel!" Canaan shakes Mahmoud's hand, but Karmel is shy and turns his head into my skirt.

I lean over and lift Karmel into my arms. "This is Mahmoud, your cousin." Karmel studies his face for a moment, then offers a narrow smile, his mouth closed. We sit on mats in the lovely domed 'aqid, shielded from the heat outside by the thick stone walls that were built in Palestine and now stand under Israeli occupation. Sitti comes in with a tray of hot tea and tiny glasses. So good to be back home.

I always know I am in Palestine when I can smell the sour, smoky scent of the traditional taboun ovens. 'Amti Saymi's house is one of the few houses in the village that still has one. Her two unmarried daughters, Intisar and Fawziya, take turns baking the traditional taboun bread each day. I visit one afternoon and join 'Amti Saymi on the veranda, where she is sitting in an armchair outside the front door, a sizeable Quran cradled in her lap. Fawziya sits next to me on one of the white plastic chairs across from 'Amti Saymi while Canaan and Karmel play in the courtyard with the children of the extended family. Canaan is delighted to find Foufou and show her to Karmel. She is a grown cat now and has kittens of her own. Intisar brings out a pot of black tea with fresh sage she picked along their privacy wall.

I turn to Intisar. *Ba'ad btikhbazu khubiz taboun?*—Do you still bake taboun bread?"

Ta'ban—Of course. *Kul yom*—Every day.

I commend her on her hard work. *'Atik al-'afiyeh*—May you have vitality.

Allah 'afiki—May God grant you vitality as well.

Intisar explains how most people in the village are either farmers or have taken jobs in the city, so they no longer have goats of their own. Without goats, they don't have the goat dung that serves as the fuel for the taboun oven. The fire is replenished each evening with sun-dried dung, offering the perfect temperature for baking over a bed of stones come morning. A taboun oven is always burning.

My eyes are wide open with excitement. *Biddi akhbaz ma'akum*—I want to bake with you. The two sisters look at each other and smile with a mix of skepticism and delight.

Intisar's eyes are full of doubt. *Anjad?*—Seriously? *Lesh, wasikh*—Why, it's dirty.

Mish meshkaleh—No problem. *Wenta btikhbazu?*—When do you bake?

Intisar offers me more tea. *Yom ana, yom Fawziya*—One day me, the next Fawziya. *Al-yom khabazit Fawziya, bukra ana*—Fawziya baked today. Tomorrow is my turn. Intisar tells me to come tomorrow morning at six, hoping that's not too early for me.

I arrive the next morning. Intisar greets me with a fresh smile. We sit for a few minutes to have a cup of tea, then Intisar brings out a steel tub filled with dough covered with a cloth. She beckons me to follow her to a free-standing stone building with a flat, sheet-metal roof the size of a large outhouse over by the goat pen. I follow her through the simple wooden doorway, ducking my head as I enter, the intense heat hitting my face like a bonfire. Intisar squats down and scrapes ash away from a metal cover with a scrap of wood, then lifts the metal cover off with a rag and sets it aside.

Intisar lifts the cloth off the dough, revealing a swollen mass. She cuts into the dough with cupped hands, scoops up a section, and sprinkles flour on it, then passes the dough back and forth from one hand to the other, rotating it as she works. The round section of dough quickly becomes a shape that is neither round nor square, nor perfectly flat. With a final throw, she places the dough on the stones. The loaf immediately takes on the lumpy shapes of the stones below. She covers the oven with the metal disk and scrapes ash back over it to seal in the heat. After a few minutes, she retrieves the golden-brown bread below, the lumps and bumps from the stones even more pronounced, some crispy.

Nasser bihab imkamish, mish heik?—Nasser likes it crispy, right?

Ah—Yes. My voice trails off. I wish he were here to enjoy this delicacy.

She sets the stiff loaf aside on an open section of newspaper. Now it's my turn. I cup my hands together and lower them into the cool, elastic dough, scooping up a section by cutting it from underneath with my hands. I sprinkle on some flour, then slowly pass the dough from hand to hand, rotating it as I flip it from one hand to the other. The dough becomes flatter with each pass, collapsing over the edges of my hands. *Heik mnih?*—Is that good?

Ah, mnih, hutti—Yes, that's good, put it in. I flip the dough onto the stones, but it lands to the side. Intisar laughs. *Ma'alesh*—It's okay. She shifts the dough to the center and covers the oven.

Dusting our hands with flour, we continue the process, sweat trickling down our foreheads, until we have a stack of loaves ranging from off-white to nearly brown. *Khalasna!*—We finished! Intisar's face is smooth with pride as she rises to her feet and pushes open the door with her shoulder, letting a rush of cool morning air onto our damp faces. I follow her into the kitchen, cradling the stack of taboun bread in my arms. The warmth of the bread permeates my chest while the delicious smell of the bread tantalizes my taste buds. Intisar wraps a few of the loaves in newspaper.

Hathol ilkum—These are for you.

I gladly accept the loaves to share with Canaan and Karmel, honored to take part in this age-old tradition. *Yislamu ideiki*—Bless your hands.

Yislamu ideiki anti!—Bless *your* hands.

It is September 12, my 31st birthday and I decide to have a party at Nasser's family home in Jalameh. I make several cakes as is customary here and a large platter of tabouleh with a side plate of romaine hearts. Canaan loves what I call "squirgle cake," which is a vanilla-and-chocolate-swirl Bundt cake, so I include it in the lineup. I also make banana bread because people don't know it here, and almond cake with chocolate specks I know from Germany, only there they make it with hazelnuts. As Nasser's brothers and sisters arrive with their families, the assortment of desserts grows across the coffee table on the veranda. The tabouleh is an island of green among a sea of desserts.

Suhaila is arranging some cookies on a plate when a car with yellow Israeli license plates stops in front of the house. Huda walks up to the driver, who gets out of the car and hands her a bouquet of fresh flowers. He is from a flower shop in Afula, which is the first Israeli town across the Green Line, about 20 minutes north of Jenin. Huda hands them to me. *Hathola ilik min Nasser, ya Christa*—These are for you from Nasser, Christa. *Kul saneh wa anti salmeh*—Happy Birthday. My heart bubbles with joy at the sight of the gorgeous bouquet: pink and white lilies like I had in my wedding bouquet and dense, velvety, purplish-pink flowers tucked in among smaller flowers and greenery. I later learn the velvety flowers are called cockscomb or *deek* in Arabic because they look like a rooster's head. My heart expands in my chest, my cheeks locked in a smile.

One of Nasser's nieces leans into the bouquet with wide eyes. *Haqiqeh hathola?*—Are they real? Throughout Jalameh, there are several different kinds of flowering bushes along the privacy walls, such as the fragrant, white jasmine flowers or the bright pink or purple paper flowers, known here as *majnoun*, which means "crazy" in Arabic, maybe because they grow like crazy! Fresh-cut flowers are not common here. Some families have plastic flower arrangements in their formal living rooms. Nasser's sisters eye each other and smile at me.

I take the gorgeous bouquet from Huda and thank the Israeli delivery man. I realize he had to cross the border into unfamiliar territory. I wonder how Nasser got the flower shop to deliver all the way to a Palestinian village in the West Bank. The man shifts his weight as he looks at all the faces witnessing the delivery, his face still, expressionless, as if paralyzed by a stroke. He can hardly speak English, and no one present can speak Hebrew. I thank him just the same, tilting my head toward him and smiling. His eyes soften for a moment as we share the same space, then he takes a step backward, gets in his car, and drives away.

Maha brings out a large jar filled with water and arranges the flowers among the desserts. Tucked into the flowers is a handwritten card. "To Christa, Happy Birthday! Love, Nasser." Nasser's nieces and nephews are eager to try all the treats in front of them, but first, the adults initiate a round of singing "Happy Birthday" in Arabic. I don't know why, but this song is always sung in the Egyptian accent with the "j" of jamil, Arabic for "beautiful," pronounced "g" as in "goat."

Sana helwa ya gamil,
Sana helwa ya gamil,
Sana helwa ya Christa,
Sana helwa ya gamil.

The song is a simple repeating verse of "Beautiful year, beautiful one," sung to the tune of "Happy Birthday to you" in English, including my name in the third verse. The tops of my cheeks are cramping from smiling so much. *Shukran. Shukran kithir. Yallah?*—Thank you. Thank you so much. Shall we?

Now the party can begin.

Abu Samir's family owns the land behind Sitti's house that extends to Tariq Burqin, the street through which Sitti was brought to the village on horseback for her wedding. I have become good friends with 'Aida, who is married to Abu Samir's son Khalid. They live right next door beneath Abu Samir—the mayor whom I had talked to about the garbage in the village on our first trip to Jalameh—so they already know I am passionate about keeping the village clean and beautiful. There is only a narrow dirt path leading from the back of the house to the street. The land itself, full of weeds and garbage, is my view from the kitchen window.

Khalid listens closely when I ask if I can clean up the land behind Sitti's house and plant some bushes along our pathway to the road and some flowers outside the kitchen window. I assure him I know it is their land, but I want to make it more beautiful for both of us. Intrigued by my request, he discusses it with his father and brothers. A few days later, he tells me I can do whatever I want, adding they should really be the ones to clean it up. I thank him profusely. I am glad to do it for all of us.

Nasser is surprised the neighbors agree to let me plant on their land given the tension between the two families for years over that parcel of land. Planting is a sign of ownership. He is worried they will think we are trying to claim it by planting on it. I assure him they are fine with it. Besides, the access pathway to the road does belong to Nasser's family, and on the rest, I am simply planting flowers. Nasser tells me not to plant any trees—they are a whole other matter—because trees outlive those who plant them. I promise not to plant any trees on the neighbor's land.

Nasser's eldest brother Ghazi works at a nursery in Jenin. He and his wife Amal are both knowledgeable about plants. They help me pick out bushes for the hedge. I also choose deep red flowers with large, shiny reddish green leaves that will become quite tall, known as *zanbak*—Canna Lily in English—to plant in a circle outside the kitchen window. While I am looking around the nursery, I notice an area with some scrawny trees, one with a single tiny orange on it. I think of the orchards of Jalameh that have all been uprooted by their owners because they cannot afford to water them. Ghazi catches my gaze, and we walk over to them.

Shou naw ish-shajar?—What kind of trees are these?

Hay klementin u fi tin u hathi limun—This one is clementine, there are fig trees, and that one is a lemon tree.

The word *limun* sends a bolt of energy through my veins. My eyes lock on the lemon tree with its sparse green leaves scattered across its thin branches. I remember the lemon tree in the courtyard in Gaza hanging over the wall. I also recall the prominent lemon tree in the children's story *Sitti's Secrets* by Naomi Shihab Nye. My friend Annette got this book for Canaan as a gift when he was born. It's about a young Palestinian girl who grows up in the US and travels to Palestine to visit her Sitti, who has a lemon tree in the courtyard of her house. She and her grandmother make lemonade with fresh mint. I want my children's Sitti's house to have a lemon tree. A house without a lemon tree is like a mosque without a minaret. I think of Nasser's warning not to plant any trees on the neighbor's land.

Ghazi senses my excitement. *Shou, biddik limuneh?*—What, you want a lemon tree?

Ah, bas wen ahatha?—Yes, but where would I put it?

Hattiha 'and id-dawali—Put it by the grape vines.

My heart is racing now. *I can plant a lemon tree.* Ghazi promises to deliver the bushes and flowers along with the lemon tree. I can hardly wait to plant them, especially the lemon tree. I gather several of Nasser's nieces and nephews, and we go to work picking up garbage and clearing stones from the neighbor's land. My heart burns at the sight of all the garbage. I tell the kids about the time I organized a clean-up day and repeat the same message. *Khalli Falastin halweh*—Keep Palestine beautiful.

We collect plastic bottles, chip bags, metal scraps, broken glass, and other odd objects and throw them in black buckets that we empty into a larger garbage bin. We set the stones we collect off to the side of the road. Collecting the stones reminds me that I want to build a *silsileh* one day. These meticulously hand-laid walls of stone form terraces to support olive trees on hillsides. I pause to admire how quickly we can transform this area simply by clearing the garbage. It already looks better.

Ghazi delivers the plants and supplies me with a shovel. Canaan and Karmel's cousins fill black plastic buckets with water while I dig the holes. I have them pour water in each hole before I place the bushes into their new homes. We do the same for the flowers. I save the lemon tree for last. Sure enough, there is a perfect spot for it between the grape vines and the guava tree. I dig a larger hole and have the children pour an entire bucket of water into it. The dry earth softens and turns a rich chocolate brown. I carefully position the lemon tree in the hole, then fill in the surrounding dirt. Canaan and Karmel stomp on the loose soil to pack it down.

My heart swells as I admire the lemon tree, its narrow trunk freshly anchored in the soil. At last, Sitti's house has a lemon tree. Having planted this tiny tree with my own hands, I, too, feel anchored in the soil. My roots, which sprouted on that first trip to Jerusalem and Gaza back in 1986, are growing deeper like the people in Salem's paintings, roots that now extend to my children. I suddenly feel the power of having that connection to the land, not any land, but one's homeland. I look forward to the day when we can all enjoy the harvest.

It is late October. Families all over Palestine are busy picking their olives. Many businesses are closed, and the universities are on break so that everyone can join in on the harvest. Farming families depend on the harvest for their own supply of olive oil and sell their surplus to support their livelihood. Nasser's maternal grandmother Sitti Sabha used to keep a giant ceramic jug called a *butta* filled with olive oil from the previous year before she would sell her oil from the current harvest to make sure the family would have enough supply for the year. Besides pressing olives into oil for consumption, people also make soap and pickled olives. In fact, Canaan and Karmel's Sitti washes her hair with olive oil soap.

I have never been in Palestine for the olive harvest since we only came here in the summer. Now that we have our own car, we visit Nasser's sister Suhaila in the village of Rummaneh one day after school during the olive harvest since they have olive trees. After dinner, Suhaila takes us to an unfinished room in their house. Piled on the concrete floor is a mountain of green olives. *Hathola laqatnahin*—This is what we picked so far.

I am hopeful I will have a chance to pick olives. *Ba'ad fi?*—Are there still some?

Ah, bethul sway. Bawarjiki ba'adeen—Yes, there are some. I can show you later.

Karmel is wearing a crown made out of green construction paper he made at school. Canaan and Karmel scramble toward the olive mountain, as if summoned to climb it. They fall to their knees and try to climb up, but the olives roll them back down to the base of the mountain. Canaan manages to get to the top on his second try and lies down on his back, scooping the olives with his hands to cover himself, as if he is at the beach burying himself in sand.

Karmel has also managed to climb to the top of the mountain, sitting with his legs out wide in front of him. With his construction paper crown, he looks like a little king. Canaan rolls over to free himself of the olives. Now on his stomach, he looks like he is swimming in a sea of olives as he drags his fingers in front of him.

I am worried about them climbing all over the olives. "Come on. We are going to go to the wa'ra to pick some." Karmel rolls over on his stomach like his brother and slides down the mountain. I prop him up on his feet when he gets to the bottom. Canaan is still swimming. "Come on, Canaan." A few more strokes, and he slides toward me.

Suhaila and her husband Riyadh—Im and Abu Fayyad, and their six children lead us down the hill in the village to the wa'ra. We reach a dirt road and turn off, a sea of olive trees now in front of us that extend up the rocky hillside.

When we reach their land, Suhaila leads us to one of the trees with a large plastic tarp spread out underneath it. She shows me how to cup my hands around the olives and gently pull until they release from their stems and fall onto the tarp. The olives are hard and dusty. They sound like large raindrops, some bouncing slightly when they fall. She explains how every few days, they bag up the olives in burlap sacks and take them to the olive press. There is always hot bread at the press so they can have a taste of their own oil. They will keep enough olive oil from the season for the family and sell the rest on the local market. With Riyadh's modest salary as a clerk in Jenin, the income they get from their olive trees is critical to their livelihood.

On our way back to the house, Riyadh points out his family's land in the distance, which Israel confiscated in 1949 after the signing of the Rhodes Accords. *Like Sidi's land.* Riyadh peers into the distance at his land across the Green Line, visible but out of reach. His gaze, rooted in the land, is filled with both familiarity and heartache, the absurdity like a relentless burden he invariably passes onto his children. *How many generations must put up with this madness?*

25

Villages

As an American citizen with a car with yellow Israeli license plates, I take advantage of my privilege to be able to enter Israel. I cross the Green Line often to explore 1948 Palestine—*juwa*. I want to visit places Palestinians in the West Bank cannot visit and bear witness to what Israelis choose not to see.

Today, I am driving to the Palestinian town of Kabul, not far from 'Akka, to visit my friend Ibtisam, whom I met when we were both graduate students at the University of Wisconsin–Madison. As an American, I only receive a three-month tourist visa upon entering Israel, but I am staying longer, so Ibtisam will help me renew my visa. I pass through the Jalameh checkpoint without incident and continue north toward Nazareth.

With each mile, I am one mile farther away from the Palestine I know. Before I even reach the Israeli town of Afula, I see a single, tall arched window of stone in an otherwise flat, grassy landscape. I can only imagine the rest of the building that used to stand there. It must have been quite prominent, judging from the size of the window. I don't know yet that this window is all that is left of the Palestinian village of Zir'in.[86]

Farther north, just before the Somekh Junction, I see a whole landscape of blackened stone buildings up on a bluff. My throat tightens as I peer intensely at what looks like a ghost town from another century. The windows are hollow, like the eyes of a skeleton, and the stone buildings all partially destroyed. Between them, overgrown grass hides whatever paths used to separate them. I can't help but think of Deir Yassin. I wonder if this is what it looked like after Jewish militias attacked the village. Chills run up my spine, and I feel a sickening in my stomach. These places are real. People lived and died here or were driven out, never to return. The ruins become a blur as my eyes fill with tears. I blink several times to bring the road into focus as I leave the ruins behind and continue north.

When I arrive at the road to Kabul, I turn right and drive along two-story, concrete houses until I reach a bend in the road—my landmark that I have arrived at Ibtisam's. I pull into a steep driveway that opens to a courtyard framed by two houses with young children playing out front. They are taking turns driving a kid-sized electric car around the courtyard that looks like a mini 4x4 off-road vehicle, a fancy toy compared to the plastic trikes the children in Jalameh ride on. One of them runs into the house when I ask about my friend Ibtisam. Moments later, Ibtisam comes out, her long, curly, black hair framing her smiling face.

"Hello, my dear, how are you? So good to see you." We exchange kisses on both cheeks. "This is my brother's house." She points to the house from which she just appeared, and then her gaze shifts to the other house. "My mother lives over there."

She asks me about the drive and the kids. In miles, I have not traveled far, but here it already feels like another world. I tell her about the blackened ruins I passed.

"Yes, I think it may be Hawsha.[87] Many villages in this area were destroyed in 1948. They are everywhere."

"It's a whole village. So many houses still standing. Such an eerie site."

"You know, my mother is from a destroyed village just next to Kabul. The village of Damun."

Her words ring in my ears. *Just next to Kabul.* "Really? Can we go there?"

"Sure, I can show you. But let's go say hello to my mother first. Maybe she will come with us."

We find her mother washing clothes in a plastic tub on a table in the living room. Ibtisam whispers in my ear as we approach her. "She still washes all her clothes by hand." *Like in Gaza.*

Yama, ajat Christa, sahabti min Madison—Mama, my friend Christa is here from Madison. Her mother looks up surprised, then smiles as she pushes the clothes deeper into the water, shakes off her hands, and dries them on a scrap of cloth on the table.

I extend my right hand to her. *Salam 'aleikum*—Peace be upon you.

'Aleikum as-salam! Ahlan wa sahlan!—Peace be upon you! Welcome! She takes my hand and leans forward to kiss me on both cheeks repeatedly, then invites us to sit down on a sofa against the wall and disappears through a doorway.

Rather than sit down, we join her in the kitchen, a sizeable room with concrete walls, the only light seeping through the ornamental bars of an open window over the kitchen sink. A line of cupboards extends below the black granite counter, their contents hidden by a cloth hanging on a string. Ibtisam's mother is standing in front of a two-burner stove by the sink with a teaspoon in her hand, her head bowed forward as she gently stirs the pot to keep the creamy foam of the coffee from boiling over. The rest of the kitchen is open space, not even a table or chairs. The scent of cardamom finds its way to my nose from the tiny pot. I know Ibtisam from our world in Madison. Now, I am in her world.

We return to the living room to sip the sweet, strong coffee from tiny cups. I gather my courage and address Ibtisam's mother. *Anti min Damun?*—You are from Damun?

Her sullen eyes dart at me, as if I uncovered a hidden secret, then sink to the floor with the weight of her village's name. After a moment of silence, she looks up at me.

Ah Damun—Yes, Damun. Then she lifts her gaze toward the wall behind us and points with her eyes and her finger. *Damun hun*—Damun is right there. I tell her I want to go see it. Will she take me? She pauses, then raises her brow and lets it fall as she shakes her head. *Damun mudammara*—Damun is destroyed. I know, I tell her in Arabic, but can we still go there?

"I know," I tell her, "but can we still go there?"

Al-bir yama, btiqdari itwarjiha il-bir—You can show her the well, Mama.

Ah, al-bir—Yes, the well. Her eyes sink again to the floor.

She leans forward to stand up, then summons us to follow her to a fenced-in area just behind the house where she is growing *qaria'*, a type of light-green squash that hangs from vines above our heads, narrow at one end and fat and round at the other. When we are back inside, she has me try some she made earlier. I am honored to taste the tender, delicate squash she grew herself stuffed with rice and meat I can actually eat since I am no longer a vegetarian.

Yislamu ideiki—Thank your hands.

She smiles. *Wa ideiki*—And your hands.

When we walk out to the courtyard, a slender woman with reddish-brown hair calls out to us from a window overlooking the courtyard. Ibtisam explains that the woman is her sister-in-law, who runs a salon out of her home. She wonders if I am leaving already.

La, Christa bidha itshuf Damun—No, Christa wants to see Damun.

I wave to her and smile. Ibtisam promises we'll stop by her salon on our way back.

The three of us get in my car and drive to the main road, then turn right to head north. After a short while, Ibtisam and her mother direct me to turn right into a gravel road. There are no houses, no buildings, just a thicket of young trees on both sides. Farther ahead, Ibtisam's mother has me stop the car.

Hun al-bir—Here's the well. Her mother's voice is quiet. She stands still at the side of the road, her hands clasped together in front of her.

"Here is the village well." Ibtisam echoes her mother's words in English, pointing to a square mass of concrete protruding from the ground. I wonder what else used to be here. Was it the center of the village? The well appears to have been updated and is still in use, the area around it flat, a dense orchard of fruit trees extending beyond it. There is no longer room for any houses. Ibtisam explains that this land belonged to the village of Damun and was confiscated by the State of Israel and given to the settlements of Yas'ur and Ahihud to cultivate.

Yas'ur was established in 1949—Israeli historian Benny Morris' parents among the founders—on the destroyed Palestinian village of Al-Birweh—the birthplace of Palestinian poet Mahmoud Darwish. Yas'ur cultivates the lands of the villages of Damun and Al-Ruways, both captured by Jewish forces on July 15, 1948, and destroyed shortly thereafter.

I later learn that Ibtisam's maternal aunt, who was married to Mahmoud Darwish's paternal uncle, along with her nuclear family, were residents of Birweh. She became a refugee in Lebanon and lived the rest of her life in the Ein Al-Hilweh refugee camp in southern Lebanon. Ibitsam's mother only saw her sister twice since they were forced out of their homeland in 1948.

I try to see past the tiny trees to imagine what it used to look like. *Wen kanat darkum?*—Where was your family's house?

She points with her eyes, lifting her finger toward the thicket of trees. *Hunak*—there. My face tightens as I try to imagine her house, her life, this elderly woman as a young girl. My heart seeps into the earth, seeing her now standing there, her memories and this well the only proof of her childhood home, the whole village simply gone.

My eyes plead with Ibtisam. "So that's all that's left of the village?"

Al-maqbara, Yama—The graveyard, Mama. Ibtisam turns from her mother to me. "There is also a graveyard." We get back in the car and drive a bit farther until we come to an open area covered in stones. *Hun, Yama?*—Here, Mama?

Ibtisam's mother's eyes gaze at the field of stones. *Ah hun*—Yes, here.

The elevation is higher here, so we can see for miles. When I look at the ground covered in stones, I realize the stones are grave markers, some arranged in a long oval pattern, some larger headstones visible but no longer upright. I spot a few prominent graves of large cut stones sinking into the earth. The graves, like saber—the resilient cactus plants—call out to me. *We are still here.* My body hears them. *Yes, I see you.*

It is confusing to me that Ibtisam's mother lost her family's village but can still live in Israel. I learn she is from the generation of so-called "internally displaced" Palestinians whose villages were destroyed in 1948 but who ended up living in other towns and villages in Israel. Those who fled the area altogether became refugees. Neither the internally displaced Palestinians nor the refugees are allowed to return to live on their lands to this day.[88] I try to imagine which is worse, living right next to what was once your home, like Ibitsam's mother, or off in Jordan, Lebanon, or Syria with home only a distant memory, like her sister. Either seems like too much to bear. The village is right there, and yet it's gone. Its people are right here but unable to return, even from the next village. I breathe through the absurdity. My heart aches that these Israeli towns can plant trees, use the well, and sell the fruit—right before Ibtisam's mother's eyes.

I don't know what to say. *Shukran*—Thank you. I look into her faraway eyes with deep gratitude and sadness, worried our visit to Damun reopened a deep wound that may never heal.

After witnessing how the village of Damun was virtually erased from the landscape, I can't help but notice large clumps of thorny saber growing on the hillsides whenever I drive *juwa* along the roads in 1948 Palestine. I have seen how villagers plant saber as a natural barrier between lands in the wa'ra of Jalameh. Now, they seem to be everywhere I look. Their bright green, oval-shaped cactus leaves and over-ripened, reddish-green cactus pears jutting out in complex formations call out to me like thorny ghosts of the past. The word *saber* in Arabic means "patience." There they sit, resting on the hillsides, waiting for the return of their inhabitants. I want to know the names of these villages, their stories. *What happened to the people who used to live here? Where are they now?*

When I get back to Jalameh, I find myself talking again and again about the destroyed villages. I learn from someone who works at my sons' school that there is an oral history project underway at Birzeit University near Ramallah that is currently documenting the history of the destroyed villages. I meet with the director of the project, who explains that they are compiling a book on each village with pictures and testimonies.

I think of two books Nasser and I have in our home in Madison from Walid Khalidi: *Before Their Diaspora* and *All That Remains.* One tells the story through photos of Palestine before the Nakba, the other documents the location and remains of many of the Palestinian villages destroyed in 1948, only now I have seen some of the ruins myself.

In his office, the director pulls out a map of Palestine, which has all the destroyed villages marked with red dots, and hands it to me (see Map 9). My throat tightens, my eyes become heavy, and my cheeks constrict with the threat of tears as I gaze at all the red dots scattered across what is now the Israeli landscape, among them Zir'in, Damun. *Places where Palestinians lived only 50 years ago.* All these villages were literally wiped off the map, the landscape redefined as another country. My head is about to explode with sadness, anger, and frustration that people can be driven off their land, their homes destroyed, and barred from living on their land or returning to their homeland all together.

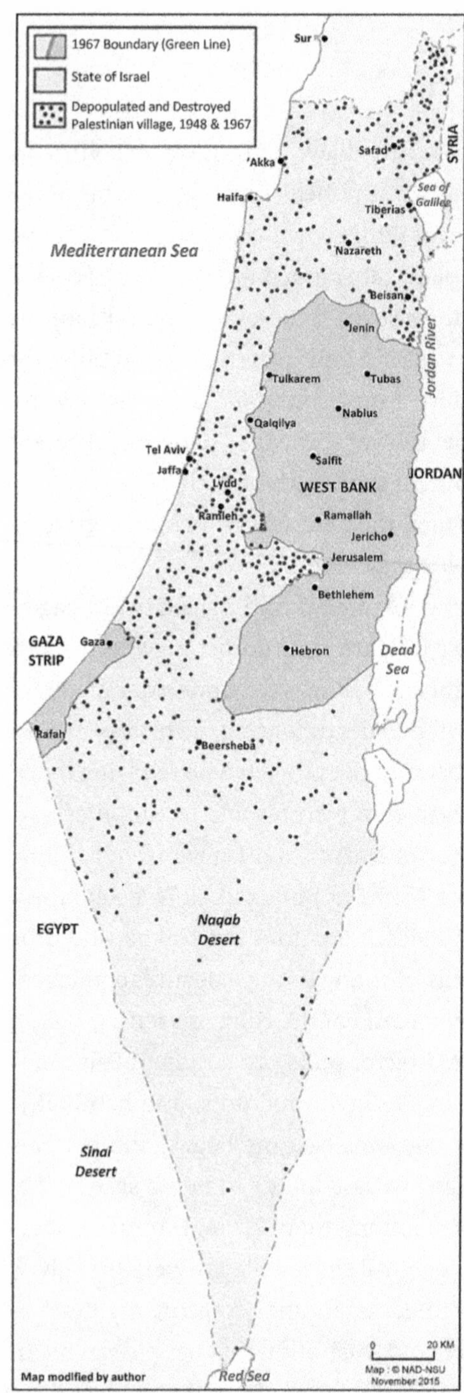

Map 9: Palestinian Villages Depopulated and Destroyed by Israel, 1948 and 1967 (Source: Palestine Portal)

I take this treasure map in my hands, grateful that I now have a key to the past, a way to see what is no longer there. From that day forward, I carry that map with me in the car whenever I enter 1948 Palestine. My eyes comb the landscape, searching for clues, clumps of saber gathered on the hillsides, patiently waiting for someone to notice them, begging me not to forget. No sooner do the saber call out, *Over here!* then I pull over to check the map. Sure enough, there is a red dot to match my location.

Mostly, I find the saber on the distant hillsides. But in this moment, both the saber and the remnants of stone houses are not far from the road. To my astonishment, there is a driveway, so I pull in, take a deep breath, and look at my map. I have found the village of Indur, a red dot on the map, now just a gravel road at the base of a hillside.[89] I venture in, surprised that the road continues into the village, up to the left and the right, as if it still leads somewhere. Patches of the hillside are covered in saber. Only the road is clear. The few remains of homes peek out of a lush green landscape of overgrown bushes and trees.

I circle back toward the entrance to the village, stop the car, and get out to take in the stillness of this place that is no more. In the distance, I spot a group of people. Surprised to see anyone in this quiet space, I stop in my tracks and listen, not sure I want them to see me. They are sitting off to the side of the road in the shade having a picnic, an older woman sitting on a blanket, her hair covered with a scarf, an older man, his hair speckled with gray, and a younger couple with children. Faintly, I hear them speaking Arabic. *They are Palestinian.*

I approach them slowly, smile, and say hello. *Marhaba.*

They respond with equal curiosity. *Marhaba.*

Hatha shou?—What is this? They seem confused by my question, their faces tightening. *Qariya?*—A village?

Their faces soften. The older woman answers, raising her chin with pride. *Hath baladna Indur*—This is our village Indur.

Kif, antu min hun?—So, you are from here? *Wen saknin halla?*—Where do you live now?

They point toward the main road, then explain that they come here every year to spend time in their village. *They are internally displaced Palestinians, like Ibtisam's family.* Sometimes soldiers come and drive them away or tell them they are trespassing. *Trespassing on their own land, in their own village.* Today, they are lucky. It is only them and me. It is a solemn picnic. I lower my eyes and wish them well. They offer for me to join them, opening their hands to the display of food on the blanket, but I decline and step away. I want to give them the space to have a picnic in a village that no longer exists, except in their hearts and minds.

Their presence here feels bittersweet. They are fortunate that the remains of their village are accessible since they are Israeli citizens, and yet they cannot return to live on their own land. Some destroyed villages are surrounded by fences or rebuilt as Israeli settlements or towns, making them off-limits to Palestinians. Indur is there, but it is gone, the remains of houses inhabited only by trees.

There is no dot on the map of Israel for Indur, only for the nearby Israeli kibbutz of Ein Dor, founded in 1948. The Palestinian village of Indur was destroyed on May 24, 1948, ten days after Israel was founded. Like so many other Palestinian villages that Jewish forces seized and destroyed in 1948, the nearby settlement took on a Hebraicized version of the Arabic name. The same year Ein Dor became a dot on Israel's map, Indur disappeared. But the red dot on my map confirms it was there. The day I happened upon the village of Indur, I saw how its descendants keep the memory of their village alive even if it has been erased from the map. The enduring family, the resilient saber, the stone remains, persist in its absence.

Like Indur, Palestine itself is no longer on the map. The same place, a new name. And yet, Palestine has not been forgotten. The people of Palestine still exist—some still on their land, others resettled in other towns and villages, and still others in refugee camps or in exile. They are all Palestinian. Wherever they may live now, they keep the memory of their homeland alive. The lost villages that make up much of Palestine are more than dots on a map. They are home.

When one place has two identities, two names, which one is real? Can one place be two? Can two peoples coexist on the same land? The land is there, but can they make room for each other in their hearts and minds? All I know is that I carry a new load with me for Ibtisam's mother, the burden of knowing that she has to live the rest of her life somewhere else when all she ever dreamed of was going home.

In December, my father combines touring historical sites in Egypt, Jordan, and Israel with coming to visit Nasser's family and me. Though having traveled the world, it is his first and only trip to the Middle East. We never talk about how it feels for him as a German, who served his fatherland as a child soldier, to visit the Jewish homeland. He is focused on his lifelong passion of culture and art. He has taken me to numerous orchestral performances with Gidon Kremer, the famous Israeli violinist. And yet his favorite music of all time, the operas of Richard Wagner, are banned in Israel, given the Wagner family's affiliation with Hitler. I imagine he must admire the young Jewish state with all of its cultural offerings.

At the same time, I want him to experience what I have come to know as Palestine, which exists in Israel's shadow. I want him to know the other side of the golden coin Israel has become. I want him to feel the loss, the heartache, and the struggle that befell the Palestinians when Israel was born. He has experienced the warmth and generosity of Nasser's family, traveled through Israeli checkpoints, and seen what Palestine is now, but I want to show him what he may otherwise not see. I take him to Yalo—one of three villages Israel destroyed during the Six-Day War in 1967.[90] I tell him about the fate of the hundreds of Palestinian villages destroyed during Israel's War of Independence, how hundreds of thousands of people were forced to leave their homes, how the villages are still there but have become ghost towns or parks, or grazing lands for the livestock of Israeli settlements.

The dirt roads of the village are clear and open, the remnants of concrete and stone homes visible through the brush. The rains have yet to come, so the land is bone dry, the tall grasses of the previous season stiff, blending into the dusty dirt road as we drive through the village at a walking pace. Even though the season of saber is long over, a few saber are still flowering. I pull over when I spot pale-yellow, cup-shaped flowers in bloom growing out of the saber to form a crown at the top of a cactus leaf, the clusters of leaves like the heads of fair maidens gossiping and giggling in their youth, leaning into each other so that others cannot make out what they are saying.

This miraculous display of life stands in stark contrast to the rubble nearby each prominent cluster. My eyes follow the natural borders of saber

Palestinians planted between their properties. The clusters stand taller than the rubble of the homes between them. The still-flowering crowns are a celebration of their resilience and a reminder that they bear witness to the destruction carried out only a few decades before. The older leaves that form the trunk are anchored to the earth. I watch them reminiscing about the lost life of the village while they patiently wait for the villagers to return. Even though the surrounding brush has turned golden brown and the dirt road to dust, the bright green of the cactus leaves and the pale green and yellow crowns of saber bear witness to the absence of those who once lived here. No wonder saber is a Palestinian symbol of rootedness in the land.

I examine the delicate flowers I am meeting for the first time, though the grave silence reminds me of the voices I should hear. I explain to my father how this plant is an overt reminder of the life that once flourished here. In 1948, the year Israel declared statehood and destroyed over 500 Palestinian villages is not that long ago, but 1967 is even more recent—the year I was born. *It is my lifetime.*

While I was in my mother's womb, the Israeli army was wiping this village and neighboring Imwas and Beit Nuba off the map. Those driven out of these villages still have their whole lives ahead of them. Their village is not a distant memory passed down by their mothers and fathers. The silence is chilling. The rubble weighs on me, as if it could bury me on the spot. I try to imagine their homes still standing, people coming and going, the sound of their voices, the aroma of midday meals traveling between their homes. I stare into the faces of the cactus flowers, full of gratitude that they faithfully show up each spring and that I get to witness the saber giving birth to itself against all odds. I feel as if I have uncovered a simple yet profound truth.

My father listens as I speak, his body still, his gaze cast on what was once there. I don't know if he can see what I see or feel what I feel. I don't know if his heart aches at how history plays out here. Not everyone can see what is no longer there. I know my father as a practical man, someone who makes the best of what he has and keeps moving forward. Here I am, asking him to look back for a moment and appreciate what fuels the fire of Palestinian determination to live in Palestine.

After Yalo, I show my father the ruins of a church, the only remains of the nearby destroyed village of Imwas. I think of the countless ancient churches he took me to visit in Europe, the layers upon layers of history. *Is it easier to accept how the landscape and the people that inhabit it change over time, how some civilizations cease to exist, how spaces are reconfigured and renamed when the history is completely buried?* Here the people of these ruins are still among us, and the rubble remains visible, not to mention the trees and plants they once cultivated laced between destroyed homes. I am inspired again to deepen my work to right the wrongs of history, first by acknowledging what happened and then exploring what is possible.

The most memorable phrase from the Holocaust is "Never forget." So, too, is Palestinian memory the starting point of a Palestinian future that moves beyond loss. Just as no one can ask the Jews to forget their suffering, Palestinians have a right, an obligation, to keep their memories alive. They are forever woven into the fabric of their sense of self. *What will it take for Israelis to acknowledge this living memory, to see it as part of their own story?*

26

Contradictions

Meanwhile, my own story in Palestine is unfolding. I find myself in an educational role after one of the parents at my sons' school tells me that an association in Jenin is looking for someone to teach business English to local businesspeople. When I meet with the director, he hires me on the spot, eager to have a native speaker of American English offer instruction. My brother Dieter, who has become a teacher of English as a Second Language (ESL), offers suggestions for materials to develop a curriculum. I launch the course, delighted to find the participants eager to learn. Now a couple of days a week, I go to work in Jenin, no longer simply a visitor. *I am living in Palestine.*

With teaching front and center on my mind, my heart races when I learn from one of Nasser's nieces that the teacher hit her with a ruler at the local girls' school because she forgot to bring a pencil. I look into her sad, blue eyes and acknowledge her pain. *Besirish heik*—That's not okay. She tells me the teachers hit the students all the time for the stupidest things. Everyone knows, even the principal of the school, but they do it anyway.

That evening, I talk to her parents, drawing on one of the deepest cultural norms I know. *Ma fi ihtiram fid-darab*—There's no respect in hitting. They agree it's unacceptable and have even talked to the principal, but the teachers take it out on the students if the parents complain. How are these children supposed to learn if they are afraid of being hit? And how are they supposed to respect the teacher?

I check in with Nasser's other brothers and his sister in the village and their children, and they all report similar stories of teachers hitting the students for forgetting their homework, not speaking in formal Arabic, speaking out of turn, or not knowing the right answer to a question. The same thing happens at the boys' school. Not all the teachers hit the students, but the children describe those who do as mean and scary. Most of the time, the boys laugh it off, but sometimes they really get hurt.

I also talk to Amal, my sister-in-law, who is the English teacher at the girls' school. The children told me she is strict, but she never hits them, so I feel comfortable reaching out to her. She explains that it has gotten harder to control the classroom. "The kids do not show the same respect to their teachers that they used to. Some of the teachers don't know what else to do to get their classrooms under control." She goes on to tell me how little teachers are paid. *Thaman-miyit shekel bas*—Only 800 shekels, which is about 200 dollars a month. I know she enjoys the status of being one of the few women in the village who works outside the home, but she is clearly frustrated by her job and salary.

I check in with Nasser's sisters, who live outside the village, and find out the problem is worse in the villages than in the cities and more common with younger children than older ones. I have been taking notes on my findings and write up my results as a study that draws on the traditional values of honor and respect. I talk to one of Nasser's cousins, who works at the Ministry of Education in Jenin. He suggests I share my study with the office. His supervisor is concerned about my findings and encourages me to take my study to Ramallah to the Ministry of Education.

The next day, I make the hour-and-a-half drive to Ramallah to meet with the Minister of Education. He greets me with a raised brow and controlled smile when I explain my findings that are both inconsistent with the local culture and interfere with learning. The minister sits up tall with his shoulders back, his chin held high and assures me that there is no such practice. "We have a law against it. It doesn't happen."

"You may have a law against it, but it is happening."

He leans back in his chair. "There may be isolated incidents, but we don't have a problem."

"These are not isolated incidents. And the examples the kids gave me are consistent with each other and across schools."

He leans forward as I hand him my study. "Who asked you to conduct this study?"

"No one. I was surprised to find out this is going on, and so I decided to do it. I have the names of the teachers if you need them." He flips through the pages of my study. When he reaches "Findings," his gaze narrows, locked on the page. He tucks his chin, and his shoulders slouch forward as his confidence sinks to the floor. He is silent for a few minutes, then looks up at me as he sets the study on his desk.

He breaks his silence. "It's possible that we may need to review the law with the local ministries as a reminder. You know, it is difficult to teach under occupation."

"There is enough violence against Palestinians from the Israelis. We don't need to be directing any violence against our own kids."

He smiles and gets up from his chair. "Thank you for bringing this to my attention." He offers me his hand.

"You're welcome. I hope for the sake of the kids that something changes soon."

He walks around his desk and accompanies me to the door of his office. "I will see what I can do."

"Thank you. I appreciate you looking into this." I take a deep breath as I walk back out into the bright sun. *Maybe, just maybe, I can make a difference for these children.*

The next afternoon, several of Nasser's nieces and nephews come by the house after school. Their eyes are wide, and their voices are bubbling with excitement.

Khaltu Christa, ma darabna al-mu'alameh al-yom!—Aunt Christa, the teacher didn't hit us today!

As delighted as I am about the news, it's only been a day. I doubt the minister has already done something. The children assure me the teacher hits someone every day, but no one got hit today, not even at the boys' school. I can hardly believe what I am hearing. I smile at them, their eyes full of light. I insist they let me know tomorrow, too, what happens at school.

I go see Nasser's cousin, who had advised me to take my study to the Ministry of Education office in Jenin. He offers me a nervous smile and tells me that the study may already be having an impact. His office in Jenin got a call the same day I visited the ministry and was instructed to set up meetings with the principals, who were notified by phone that the hitting has to stop.

Later that evening, I go visit Nasser's brother Jamal and his wife Samira. Jamal confides that several parents in the village are asking him who this American thinks she is, coming here to tell them how to run their schools. He says he told them he agreed that it isn't right what the teachers are doing. He tells me not to worry; more parents are happy with addressing the issue than are upset about it.

The next day, the children come by the house after school to report the same news. No one got hit again today. My heart fills with gratitude to be able to make a difference in the lives of these children, and so quickly. I can't take my eyes off their smiling faces. Their bodies are relaxed and full of life. The fear I saw in their eyes has vanished. I tell them to be sure to do their homework and listen to their teachers so they also feel good about the change. They assure me they will. They fly out the door like butterflies going to the meadow, their wings fluttering in the afternoon sun.

Nasser's sister Suhaila invites my father and me to dinner at their home in the village of Rummaneh. It is mid-December, and the winter rains have yet to wash over Palestine. Suhaila has prepared a delicious spread of platters of spiced rice topped with tender lamb and roasted almonds, which she serves with tiny bowls of yogurt and tomato cucumber salad laced with lemon and fresh mint. The meal is carefully laid out on a vinyl tablecloth on the floor, surrounded by large rectangular mats on three sides. My father cannot sit on the floor, so they invite him to sit on a white plastic chair and set a small plastic table in front of him before handing him his plate piled with rice and meat.

"Thank you! This is wonderful!" His voice is loud, but his blue eyes glisten with gratitude. I translate my father's words.

Suhaila welcomes my father as their guest. *Ahlan wa sahlan!*—Welcome! She offers him more food, but he holds up his hand in protest. My father doesn't usually eat rice, being mindful of his heavy stature, so he is already being a good sport.

The open western window brings a pleasant breeze into their living room, which grows dimmer and dimmer with the setting sun. Suhaila instructs one of her sons to switch on the lights before serving her famous *knaffeh* for dessert. I savor the cheese-filled, wheat-string pastry topped with its signature bright orange spice with Arabic coffee laced with cardamom, the perfect accompaniment. My father delights in the robust coffee and eagerly holds his tiny cup out for a refill.

Suddenly, the lights switch off, leaving us all in the dark. *Imqata'a alkahraba*—The power is cut. Suhaila's husband explains that the power often goes out in their village as a form of collective punishment for their resistance to Israeli occupation. Suhaila resorts to candles. The dishes from dinner are piled in the kitchen, but without electricity, the water pump doesn't work. The only way to do the dishes is to haul water up from the basement cistern and fill pitchers to pour water onto the dishes by hand. I always help do the dishes when I visit. This time will be no exception.

The village has a backup generator, but it doesn't always supply enough electricity for the whole village. Usually, there are only four hours each night. That is when Suhaila does load after load of laundry so she can use her washing machine. She piles the wet clothes in the bathtub until she manages to wash them all. With her new baby, she has seven children, so there is a lot of laundry. Besides the limited access to electricity, the Israeli government has yet to allow the village to connect to the main water supply, so villagers have to truck in water to store in reservoirs.

I help Suhaila carry the dishes over to the hallway by the stairs, where we have more room to set up a makeshift dishwashing station by candlelight. I sit down on a wooden stool while her daughter Nadine pours the water slowly from the tiny spout onto my hands so I can rinse the food remains off the plates into a large metal wash tub. Then I wash them one by one, saving the large aluminum platter for last. I cannot help but think of when

I did dishes in Gaza, squatting by the faucet. At least there, we had running water. Now and then, Nadine returns to the cistern below to refill the water until we have completed our task. I lean back to stretch my aching back.

Yislamu ideiki, ya Nadine!—Thank you, Nadine!

Her eyes sparkle in the candlelight. *Yislamu ideiki anti! 'Amilti kul shi!*—Thank you! You did everything!

We return to the candlelit living room, where Suhaila is setting out tea and insisting we stay the night. I thank her again for an enjoyable evening but decline her invitation. Here we are sitting together by candlelight while President Clinton is being wined and dined by Prime Minister Benjamin Netanyahu in Jerusalem. The stark contrast in living conditions between Israelis and Palestinians is haunting me in the dim light. *Why shouldn't both peoples have equal access to resources?* Nasser's father's words come to mind again. *The war is not over.*

After spending the last four months in Palestine living in Jalameh, it is time for Canaan, Karmel, and me to go back to the US to see Nasser for the holidays. We need to get to Ben Gurion Airport in Tel Aviv in the middle of the night for a pre-dawn flight. New restrictions are in place at the border. No longer can a taxi driver from Israel enter the West Bank, so we will have to walk across the checkpoint. It is midnight when Nasser's brother Jamal drives us to the checkpoint. He helps me carry our luggage to the gate, where a group of Israeli soldiers are standing with their M16s hanging loosely across their chests.

It is unusually warm for this time of year. The night air is thick and moist, though the heavy rains have yet to fall. There is no moon to brighten the darkness beyond the floodlights. The checkpoint is just a concrete shelter for the soldiers in the middle of the road, with a simple metal gate on each side to block the road.

Jamal helps me get the luggage to the checkpoint, but he cannot cross with me. I cannot carry Karmel because I have to manage our suitcases and handbags. Canaan stands close to me, watching the soldiers as they gather in front of us. I urge Karmel to stay close by us, but he starts running around the luggage.

The soldiers ask for our passports and where we are going. They flip through the pages, glancing up now and then. Suddenly, Karmel darts forward and throws his arms around one of the soldier's legs, his face buried in the soldier's heavy olive-green army pants. I call out to him to come back as my eyes meet the soldier's. We know we are on two sides of a bitter conflict, but Karmel doesn't know he is hugging the enemy. His ignorance diminishes the tension between us. I smile as an apology that my son has crossed the invisible line that divides us. This soldier is our gatekeeper to travel home.

I reach for Karmel's arms to release his embrace, but he hugs him tighter. The soldier's eyes soften, as if Karmel has pulled him out of his role as a soldier for a moment. We both reclaim our identities as occupier and occupied when one of the other soldiers hands me back our passports and grants us passage across the Green Line. Karmel finally releases his embrace. *If only there were no borders between us.*

We walk a few steps past the group of soldiers. I drag two of the bags awkwardly behind us, then briefly return for the rest. The taxi driver is standing by the passenger door waiting for us, his arms hanging neatly with his hands folded over each other. The driver steps forward to load our bags into the back of his car. His movements are quick and precise, as if we are making an escape from prison. I load Canaan and Karmel into the back seat of the car and climb in next to them. It feels good to sit down.

The driver slams the trunk and gets into the front seat. *Yallah? 'Al matar?*—Ready? To the airport?

Yallah. Canaan looks out the window at the dim landscape whirling by the window. Karmel snuggles close to me, his bright blonde hair casting a subtle glow, his body softening as his eyes close. We are on our way. With no traffic at this late hour, we sail through the night. At the entrance gate to the airport, the security guard asks our driver for our passports and airline tickets in Hebrew, then hands them back and waves us through. At the main entrance, we give our luggage to a man with a large flat cart so I can carry Karmel, keeping Canaan close by my side. We thank our driver and wave goodbye, then follow our luggage cart over to a group of airport officials for questioning.

Once they realize we are coming from the Jenin area, one official instructs another to wheel our luggage to the side for inspection in a curtained-off area at the far end of the airport. Other Palestinians are also undergoing the same "special treatment." The officials set our suitcases on a large counter, where they go through everything item by item, piling our belongings onto the counter, while another official asks me some of the same questions: *Where did I travel in Israel and why? How long was I there? Did anyone give me anything to give to someone else? What did I buy? Who packed my bags? He asks me some questions more than once.*

Canaan is restless, and Karmel is becoming heavier in my arms by the moment, unable to keep his eyes open. Finally, they let us sit down and wait for our luggage. An hour and a half pass before they complete their inspection and repack our belongings.

One of the inspectors invites us to proceed to the gate. I take a deep breath as soon as we are settled in our seats. It has been an exhausting night. It is still dark. I close my eyes for a moment until I can feel the plane moving, then glance out of the window, wishing I could see something other than runway lights. The engine begins to roar. We are on our way to visit Nasser in the US. I can't wait to see him, but I also can't wait to get back home to Palestine.

While in the US, we celebrate Karmel's third birthday, followed by Christmas and New Year's. As nice as it is to all be together, Nasser and I feel it is important for Canaan and Karmel to have this extended period in Palestine. They are really starting to pick up Arabic. With another few months there, they will both be speaking without even thinking about it. Again, we will make the sacrifice of splitting up our family, leaving Nasser to manage the restaurant and the show circuit while I return to Palestine with our children.

Before we go back to Palestine after the new year, I research disciplinary strategies in schools so I can share my knowledge with the school administrators at my children's school when I return. As a new private school, it aspires to be a model for public schools in the area. Back in Palestine, the principal is delighted with my knowledge and enthusiasm and hires me as a consultant to contribute to the school's development. I am offered an apartment in Jenin, where my sons and I adjust to the isolation of city life.

Family members call ahead instead of simply stopping by, so our routine is calmer, more predictable.

My interest in discipline quickly expands to all areas of the school. I develop a teacher training program to better meet the needs of students with different abilities, foster coordination among teachers to integrate subjects across the curriculum, establish a school-community relations program that builds bridges between teachers and parents, and ultimately assist the principal in conducting teacher evaluations in order to make staffing recommendations for the following year. Unfortunately, one of the teachers falls back on the old practice of hitting a student with a ruler and is fired. Still, the morale of other teachers, staff, and students soars as the school comes together as a community where teaching and learning go hand in hand.

I look forward to driving each day to work after Canaan and Karmel board the yellow Mercedes school bus we can see each morning from our second-story balcony, the name of the school painted on the side in Arabic and English. Canaan is dressed in his gray slacks and a white oxford shirt with a gray sweater over it, Karmel in his burgundy sweatsuit with the school logo on the front. Some days, I drive an hour and a half south to Birzeit University where I am taking an Arabic class, listening to the popular *sha'abi* songs of Lebanese singer Fares Karem (Lebanese) on the way that Nasser's nephew Mahmoud gave me. In class, we discuss the challenges of living under Israeli occupation and the events leading up to that reality. We also read Palestinian author Ghassan Kanafani's novel *Return to Haifa*, which I had only read in English.

On days I work at the school, I enjoy a simple lebneh and za'atar sandwich served with a wide smile by the lunchroom attendant each day. I greet the women who clean the school from top to bottom each day by pouring water on the tile floor and using a squeegee and rags to clear the dust from the smooth stone floor, restoring its brilliant shine. Seeing the teachers and students in the classrooms fully engaged in teaching and learning fills my soul with hope and pride that Palestine indeed has a future.

One day, one of the cleaning ladies, who lives in the Christian village of Zababdeh, invites me to visit her on my way home. She throws her arms up to greet me when I enter through the gate of the privacy wall. *Ahlan wa sahlan! Tafaddali*—Welcome, please come in! I join her on the veranda, the mild breeze beneath the overhang a welcome relief from the afternoon sun. She disappears into her house, then returns with a steel teapot and two glasses neatly arranged on a tray.

Qadesh suker ahattilik?—How much sugar? She laughs when I remind her that I prefer no sugar at all.

'Amilit ish-shai min mayit is-sama'—I made the tea from sky water. I look at her, confused. I know the word for water but don't know the word "sky" in Arabic. She holds up her hands toward the sky. *Mayit is-sama'. 'Anna bir*—Sky water. We have a well.

Now I understand. I have heard that the best tea is made from rainwater, but I have never tasted it. I take a sip. The tea is so smooth; it slides down my throat like liquid silk. *Wallah zaki, yislamu ideiki*—It's really delicious, thank you. *Shou hateiti fi?*—What did you put in it? I am accustomed to fresh mint or sage in tea, but I don't recognize the distinctive flavor.

Zayit man. She goes back into the house and brings out a bundle of stalks with tiny, dried leaves. I hold it to my nose and breathe in. *Yes, that's it.*

Khuthi—Take it.

My eyes gleam with gratitude. Not only did I get to drink tea from sky water, but I also got to try a new herb, *zayit man*.

The next day at work, the lunchroom man greets me with particular enthusiasm. He offers me a sandwich, then hands me a black plastic bag.

Shou hatha?—What's that?

Zayit man.

My heart dances with delight.

Mish ithabih?—Don't you like it?

Ah wallah, bahabu kitir—Yes, I love it so much.

Bitla' hun fil-montiqa hay—It grows in this area.

Shukran kitir—Thank you so much. I bite into the soft pita bread with a smear of lebneh and sprinkle of za'atar. A few minutes later, he offers me a cup of tea with *zayit man*. Now, I am not sure whose smile is wider, his or mine.

I come to know the students by name, and they all greet me in the hall as "Miss Christa." Sara often looks sad, so I put my arm around her and ask *Kifik?*—How are you? She says she's fine, but I don't believe her. She confides in me that one of the teachers put her desk in the corner of the room and stopped calling on her because she can't answer the questions. The other students tease her for not being smart enough. I suggest that the teacher put her desk back among the other children and let her volunteer what she knows instead of putting her on the spot. Sara begins dancing through the school, her head held high. Now, all the students treat her with respect.

I begin to wonder if education is my calling. Toward the end of the school year, there is talk of having me return as school director the following year to a new position above the principal. Although an exciting opportunity, I feel awkward committing to such a position when I haven't formally studied education. I wonder if I would be able to get credentials in school leadership. Maybe I could really play a role in education here. After all, the children are the future of Palestine.

27

Beisan

The seasonal rains set in while Canaan, Karmel, and I were in the US, so farmers have planted their winter crops. I am driving back across the Jalameh checkpoint with Canaan and Karmel when I spot Nasser's aunt 'Amti Saymi sitting at a roadside stand behind a wooden table piled high with romaine lettuce, her long white scarf loosely framing her golden face. I pull over to say hello and ask her what she is doing there.

Hatha ardna!—This is our land! She casts her right arm behind her, then raises her eyes and both arms to the sky as she thanks God for the land and the harvest.

Min zara' al-khas?—Who planted the romaine?

Her sparkling eyes open wide as she places her hands on her chest. *Ana!*—I did!

She grabs a knife off the edge of the table and rises to her feet, her long white dress brushing against the moist earth below. We follow her into the vast field of neat rows bursting with green. She carefully tucks the front of her dress into the wide, striped silk sash around her waist, then bends over to cut a bulky head of romaine from its stem. She hands it to me like a bouquet of flowers, then cuts another for Canaan, who cradles it in his arms like a baby before biting into it with an audible crunch. I break off a leaf and hand it to Karmel to nibble, ignoring the dusting of soil between the leaves, then another leaf for myself, which I gnaw from the tender, bright green end to the crisp, silvery base as if I am tasting romaine for the first time.

'Amti Saymi's deep voice carries from her solid body nourished by these lands. Over 70 years old and still farming! Her strength and determination remind me of Nasser's father. She is, after all, his sister. I wish he were here so Canaan and Karmel could witness his resolve to live off the land. At least they can experience him through her. As I thank 'Amti Saymi for sharing the bounty of her harvest with us, I see in her eyes that this land is not only her livelihood but her very reason for being. Its soil runs through her veins. It is this soil to which she returns nearly 20 years later.

One day after school, I set out in my green Ford Taurus with Canaan and Karmel to the city of Beisan, passing 'Amti Saymi's *khas* field along the way. I slow down as we approach the checkpoint, but none of the Israeli soldiers asks me to stop. Perhaps they have come to recognize me with my yellow Israeli license plates—my ticket across the Green Line. Here I am able to cross freely as an American into 1948 Palestine, while Palestinians in their own homeland cannot enter without a permit, one of the fallouts following the First Intifada, a new requirement after the Oslo Accords.[91] The soldiers don't know I am headed to Beisan.

I first heard of Beisan from Tony, Nasser's best man at our wedding. He named his youngest daughter after that city since his family experienced a similar fate when they were driven out of their village of Kufr Bir'im we visited with Johnny years ago. Beisan came under attack by Jewish militias on May 12, 1948, just two days before Israeli independence. The entire population—some 6,000 Palestinian residents—were loaded up in trucks and taken across the Syrian and Jordanian borders under British military supervision, never to see their beloved city again. As with other Palestinian cities, a complete infrastructure was made available to Jewish immigrants coming to populate the emerging State of Israel, the Jewish homeland. Their safe haven became the Palestinians' nightmare.

My mind feels squeezed to comprehend how a place can simply become something else, how for Palestinians' Beisan remains alive only in memory.

I simply must see it for myself. I want to go because Palestinians in the West Bank and Gaza cannot, even though it is less than 15 miles west of Jalameh. It may as well be a million miles away. I trust my gut, calling out to me to use the privilege of my yellow Israeli plates to go there. It is so close, and yet none of the younger generations in Nasser's village have seen it. Even if they secure a permit to cross the Green Line, Israel does not allow cars with license plates from the West Bank or Gaza to cross, and private taxis for such excursions are expensive.

So off I go with my Palestinian children, my heart racing with the freedom to move on behalf of others, my mind hyper-alert. After we pass through the checkpoint, my eyes comb the landscape that has become familiar from my trips north to Nazareth, Haifa, and 'Akka. I turn right at the Yizre'el Junction toward Beisan before I reach the Israeli town of Afula. Like so many other Palestinian towns and villages, Israel changed the Arabic name to Hebrew, so Beisan (بيسان) became Bet She'an (בית אך). Even the Arabic on the sign is a transliteration of the Hebrew, Bet She'an, to read بيت شآن instead of the Arabic name بيسان.[92]

The State of Israel has even renamed places where Palestinians still live. The sign to Nablus, where Nasser's sister Kifah lives, reads שכם in Hebrew, pronounced *Shekhem*, Nablus (Shekhem) in English, and a transliteration of *Shekhem* in Arabic, namely شخم, instead of the Arabic word for Nablus, نابلس, which is pronounced *Nablus*, not *Shekhem*. Similarly, when I drive to Jerusalem, I notice the same obscurity with Jerusalem in English, ירושלם in Hebrew, pronounced *Yerushaleim*, and اورشليم (القدس) in Arabic, which is a transliteration of *Yerushaleim* followed by the actual Arabic name for Jerusalem, القدس, pronounced *Al-Quds*.

Between Nablus and Ramallah are a number of Israeli settlements right off the main road, but their signs are in Hebrew with a transliteration in English below, catering to their Jewish-only residents. *No Arabic. No need for Palestinians who live in the area to know their names. They are not intended for them.* I have even experienced signs exclusively in Hebrew when I have made a wrong turn with no idea where I landed. My only recourse was to turn around.

My heart burns when I witness this deliberate renaming of Palestine. Though many historical names in the area exist in all three languages, Israel is choosing to selectively erase Arabic names. It is one thing to remove villages from the map with no recognition of where they once stood, yet another to take on the Hebrew version of the very names of those erased places, as many settlements adjacent to destroyed villages have done, but to rename places where Palestinians are still living feels like adding insult to injury. Changing names or failing to mention them does not sever Palestinians' connection to those places. In fact, it exacerbates the longing for home denied so many.

When I drive around in 1948 Palestine, the clusters of saber let me know where Palestinian villages once stood. The map of the destroyed villages confirms it. If I listen into the wind, I can hear them. And where only ruins remain on hillsides, they call out, *I have a name. I am a place. You cannot erase me.* My senses search the landscape. I cannot smell the smoke from the taboun ovens. No cardamom-laced coffee over the fire or sage-infused tea. No voices of children in the streets. I don't hear the chickens, sheep, or goats. No wedding cries or wailing at the death of loved ones. The people are displaced, but the land remembers.

As we enter the city of Beisan, I slow way down. There is no one in front of us or behind us. The road is neatly paved with curbs along the sides of the road. As my eyes creep onto the sidewalks, a bolt of lightning races through my body at the sight of familiar rugged, stone façades of pre-1948 Palestine with rectangular windowpanes framed at the top in vertical stones, just like Nasser's family home. It is quiet, as if no one is living there. It is midday. Perhaps people are at work. It's just Canaan, Karmel, and me.

The weathered stone houses in Beisan bring me back in time. I think of the hands that built these houses, the voices that filled them. I feel restless with the silence. My head is filled with images of men and women walking and children playing, but I see no one, my own children filling the void. One modest, square house with a simple veranda on one side catches my eye. I gaze at the rough stone, as if it contains hidden messages. No one appears to be home, the curtains in the narrow windows drawn. I look at the door and think of those who left in 1948, walking out of this door for the last time. *Where are they now? Do they still have the key to this house like so many others who lost their homes, their homeland?*

I have Canaan and Karmel sit down in the shade to escape the relentless sun beating down on my head, take a deep breath, feeling the stone beneath me, taking a moment of silence for those who no longer live here.

I brought along a small blue cooler. I want to eat with my sons in this place, like the family I met in the destroyed village of Indur, having a picnic in their village even when they are barred from living there. I take out a container of lebneh surrounded by a deep green moat of olive oil and place it in the sun on the stone veranda. The oil glistens, the lebneh blinding in its whiteness. I pull out a bag of fresh za'atar with sparkling water droplets on the velvety, olive-green leaves. Then I take out a few cucumbers, still fuzzy with freshness, and a cluster of green grapes, both grown in Jalameh. Lastly, I lay a plump loaf of pita bread in the sun, its golden color blending into the stone.

I look down at my simple spread, a traditional Palestinian breakfast I have brought home to Beisan. I break off pieces of sun-warmed bread for Canaan and Karmel. We each dip it in olive oil and lebneh. I press my bread against the fresh za'atar leaves that stick to the olive oil and lebneh like young children to their mother's side. When I bring this constellation to my mouth, my tongue comes alive with the multitude of flavors—the tangy lebneh, the spicy olive oil-soaked bread, the intense bite of the za'atar. I hand Canaan and Karmel each a cucumber, the crunch when we take a bite the only sound. We follow with a couple of cool juicy grapes for a perfect finish.

Canaan and Karmel cannot fully appreciate why we are having a picnic on this stone veranda, but I chew slowly, my whole body engaged in this ceremony of memory. *How many breakfasts of lebneh were eaten on this veranda? How many smiles spilled over into laughter? How many times did the shade of this veranda comfort the family who lived here? How many children ran around it, hiding at each corner?*

My throat and chest tighten with these images as I dip bread into the rich, green oil. I realize I am biting into the cucumber with defiance, chewing with heartache. The cool sweetness of the grapes softens the pain of the memory of those I never knew, of the unbearable silence. My legs crossed, I sit there, bite after bite, crunch after crunch, sweetness after sweetness. No one appears. I put the food away and sit a moment longer in silence, my heart sinking into the weathered stone as I reach out, in my mind, to those who once lived here.

I don't bother to go farther into town to see the Roman and Byzantine ruins surrounded by springs that have become an archeological treasure of the State of Israel. I am not here to sightsee. I don't care to see anyone, talk to anyone. I need the silence. I am relieved we were able to eat on that veranda in peace, albeit a sterile peace of emptiness.

I bid the house farewell, thank it for hosting us, and wish it well in its solitude. I cannot help but wonder if one day, the descendants of those who once lived here will return to their city, touch the rough stone walls of their home, meet those who live there and ask, *What now?* The lemon tree we planted behind Sitti's house and the changes taking place in the schools suddenly seem like drops of water in the sea. I wonder yet again how and when the question of Palestine will be answered. I take one final glance at the house and pull away, the strings of my heart tugged and ripped apart. As the houses disappear behind me, I think about how lives were interrupted, rerouted, and forever changed. I wonder at the power of people to rewrite history, reconfigure place—how memory keeps Palestine alive.

The farmland I pass on my way home—now cultivated by Israelis—raises so many questions for me. I didn't grow up as a farmer. My parents moved nearly every year of my childhood. I have little connection to the places I have lived, and yet I feel the stark absence of the people who once lived here. I feel the memory of the place in the names of Palestinian daughters given the name Beisan. I think of Tony's daughter. That young girl—now a grown woman—carries the memory of Beisan and the story that goes with it, even though she may never set foot there. Through her name, she tells the story of Palestine, loss, and dispossession.

When I get back to Jalameh, I explain to Nasser's nephew Mahmoud that I went to Beisan. His eyes light up like a spark in the night, and his whole body snaps upright into alignment.

Shufti il-bir?—Did you see the spring? His eyes are wide and hopeful. I tell him about our breakfast on the veranda. He smiles and tells me I have to see the spring near Beisan with pools and waterfalls called *Sakhne*, which means "hot" in Arabic. Years ago, people from Jalameh would go there to enjoy the crystal-clear water and shade by the spring. Now, they can only see it if they sneak across the Green Line through the hills of the Palestinian village of Faku'a.

His eyes are narrow and focused. *Wallah, lazem itshufiha*—Seriously, you have to see it.

Yallah, warjini—Okay, show me. I laugh off that possibility. But then I tell him how easily I pass through the checkpoint, how no one even stops me to ask for my passport. We decide to give it a try. Maybe the soldiers would assume he was from "inside" and not question him. If they stop us, I will simply say I didn't know he couldn't cross with me and turn back.

The next morning after Canaan and Karmel are off to school, I pack another picnic of lebneh with olive oil, za'atar, cucumbers, and grapes. Mahmoud and I head out of the village mid-morning. He is clean-shaven and sits up straight in the passenger seat as we approach the checkpoint. I slow down, smile at the soldiers, and wave but keep moving forward. They wave back and immediately return to talking amongst themselves. I continue through the checkpoint, my eyes focused on the road ahead, picking up speed as I pass. I don't look back.

My heart is pounding in my chest. I don't say anything until we are well out of range of the checkpoint. Suddenly I can breathe, releasing the air from one side of the checkpoint into the other. It is one thing for me to cross the border so freely, but the risk of passing through the checkpoint with someone from the village races through my body to my fingertips like a cosmic shift. Even the impossible is possible. *Why shouldn't he be able to see this beautiful place?*

We take the same road I traveled the day before, then veer off to an area full of trees until we come to a clearing. Mahmoud has me park the car off the side of the road. *Hun il-bir*—Here's the spring. We walk through a dense cluster of trees, blue cooler in hand, until we reach a natural pool with rough boulders at the edge of the water that continue down deep, as if carved out of the earth, the reflection of the trees floating on the surface. The water is crystal clear with a bluish-green hue that becomes darker the deeper my eyes sink into its depths. I squat down at the edge and run my fingers across the sparkling water. I have missed swimming. There are no pools anywhere near the village, and Palestinians in the West Bank have no access to the Mediterranean Sea. Mahmoud takes off his shoes and shirt and lowers his body into the water, his feet guiding him down the side of the pool. He hangs onto the stone edge. *Yallah!*—Come on!

I didn't really expect to be able to swim. I thought the pool would be shallow, with a trickle of water feeding it. I didn't think I would get more than my feet wet. The heat of the sun is intense, even through the trees. The refreshing thought of immersing myself in the water draws me into its depths. I sit at the stone edge of the pool. Slowly, I lower my feet into the clear water, letting them follow one of the boulders below until the water is up to my shoulders, my dress suspended in slow motion. I release my hands from the stone edge and allow myself to float out into the middle of the pool, as if I am in outer space. The water is invigorating, and my entire body feels strong and light, as if infused with a magical energy from the earth.

Mahmoud is all smiles. *Helu?*—Beautiful?

Ah, katir helu!—Yes, very beautiful! *Zay ij-jineh*—Like paradise.

The fresh water seeps into my mouth as I immerse my head, my scalp relaxing from the heat of the sun as the water saturates each strand of hair. I can't believe this gorgeous place is right here, just minutes from the village, but no one can come. All those brutal, hot summer days with no relief.

We swim over to the other side, examining the rock formations above and below the water, then swim back to the edge where we had entered the pool. We sit at the edge for a few minutes to dry off, then move aside to have our picnic, asserting a Palestinian presence in this place.

The sun sinks lower in the sky. It is time to go. We don't want to push our luck. My dress is dry, but my skin still feels energized. The heat trapped within the car billows out, engulfing my gratitude. The air conditioning offers relief but is a poor substitute for the refreshing waters of Beisan.

We make our way back toward the road to Afula, then head south to the checkpoint. Getting back across the checkpoint is no problem. The other cars all appear to be settlers, also with yellow Israeli license plates, on their way home to the nearby Israeli settlements Ganim and Kadim. All the settlers are armed and aren't shy to show it. One of the cars next to us has a rifle on the dashboard. I turn my head away from the rifle and look ahead as I move forward, waving at the soldiers as we pass through the checkpoint. Beisan is no longer so far away.

28

Spring

The land has woken up from the winter rains of the past several months, casting a blanket of green over the landscape. The air is clear and warm, the earth moist with the promise of life. What a gift Canaan, Karmel, and I all get to experience spring in Palestine for the first time together. Soon it will be *'Eid al-Adha*—the Celebration of Sacrifice—to commemorate Abraham's willingness to sacrifice his son to God. That year in 1999, the Eid fell on March 28, 70 days after *'Eid al-Fitr,* which marks the end of Ramadan. Since we were still in the US then, we got to celebrate with Nasser. Each year, these holidays shift earlier by about 10 days as dictated by the Islamic lunar calendar. It is the sighting of the first crescent of the moon at dawn that declares when the festivities may begin.

When the day comes, Canaan and Karmel can't wait to get their *'eidiyeh*—Eid money—so they can go buy treats and trinkets at the local shops with their cousins. I tell them they have to get dressed in their Eid clothes first since everyone traditionally wears new clothes on the Eid. Women even wear their wedding jewelry, which usually includes heavy 21-karat gold bracelets and necklaces, as well as rings and earrings. Canaan puts on his plaid dress shirt and mustard-colored corduroys while I help Karmel button up his striped dress shirt and green corduroys and tie his brown hiking boots.

Nasser and I usually give them 10 dollars for each year of their age for the Eid, but since we are in Palestine, I give them 10 shekels for every year instead, even though the exchange rate is four shekels to the dollar. So, Canaan gets 60 shekels since his birthday is soon and Karmel 30 shekels, which is a lot of money for a kid to spend in the village shops. I tell Canaan to put both their *'eidiyeh* in his pocket until we get to the village. "Make sure you take him to buy something."

When we arrive at Sitti's from our apartment in Jenin, we all go next door to Jamal's house for the traditional breakfast for 'Eid al-Adha, slow-baked lamb in its own juices. All of Nasser's siblings are there, including Nasser's sisters Nawal and Maha, who recently moved back to Palestine from Saudi Arabia after Nawal's husband passed away from a heart attack. Now, it is up to her eldest son to support the family with his work at Ford Motor Company in the US, the same son who lived with us while a student at the university when Nasser and I first got married. We gather around a shallow aluminum pan, each dipping bread into the juice and scooping up pieces of meat so tender it falls apart in the pan. Canaan and Karmel delight in this special treat.

On the morning of 'Eid al-Adha, it is customary to slaughter a lamb for those who can afford it and give one-third to those in need, one-third to the extended family, and keep one-third for the immediate family. I ask Jamal if he slaughtered a sheep for the Eid.

La, Faisal illi bithbah—No, Faisal's the one who slaughters. *'Atana lahmeh minu*—He gave us meat from it.

It is not long before we finish the pan. My eyes connect with Jamal and Samira's eyes in gratitude. *Yislamu ideikum*—Bless your hands.

U ideiki. Bi 'aris Kana'an inshallah—And your hands. To Canaan's wedding, God willing. I laugh at this common expression of gratitude because Canaan is not even six years old.

After breakfast, we walk through the village with Jamal's family to visit Nasser's other brothers, Faisal and Ghazi, who live next door to each other down Tariq Burqin. They join us to visit their sister Huda and Nasser's aunt 'Amti Saymi. Canaan and Karmel are swept away by their cousins to go to the shops. Soon, we hear *pops* from cap guns and a series of crackling sounds as fireworks explode on the street.

Suddenly, one of the cousins comes running back with Karmel, whose eyes are filled with fear after a pack of fireworks explodes in his pocket. My heart drops through my stomach. I rush home to Sitti's house to find his front right pocket blown to shreds, leaving a red mark on his skin from the blast. No sooner do I give him a new pair of pants than he wants to go back outside and play. "No more fireworks!" I insist.

Canaan and Karmel get out their bikes I bought them in Jenin, Karmel's outfitted with training wheels. They take turns riding down the street in front of Sitti's house with their cousins. One cousin is riding Karmel's with another cousin standing on the frame of the training wheels when one of the plastic wheels snaps, and the metal frame drags the bike to a halt. I do my best to console Karmel, then turn to his cousins.

Khallas, kharban. Fishi bisiklet—Enough, it's broken. No more biking.

Karmel goes back outside to his cousins, and they take him to Ghazi's house to go on the slide, though it is only a frame of a slide, so they take turns hanging their arms and legs over the bars to slide down. My heart soars that Canaan and Karmel finally get to celebrate the Eid with their cousins and spend their *'eidiyeh* in Palestine. Visiting family, playing in the street, it is truly a happy Eid!

On the second day of the Eid, we visit Nasser's sister Suhaila in the village of Rummaneh. We walk to the hills of the wa'ra among the olive trees, where I watch her husband Riyadh clip the new shoots at the base of the trunk of each tree. When we approach rougher terrain, he points out a huge boulder with rusted metal protruding from it, an official border marker from the Six-Day War of 1967. Just beyond it is the Israeli checkpoint between the villages of Rummaneh and Salem that straddle the Green Line.

Even though Riyadh has relatives there, he cannot cross over, nor are they allowed to come to Rummaneh. Two villages within walking distance of each other but worlds apart. It reminds me of how Nasser's village of Jalameh is cut off from the villages of Sandala and Muqeibileh. Riyadh gazes into the distance at his land on the other side of the Green Line, visible but out of reach.

In spite of this painful truth, I admire how this man can find joy in what he still has as he tends to his olive grove, explaining the impact of the lost land across the Green Line on his family's livelihood. His gray hair is testimony that he has carried this pain his entire life. I wonder how many men have suffered the same fate. At the same time, he is hopeful that one day, he or his sons will get back their land. He has not surrendered nor forgotten the transgressions against his family and village. The battle for justice is not over. I am reminded that mine is just beginning.

As we walk among the olive trees, Riyadh and Suhaila show me the first *zamatot*, peeking out through the rich soil in dense clusters anchored between the rocks. The lovely pink of these velvety cyclamen flowers is surrounded by two-toned leaves. Their rich color and distinctive pattern are the first rebuttal against the idea that the land of Palestine is a barren desert. As my eyes scan the wa'ra, I spot more and more of them. Although they gather in clusters, they are close enough to the next ones to exchange glances, and so the hillside is bustling with activity. Other flowers have yet to arrive. The zamatot have the hillsides to themselves.

Suhaila explains that you can roll the leaves of zamatot just like dawali. She shows me another, much larger leaf called lisayneh, though zamatot is said to be the most delicious. I pick some of each to take back home to make for dinner. The zamatot leaves are much smaller than grape leaves, so they must be worth the trouble. We end up picking enough leaves for a small pot, which I faithfully roll and cook the next day for dinner. Canaan and Karmel pop one rolled zamatot or *lisayneh* into their mouths after another, the zamatot as delicate as their fingers.

I find the zamatot much finer in texture and taste than the *lisayneh*, but without them, I wouldn't have had enough to fill the pot. Taking part in this ritual is like I am in on a family secret reserved for those with an intimate connection to the land, who still walk it and know what to pick when and how to prepare what they have gathered, a secret I have now shared with my children.

Soon the hillsides are bursting with wildflowers, the almond trees adorned in pink and white flowers, olive trees covered in white blossoms. One morning, we oversleep, so we are all stressed and out of sorts. I plan to drive Canaan and Karmel to school since they missed the bus. We are almost there, having made our way through Jenin and Zababdeh, when I notice the landscape is filled with red and black specks. Canaan and Karmel are surprised when I pull over and have them get out of the car to enjoy the spring landscape of Palestine instead of going to school.

Even though there is a magnificent display of yellow, pink, and purple wildflowers, we are all transfixed by the *hanoun*. The stems of these bright red poppies with large black eyes are so thin they bounce wildly in the warm breeze. I hear them call out, *Come dance with us!* Canaan and Karmel are mesmerized by their new friends anchored in the fertile soil. Their small hands reach down and pick the delicate stems. Tall flowers brush against their pant legs as they carry these tiny bouquets through the lush landscape. We are right at home, energized by the delightful display of life surrounding us. It is just us and the land, like long-lost friends getting reacquainted. The stress of the morning has dissipated, and we all play like children, free of worry or responsibility.

It is years later that I learn that hanoun are believed to grow from the blood of martyrs. The poppies are a reminder of those who have sacrificed their lives for their homeland. I feel honored that they chose to come out to greet us that day, to invite us to spend the morning with them just as they opened their eyes. Somehow, without knowing it, we intuitively took part in celebrating our love for Palestine.

In the afternoon, when we recount our morning with the wildflowers to Nasser's nephew Mahmoud, he wants to show me, Canaan, and Karmel the onions he planted just before the winter rains, now ready to harvest. We make our way from his house at the edge of the village to his cultivated land, the checkpoint, and the dirt road the Israeli army patrols along the Green Line, separating us from the rest of the village lands visible in the distance.

Nasser's sister Naziha is visiting from Jordan and walks with us. The sun is high overhead, though not yet blistering. As we make our way along the dusty dirt road, Naziha points out prickly stalks growing at the edge of the crops. She squats down, her long skirt settling in the dust. *Shinareh!* She breaks one of the stalks at the base with a snap of her wrist, then peels the outer layers of the hearty stalk in green strips, revealing a lighter green, moist interior. She snaps off a piece and hands it to me, her wide smile encouraging. *Kuli*—Eat it.

It crunches softly between my teeth like a cucumber, its fresh flavor sweet and nutty. The juicy flesh quenches my thirst instantly. *Zaki!*—Delicious! I try to pick my own, only to release my hand instantly as the thorn-covered stalk defends itself from my ignorance.

Naziha clarifies her technique. *Min tahit*—From underneath.

I snap the plant at the base, its weight collapsing in my hand like a fallen tree. Naziha shows me how to get to the prize at the center. I continue peeling from where she started, working my way around the perimeter of the stalk until the juicy center is glistening in the sun, each bite energizing my core. I offer her some, but she has already found another stalk. Such a generous land, whose people know it well.

Mahmoud calls our attention to his field of yellow onions, their scraggly stalks peeking out of the earth below like umbilical cords still attached to their mothers. *Hayhum*—Here they are.

I can't help but admire his harvest. *Mumtaz! 'Atik al-'afiyeh!*—Amazing! To your vitality!

Mahmoud's pride fills the landscape as he pulls at one of the stalks to reveal the shiny, golden skin gleaming in the sun. Soon, he will harvest them all to sell at the market in Jenin at a good price since he is one of the few farmers growing onions this year. He is really living off the land.

He invites us over for coffee but first leads us to a glass greenhouse adjacent to his house. Inside are gorgeous flowering plants, including *ferawleh* spilling out over plastic containers hanging from the wall. Canaan and Karmel's eyes grow wide with delight when Mahmoud offers them some of these homegrown strawberries. Their delicate fingers latch onto the gleaming red berries, which quickly disappear in their mouths. I have never seen strawberries in Palestine. What a treat! When he realizes how thrilled they are to eat berries, he promises to show them local berries known as *tout*.

We walk out into the fields west of the village to a cluster of towering trees not far from the village school that once served the three adjacent villages before the Green Line severed them from each other. Mahmoud reaches up and hands Canaan and Karmel a handful of plump black berries, the same berries that grow behind our house in Madison on our mulberry tree. He picks more from another tree, only now they are white, like albino berries. Two trees, close enough to hold hands, one producing black berries, the other white. I pick some of the black ones, their delicate membranes bursting with juice as I press them against the roof of my mouth. I expect the white ones to be devoid of flavor, but they are just as sweet. If I close my eyes, I can't even tell the difference between the two!

Canaan and Karmel want to pick their own, but the branches waving in the wind overhead are out of their reach. Mahmoud channels them a steady supply. We pick as many as we can reach, then head back to the village, our bellies full of *tout* from Palestine, their juice now running through our veins.

The wildflowers brought to life by the winter rains have given way to lush green grasses when I return to the destroyed village of Yalo near Ramallah in April to join a group of former residents and their descendants to visit the ruins of their village, then re-walk the same path they followed when the Israeli army forced them to evacuate on foot to make their way to the city of Ramallah in the midst of the Six-Day War of 1967 over 30 years ago.

We begin our journey in the morning as a caravan of cars from Ramallah. We arrive at the main entrance of Canada Park, established in 1975 on the site of these three villages in an effort to hide their remains. I wish I could ask Nasser's friend Johnny, whose family was driven out of their town of Ramleh in 1948, what he thinks of a park in Israel being named Canada Park.

We leave our cars in the parking lot and walk into the "park," the older residents of Yalo taking the lead. One woman in a traditional black, embroidered dress and a long, white head scarf must be in her 60s, a grown woman when her village was reduced to rubble. Her brow is firm and her gaze steady. Her feet follow the path with no hesitation. Her entire gait flows forward from her forehead to her footsteps.

We walk for some time before the women leave the path and continue up a gravel road. My eyes follow the road as it winds up the hill out of sight. I spot clusters of fruit trees on either side of the road, then the stone corner of the remains of a house. *This must be a village road.* My heart descends into my stomach as my eyes scan the landscape for more remains, but there are no houses in sight, only rubble amidst clusters of saber.

The group proceeds up the road. At one point, one of the older women points out the names of the families who used to live here, as if their houses are still standing. Then she leaves the road and walks between the invisible houses surrounded by fruit, almond, and olive trees. The woman's voice is heavy. The more names she utters, the more disbelief in her voice, until it falls silent.

We reach a plateau with the ruins of a high wall, where the village center used to be. Along the way, we see the concrete rubble of what must have been newer homes. Another woman points toward a pile of stone rubble surrounded on one side by a cluster of fruit trees.

Hun kan dar Sitti!—This was my grandmother's house!

She kneels down and pushes away some of the rocks with her bare hands. Those who brought hand tools with them offer her a spade, but she keeps clearing rocks that were once the stone walls of her grandmother's house until she has made a small depression in the pile. Her eyes are wide open. Her gaze is focused on her hands. Suddenly her shoulders are still, and I hear her gasp. She picks up a triangular shard of white china with the remnants of a deep blue floral pattern.

Hathi min sahoun Sitti—This was my grandmother's china.

Her eyes dart up at those of us standing around. *Kunna nokul minhin*—We used to eat off them.

She continues digging and finds a few more pieces and tucks them into her pocket. Then she gets up and walks toward the back of the destroyed house. She bends over again and tugs at a piece of metal protruding out of the rubble.

Ya Allah, makinat al-khayata!—Oh, my God, my grandmother's sewing machine!

Now, the tears flow freely down her smooth cheeks, her dark eyes scrunched in heartache. The earth below will not surrender the machine. She runs her hand back and forth over the frame, as if it is her grandmother's arm. *Kanat Sitti itkhayat huna 'and ash-shabak*—My grandmother used to sew here by the window.

The woman's image blurs as my own eyes pool up with tears. I take a sip of water, hoping to swallow the lump in my throat, but it remains stubborn. I look around, scanning for a neighbor's house next door or across the street. Piles of rubble are all I can see. It has been nearly 32 years since the village was destroyed, but the wounds feel fresh and open. A whole community of people with the rug ripped out from under it.

I follow along with the group as we proceed back to the center of the village, then downhill to an open, flat grassy area scattered with overgrown fruit trees. The grass is long and soft, bending easily in the warm breeze. We follow the older women off to one side, where they point to a lush green area.

Hun il-bir. Zaman kan fi maya kitir. Hala bas nitfeh—This is the well. There used to be a lot of water flowing here. Now, there's just a trickle. The woman raises her arms up to the sky and continues speaking softly to herself in Arabic.

I walk over to the well. The ground is moist, but the wide channel only hints at how much water used to flow here. I try to imagine the sound of the water running through the village. Here, water is like gold. Some of the women bend down, running their hands between the long grass, occasionally tugging methodically at green leaves with one hand and holding them with the other against the front of their long dresses, a micro-harvest from their village lands.

A couple of men direct us to follow them to an open area in another part of the village, where they point out an intact, rectangular foundation. *Hatha kan madrasat il-awlad*—This was the boys' school. *Hunak madrasat il-binat*—There is the girls' school. He points to a stone doorway still standing. His voice is solemn. *Dammaru kul shi*—They destroyed everything.

I try to imagine the desks in the large rectangle, the voice of the teacher, the view from the windows. I wonder where the students are now, how their lives were displaced with their families, and how this village became only a memory, a story to pass on to future generations. And yet, this walk is showing the younger generation what happened to their village. What is lost but still there.

The sun is high overhead when we begin our walk out of the village just as its residents must have walked nearly 32 years before. The drivers of the group go to get the cars and will meet us ahead. We walk along the main road toward Ramallah, passing by the Israeli settlement of Mevo Heron built next to the destroyed village of Beit Nuba, which like Yalo and the nearby village of Imwas, was destroyed in 1967. We continue on, the afternoon sun high overhead, radiating off the asphalt.

I try to imagine what it felt like to walk away from home, never to return. It is over 20 miles to Ramallah. Then, it was June 7, 1967. It would have been an exhausting walk in the brutal heat of summer. *Where would they go? How would they rebuild their lives?* Up to 10,000 people from three villages were forced to leave their homes that day.

The lump in my throat has become a stone in my stomach. I feel heavy, carrying this load in my body. This loss in my lifetime, going back to the year of my birth. Now and then, I look back at the hilltop of Yalo in the distance. A beautiful setting for a village, a village that now only exists in the minds of its residents and their descendants. The village lands are still there, and the descendants are still alive. I wonder if one day, Palestinian hands will again tend to the trees and laugh in the streets of Yalo, Imwas, and Beit Nuba, just as I wonder if Palestinians will ever be able to return to their villages destroyed in 1948. Saber, the clusters of cactus, are still waiting. Palestinians the world over are still waiting. *How long must they wait?*

29

Haifa

My apartment in Jenin is on Haifa Street, a road that once continued all the way to the city of Haifa on the Mediterranean Sea. Now it is interrupted by a roadblock that cuts Palestinians in the West Bank off from their beloved city, where Mount Carmel is located, the mountain after which Nasser and I named our son, Karmel. Haifa, once a center of Palestinian commerce and trade, is one of several Palestinian cities where most of the Palestinian inhabitants were driven out leading up to Israel's declaration of statehood in 1948.[93]

It is nearly the end of the school year in May 1999 when I set out to explore the city of Haifa with one of the school administrators, whose family is originally from Haifa. He grew up in Jordan, and he and his wife raised their children in the United States. As American citizens and nonresidents of the West Bank, we are able to pass through the Jalameh checkpoint without a permit. From there, we head west to Haifa Street on the other side of the Green Line, then cut over toward the sea to enter the city from the south.

As we make our way north along the coast, we pull over by the ruins of a castle-like structure known as the Caferlet Castle, which dates back to the seventh century and was built to protect the village from Byzantine invasion, then later the Crusaders. The hillside is covered with saber. *It's another destroyed Palestinian village, Kufr Lam, another red dot on the map.*

I later learn that Israel took over the village and drove out its residents on July 16, 1948, as part of its campaign to ethnically cleanse Palestinian villages that remained after the first incursion in the area in April and May 1948. The following year, they established the *moshavim* HaBonim and Ein Ayala on village lands with new Jewish immigrants from Great Britain, South Africa, and Eastern Europe, respectively. *The same place renamed—one population to replace another.*

Just south of Haifa, we pull off to an archeological site with stone archways drawing attention to ancient settlement in the area. The signs make no mention of the destroyed Palestinian village of Atlit that once stood here only 50 years earlier before Jewish forces took it over on May 15, 1948—only one day after Israel declared statehood. Instead, tourists are led to link an ancient Jewish presence to the modern State of Israel. The fact that Jews established a colony nearby in 1903 by the same name only adds to the confusion. My heart shifts between feeling sad and angry at these efforts to "prove" a Jewish presence without acknowledging the presence of Palestinians here or the state's role in their absence.

We continue north toward Haifa, only to spot the ruins of the destroyed Palestinian village of Al-Tira up on the hillside, famous for its almonds, giving it the name Tirat al-Loz. Stone remains peek out from among the trees, searching for their residents that fled when Jewish forces attacked the village in that spring of 1948.[94] We pull over, but the hillside is too overgrown to get any closer to the ruins. Such a gorgeous setting overlooking the Mediterranean Sea, now enjoyed only by the residents of the Jewish town of Tirat Carmel, built on village lands.

When we reach Haifa, I notice a number of older two-story stone buildings that stand in contrast to the newer Israeli buildings with smooth façades. These were likely once Palestinian businesses, but the signs above them are all written in Hebrew. Now, they are Israeli, like a sign on a storefront that changes from "open" to "closed" with the flip of the wrist.

We follow the older buildings up the slope until the school administrator's eyes lock onto the hillside. "This is the area where my family lived just before I was born."

Prominent Arab villas stand like crowns at the top of the hill. We walk up a stone staircase that is nearly rubble, though it appears to be under renovation. We climb the first few newly set steps, then carefully navigate the mix of loose dirt and stone. On our left is a row of one-story stone houses, walls nearly intact, but the rooftops are caved in. We climb down a narrow passageway between two of the homes that appear sunk into the ground.

"This is my parents' house. My mother was pregnant with me when they fled in 1948 once the shelling started in 1948. I never got to live in this house."

I look into this man's sunken eyes as he speaks. Now, when he says, "I am from Haifa," I have a better understanding of what he means.

We pass a window with no glass, no frame; it's simply a gaping hole. As I gaze into this void, I see the twisted metal frame of a bed. The floor is uneven, covered with loose stone and broken fragments of the ceiling. I turn away from the open window. We spend a few moments there in silence, then return to the crumbling staircase and walk farther up past other homes reduced to rubble. Now, the large villas at the top of the hill come into full view. I look up as the arched windows stare at me through prominently covered verandas. He explains the one on the left is the home of the Kanafani family. Hearing that name reminds me of Palestinian author Ghassan Kanafani, who experienced his own exile from the city of 'Akka in 1948.

I stare into the pointed, arched windows on the second floor, all gaping holes that stare back at me with drooping eyes. I turn around to look at what they are seeing. Beyond the rubble at my feet lies the vast harbor in the distance, with several ocean liners and enormous cranes to unload them. It is as if I am standing on a magic staircase. By simply turning my head, I move from the modern harbor back in time to the devastation and destruction of 1948 right in front of my eyes, right underneath my feet.

When Golda Meir—who grew up in Milwaukee, Wisconsin and later became prime minister of Israel—walked through the empty streets of Haifa after the majority of its 60,000 Palestinian residents were successfully driven out of their homes that spring of 1948, she could not help but link their suffering to that of the Jews in Europe:

> *"It is a dreadful thing to see the dead city. Next to the port I found children, women, the old, waiting for a way to leave. I entered the houses, there were houses where the coffee and pita bread were left on the table, and I could not avoid [thinking] that this, indeed, had been the picture in many Jewish towns [i.e., in Europe, during World War II]."*[95]

I wonder if she felt any remorse for this new round of suffering. After all, it was Christian anti-Semitism in Europe that led to the persecution of Jews, not the Palestinians. Why must they pay the price by being forced to forfeit their villages, towns, cities, farmland, homes, property, and businesses?

I also wonder what these homes have witnessed all these years. How the city of Haifa has become an Israeli city. How the Palestinian residents who fled for their lives were never allowed to return. How the rain seeped into their rooms, and the rubble settled on their floors. We walk closer, stepping carefully. I look up at the doorway of the Kanafani villa, a gaping hole, the front staircase gone. *I have to go in.*

I climb up the stone foundation from the side, revealing the floor tiles, loose and broken, nearly identical to the tiles in Nasser's family home, with soft green, mustard-yellow, and chocolate-brown geometric designs framing the floor and filling the center like an exquisite carpet. I try to imagine this family living in such a stately house overlooking the Mediterranean Sea, then having to leave it all behind. I pause for another moment of silence, then jump back down onto the dry earth and gaze into these hilltop eyes, sad but steadfast in their stillness.

Just below the deteriorating villas, I notice laundry hanging on the second floor of a modest, two-story home surrounded by open areas where houses once stood. The window and door frames are filled with modern replacements. The walls on the verandas are painted white, reflecting the bright sun. I slowly walk up the long, newly added staircase and knock. A woman with dark, curly hair opens the door, her eyes narrow as she peers out to find a stranger's eyes.

I smile, hoping she won't close the door. "Hello. Do you speak English?"

She opens the door a little wider. "Yes, a little. What do you want?"

"I was just walking in the area." I turn my head toward the crumbling homes. "I wonder if you can tell me about these houses." My eyes lock on hers.

She looks past me for a moment, and then her eyes return to mine. "It is a neighborhood. What is there to say?"

I turn again, this time pointing to the staircase. "It looks like they are working on it. Are they fixing it up?"

Her eyes widen a bit as she swings the door open a little farther. "I don't know what they are doing. It is taking a long time."

I catch a glimpse of the interior of her apartment and notice layers of paint have brought this old home into the present. "Do you live here?"

"Yes, this is my house." Her grip on the door is firm now.

My eyes scan the ancient stonework visible in the walls. "What a beautiful house. How long have you lived here?"

Her eyes narrow again as she shifts her weight. "Since 1948. My family got it then."

Her words pierce my heart. I am forcing my smile now. "I see. What about those houses? Whose are those?" I look up the hill at the villas.

Her eyes narrow farther, her body stiffens as she begins to close the door. "I don't know about them. Nobody lives there."

"Sorry to bother you. Thank you."

She closes the door. I walk back down the long staircase. I can still see the houses on the hill watching me.

In May, Nasser comes from the US to visit Canaan, Karmel, and me. We drive to Haifa to show Karmel "his mountain." We have told him about it his whole life, but he is just old enough to understand that Mount Carmel is an actual place. We arrive in the city and come across a modern shopping district, where Canaan spots Power Rangers and Transformers in one of the store windows. He pleads with us to get him one. I cringe after watching him happily buy balloons and other trinkets from the local shop in Jalameh for next to nothing. Now, he wants one of those fancy Western toys for 50 dollars—a quarter of a Palestinian teacher's monthly salary. He has been free of the pressure to buy these toys, but the Israeli stores with their Western wares tempt him. Nasser and I give in, wanting him to have a positive memory of this historic place.

We get Karmel one, too, in parity with his older brother.

We head up the winding road through town, braving the traffic past two-story buildings with storefronts and apartments. We pull over to buy some snacks at a local shop. The sign is in Hebrew and Russian. The labels are in Hebrew. The people in the shop are speaking Russian and Hebrew. Canaan and Karmel each pick a snack. Nasser finds some nuts we can share. Then we each choose a juice from the cooler, images of fruit our only guide. The man behind the counter tells us the total in Hebrew. Nasser hands him 20 shekels, hoping it is enough, relieved when the man hands him some change.

We follow the road to a higher elevation with a lookout point. We walk to the edge of a platform overlooking the sea, neatly arranged bricks beneath our feet. Nasser points beyond the iron railing. "This is your mountain, Karmel." Karmel looks up at his father, his hazel eyes squinting from the overhead sun. Karmel's eyes follow his father's hands as they sweep across the landscape. "All of this is yours!"

I follow Karmel's gaze taking in the view of the city overlooking the Bahá'í Temple, the harbor below, and the sparkling, deep-blue Mediterranean Sea beyond. Karmel starts skipping around the platform, his body small but solid, his blonde hair gleaming in the midday sun. He pauses to take another look, the soft curls in his hair forming neat clusters on his head.

Why should Palestinians be barred from returning to their destroyed villages or homes in these treasured cities of Palestine? It is one thing for the Jews of Europe and the Middle East to flee to Palestine as a place of refuge and quite another to take over the country as Israel. The more powerful Israel becomes, the more Palestine is pushed into its shadow. And yet, *Palestine still exists, but how can its recognition on the map be restored so its people can live a life of dignity?*

We head back toward Jenin along winding roads through the dense forest across the top of Mount Carmel. Occasionally, we can see for miles in all directions. Soon, we arrive in the Druze village of Daliyat al-Karmel. As we walk through the market, Nasser is pleased to find many items handcrafted from wood like in the old days, such as small stools with handwoven straw seats and traditional brooms hand-sewn from grass like the ones we use to clean Nasser's family home. Plastic versions of these same traditional handcrafted items are sold in Jenin. We buy some stools and a broom.

Everyone is speaking Arabic, though signs are in Hebrew and Arabic.

Daliyat al-Karmel feels untouched by history, as if the villagers have remained hidden from the conflict for decades. This village thrives in part because Israel made a strategic decision to favor the Druze from the earliest years of statehood to divide and conquer Palestine. The Druze, unlike other Palestinians, are trusted to serve in the Israeli army. The impact of their special status on their village and livelihood is clear. Here they are allowed to carry on with their lives in their homes and on their land while other Palestinian villages around Haifa and elsewhere in Palestine were wiped off the map. That's what it means to be special in Israel, to be allowed to exist. How can the "light unto nations" exist at the expense of another nation?[96]

On May 14 of that year, Canaan and the State of Israel are another year older. Israel turns 51—51 years since the Nakba—as we mark Canaan's sixth birthday. Nasser brought punch balloons from the States for his birthday celebration so Canaan can have a punching bag match with his cousins. Like on my birthday, I make a number of cakes and a large platter of tabouleh. It feels like a crazy turn of the tables that we are living in Palestine and Nasser in the States. *Like the Palestinian people, our family is fragmented.*

Nasser gets to visit Canaan and Karmel's school and meet their teachers, who tell him how sweet Karmel is and how proud they are of Canaan, who is at the top of his class. Nasser laughs and corrects Canaan when he hears him cite verses from the Quran he learned at school. When Canaan closes the verse with the incorrect phrase *saraq Allah 'athim,* which means "God's stealing is great," Nasser corrects him with *sadaq Allah 'athim*, "God's truth is great," a single sound changing the whole meaning. Back in Jenin, Nasser witnesses our morning routine of getting up and out the door to catch the school bus. We have a whole new life in Palestine.

30

Encounter

It is Saturday, the first day of the work week in Palestine. Canaan and Karmel have already caught the bus to school. I have a meeting with the school director at 10:00 a.m. to discuss teacher reviews I have prepared for end-of-year teacher evaluations. I travel the familiar route from my apartment on Haifa Street in Jenin through the market up the hill toward the village of Zababdeh. On the final stretch, I see a line of cars ahead of me and come to a complete stop. Another car pulls up behind me. No one is moving. No vehicles are coming from the other direction either. I peer out my window. All I see is the line of cars and trucks. Amidst the blur of intonation expressing anger and frustration, I manage to make out what they are saying. *At-tariq imsaqqir*—The road is closed. It doesn't make sense. There are two roads to get through this area used by the Israeli army for target practice. Even if one is closed, the other is always open.

I check the time on my cell phone. It is 9:45 a.m. I don't want to be late for my meeting. I become impatient and get out of the car. There is already a line of cars and trucks forming behind me. I look to the front of the line, but even standing, I can't see what's going on ahead, so I walk forward, spotting an army Jeep in the distance. The other drivers peer at me as I walk past them, frustration heavy on their brows. The farther I walk, the more their expressions turn to worry.

One of the drivers addresses me in Arabic, his voice almost shaky with fear. *Esh bitsawi?*—What are you doing? *Irja'i 'as-sayara*—Go back to the car.

I know confrontations with soldiers don't usually end well for Palestinians. Perhaps they are as much concerned for my safety as their own. I continue walking forward without a word, making eye contact to show appreciation for their concern. I don't want the soldiers to know I speak Arabic. English is my only recourse to step outside of this divide. My flowing, black skirt and matching vest are blowing in the breeze, my creamy silk short-sleeved shirt and long golden hair reflecting the bright, hot sun. I approach the soldier at a normal pace, neither hurrying nor hesitating, my arms hanging loosely at my sides.

Farther ahead, I see an Israeli soldier facing the line of vehicles, both hands gripping an M16 across his chest like a seat belt, the barrel pointing at the sky. I approach his squinting eyes, partially shaded beneath his olive-green helmet, and stare straight into them, as if our mutual gaze guarantees my safety. Behind him are several Israeli army Jeeps blocking the road, each with soldiers peering out of the back, M16s in hand, resting on their crouched knees. The closer I get to the one soldier,, the tighter he grips the M16 to his chest. He calls out to me in Arabic, then Hebrew. I respond to neither. Then he turns his head nervously toward another soldier and says something in Hebrew. I wait until I am just a few steps away to address him.

"Do you speak English?"

His shoulders relax slightly, and he lets his M16 slide down his chest a few inches before answering me in perfect American English. "The road is closed. You can't get through."

My eyes sharpen. "What do you mean the road is closed?"

"Just what I said. It's closed." He tightens the grip on his M16 as he regains his stiff soldierly composure. "Let me see your ID."

I reach into my purse and hand him my American passport. He lets his M16 hang loosely for a moment as he flips through my passport. "Ah, you're American." He hands it back to me and resumes his grip on his M16. "We have shooting practice today. You'll have to go back."

"But there are two roads. One of them has to be open. I come by here every day. I know."

"Both are closed today. You'll have to go around."

My frustration is mounting. "There is no 'around.' This is the only way through." I point to the school grounds in the distance. "I have to get over there to the Arab American School. Look, you can see it from here. I have a meeting in ten minutes. This is the only way."

"Sorry, you can't pass here today."

His familiar American English doesn't match the intensity of the situation. I switch my tone, as if we are tourists getting acquainted. "So, where are you from?"

Again, his brow softens. "California."

So, he *is* an American. I cling to this connection we share like a lifeline.

"Really? My sister lives in California. What are you doing here?"

"I live here now." He pauses. "What about you? What are you doing here?"

"I live here, too. I am here with my two children. My husband is from here."

"He's Palestinian?"

"Yes." He seems surprised, and his face hardens. *I am one of them.*

As I carry on a casual conversation with this Israeli soldier, I can't help but wonder how this 18-year-old from California is able to interrupt the daily lives of people halfway around the world. Does he have any idea what he's doing? My chest burns inside. He probably came to Israel to make Aliyah and serve the Jewish homeland.[97] But in reality, he is keeping ordinary people from doing ordinary things. I look back at the long line of cars behind me. My mind is racing with the absurdity of it all, but I quickly get back to the subject at hand.

My voice is firm. "Listen, I'm going to be late. I have to pass through here now. You'll have to open the road."

He chuckles and tilts his head apologetically, his tone friendly. "Sorry, I can't. It's closed. You see them shooting down there. It's not safe."

Yes, they are practicing to shoot the people in the line of cars behind me. I can hear the faint echo of gunshots in the background. I regain my composure, blocking the sound of gunfire out of my mind. It is just him and me. I loosen my arms, letting my hands fall open, palms facing upward. "Come on, haven't you ever had somewhere you needed to be? I have to get through. And so do all these other people. We all have somewhere we need to be."

"I can't."

"Look, I know you can. You just need to call someone to let you open the road. There is no other way to get over there. There is no going around."

He shifts his weight in his steel-toed, black boots, mulling my words over in his mind. Finally, he pulls out a walkie-talkie and steps aside, speaking Hebrew. Another soldier comes over, and they carry on a tense exchange, occasionally looking in my direction.

I stand there with my arms folded, waiting in the already hot morning sun. *Am I wasting my time pleading with a soldier? Isn't he simply doing his job? What makes me think they will listen to me?* I glance behind me at the growing line of cars creeping into the distance. My eyes meet some of the drivers within view. They must think I'm crazy, standing up to the soldiers. *They know better than to take that risk.* I turn back to the soldier. He puts down his walkie-talkie.

"Okay, you can pass."

Is he serious? Can I trust his words?

"You're going to open the road?"

"Yes, just for you."

I look again at the line of cars, my heart pounding in my chest. I can't accept that they only open the road for me. I reply slowly, adding weight to each word. "No, we all need to pass. I'm not going through unless we all go through. You need to open one of the roads." Fear now surges through my veins, the sweat prickling under my fitted silk shirt. *What am I doing? This is my chance to pass, to get on with my day.* But I don't care about my meeting anymore. It's not about getting through. It's about getting this soldier and the others behind him to see how many lives they are disrupting for no good reason. *For shooting practice.*

He stands there for a moment, sensing I am not going to back down, that it is no longer about the road. "One minute." He raises his index finger and steps aside, then returns to his walkie-talkie and another exchange in Hebrew with the soldier next to him. The other soldier seems annoyed by my request and frustrated that the soldier from California is considering it. He rolls his eyes at me but cannot help himself from laughing, amused by my persistence.

The first soldier takes a few steps toward me. "Okay, okay, we will open one of the roads."

My eyes are glaring. "For everyone?"

"Yes, yes, for everyone." He sounds exasperated. "Now go get back in your car."

I let my arms fall to my sides. I can hardly believe it. They are going to open the road and let everyone pass. I look the soldier in the eye with gratitude. "Thank you." I really mean it.

I turn around to face the line of cars and make my way back to my car. As I pass the unsettled drivers, I utter under my breath so each one can hear me, *Biddu yiftah at-tariq*—He's going to open the road. Their brows soften at the prospect of getting through, disbelief in their eyes. I get back in my car, start it, and wait for the line to move. The brake lights on the car ahead of me go out as it rolls forward. When I reach the point where I had been standing moments before, I give a final wave to the young soldier from California and smile as I pass him. He waves back and smiles.

I look back to see the cars coming through, bumper to bumper, a cloud of dust trailing behind them. I am torn between feeling proud that I was able to convince the soldiers to open the road, and a deep sense of anguish, knowing that if any of these other drivers had tried to do what I did, they would have been beaten, detained, or shot. *Was I able to break through that barrier because I am an American? A woman? Both?*

I arrive at the school by 10:30 a.m. Another day in Palestine.

Shortly before I travel back to the States with Canaan and Karmel, Nasser's nephew Mahmoud gets engaged through the Islamic tradition of *katib al-kitab*, where he and his bride are essentially "written" to each other. I am thrilled to be invited to her family's home. In Palestine, getting engaged is a celebration for the groom's family because they are gaining a daughter-in-law and the potential of children who will carry their family's name. For the bride's family, it is both a celebration and a day of mourning because they are losing their daughter to the husband's family. No wonder the air is heavy when I arrive, almost like a funeral. Still, congratulations are in order. I kiss her mother repeatedly on both cheeks, then shake hands with each of the women sitting on mats along the perimeter. *Mabrouk*—Congratulations.

Allah yubarich fich—May God bless you, the older women tell me in the traditional dialect of the village with its distinctive "ch" sound instead of "k."[98] *Allah yikhalli awladich*—May God keep your children. Perhaps the younger women among them are cousins of the bride.

I kiss Mahmoud's fiancée on both cheeks, her long, sleek black hair draped over her shoulders like a cape, then take a seat on one of the mats across from her. The older women are talking amongst themselves, their hands joining in on the conversation, their bodies relaxed in their long, black, traditional dresses adorned with colorful tatriz embroidery, their legs crossed beneath them. The younger women sit quietly, occasionally exchanging a few words, their bodies constricted in narrow, long synthetic skirts, forcing them to sit on their knees. One of the older women offers me *baklawa* pastries and a tiny cup of Arabic coffee, the perfect accompaniment to the sweet honey-soaked layers of the pistachio-filled filo pastry.

Then, as if rising from below the earth, comes the distant sound of rhythm. The bride's mother enters the room holding a traditional tableh drum under her arm, hitting the top with her hands and the tips of her fingers. Her voice chimes in, low and rhythmic, as if coming from the hollow cavity of the drum. As the bride enters the room, her mother's hands beat harder against the drum, quick and repetitive, almost hypnotic, carrying the sound into the depths of our souls. I rock my shoulders back and forth as the vibrations resonate through my body, pulling me into a trance.

One of the older women gets on her feet, her hair covered with a thin white scarf that trails down her back in soft folds over the stunning embroidery of her long black dress. She surrenders her body to the music, turning several beats sharply to the left, then the right, keeping her hips and torso tightly in line with each other. Her head turns in the opposite direction of her torso, then back as her body changes direction to the beat of the drum. Her bare feet bounce to the rhythm from beneath her hemline. When another woman joins her, they raise their arms to their sides, holding them like trophies. I am intrigued by how their hips remain centered under their torso, unlike belly dancing, where the hands, chest, and hips all move in isolation from each other.

One of the women turns to me and stretches out her hand, inviting me into the center to form a constellation of planets circling in one powerful orbit. The bride's mother lets her hands fall harder against the drum, creating the deep *dum* sound with the flat of her hand, then a single sharp *tak* with her fingertips at the edge of the drum. My body follows the rhythm, my core tight to hold my shoulders, torso, and legs locked in line.

At first, my movements are stiff and deliberate, but then I follow the women as they bend their knees on the third beat, then spring in the other direction, their heads turning the other way. Now, all I feel is the change in direction as our bodies move in unison—*dum-dum-tak*.

Another older woman gets on her feet but stays to the side. She places her hand cupped above her mouth, releasing the traditional shrill ululation with a final rise in tone ending in *yih*. The tension builds in my chest as we collectively mark this moment, where this young woman becomes officially betrothed to Mahmoud, as if the music itself is transforming her from girlhood to wifehood, rearranging molecules and brain cells to step into this new role. The repetitive rhythms of this ritual extend throughout the room, building in intensity.

One of the older women draws the bride to her feet. I feel her hesitate as if surrendering to the music is the crossing of a threshold from which she can never return. She succumbs to the rhythm. I take her hand and look into her eyes. We circle around each other, her final moments of girlhood being released into rhythm. I am honored to share in this persistent custom of committing two people to marriage, a rite of passage that follows their journey from the womb to mother's breast, to living among extended family, and onto building a life, a home, and a family of their own. *This, too, shall be.*

I breathe in the air of trust and inevitability. Life continues here in spite of all of the political turmoil and limitations under occupation. Unfortunately, I will miss their *hafleh*, or wedding celebration, at the end of June. I will already be in the States by then. There his bride will appear in her wedding dress, surrounded by female friends and family with Mahmoud by her side. They will sit like king and queen while female family and friends dance the night away behind closed doors. The men of the village will line the streets, holding hands, dancing traditional dabkeh in unison, their feet skipping and stomping, their hands clapping. The leader will spin a cloth from his extended arm overhead, occasionally lowering his body to the ground and rising again to his feet with ease, or breaking off at times to offer a prominent display of strength and agility.

Some villagers will watch from their rooftops as the sound of the music carries throughout the village into the night. No joining of bride and groom goes unnoticed. It is as much a private declaration as it is public. The persistence of life despite the occupation reminds me that people will carry on here regardless. At the same time, without change on the ground, this couple will face the same humiliation and restrictions on their lives and livelihood as their parents' generation.

Even though it is time for my sons and me to go back to the US, my connection to Palestine has never been stronger, and I am more determined than ever to make a difference. No longer am I on the outside looking in, trying to make sense of this place. I am beginning to see how by simply drawing on my own skills and embracing the local culture, I can contribute to people's lives here.

Who knows? Maybe education is my calling. Palestinians are already said to be the most educated people on Earth. Their commitment to education has served them well by preparing for a future, where their fight for self-determination in their homeland will become a thing of the past. Even though I am leaving home behind, I am more focused than ever. I, too, will invest in Palestine's future and help bring Palestine out of the shadows so this generation—and my own children—can live a life of dignity.

PART IV

STEADFASTNESS

Al-Aqsa Intifada and the Collapse of Oslo

2000-2007

31

Fieldwork

Inspired by my work as an educational consultant, I decide to go back to school at the University of Wisconsin–Madison in the fall of 1999 to get my doctorate in educational administration. I learn about the history, impact, and development of secondary education and higher education and apply all my knowledge to the Palestinian context. I am hired as an assistant to the dean of the School of Education, who is also my doctoral advisor, to draft a strategic plan for the university's School of Education. This experience gives me the idea to develop a strategic plan for Palestinian higher education for my dissertation.

My first opportunity to share what I have learned in my research on Palestinian education generally, and Palestinian universities, in particular, is at an academic conference in Washington, DC. I give a paper on "Higher Education in Transition: Current Realities in Palestinian Universities" to highlight not only the history of higher education in Palestine but also the changes that have taken place in the education sector since the Oslo Accords of 1993 and Oslo II Accords of 1995.[99]

The following year in late summer of 2000, I travel to Palestine for my fieldwork to conduct interviews with administrators, faculty, and staff from all 10 Palestinian universities in the West Bank, Gaza, and Jerusalem that exist at that time, as well as private educational institutions, such as the

Qattan Foundation in Ramallah, and officials at the Ministry of Education and Higher Education that formed after the Oslo Accords.

It feels strange to come to Palestine and not see Nasser's family, but I am on a tight schedule to get back before Canaan and Karmel start school. I arrange to stay with my friend Najat, whose family has a house in Ramallah, so I am centrally located. She is also doing her doctorate in Madison on the Palestinian poet Mahmoud Darwish, who lives in Ramallah. At least I am not completely alone.

I follow through on my rigorous interview schedule, beginning with the Arab American University in Jenin. It has been two years since I spent the year in Palestine with my sons and worked at the school affiliated with the university. Then, the university was only under construction, but now, some of the buildings are finished, and the first students are enrolling. It is the only private Palestinian university and fills a much-needed void in the northern part of the West Bank, especially for female students whose families are uncomfortable with their daughters having to commute to other cities farther south.[100]

The following day when I arrive in Nablus to meet with the president of Al-Najah National University, the largest university in the West Bank, I am met with an Israeli checkpoint blocking traffic in and out of the city. This checkpoint is one of many flying checkpoints the Israeli army sets up randomly, in addition to the hundreds of regular checkpoints across the West Bank. It reminds me of that day when I was trying to get to my sons' school, and the road was closed. Standing in the hot sun, I insist the soldiers let me through so I can get to my interview. The soldiers talk amongst themselves, laughing at my determination. When they realize I am not going anywhere, they finally allow me to pass, though the checkpoint remains. I don't want to be any later than I already am. The president of the university is surprised I am late. I point out that even as an American, I am subject to the same delays under Israeli occupation.

In Ramallah, I conduct interviews with several administrators and faculty at Birzeit University, the most prestigious Palestinian university, where I took Arabic language classes during my last trip to Palestine. As the most elite of the Palestinian universities with an array of rigorous programs, it also stands out above the rest in producing local leaders, such as Marwan Al-Barghouti.

He ultimately becomes known as the Palestinian Nelson Mandela when he is imprisoned for life in 2002 for his leadership role in resistance activities related to the First and Second Intifada.

Another day, I meet with the president of the Open University in the lovely outdoor courtyard of The American Colony Hotel in Jerusalem. With its numerous satellite locations in towns and cities across the West Bank and Gaza, it operates more like an independent study opportunity, providing Palestinians access to higher education, who might otherwise not be able to attend a university because they are working or cannot travel.

After the interview, I realize I am near Damascus Gate, which is close to the Browns' house my brother and I had visited 14 years earlier. I have lost touch with the family—as I have Salem and his family—and don't expect them to still be living there, but I feel drawn to go to the house before my next interview at Al-Quds University. There is still a taxi lot by the gate, the same one we walked across from the Browns to venture into the Old City. Now, the road is much wider, and there is a privacy wall all the way along the neighborhood. I see an opening and head in that direction.

I end up in a small street that feels familiar, but all I find is a much larger two-story house. *I must have made a mistake.* I retrace my steps again, looking back toward Damascus Gate, then into the street. I am about to give up when I realize that a second floor has been added to the original one-story home. Now, I see the familiar old stone walls, the front steps, and the beautiful arched windows. In my mind, I can see Eleanor standing there on the front porch with Jessica and Benjamin that first day we met, but now, I am alone, staring into the past from a very different present. I am married to a Palestinian, I have children of my own, Palestinian children, I speak Arabic, and I have a master's degree in Middle Eastern Studies. I feel the passing of the years, and my heart tugs at the loss of their friendship. I take one last look at the stone walls of the house that was my first home here, then turn away.

I get a taxi across the street and head to Al-Quds University, the only Palestinian university in Jerusalem. Although it offers a wide range of faculties, it serves as the only medical school in Palestine. I don't know then that in three years, the Israelis will build a wall that will cut the Abu Dies campus in two and cut East Jerusalem off from neighboring Palestinian villages in the West Bank.

That evening, Najat and I meet up back in Ramallah and have dinner in Jaffa, just a 30-minute drive away, accessible to us because of our American passports. So much history still separates these two cities that it feels like a world's journey. The cool evening breeze magically washes away the heat of the day. There is something reaffirming about simply being in this place treasured by Palestinians the world over. Part of me wants to turn back the clock so that I am surrounded by the Palestinians who once lived here, but there is no going back, only forward.

Maybe someday, those who fled Jaffa in 1948, like Salem's family, will be able to see their hometown again, even live here. I am hopeful my research in education will somehow contribute to raising awareness of the plight of the Palestinians in their struggle for self-determination in their homeland. But awareness is not enough in a part of the world often written off as too complicated and laden with conflict. *How will there ever be peace unless Palestinians can live in the places they call home?* Jews the world over repeated the words, "Next year in Jerusalem" for centuries. Why impose that longing on another people, who just decades ago walked these streets, fished this sea, and worked this land as their homeland?

The next morning, I travel by taxi to Bethlehem University to meet with several faculty and administrators. They have an impressive campus with their own School of Education to train future teachers. Here I witness the power of education to provide hope by building the capacity for a future Palestine. By the time I meet with everyone, it is too late to see the city, "the little town of Bethlehem," I only know from Christmas songs. It will be nearly two decades before I make it back to Bethlehem.

I set out early the next morning by taxi to the city of Hebron, the southernmost Palestinian city in the West Bank. The rolling hills covered with olive trees slowly give way to dry rocky terrain that reminds me of the Dead Sea basin. The taxi driver points out caves in the distance, where some Palestinians still live as they did thousands of years ago. It always amazes me how drastically the landscape changes from region to region. The distances are not that far, and yet the terrain feels worlds apart.

In Hebron, I conduct my interviews at two institutions that provide access to higher education for Palestinians living in these remote areas, the Polytechnique University and Hebron University. Fortunately, I have time to visit the Old Market, where I purchase a traditional hand-painted, pale blue ceramic tableh drum from a small shop on the ancient cobblestone main street of the Old City. This antique is a real treasure compared to the modern steel drums available in the market. The sheepskin is still as taut as ever, giving it a beautiful full sound when I tap my fingers at the edge and center with the simple rhythm *dum-dum-tak*.

I visit the Ibrahimi Mosque, which has a heavy Israeli and Palestinian security guard presence. It has only been six years since the massacre when an Israeli in uniform gunned down 29 Palestinians during Ramadan prayer services. Tensions are increasing as the Jewish settler population just southeast of the holy site grows, encroaching on city residents. This site is sacred to both Muslims and Jews, said to be the final resting place of Abraham's family. The Jews' deep attachment to the site and increased presence in the city lead to frequent clashes between Palestinian residents of Hebron and Israeli settlers in the area, resulting in an ever-increasing Israeli military presence.

In conjunction with the Oslo Accords, the Hebron Protocol of 1996 formally divided the city into H1 and H2 zones that fall under the Palestinian Authority and Israel, respectively (see Map 10). Years later, the separation and antagonism between Palestinians and Israeli settlers in Hebron will grow to the point that Israel completely shuts down the market in the Old City where I bought my drum. Who knows when I will ever get to see that main street of Hebron flourish once again?[101]

Back in Ramallah, during my interviews at the Ministry of Education and Higher Education, I sense frustration as these newly established ministries try to get all the universities to coordinate their programs to avoid duplication and prepare for certification to improve the quality of program offerings in their state-building efforts. The universities are used to operating independently, so there is some resistance to this oversight.

I leave my trip to Gaza for last, where I will also visit two universities. I arrange for a private taxi with yellow Israeli license plates to take me from Ramallah to Gaza. The driver will stay with me for the whole day. I wear a two-piece black outfit with a long-sleeve blouse and a long skirt. I also have a sheer black scarf I bought in Jerusalem to cover my hair when I visit the Islamic University to show respect.

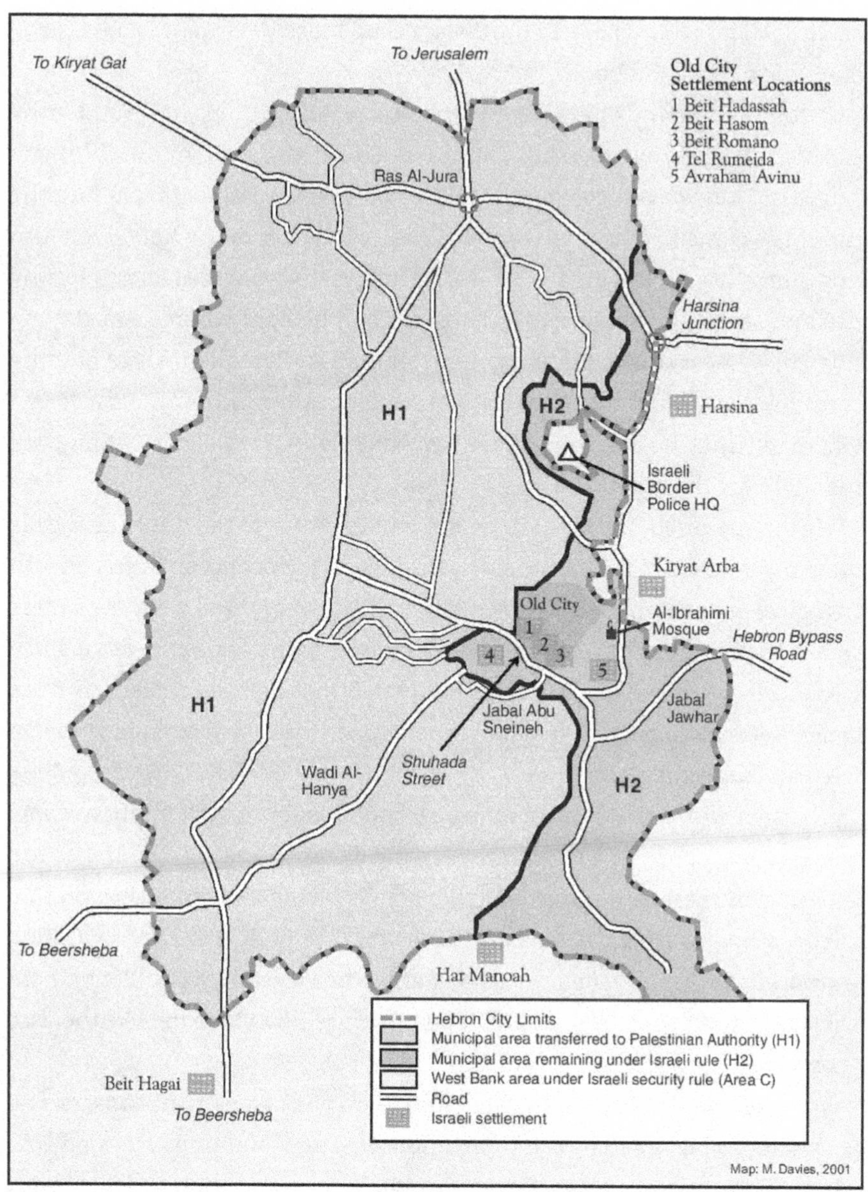

Map 10: Hebron Protocol, January 15, 1997 (Source: PASSIA)

Getting into Gaza is not easy, but with my scheduled interviews, I am able to enter this otherwise closed area. The checkpoint is no longer the simple steel gate across a two-lane road I had encountered back in 1986. Now, the entire area leading up to the checkpoint is paved in concrete and there are

Israeli soldiers everywhere. In the distance is a massive entrance gate several lanes wide, like a toll booth.

Before we get anywhere near the gate, a soldier comes up in full army gear, his M16 slung over his shoulder. The taxi driver hands him my passport. They exchange words in Hebrew, then the soldier peers into the car and asks me in a heavy Hebrew accent what I am doing here. I tell him I have meetings scheduled at Al-Azhar and the Islamic University for my research at the University of Wisconsin. Then he asks where I am staying in Israel. I know it is safer to say Jerusalem than Ramallah, since coming from the West Bank raises security questions. After inquiring how long I will be in Israel, he asks me where I am staying in Gaza. I clarify that I am only here for the day.

He flips through my passport again, hands it back to the driver, and calls out to the soldiers at the gate to let us through. They peer at us from beneath their olive-green helmets, their M16s reaching toward the sky. My eyes meet each of theirs through the glass of my window as we pass. I know that since the Oslo II Accords of 1995, the entire Gaza Strip has been sealed off from all sides. The soldiers are the gatekeepers. Only the Israeli settlers who live here can come and go freely.

The area along the road past the checkpoint is more built up than it was 14 years ago. I spot some red rooftops in the distance and wonder if they are settlements. I can hardly stomach the Israelis taking any more land on this narrow strip away from the Palestinians who live here. It is already among the most densely populated places on Earth. The Palestinian population here has nearly doubled to over a million people since I was here in 1986, the vast majority of them refugees from 1948.

We enter the city and head toward the sea on one of the main roads framed by buildings higher than the one- and two-story buildings I remember. Palestinians of all ages are walking down the sidewalks, the streets filled with a mix of newer cars and the old "toy" cars I remember. Only the youngest girls do not have their hair covered. It all looks familiar, but I don't recognize any building in particular. I want it to be familiar. *I was here.*

After my interviews at Al-Azhar and the Islamic University, I direct the taxi driver to Omar Mukhtar Street to look for Salem's house. He drives north along the coastline and pulls over. *Hun Omar Mukhtar*—Here is Omar Mukhtar.

Biddi amshi sway—I want to walk a little.

The sun is hot against my face as I gaze out at the sea, the black scarf covering my hair. I scan the area, remembering the sandy open clearing from years ago, where a few two-story buildings now stand. I look back at the sea to orient myself. My gut guides me at a diagonal toward a group of buildings. I follow the path until I reach a narrow street with a solid block of two-story houses on both sides, just like the houses of long ago. *Can this be it?* The houses are more built up than before. *Maybe I have it wrong*. I look back at the sea, then at the houses. *No, this is it. I am sure of it.*

The open sewer that once ran down the center is paved flat. My eyes skip from front steps to front steps, searching for Salem's door. I keep walking forward until I reach a narrow side street, where I saw the soldiers looking at me through the side window. *This is the house.* I stare up at its tall façade. The open courtyard must be gone. I go around the corner and find my window with a view of the sea, then look down the narrow passageway. A few children are playing in the distance.

I call out to them, smiling. *Allo*—Hello. They giggle and look at each other. *Ana Christa*—I'm Christa. *Kifkum?*—How are you?

More children appear, as if they can walk through walls. They look at each other, then back at me. I realize they don't know me. They are the next generation of Palestinians born under Israeli occupation. I smile as I walk past them, their eyes staring at me. Some of them smile back at me, while others tuck their chins. I wave goodbye and head toward the sea. This was once my home. I can feel my footsteps walking the familiar path of the past. Now that I recognize it, I am surprised at how little it has changed.

I continue to the beach. I want to find the shipwreck. I scan the horizon, looking for metal protruding from the bluish-green water, but all I see are the vast open waters cascading onto the shore. I sharpen my gaze until, just beyond the waves, I spot the shipwreck. I take a deep breath, overcome with a sense of relief. I need proof I was here, that it was not a dream. I take one last look at the sea and head back to the taxi. It is getting late, and I still have to get back to Ramallah. The driver is patiently waiting. *Khallasti?*—Are you finished?

Ah, khallas—Yes, all done. *Yallah*—Let's go.

It is hot, but I leave my scarf on until just before we get to the checkpoint.

The sea and the faces of the children in the passageway are swimming in my head. Something in me feels like I have come full circle. I found the Browns' house in Jerusalem, and now, I found Salem's house in Gaza, early beginnings that set a lifelong journey in motion. My heart swells with gratitude. I take a deep breath as several soldiers approach the taxi. I hand my passport to the taxi driver. I know the drill. Another exchange in Hebrew. Flipping of pages. Peering into the taxi. Waving us through. The concrete plaza. The watchtowers. Army helmets and M16s. *I am leaving Gaza prison.* My interviews all complete, it is time to go back to the US. I leave without seeing Nasser's family. I was in Gaza but did not see Salem's family. Just me on my own in Palestine.

The two weeks of my fieldwork in August 2000 have passed, and I return to the US laden with material that will become my doctoral dissertation. I realize it is not for me to define Palestine's educational future with a strategic plan through my research but rather to make sense of the past and present as a Palestinian framework for thinking about the future. When I sort through my interviews, I recognize the central role the university has played in stateless Palestine.

I break down that empowerment process into three distinct periods: first, the universities' role in giving Palestinians space to articulate a Palestinian national identity during the early years of the Israeli occupation since universities were the only places where Palestinians could gather; then as centers of resistance to Israeli occupation beginning with the First Intifada in 1987 through the Madrid Conference in 1992; and finally in preparing Palestinian society for statehood following the Oslo Accords. I am hopeful this framework will deepen the world's understanding of how the Palestinian struggle for self-determination has evolved over time from resistance to state-building. Without a clear path to statehood, however, I fear the frustration will boil over into chaos.

Sure enough, the empty promise of statehood through the Oslo Accords becomes a time bomb that by September 2000 explodes. It is on television back in the US that I witness the spark ignite when Prime Minister Ariel

Sharon—accompanied by a thousand Israeli soldiers—visits what Muslims call the Noble Sanctuary and Jews refer to as the Temple Mount in Jerusalem. This confrontational act only adds insult to injury and gives birth to the Second Intifada, what will come to be known as the Al-Aqsa Intifada.[102]

This new uprising is marked by a generation of Palestinians who grew up under Israeli occupation and a peace process that reduced the Palestine Question to one of squeezing a future Palestinian state into fragments within the 1967 borders. These young Palestinian men and even women resort to carrying out suicide missions in Israel—places from which most Palestinians no longer have access—as if to communicate that if the lives of Palestinians cannot be normal, neither will those of Israelis. In response, Israel cracks down hard on Palestinian communities and, by 2002, begins erecting a prefabricated 25-foot wall across the West Bank and near Jerusalem on or near the Green Line to allegedly protect itself from future attacks.

I learn that Israel calls this concrete snake *gader hafradeh,* which literally means "separation fence," Palestinians *jidar*, Arabic for "wall." Ironically, the Hebrew *gader* and the Arabic *jidar* are derived from the same word but have different meanings that mirror the divide of this *de facto* border between Israel and the West Bank. Over time, particularly in areas with a heavy presence of settlements, the Wall is constructed deep inside the Green Line within Palestinian territory, cutting communities apart, isolating villages, blocking farmers' access to their land. In rural areas, the Wall is a fence with barbed wire and security ditches. The result is interactions between Jewish Israelis and Palestinians in the West Bank are more restricted than ever. With separation comes mounting antagonism.

Soon after I return to the US, the situation quickly degenerates from bad to worse, creating a stranglehold on Palestinian lives from all sides. Israel freezes tax revenue to the Palestinian Authority, so the ever-growing web of public employees—including schools and universities across the West Bank and Gaza—are forced to work without pay. Israel's use of collective punishment is nothing new, but during the Second Intifada, Israel takes its dismay with Palestinian resistance to a whole new level with the reinvasion of Palestinian cities, and increased raids and checkpoints. Whatever hope people had that relations between Palestinians and Israelis would normalize—that Palestinians could build a state and a future next to Israel—is shattered.

32

Sham (شام)

In the midst of the chaos that ensues overseas with the outbreak of the Second Intifada, Nasser and I have much to celebrate, much to be grateful for. As my father always said in German, *Alle gute Dinge sind drei*—All good things come in threes. This phrase comes to mind when I learn I am pregnant with our third child. I touch my belly and try to imagine this new life emerging within me.

Back at work, I continue developing tables, charts, and worksheets for our upcoming unveiling and distribution of the strategic plan for the School of Education. By spring, my final two classes required for my doctorate, as well as my position with my advisor, come to an end. The timing couldn't be more perfect. Now, I will have the summer to work on my dissertation and get ready for the birth of our third child. *Another Palestinian child.*

At one of my prenatal appointments, I find out what I am having. I could not imagine having a boy, and I had two. Now, I am having a girl. My brain is adjusting to a whole new being, a daughter, a princess of Palestine. I can't wait to tell Nasser he will be the father of a daughter and Canaan and Karmel that they will be big brothers to a baby sister.

Not long after I learn the news, her name comes to me in a dream: Sham (شام). I don't know this name. I only know the word for "sun" in

Arabic, which is *shams* (شمس). Nasser explains the meaning of Sham. "It's the historical name for Greater Syria, which was Syria, Lebanon, Jordan, and Palestine. In Arabic, we say *Bilad ish-Sham*—The Countries of Sham." He describes how a great deal of poetry and songs have been written for the love of Sham and that people still refer to Syria or even the city of Damascus as Sham.

All our children's names are places of great significance to Palestinians. Canaan is the ancient name of Palestine, Karmel the mountain in Haifa, and now Sham, the whole region of Greater Syria. *A big name for a little girl.*

In March, Palestinian musician Simon Shaheen (Palestinian) and his orchestra perform on campus in Madison, including some of Marcel Khalife's music. I wear a Palestinian dress embroidered with tatriz, a gift from one of my sisters-in-law, that is both traditional and modern, with cross-stitch framing the neckline and bright orange satin sleeves. I also wear my gold necklace, earrings, and bracelet from our fifth wedding anniversary.

I am five months pregnant but hardly showing. The music is both uplifting and soothing as the violins sing and the musicians' hands fill the hall with a base rhythm on traditional drums for all the other instruments to dance around. The delicate plucking of the *qanoun* table harp warms my heart, and the soft flute known as *nay* seeps into my ears and through my veins.

I am delighted that Sham's ears have developed to be able to hear the music and that Canaan gets to experience the music live that filled his ears every day for the first year of life when I would dance with him around our living room in Detroit. I watch as Canaan and Karmel are compelled to move to the music. They make their way to the stairs at the end of our row, scramble down to the front of the hall by the stage with swooping arms, then up the other staircase and back around. Their movements are met with smiles, not sneers, as concertgoers delight in their enthusiasm. I feel fortunate that it is socially acceptable to move to the music rather than be expected to sit in stillness and silence like the European classical concerts I grew up attending with my father.

The big hand is five minutes away from striking midnight when I glance over at the clock on the wall just after I give birth to our new baby daughter Sham. She just made it to be born on July 7. *Seven seven.*

"It's Sham." Nasser's voice is trembling, his eyes tender as they witness the miracle of his daughter's birth. I gaze at our beautiful newborn daughter, so complete, so perfect, so whole. I examine her delicate fingers and toes and am mesmerized by her strawberry-blonde hair that veils her tiny head. Her eyes, steel gray, are staring at me in total silence as we gaze into each other's souls. When I left home, we were four. Now, we are five. I encourage Canaan and Karmel to each come up to her. I watch them examine her tiny hands and hold her delicate fingers. I am grateful that she has two strong brothers to watch over her.

I don't know then that Sham is born 64 years to the day after the Peel Commission of 1937 that first recommended the partition of Palestine.[103] *Who would accept to partition their homeland?* Since then, only a fraction of what was once Palestine remains in Palestinian hands, and more land is taken each year for "security reasons" or settlement construction. Palestinians hold onto what is left of their homeland, even though it is beginning to look like a piece of Swiss cheese. Palestinians are left to live in the holes cut off from each other while Israel controls all the areas in between. To Israelis, Palestine is Israel, and to Palestinians, Israel is Palestine. They are one and the same. *What is the secret to keeping the land whole so the suffering stops?*

Sham is two months old when her grandfather Opa comes to visit in honor of me defending my dissertation proposal for my doctorate at UW–Madison. It is scheduled, in fact, on my birthday, September 12. But the morning of September 11, 2001, Opa, Nasser, and I witness the news reporting live that one of the World Trade Center towers in New York City is on fire. The newscasters are scrambling for information, not sure how to interpret what they are seeing. We all stare at the screen in disbelief. *What is happening?* They report a plane crashed into it. Smoke is billowing out of the side of the North Tower.

As we struggle to make sense of what just happened, we witness a second plane fly into the other tower and explode. Now, smoke is billowing out from both towers. The images shift to chaos in the streets, smoke and dust gushing around corners, broken glass, people fleeing for their lives, and from a distance, people jumping out of the windows in the hope they will survive. Then we hear reports of a plane crashing into the Pentagon and another plane crashing in a field. *Was it meant for the White House?* And then, right before our eyes, one tower collapses, then the other, sinking down as if the earth is swallowing them whole. My heart crumbles with the weight of the rubble filling the streets of New York City, now in a state of emergency.

Scheduled to defend my dissertation proposal the next day, I am not sure I can focus but decide not to cancel. I review my main argument that Palestinian universities have been vehicles of social and political change, but I cannot escape the images of the sinking towers and soot-covered faces. All evidence of the disaster points to the Middle East, and I am presenting on Palestine.

At the start of my defense, my professors want my take on the Twin Towers attack, which I sum up as anger toward the West in general and America in particular for failing to address long-standing grievances in the Middle East. Maybe this attack will serve as a wake-up call for the US and even lead to some shift in American policy that can pave the way to peace and prosperity for the region. Achieving peace in the Middle East is a tall order, so I am relieved when we manage to shift our focus to my dissertation proposal.

Two hours go by, and I pass my defense. I have the green light to write my dissertation. My mind is racing with excitement to launch this next and final phase of my doctoral studies so I can share my findings with the world.

Nasser is busy working on making his own contribution. In the wake of 9/11, and with heightened tension in Israel and Palestine, Nasser drafts a peace plan he calls "Proposal for an Alternative Configuration in Palestine-Israel." The following spring, he connects with students on campus, who organize a number of events to raise awareness about the situation in Palestine, including a lecture by Israeli historian Ilan Pappé. Nasser establishes the

Alternative Palestinian Agenda as a platform for his vision for peace, which receives the endorsement of Dr. Haidar Abdel Shafi, who founded the Red Crescent Society and also served in a number of leadership roles, including as leader of the Palestinian delegation to the Madrid Peace Conference in 1991.

In the midst of these events, Israel launches Operation Defensive Shield, during which it reoccupies Palestinian cities with tanks and armored vehicles, reducing the new road to Jenin that Nasser's mother celebrated only a few years ago to crumbled asphalt. In response to the large number of Palestinians who snuck across the Green Line to conduct suicide missions, particularly from the Jenin Refugee Camp, the Israeli army bulldozes vast areas of the camp after 10 days of intense fighting in what will come to be known as the Battle of Jenin. Refugees of the Jenin Camp—who already lost their land, their homes, and their livelihood when they were driven out of their original homes in Haifa and surrounding areas in 1948—are once again forced to live in UN tents until their destroyed or severely damaged concrete block homes can be rebuilt. The widespread devastation in the camp that renders thousands homeless is also a form of collective punishment to this community of refugees who dared to challenge the occupation of their homeland. Less than a decade after the signing of the Oslo Accords, Israel also bombs the entire infrastructure of the Palestinian Authority, including the airport in Gaza, which was only completed in 1998.

Our attention is shifting. Having sold our restaurant, the Shish Café, to a family from Syria, Nasser and I have one last fling with the restaurant business on campus with Café Sham in a building slated for demolition within the year, though we continue selling roasted almonds, crêpes, and smoothies at festivals and art shows in the summer.

By the fall of 2002, Nasser begins his doctorate in anthropology at UW–Madison, hoping it will help him advance his peace proposal. As he gains support for his vision, we organize a workshop in Madison and invite a cross-section of Palestinian society to attend to get their input on the plan. I am thrilled that Nasser and I are working together to make a difference in Palestine. We are both students again, just like when we first met, and yet now, we are presenting a vision for Palestine and Israel to the world. *What more could I hope for?* However, as much sense as this vision made for the future of Palestine and Israel to move toward a shared future, it would only be a matter of time for us to realize that vision alone cannot lift Israel's shadow.

In 2002, our daughter Sham turns one, and the State of Israel seizes yet more of her Sidi's land, the land where we hoped to build a house someday. The olive and almond trees are uprooted in order to build the Separation Fence. I can't imagine the trees are gone, that Sham will not see them, that we will never again get to pick almonds and crack them open with nearby stones in the afternoon sun, nor see the *surou* trees standing tall. I can't imagine a border fence in their place. It is as if a piece of Palestine has been obliterated, uprooted, though its people remain steadfast.

I wonder what the Israeli bulldozer drivers felt when they dragged those trees out of the earth, ripping them from the only land they ever knew, severing them from the soil, their life source that would have enabled them to bear fruit for generations to come. Perhaps it felt noble being part of a project to achieve greater security for Israel. Perhaps it was simply a job to do before heading home for dinner, just another day.

As when I did my fieldwork, Nasser travels to Palestine alone to conduct interviews for his dissertation on Palestinians who voluntarily engaged in martyrdom operations—the *istishhadiyin*. When he comes back home, he pulls two bulky packages out of his suitcase wrapped in black plastic bags, one clearly heavier than the other. He carefully unwraps the heavier one to reveal an opaque plastic jar with a white lid. Through the milky white jar, I see the deep-green hue of olive oil.

Nasser's eyes lift to meet mine, his gaze intense. He looks right through me as he tells me it's the last oil from that land with the olive and almond trees. My whole body tightens as my eyes fight back the pooling of tears in silence. My eyes stare at the jar, but all I can see are the trees firmly rooted in the soil. My brow tightens as I gaze at the wide jar in his hands like the remains of a dead body brought home from war. The trees didn't survive this war. This container holds all that is left of them. He pulls out the other bag and carefully opens it to reveal almonds from the trees still in their sun-roasted shells. *The last harvest.*

"What about the *surou*?" I am hopeful that at least the tall, narrow evergreens survived this assault. Nasser confirms that they destroyed everything. Not a single tree remains.

The next morning, Nasser heats a loaf of crusty sourdough bread. He opens the jar and pours some of the rich, green oil into a shallow bowl, then sprinkles salt, which quickly dissipates into the thick liquid. My eyes sink into the bowl. Nasser breaks off a piece of the steaming bread, dividing it in two, and hands one to me. I take a deep breath as we take turns dipping the warm bread into the gleaming oil. I watch how the bread drinks the oil, let it drip for a moment, tap it on the edge of the bowl, then place it in my mouth. The pungent taste of this last harvest awakens every taste bud. I cannot help but think of the trees, of the summers we ate almonds on that land. I chew slowly, savoring every bite, not wanting to swallow, as if the trees would truly vanish even from memory if the olive-soaked bread disappeared into my stomach.

Eating that oil feels like both an honor and a surrender. We got to eat from the last harvest, but knowing Israel won the war, at least that part of the war. Israel destroyed the trees, took the land, and for what? A fence. No one in the village could stop them. Not even the trees could stop them. They had to surrender, both the people and the trees. Now, the trees live on in our memory, in our bodies. *We are the trees.*

33

Rachel Corrie

All the years I traveled to Palestine, I was aware of my privilege as an American. I know the Israeli army can detain or kill Palestinians without consequences, but I have never worried that anything could happen to me. I am an American citizen, and by extension, I am Israel's benefactor. *I am untouchable.* It is this belief that lets my eyes lock onto those of the soldiers at checkpoints, gives me the courage to demand the soldiers open the road when it's closed, keeps me committed to holding the State of Israel accountable for land confiscations, harassment of Palestinians, violations of human rights and international law. *My privilege is my protection.*

When I first hear of Rachel Corrie's death in Gaza, I am in disbelief. Aware of her own privilege as a White American, Rachel attempted to make a dent in the injustice in Palestine until her life was cut short in Gaza. *A European-American girl in her twenties run over by an Israeli bulldozer. It can't be true. Israel wouldn't dare kill a Westerner, especially not an American.* The Israelis crossed the line and plowed through her veil of protection. Rachel is dead. My belief is shattered with her death.

I learn Rachel went to Gaza to protest the demolition of homes in Rafah, that she put her body between a Palestinian home and the bulldozer, and that the bulldozer ran right over her. That was March 16, 2003, just days before the outbreak of the Iraq War.[104] Officially, the Israeli army was conducting a military operation to demolish Palestinian homes, seize weapons, and locate smuggling tunnels across the border with Egypt. Rachel and seven other International Solidarity Movement (ISM) activists were engaged in nonviolent direct action to protest the home demolitions when one of two bulldozers involved in the operation ran over her and killed her.

I recall seeing the border in Rafah when I was in Gaza in 1986. It was then that the director of Save the Children showed me the beginnings of a water treatment facility buried in the sand. I saw the way families, separated by the border, called to each other across the fence. Now, Israel has started an operation to bulldoze homes in Rafah, allegedly to give a wider buffer on the border with Egypt, similar in principle to the clearing of the Lebanese border areas in 1948, but instead of whole villages, houses were the targets. The people of Rafah lost their homes and their dignity. Rachel lost her life.

Rachel's parents' lives are shattered with her death. A further slap in the face are the disappointing outcomes of a series of investigations and court cases from 2005 through 2015, culminating in Israeli Supreme Court hearings that absolve the Israeli military of any guilt or violation of human rights. The Supreme Court deems her death an unfortunate accident and claims the driver of the bulldozer could not have seen her. Moreover, the court rules that the Israeli military cannot be held accountable for violations of human rights because the incident took place during wartime. Nasser's father's words ring in my ears. *The war is not over.*

Despite Rachel's parents' frustration over the lack of justice for their daughter's death, they carry Rachel's message forward through the establishment of the Rachel Corrie Foundation for Peace & Justice.[105] I recall my time in Gaza, where I witnessed the hardship of living there, the heavy Israeli military presence that rode past my window and nearly got my brother shot on the beach. I recall my own experience of standing up to the army to open the road closed for shooting practice. *Could that have been me? My brother? How will I respond the next time I come face to face with the Israeli army?*

34

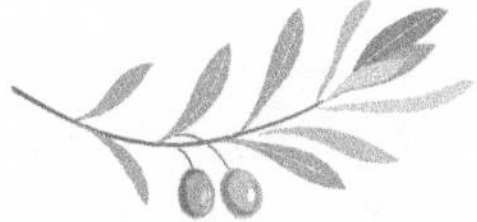

Opportunities

While working on my dissertation, a number of opportunities come up that increase my involvement in education, both at home and abroad. First, in the fall of 2003, I interview for a position as a diversity officer for the University of Wisconsin System Administration and get the job. I am thrilled to be working to increase access for underrepresented groups among students and faculty alike across the entire state of Wisconsin. Later that year, Ismael Abu-Saad, one of the Palestinians who attended our Alternative Palestinian Agenda workshop in Madison, invites Nasser and me to a conference he is hosting at Ben-Gurion University of the Negev the following summer in his capacity there as a professor of education.

After I give a paper presentation on "Making Space for Democracy: Palestinian Universities and Democratic Transformation in Palestine" at the Center for International Education Society (CIES) conference in Salt Lake City, Utah, the following spring, a professor from the Technical University in Dresden, Germany invites me to participate in a Peace Education Symposium that summer in Dresden. What an opportunity to not only be part of bringing people together around the Israeli-Palestinian conflict but in Dresden, of all places, the first East German city I ever visited just prior to my junior year abroad in Freiburg back in 1985. I accept the invitation, where I will be the only "outsider" who is neither Jewish, Palestinian, nor Israeli. The professor is hopeful my perspective will help build bridges around the theme of peace.

Meanwhile, Nasser is back in Palestine organizing farmers into the Palestine Fair Trade Association he established along with an export company for olive oil under the name Canaan Fair Trade. The price of olive oil had sunk so low that farmers were opting to work as day laborers in Israel to make ends meet.[106] He applies the same principles he learned about from fair trade coffee shops in Madison to the olive oil sector in Palestine to help farmers earn a living wage so they can support their livelihood from farming as their forefathers did for millennia.

Nasser also develops relationships with companies to support his effort, including Dr. Bronner's Magic Soaps, which helps Nasser secure organic certification so he can sell the farmers' products at a premium. Through the export company, he commits to purchase olives from small-scale Palestinian farmers to sell on the global market to socially conscious companies and consumers. So instead of farmers giving up on farming or selling their olive oil at rock-bottom prices to Israeli companies that market it as an Israeli product, the fruits of their labor are making it onto the shelf around the world as a product of Palestine.

Nasser also establishes women's cooperatives to create artisan Palestinian products traditionally produced by women, such as olive oil soap, sun-dried tomatoes, za'atar, and hand-rolled maftoul, like I made with Nasser's mother years ago. Working in these cooperatives gives women a greater voice in their communities and enables them to contribute to their family's income. It also gives the world access to delicious Palestinian specialties usually only enjoyed by Palestinians in their homes.

While Nasser is in Palestine, I manage to finish my dissertation and distribute it to my committee in time for the 2004 spring graduation, but I am met with requests for revisions that I simply don't have time to finish before I leave for Germany. I have a big summer ahead of me and thought I would have my dissertation behind me and my PhD in hand. Unfortunately, I have to set it aside and revisit my revisions in the fall when we are back in the States.

Canaan, now 11, plans to participate in a summer science program at UW–Madison, so he and Nasser will meet up with Karmel, Sham, and me in Germany so we can travel together in Europe after my symposium. It is a perfect plan. It is July 2004, my first time back in Germany since I spent the year there in 1989. The two Israelis are from the same university, though one lives on a settlement in the West Bank. One of the Palestinians works at an Israeli university and the other at a Palestinian university in Jerusalem. We each present a paper on prospects for peace in Israel and Palestine, followed by discussions facilitated by our host.

It is my first experience meeting a settler. *I am befriending the enemy.* We believe our friendship is no accident. It is necessary. Through our connection, Jenin now holds a special place in her heart, and I can associate a face and a name to a settler. Our friendship pushes the envelope on our understanding of space and community. She lives behind a security fence, self-imposed to protect her settlement from her enemy—the surrounding Palestinians who want nothing more than for her and her community to disappear. I have witnessed firsthand how Israeli security translates into the loss of yet more Palestinian land.

Here we are in Germany, my father's homeland, the very place that carried out the Holocaust that enabled Israel to be born as a nation. I am a German American whose life path has made Palestine personal, and she is an Israeli Jewish settler of German ancestry. We know it is challenging to meet in that contentious space. There is no neutral ground. I cannot ethically or logistically go to her home on a settlement, and as a settler, she cannot safely travel to Jenin, so our meeting place becomes our academic conferences. We dream of creating some academic work out of our story, but we never do find enough common ground to make that intention a reality. Perhaps there is still too much space between us. I am not sure how to narrow that divide.

At the symposium, the five of us become a community just the same. We walk the streets of Dresden in our free time. I serve as their tour guide since none of them have ever been there before or speak German. They get to see the former East German city of Dresden through my eyes. As we walk among the still blackened and only partially renovated palaces, churches, and museums of the Old City, then across the bridge to the New City with its broad pedestrian zone lined with shops and restaurants, I am bridging the past with the present in my mind. My German life is merging with my Palestinian life. I even get to visit the first East German family I met back in 1985, their Russian Lada replaced by a black Mercedes sedan now that two Germanys have become one. *Will Palestine and Israel ever become one?*

After Nasser and I travel through Europe with Canaan, Karmel, and Sham that summer of 2004, including visiting my father in Munich, where he has been living since he retired from the university, we fly to Jordan. It is our first time traveling to Palestine through Jordan. It is also Sham's first trip to Palestine. Previously, we always traveled to Palestine via Tel Aviv, but now that Canaan and Karmel are residents of the West Bank, they are no longer allowed to travel through Tel Aviv without a *tasrih*, or permit. Applying for a tasrih can be a lengthy process with no guarantee of getting one. Even if we got one, we would need another tasrih to return to the airport to go back to the States since they are only valid for one day. Traveling through Jordan has its own complications of having to stay overnight and pay extra fees to both the Jordanians and the Israelis to cross the Allenby Bridge into the West Bank, but the advantage is that we get to visit Nasser's sister Naziha in Amman.

Naziha's eldest son Abdullah picks us up at the airport, approaching us with long, quick strides and dressed in a long-sleeved white cotton robe with a thin white crocheted skull cap on his head. His full beard distracts me from his kind eyes. I have never met any of Naziha's sons because they all live in Jordan and are not allowed to travel to Palestine until they are over 50, presumably since at that age they are too old to fight for their homeland. I have only met Naziha's daughter Nadia, who lives in Jalameh through marriage. Naziha can no longer travel to Palestine. The last time she visited was during the Second Intifada. Because of all the unrest, roads were blocked, and the bridge to Jordan was closed, so she was not able to go back to Jordan and overstayed the time limit on her tasrih—her permit to enter the West Bank. Ever since then, Israel has not issued her a tasrih. Now, she is like a refugee, barred from her homeland.

We arrive at a quiet residential street with one- and two- story stone houses, square with flat rooftops situated on a steep hill. A young girl sees us pull up and runs down some stairs out of sight. Abdullah carries some of our luggage across the entranceway, a bridge that leads to a large wooden door. "*Yama! Wasalu dar Nasser!*—Mama, Nasser's family is here!

Naziha appears in the doorway and reaches for Nasser's shoulders. *Kifak, ya Nasser?*—How are you, Nasser? She then takes my hands and kisses both cheeks. *Ahlan wa sahlan, ya Christa! Ahlan wa sahlan, ya Im Kana'an!*—Welcome, Christa! Welcome, mother of Canaan! She greets Canaan and Karmel, then Sham, who clings to me, hiding her face in my neck.

Naziha looks the same to me with her smooth skin over high cheekbones, like her mother. She invites us into the modest living room, where her husband is sitting on a brown velvet sofa dozing in front of an older TV. He opens his eyes as we enter the room. His sleepy eyes now alert, he rises to his feet as we each greet him. No sooner does he greet us than he seems tired, as if all his energy is sinking into the sofa. I don't know this is the last time I will see him, since he will die of a heart attack just a few years later.

Because Naziha is the eldest of Nasser's 10 surviving siblings, her children are close to our age, even though they are Nasser's nieces and nephews. In fact, it turns out her son Abdullah and I were both born in 1967—*sanat al-harb*—the year of the war, as I always say, referring to the Six-Day War when Israel occupied the rest of Palestine. Like Nasser's eldest brother, Ghazi, who was also born in the year of a war, in 1948, during Israel's War of Independence, the year that Palestine was wiped off the map. *Both born in a cave.*

Abdullah's wife Maysoun appears in the doorway and greets me like a long-lost sister with several rounds of kisses on both cheeks, then invites us into the next room to eat from a large platter of chicken and yellow rice laced with peas, carrots, and raisins. *Kabseh*, she calls it, is a dish famous in the Arabian Gulf region, along with tiny bowls of Arabic salad. The colorful mix of tiny cubes of tomatoes and cucumber, chopped onion, and parsley makes me feel right at home. Tired and hungry, we gladly sit down on large mats around an abundant display of steaming food. The tangy salad perks up my spirits, and the delicate spices in the rice and chicken warm my soul.

After dinner, several older boys take Canaan and Karmel to play outside. It has been nearly five years since I spent the year with our sons in Palestine, so they have lost most of their Arabic, but they all seem to communicate just fine with gestures and a mix of English and Arabic. Sham and I visit with Maysoun. One of her daughters appears in the doorway, close in age to Sham. They connect even without speaking and disappear into another room to play. In the privacy of her own home, Maysoun leaves her shiny jet-black hair uncovered, the long, layered curls extending down her back. When she places her hand on her belly, I realize she has another child on the way. While we talk, she remains fully attentive to her young children, her movements quick but smooth, full of energy, as if her feet aren't even touching the floor.

With the children busy playing, she invites me into the diwan which is a large room with a high ceiling elegantly furnished with old-world flair: leather cushions, brass platters, carved wooden trays and tables covered with glass, heavy wood-framed upholstered chairs and sofas, like a queen's chamber. Sheer curtains in gold thread and heavy velvet drapes cover the walls floor to ceiling. She explains most of the furnishing are from trips to Syria she and Abdullah have taken, always bringing back treasures from the traditional markets. Her eyes brighten when I tell her Nasser and I hope to go someday with our children so they experience an independent Arab country and the rich culture of the region instead of the soldiers and checkpoints of Israeli occupation. Unfortunately, we never make it before the war breaks out in Syria years later.

We feast on roasted nuts with juice, and the girls appear like butterflies just in time for black tea laced with sage. The girls flutter away as Abdullah's wife insists on making me Arabic coffee, so I follow her to the kitchen. The rest of the house is lined with traditional cotton mats like in Jalameh. The children run about, dodging clothes and bedding, along with a few plastic toys for the youngest among them. I stand in the doorway of her kitchen while she makes coffee, then we return to the diwan. Sitting on the stately armchairs reserved only for guests, I feel like a princess. As we sip coffee laced with cardamom, she radiates with happiness, and I with gratitude, to know this devoted wife, loving mother, and new friend.

While Nasser and I and the kids are in Jordan, we take an excursion to the desert of Wadi Rum and the ancient city of Petra that my father visited the year he came to Palestine, as well as Aqaba on the Red Sea, our chance to be tourists in the Middle East. We all have our first camel ride—so much higher than a horse! Getting onto these somewhat awkward beasts is one thing when it is kneeling on the ground, but it is especially unsettling how it leans back and then forward to get on its feet and then does the same in reverse to lower itself to the ground so we can get back off, hanging on for dear life. Our guide leads us through a deep valley scattered with foliage in an otherwise desolate rocky landscape. The camels' wide, soft feet make the ride smooth and cushioned like a Cadillac. They keep a steady but slow pace, and yet we cover quite a bit of ground during our 90-minute excursion due to their long legs. The ride is calming and clearly the best way to travel across such uneven terrain. Nasser and I laugh when Karmel falls in love with these giant creatures, declaring his intention to someday have one as a pet.

In Wadi Rum, we rent a 4x4 truck and head out into the desert, the roads hardly distinguishable from the vast sandy landscape. It doesn't take long before our wheels are embedded in the soft sand, leaving us stranded in the middle of nowhere. No amount of trying to go forward or backward gets the vehicle to move other than deeper into the sand. Fortunately, a local man drives by and offers to help. No sooner does he fiddle with the controls than the vehicle jets forward, as if the sand has turned to concrete, noting we didn't have it set to four-wheel drive. We thank him profusely and carry on with our adventure, occasionally stopping to climb colossal boulders with jagged cliffs protruding out of the ground like spaceships that crash-landed in the otherwise reddish sandscape.

The hidden city of Petra is like a treasure hunt. We walk for some time in a deep crevice like a split in the mountain from an earthquake. The entire length of it has canals carved into the side of the towering mountain walls that used to bring fresh water to the city, still out of sight. Finally, the split opens to an elaborate façade carved right into the mountain. We enter a doorway to find entire rooms carved out of the mountain, these cool, damp, and dark spaces offering relief from the dry heat and bright sun outside. I try to imagine this hidden city thriving in its prime, the only way in or out back through the narrow split in the mountain.

Traveling farther south, we know we have arrived in Aqaba when the high-rise hotels and the Red Sea come into view. Unfortunately, when we venture out in the morning, it is cloudy and quite windy, so we can't see much of the coral reef from the tiny glass-bottom boat. With the weather too cold to swim in the sea, we opt for the indoor hotel pool instead.

We spend a final night with Naziha back in Amman before making our way to the bridge the next morning, gathering in the front hall to say our goodbyes. I wonder how difficult this crossing will be. The questioning can be lengthy, and sometimes Palestinians are strip-searched. The bridge can close for no reason, leaving people in transit for hours, if not days.

When we arrive at the bridge, Abdullah shows our IDs and gives up our luggage, an area of buses visible in the distance that remind me of the city buses in Detroit from the 1970s with their rounded, tight metal seats and no AC, before they were redesigned into larger sleek buses with tinted windows. The windows are open, but the air is already hot and dusty, and there is no breeze. As the bus begins to move, we enter a closed area, fences on both sides, just a narrow dusty road, a passageway between two adjacent lands.

Geographically, the Jordan River separates Jordan from the West Bank, and yet the river is nowhere to be seen. The bus drives slowly, and the heat builds up quickly in the tight space. Time seems to stand still as we creep along in this no man's land. We only travel a short distance before the bus stops, and we are all instructed to get off. We gather our hand luggage and follow the other passengers to a narrow passageway that corrals us into a line. Standing in the hot sun, I wonder where we are, since we don't appear to be anywhere. Clearly, we aren't there yet. The only shade is when we reach the officials standing under a metal overhang, between them and us, a simple table where we set our things and answer questions.

Once we present our passports to the Jordanian border officials, who authorize our exit from Jordan, we are instructed to get on a different bus, where we wait for all the passengers to go through the checkpoint, the heat building like a sauna. When the bus finally starts to move, it is only minutes before it stops again, and we are instructed to get off. Another line, another corral, only this time we are met with Israeli soldiers armed with M16s, who control the border between Jordan and the West Bank. A series of questions follow. *How long were you in Jordan? Where are you going? How long will you stay there? Who packed your bags? Were they in your possession since you packed them? Are you carrying anything for anyone else?*

The heat of the sun is relentless. After such an exhausting journey, this piece is the most difficult of all. I have to remain strong for my children and keep them following the protocol of the crossing so we pass without incident. *I want these borders to disappear.* We get on yet another bus, the heat becoming unbearable now. No breeze. The intensity of the sun, combined with the frustrated bodies packed in the bus, is dizzying. I feel like I could faint from suffocation or exhaustion or both. Canaan is holding up well, but Karmel stares into the heat in a daze, and Sham wilts in my arms like a rose without water. My mouth begins to dry up like the desert. All I can offer them are empty words of encouragement. Our water bottles are nearly empty, and the end is nowhere in sight.

We get onto the next bus, which also only drives forward for a few minutes. I keep looking out of the dusty window, trying to spot the river. I want to know when we actually cross the bridge itself. Finally, I see a narrow, virtually dried-up rocky depression in the earth below with only a trickle of water running through it. A few sparse, scraggly bushes are growing along the banks. *Is this the Jordan River?* I wonder how Jesus was baptized here. There is no water to stand in. All the stories of this place seem to fall like a house of cards as I peer at this pitiful river through the metal fence. The narrow strip of brush along the riverbanks seems as tired and thirsty as we are. The bridge itself is unremarkable. I barely notice we are on it had I not spotted the river below. Nothing prominent to mark our passage from here to there.

Again, the bus stops. When Canaan asks me why we have to keep getting off the bus, I tell him, so that we won't want to come back. *Isn't that what the Israelis want? For Palestinians to leave and never come back?* This time when the bus stops, we are met by officials from the Palestinian Authority (PA) since we are now entering Area A of Jericho. Their uniforms are too new, too crisp, the checkpoint a mockery. I know the PA only administers the area because Israel has allowed this new layer of authority to emerge to manage the occupation, not for the autonomy of the Palestinians. My disdain is hard to hide, but at least we are one step closer to leaving this area of territorial posturing. At last, we are through. We have crossed into Palestine.

35

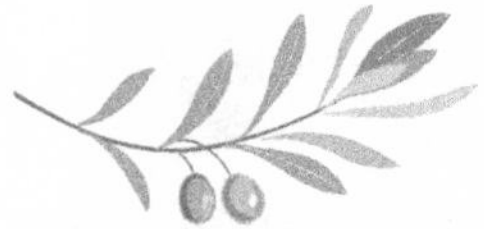

The Wall

One of the first things I do when Nasser, Canaan, Karmel, Sham, and I reach Jalameh in July 2004 is ask to see the fence Israel built as part of its Separation Barrier along the Green Line (see Map 11). I want to see what has become of Nasser's family's land with the olive and almond trees. Nasser's nephew Mahmoud eagerly volunteers to take us since he also lost land with its construction. Before we see the fence, he proudly shows us his plastic hamamot greenhouse adjacent to the Green Line, where he is cultivating *yuqtin*, the same squash Ibtisam's mother was growing in Kabul, only by a different name.

We walk down the lush green rows of yuqtin, which dead-end at a barbed-wire barrier, the neat rows torn like a shred of paper, edges ruffled. Above the barrier is a large red sign with bold white letters written in Hebrew, Arabic, and English: MORTAL DANGER—MILITARY ZONE—ANY PERSON WHO PASSES OR DAMAGES THIS FENCE ENDANGERS HIS LIFE. Mahmoud explains how Israel took 18 dunums of his land to build the fence the previous year.

The pressure in my head builds as I scan the landscape in search of Sidi's land with the olive and almond trees. I am sickened by the thought that our wish to build our house there someday is no longer possible. *If the olive oil makes it to us in a black bag, what would have become of us?* All I see beyond the tangled maze of barbed wire is a deep, wide ditch along the fence like a gouge in my heart. That life-sustaining piece of land passed down from generation to generation has carved out a place in my heart, but Israel ripped it right out of me. Even though it is destroyed, I can still see it. A ditch and a fence lie in its place, but I can still feel it. The trees are gone, but I can still taste their fruit. I could be shot dead if I try to go there, but I will not forget it.

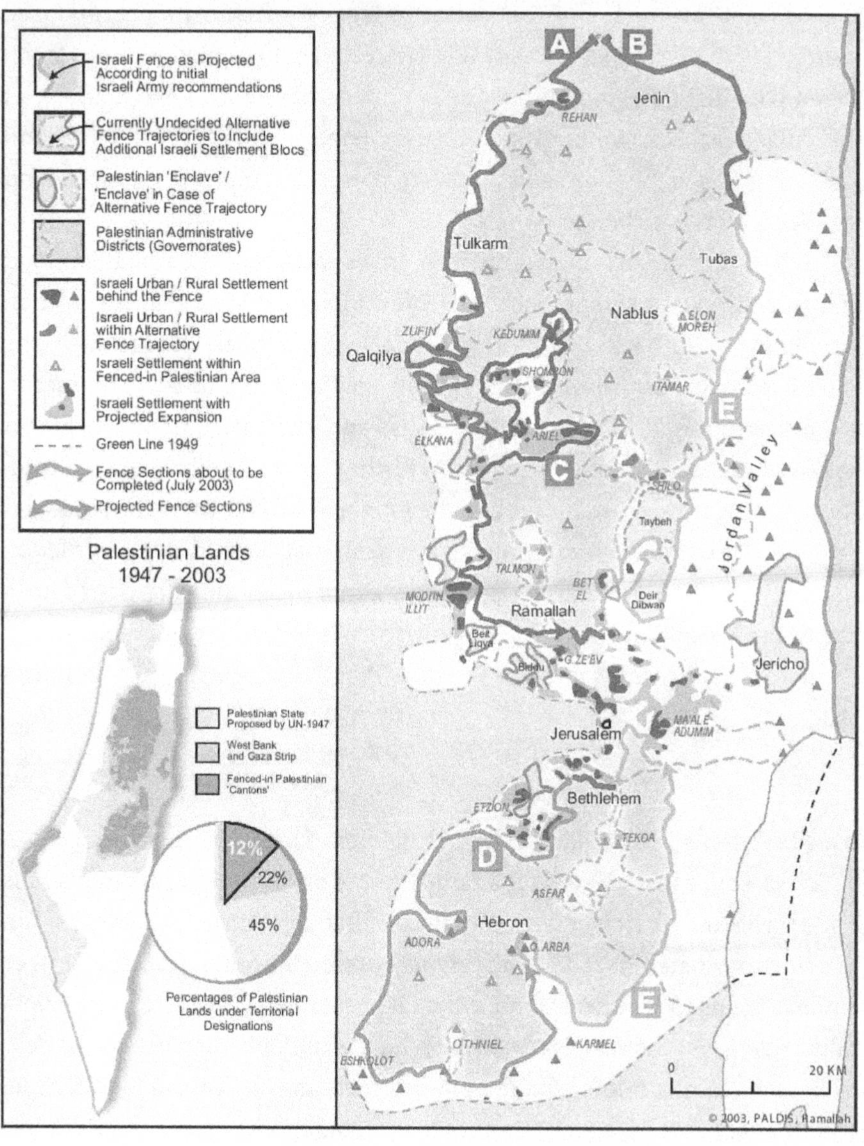

Map 11: Israel's Separation Barrier – The Wall as Planned, 2002 (Source: PASSIA)

We walk along the barbed wire. The land slopes downward, revealing the immensity of the ditch, the fence just beyond it, and a dirt road that follows the perimeter of the fence where the Israeli army patrols the border. The whole contraption extends as far as the eye can see, cutting through the open landscape like a steel centipede, the tangled knots of barbed wire its legs. In Palestine, they call centipedes—*arba'in*—"forties," but this one has not hundreds but thousands of legs. We follow its path, the red rooftops of the Israeli settlement Gan Ner visible in the distance across the Green Line just past Sidi's land. The centipede has swallowed yet more of the village lands in its path, a deliberate Israeli move known as a "land grab" that has created a "seam zone" to confiscate more Palestinian land for "security measures."[107]

In the distance, an Israeli army Jeep drives toward us, stirring up a cloud of dust behind it. As it approaches, Hebrew blares over a loudspeaker. Then Arabic. *Irja'*—Go back. We stare at the Jeep through the barbed wire, the gaping ditch and fence separating us. The soldier warns us several times to go back. Mahmoud turns toward his house and invites us to come inside for coffee. No sense in antagonizing them further, or we could all end up dead. I am burning inside. I stare through the jungle of barbed wire. The land with the olive and almond trees would have been just beyond it. Even the tall *surou* trees are no more. Now, only my memory tells me where they once stood. I think of Sidi's words. He was right. We will never build our house on that land. *The war is not over.*

Long before his death, Nasser's father planned for each of his four sons to build his house in a line near the family home on Tariq Burqin, the road his bride traveled to their wedding, a marriage that bore him 12 children. So far, the older brothers Ghazi and Faisal have built their homes. Nasser's brother Jamal takes us to his plot of land, which he has filled with young date palms called *nakhl*. On the way, we walk past the area outside the kitchen window of Nasser's family home, where I planted flowers with Canaan and Karmel and their cousins back in 1999, now full of young olive trees. I couldn't ask for a better view from the window! We arrive at the young palms spaced out across Jamal's land in rows, as if waiting to walk in formation for a village parade, their fan-like leaves at eye level waving at us in the soft breeze. One day, they will tower over us.

I joke with Jamal that once they produce dates, we can make *ka'ak* for the Eid from his dates instead buying date paste from the market. These date-filled cookies have the same name as the bread I ate with Salem in Jaffa, known by its full name *ka'akit il-Quds*—literally "Jerusalem cake." Jamal guarantees me a lifetime supply, and we all laugh. It will be another five years before Jamal builds his home on this land and Nasser another nine years on the lot next to him. Then, all four brothers will have fulfilled their father's dream of living adjacent to each other as neighbors. Perhaps there, they will be less vulnerable, even if the war is not over.

The occupation is starting to feel permanent, like no matter what I or anyone else does, Palestine will only exist in Israel's shadow. But as I gaze at Jamal's date palms, I wonder if living on what is left of the land allows Nasser's family and village to remain anchored here as the next generation while holding onto the memory of what was lost. This deep commitment to living on the land, being Palestinian, is what is known as *sumoud. Is that my contribution? To witness life here so I can share it with others, shine light on Palestine to prove it is real, still exists? Is that enough?*

Following the Israeli incursion on the Jenin Refugee Camp in April 2002, a special cemetery was established to honor the *shahid,* those who sacrificed their lives for Palestine. I ask Nasser to take me there. As we pass through the camp, Nasser points out damaged homes and whole areas that remain flattened from the incursion. It reminds me of the neighborhood I visited in Haifa, where homes that once stood became rubble or open spaces of a once thriving neighborhood, perhaps the very neighborhood where some of these refugees' parents or grandparents once lived.

We enter the cemetery through an opening in the fence. It feels like a private garden with young trees scattered throughout, providing cooling relief from the hot sun. White stone graves are neatly arranged next to each other on both sides of the narrow path. As we walk forward, we find clusters of graves aligned along the fence off the main path. I can't help but notice the dates listed on the graves, all so recent—fresh graves from the past few years. I do the math in my head and realize these are the children born after the First Intifada in the 1980s, born into an uprising, dead in the second uprising of the Al-Aqsa Intifada. I pause and look around me, trying to make sense of the loss.

Later, my mother tells me that someone at her church gave her a CD about the Freedom Theater in the Jenin Refugee Camp, and she sends it to me. The founder of the theater, Arna Mer-Khamis, was a Jewish woman committed to defending human rights. The theater was destroyed during the incursion in 2002, then later rebuilt to carry on her legacy to provide access to the arts for underprivileged youth.[108] I wonder at her courage to reach out to the Palestinians and create hope and friendship in the camp through theater. Despite all this destruction, I, too, remain hopeful, determined to move the situation in Israel and Palestine toward a more hopeful future.

I wonder what insights the upcoming conference on marginalized peoples at Ben-Gurion University of the Negev will bring. It is a long drive, but I look forward to seeing the organizer of the conference, our dear friends Ismael Abu-Saad and Kathy and their children, who have visited us in Madison several times since Kathy is from Wisconsin.

When Nasser and I leave with Canaan, Karmel, and Sham for the conference, we head south to Ramallah. We will need to pass through the Kalandia checkpoint on foot because we cannot drive our car with white license plates in Israel, then get a rental car from East Jerusalem with yellow license plates so we can continue on our way to the conference.

As we approach the checkpoint and search for a place to park, the road suddenly dead ends. Before us is the Wall towering over us. What Israel calls the Separation Barrier stands literally in the middle of the street. We must either turn left or right. We turn left, only to find that farther ahead, the Wall ends. As we approach the end, we realize the Wall is in the process of being built before our very eyes. We pull over and get out of the car.

I am stunned at the unfolding of events before me. There, right in front of me, a road is becoming a wall. To my right, the segments are already in place, anchored together as one contiguous stretch of concrete that continues into the distance. Just behind the end of the Wall, the segments are being unloaded from a huge flatbed truck onto the street, then lifted into place by crane.

The Wall is being built right before my eyes, the separation of communities being set in stone—or rather concrete—in real time. The Berlin Wall was put up in the middle of the night, so people awoke to a new reality. But this wall is being constructed—one segment of concrete at a time—in broad daylight.

I walk across the still-invisible line, where the Wall will soon cut the town of Al-Ram off from the rest of Jerusalem (see Map 12). There, on the other side I find a flatbed with prefabricated segments in full view, like a toy truck with blocks on it, awaiting a child to put the pieces in place, set the sections neatly next to each other so his mother can praise him for aligning them just right. But these are no blocks, and this is no child's play.

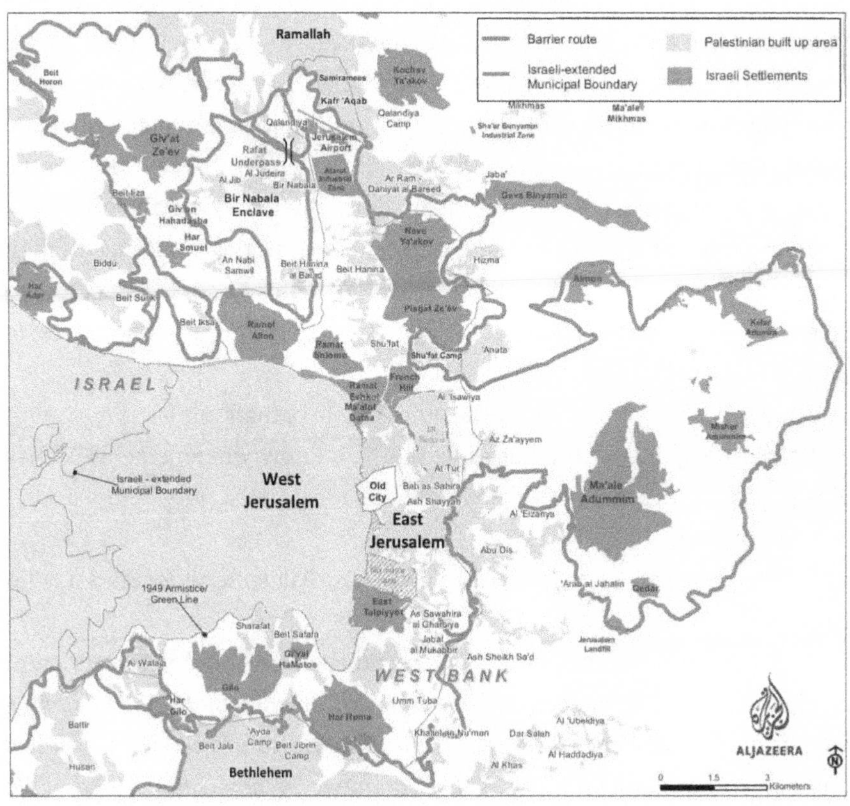

Map 12: Israel's Separation Barrier – The Wall in Jerusalem Vicinity (Source: Al Jazeera)

I am baffled at how Palestinians are walking around, going on with their day, as if nothing is happening, and yet their lives are being redefined one slab of concrete at a time. The Wall creates sides, borders, more restrictions on access, more confiscation of land.[109] My stomach turns as I witness this crude vision of security become reality. One people's security, another's confinement. Gaza is already an outdoor prison. Now, the isolation of the West Bank behind concrete walls and electric fences is taking shape in front of me. *Like in Berlin.*

I don't want to witness history, not like this. I lived to see the Berlin Wall come down, only to witness the Israeli Wall go up, right before my eyes. The weight of those concrete slabs presses down on my shoulders. I am as sad for the Israelis, who feel they need a wall to feel safe, as for the Palestinians, who have to live in its shadow. I am sad for my children, who will have to pass through this wall to see the rest of Palestine. I am sad for all the Palestinians already barred from returning to their villages, their fruit trees and olive groves, their treasured cities, the sea. The more Palestinians are confined, the less they can experience their homeland with their own eyes. Palestine becomes something only to imagine, to remember, to dream about, not to set foot on, live, and breathe. Even for those living in the West Bank and Gaza, or in areas that are now Israel, they are all limited to a piece, a corner, and left to imagine the rest. Their stories, their places, their connection to the land are left out of Israel's history books. *Is it still real? Palestine? If my daughter can tell her Sidi's story of the last sesame harvest in 1948, isn't it real?*

Sometimes people ask me, "Palestine. Where is that?"

I always respond with a question. "Do you know where Israel is?" They always provide the same answer.

"Yes, of course."

"Well, then you know where Palestine is. Palestine is Israel. Israel is Palestine."

True and so far from the truth. One and the same, and yet as different as night and day. *When does night become day and day night? Where are the borders in time and space between them? What do you call a place with two names, two peoples, two histories, two languages, many cultures, and world religions?* I am heartbroken to have those wall segments imprinted on my memory. I wonder how many years until those trucks will load the segments back up and take them away to be ground up to make roads, roads that connect the land, not divide it. *Will I get to see the Wall come down? Will I get to remember both its construction and destruction?*

I am tired of checkpoints. It is one thing to cross them as a college student in Berlin, young, optimistic, full of energy and promise. Now, I am tired. I don't want to stand in lines and breathe in the frustration of people unable to get where they need to go, witness the self-righteousness of border guards hiding behind uniforms and M16s. I don't want to wonder when the next clashes between Palestinian youth and Israeli soldiers will break out. I don't want to keep hearing about death and detention. I don't want to witness any more bombings in Gaza, land confiscations, or closed areas. I don't want to stare at olive trees through barbed wire, calling to their owners to trim their branches and harvest their fruit. Those trees that now lie on the other side of the Wall must be lonely that their owners are only allowed to visit them twice a year, once to trim—only once—and once to harvest in a hurried fashion. No lingering to sit beneath their branches. *What is so dangerous about taking care of trees?*

Like inmates in a high-security prison, these trees stand behind the Wall and fences, guarded by soldiers with M16s, who are careful not to let the farmers linger too long lest they have the chance to speak to their trees that hold wisdom and secrets in their roots, that empower, having lived for generations. They know of other times, come and gone. They give hope and promise to a different tomorrow. They remind the farmers not to give up, that one day they will again share the same space. Until then, fear contaminates the Earth, the air, and the eyes. Everyone is squinting, wondering what will happen next, trying to make sense out of senselessness. My head feels like it will explode. No matter how bad things are, I can't stomach a wall. It gets in the way. It blocks my view. It makes life hell. Hell on Earth.

I want to stand in the middle of the road, get in the way of the Wall, block its path, rewrite history, prevent it from being written this way. I know when Palestinians tried to stand in its way, they were shot or thrown in jail. No wonder people are minding their own business, as if just another building is going up to hold offices or apartments. Everyone is walking by without looking, but they know it's there. They can feel its path, as if it's emerging from the earth rather than being shoved into place. They know one day they will fight it, but not today. Today, they have to go to the market, to work, to the doctor, and get their children off to school. But someday, they will tear down that wall, just as the Germans—East and West—tore down the Berlin Wall. One day, the Palestinians, and maybe even the Israelis, will know that day has come, where they will look at it, face it, and destroy it. No one knows what will come once the dust settles, but something else will emerge in its place. Like after a forest fire, plants reemerge, but the landscape is forever changed. New realities will creep over old ones and take shape, inviting us all to begin again.

36

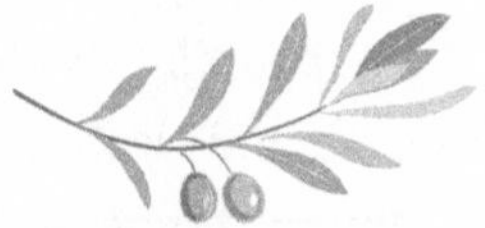

Conference

Nasser and I along with the kids make the long drive through the Naqab Desert to the conference at Ben-Gurion University of the Negev. I am blown away by the numerous contexts represented from around the world. Indigenous researchers from Canada, Alaska, Mexico, South America, and Palestine, as well as others from Israel, Europe, and the United States, are addressing discrimination in their own contexts. We are all united by this common thread, where indigenous peoples the world over face marginalization on their own land. It is the first academic conference I attend where there is no academic hype. Some presenters tell stories rather than present lengthy intellectual arguments. In spite of all the geographic differences, the stories are the same: marginalization, discrimination, incarceration, and dispossession.

The conference is contentious when it comes to Israel and Palestine. The whole mood in the room changes from serene to sharp when some of the Israeli researchers reduce the plight of Palestinians in Israel to one of policy, as if more autonomy over their affairs within the State of Israel is enough to appease the negation of their identity. *Why misrepresent their truth?* Their use of the term "Arab Israelis"—what the State of Israel officially calls the 20 percent of their population who are Palestinians and citizens of Israel—stands in contrast to my own perspective and that of others, who refer to

Palestinians as Palestinians, however fragmented they may be by the events of history that remain unresolved.

The term "Arab Israeli" is further misleading since among Jewish Israelis are the *Mezrahim*—those who immigrated to Israel from Arab countries. Other distinctions include the *Sephardim*, who are descendants of those who lived in the Iberian Peninsula and North Africa during the Islamic era until their expulsion in 1497. Numerous other distinctions are made for Jews from Italy, Georgia, Persia, Yemen, Ethiopia, and other parts of Africa, India, Central Asia, and even China. These communities stand in contrast to the Jews of European origin, who not only founded the Zionist movement but also rule the country, the *Ashkenazim*, who mostly immigrated from France, Germany, and Eastern Europe.

Yet another distinction is made for Jewish Israelis who were born in Israel (or previously in Mandatory Palestine), called *Sabra* after the cactus, ironically the same plant—*saber* in Arabic—that symbolizes rootedness in the land for Palestinians. For Israelis, it has evoked both pride among the native-born and its own discrimination from new Jewish immigrants to Israel, who feel superior to the distinctively acculturated *Sabra*. Understandably, as Jewish immigration to Israel tapers off, an increasingly greater number of Jews are born in Israel. It has become the only place they know to call home.

None of the Israeli researchers discuss any of these distinctions, which would be hugely relevant at a conference on marginalization. After all, *Ashkenazim* are the ruling class of Israel, the majority of whom were incidentally born in Israel. All other groups, including the Palestinians and the guest workers from Southeast Asia, whom Israel imports to do their dirty work as an alternative to Palestinian day laborers from the West Bank and Gaza, each have a rung on the ladder below them.

Thus, the term "Arab Israeli" is not only misleading but also problematic because it reduces the indigenous population of what was once Palestine to minority status in their own homeland, and yet the total population of Jews and Palestinians in the space of historic Palestine, regardless of status, is roughly equal. The Jewish Israelis who live in Jerusalem, the West Bank, and Gaza are counted in Israel's tally, but not the Palestinians who live there. Just because they are not counted doesn't mean they don't exist. Clearly, this selective counting based on an elaborate system of ID cards Israel endows upon Palestinians allows Israel to maintain its illusion of a Jewish majority. This strategy dates back to the start when Jewish militias and the Israeli army successfully emptied half of all Palestinians from their homes back in 1947–1948 during Israel's War of Independence.

Academics, like states, are privileged in that way, experts or rulers that they are, to subjugate others to their own interpretation to be passed off as knowledge and, ultimately, policy. But Palestinians are not plants to be categorized or neatly placed on shelves or ignored altogether, nor are they merely a backdrop to Israeli society or simply part of the landscape to be discussed in the abstract, as Edward Said so pointedly argued in *Orientalism*. They are people who have lived in the region for millennia, whose connection to the land runs as deep as the roots of the saber that can never be obliterated.

I challenge these academics directly in the question-and-answer period on their use of the term "Arab Israeli" when referring to Palestinians in Israel. "How can you call someone other than what they choose to be called? What right do you have to name them?"

"But that's what they are, Arab Israelis."

"Is that what *they* think they are? They are here, some of them. Why don't you ask them? Why don't you listen to their words? I do, and I am neither Palestinian nor Israeli. They are Palestinians, whether they are in the West Bank or Gaza, refugees here or elsewhere, Bedouins in the Naqab or Unrecognized Villages, citizens of the State of Israel or stateless subjects of Israeli occupation."

Silence. Uncomfortable silence. Minorities are not people; they are statistics, topics of makeshift policy as Band-aids to cover up injustice. They lurk in the shadows, and if they dare come out and point to their plight, they will be silenced somehow or other. My words challenge their research, findings, and categorization of "their" minorities. I am sickened as they squirm at the podium, hiding behind its elevation of their status. They stick to their guns, confirming the very truths others have spoken about the impact of state power on indigenous communities.

The irony is too much to bear that within a conference on marginalization, the marginalized are being marginalized. The very host of the conference, a Bedouin himself, who has written extensively on the state-driven disenfranchisement of the Palestinian Bedouin community in Israel, knows he can easily become a target of their wrath after the attendees leave. After all, they are colleagues at the same university, an Israeli university. Perhaps the university only agreed to host the conference in order to show how supportive Israel is of recognizing the challenges of minorities in communities around the world, all the while hijacking the narrative of their own "minorities."

Unfortunately, these twisters of the truth save their battle for faculty meetings, resource allocations, and private meetings with the administration. There is no room for truth here, not for Palestinians, who will continue to be subjugated, disempowered, and silenced yet again. That is precisely what happens. The host of the conference is later stripped of his post as director of the Center for Bedouin Studies and Development, and his access to funding for research and projects denied. Disobedience has a high price tag. Even though dignity demands speaking one's truth, it may result in further marginalization, at least until enough people hold Israel accountable for its actions.

My heart breaks at the injustice experienced at the hands of governments and institutions of power, but at the same time, I feel hopeful about the stories of marginalization shared at this conference. Somehow, the overlap in experiences across contexts is empowering, reminding us all that no matter how far we have traveled, we speak the same language, carry the same burden, and voice the same truth. I begin to realize that unleashing the power of our stories by sharing them with each other and the world can lead to the kind of transformation I've been longing for.

After the conference, it is time to return to Jalameh, which means passing again through the Kalandia checkpoint in Jerusalem. But first, we want to get some additional pieces of pottery from the infamous Armenian potters in the Old City to match our set of dishes. It is late in the day, so we make a beeline through the narrow passageways of the Old City to the pottery shop. There isn't much time to get to the checkpoint before it closes for the night. We make it, but we are all tired and quiet from the difficult journey, the weight of the checkpoint, the Wall, and the feeling that the deeper we venture into the West Bank, the more invisible we become. There we are sealed off from the rest of the world. We are on our own.

I wish the world could see us, but somehow the Wall casts its shadow even deep within the West Bank, where it is out of view, hiding the devastating impact of isolation from the outside world. No one can see us, no one can hear us, but I am not afraid. I am not alone. I am home.

Now, so many years after my first trip when I visited Salem's family in Gaza, the situation here is only getting worse. But I still want to believe the world is good, people are good, and the situation here can get better. Instead of building up this system, where some people live at the expense of others, people here must create new systems that allow everyone to live a life of dignity. But systems are powerful. They perpetuate themselves. People become complicit in the crimes of systemic power. And yet standing water becomes toxic. Water must flow to support life. Change is inevitable. Nothing really stays the same. Just as the rain comes and forces stagnant water to move again, the rain will come to Israel and Palestine. Heavy rains just came there this winter, even snow for the second year in a row. A reminder that nothing stays the same.

I am inspired by everything I've experienced in this place I call home, where lessons of patience and persistence abound. Even when the olive trees are hunched over from years of hardship, they are rooted in the land, steadfast at the core, holding their arms out to the next generation. The sun still rises to warm their branches and bring forth the blossoms of hope that, with the patience of saber, lead to a harvest of livelihood. The land has never failed them. Palestinians are of this land, the soil is in their blood, and it feeds their soul. No wonder Palestinians sing, *Biruh, bidam, nifdiki ya Falastin!*—With our souls, with our blood, we will redeem you Palestine![110]

May the hearts and minds of the Children of Abraham realize how intimately their stories have already overlapped. They have become pages in the same book. They can no longer simply be ripped out and still make sense. A bitter truth for both sides, but one with which they must come to terms. Like the leaves of saber that fuse together to become the trunk, these stories have become inseparable, however thorny they remain. Just when the heat of summer threatens all life to make it through another day, the saber bears fruit. We are in the heat of summer. The fruits are forming, however hostile the environment. Listen, look, and wait. It is only a matter of time. Sometimes I think I can already taste the first bite.

37

Dead Sea

As our visit comes to a close in late August 2004, Nasser and I take Canaan, Karmel, and Sham on one last excursion to the Dead Sea—*Bahr al-Mayit*. It is already the hottest time of year, but it is even hotter in the Dead Sea basin because it is below sea level. The strong breeze offers no relief as we gaze at the deep-blue, choppy waves crashing against the rocks along the shoreline, the pink hue of the mountains across the sea in Jordan visible in the distance.

Nasser is not a good swimmer and is worried he will sink, but I assure him that's impossible. "Just lean back, and you'll float! Keep your head up, and you'll be fine." Nasser gives it a try, cautiously lowering himself into the water, then letting himself float but soon struggles to keep his balance, tipping one way, then the other, as he tries to steady himself like a canoe. Canaan and Karmel brave the salty sea and wade into the water, then float effortlessly on their backs.

Sham tucks her head into my neck to hide from the wind. No sooner are we in the water than a wave splashes us. Sham's body stiffens as the sting of seawater permeates her eyes. I return to shore to the nearest beach shower to rinse her eyes while she shakes her head in protest. "You have to open your eyes so we wash the salt away!" I rinse her head again, then dry her face with a towel. "It will get better soon, I promise. Keep blinking." Her little eyes are red pools, tears darting down her cheeks when she blinks. I hug her tight, then walk back over to where Canaan and Karmel are floating like logs on the sea. Nasser, done for the day, takes Sham so I can join Canaan and Karmel in the water.

Nasser calls out to us from shore. He is talking to a young man who knows a spot where we can access the mineral-rich, black mud of the Dead Sea. We follow him along the rocky shoreline, stepping carefully over the large rocks. Now and then, we pass salt crystal formations growing on the rocks. The young man reaches under the water between the rocks and offers Nasser a handful of black mud. People spend hundreds of dollars on Dead Sea products because of the therapeutic benefits of the rich minerals within its water and black mud. I feel privileged that this local Palestinian wants to share his secret with us.

Nasser spreads the black mud across his chest, then on his arms, rubbing it into his skin until it is completely covered. The young man digs again and offers me some mud. I thank him and work the mud into my arms, coating them completely, then move on to my legs. When I smear some mud onto Sham's legs, she pulls back, the sting in her eyes diminishing her trust in anything to do with this odd body of water. Canaan and Karmel eagerly join in, painting their bodies with this rich treasure from the earth. We all break out in laughter at the sight of our mud-covered bodies. As the mud dries, it turns ash gray and stiffens, cracking when we move. We get back in the sea and rub our skin, and the hardened mud melts away, clouding the rough waters dancing around us. A final rinse back on shore, and my skin feels smooth and fresh, completely renewed from the mineral-rich mud.

How fortunate we are to experience the magic of this unique place together, another treasure in this distinct landscape. On our way back, we pass entire areas where the Dead Sea has dried up with large signs warning of the danger of sinkholes. I have heard that the Dead Sea is evaporating faster than the water can replenish itself due in part to Israel's use of the water that flows into the Dead Sea from the Sea of Galilee and the Jordan River. Instead of one sea, it has become two, connected only by narrow canals.

I am angry to lose this natural phenomenon and its healing properties. I am angry at the reconfiguration of Palestine, the disfiguration of her body, the way the Israeli roadways cut through her instead of following her curves, the uniform settlements that stick out like eyesores, the destruction of Palestinian homes, and the renaming of places. Just as the Dead Sea is shrinking, so are the lands on which Palestinians can live due to Israeli restrictions on the growth of village borders and ongoing confiscation of village farmland. Pixel by pixel, the picture of Palestine is disappearing before my eyes, and yet Palestine is real and alive in the hearts and minds of Palestinians the world over. It is alive in me. The question burns deeper in my soul than ever. *What will become of this place I call home?*

38

Cave of Names

Back in Jalameh, it is early morning when Nasser takes Canaan, Karmel, Sham, and me to the hills of the wa'ra at the edge of Jalameh. Along the way, Nasser points out a deep, circular depression carved into the stone. "People used to press olive oil right here. See?" There is a channel carved at one side that leads to another circle carved in the stone farther down the hill. "They would crush the olives here, then the oil would seep into the next hole." I wonder how many generations of Palestinians harvested olives here. Unlike the rocky terrain around us, these large boulders are smooth and flat. An ancient olive press still surrounded by olive trees.

Nasser continues on, stepping through jagged rocks amidst a sea of spiky plants. His feet easily navigate the rough terrain. At first, Canaan and Karmel follow him in his footsteps but eventually veer off their father's path, exploring alternate routes that sometimes lead to thick brush or drop-offs from the boulders, forcing them to turn back or take a leap down. Sham has already gotten poked in the ankles by the dry brush and reaches up for me to carry her. Nasser is farther ahead now, Canaan and Karmel scattered between us.

Nasser calls us over to an area surrounded by large boulders. "Here it is!" When we catch up to him, he is at the edge of a gaping opening in the earth. I look down and see piles of loose rubble. "This is the Cave of Names. I'll show you how to get down." He kneels where one of the boulders slopes down, putting one leg, then the other, against the inside of the opening, hanging on to protrusions of rock as he carefully works his way down.

Canaan has been watching closely and lowers his legs down the side, grabbing onto the rocky wall to climb down into the cave. Before he reaches the bottom, he leaps off, the loose rock shifting beneath his feet. Karmel follows suit, as if he has done it a thousand times. Sham clings to me, but I convince her to let me lower her down the side. Nasser guides her legs, then places his hands on her back until he can grab her around the waist to lower her to the ground. I secure my feet on protruding rocks until I can feel the rocky ground beneath me.

Canaan is already deep in the cave. Sham reaches up to me, her strawberry-blonde hair gleaming in the sun streaming down from the opening. I pick her up and follow Nasser into the darkness, breathing in the cool air as it bathes our sun-soaked skin. When my eyes adjust to the dim light, I make out a sizeable ledge like a stage where Canaan is standing, Karmel his audience.

Nasser climbs onto the stage. "People used to live in here. Let me show you where I wrote my name." I realize the entire wall is covered in names written in Arabic, some with pen or marker, and others carved into the stone. *How many names are in this cave? Who were the first ones to write their names here? How long ago?* Nasser runs his hands over the stone wall, reading some of the names aloud, then stops. "Here it is. See?" I make out Nasser's name in Arabic scratched into the stone and filled in with ink. Nasser's eyes scan the wall for an open space for them to write their names, but Canaan has already found a spot. Stone in hand, he carves his name into the stone wall in Arabic. Karmel finds a stone and climbs up on stage near Canaan to carve his nickname "Mouli" in English, short for the Arabic diminutive of Karmouli. I watch them leave a trace, their eyes focused on the wall, their hands gripping their stones.

Nasser finds a sharp stone to write Karmel and Sham in Arabic. I call out to Karmel. "Mouli, come see! Baba wrote your name in Arabic." Nasser finds another blank spot for Sham's name and begins scratching the first two curves of the letter *shin* (ش) into the stone wall. "See, Baba's writing your name!" I am hoping Sham is taking in this moment, where her name means more than the historical area of *Bilad al-Sham*. Here, she is Sham of Jalameh. I walk closer so she can see the finished product. "Sh-a-m!" Nasser traces over her name. My heart swells with pride that my children have learned this longstanding tradition. Their names are carved in stone. We are from here. This is where we belong. This is home.

It is late in the day when we are headed back to the wa'ra to clean up the olive tree trimmings of Nasser's father's trees. Several of Nasser's nieces and nephews join us along the dirt road between fields of cucumbers and watermelon until we reach the rocky hills of the wa'ra. The afternoon sun casts a warm glow on the hillside, illuminating the bright-green thorny leaves of the saber. The ground is bone dry, the brush stiff and scorched from the sun. I try my best to step onto the large boulders, but now and then, we have to walk through the brush, making it difficult to avoid the pokiest of the plants, which scrape against my ankles. I carry Sham in my arms so her ankles don't meet the same fate.

The olive trees are a pale olive-green, both their leaves and the abundance of olives hanging from their branches covered with a thick layer of dust. I rub my fingers on one of the olives, and its thick skin brightens. I look around at all the olive trees, each one unique in its stance and structure. Some of them are leaning one way, but their branches reach in the other direction, as if to balance their own weight. The younger trees stand more upright. The older trees' branches are kinked and knobby, like an old man's hands, the younger trees smoother and more uniform.

When we arrive at Sidi's land, Nasser points out the trimmed branches piled beneath the trees. He drags some of the branches together, then carries them over to a clearing and instructs the next generation to pile up all the brush there. He calls out *Yallah* to set the whole operation in motion. They scramble in all directions, scraping together as many branches as they can carry and dumping them in the clearing. Canaan and Karmel each carry so many branches that I can hardly see their faces. The branches bounce and settle as they toss them onto the pile, which quickly grows into a tangled mound. I find Sham with some of the younger children, climbing the trees, easily navigating their open branches in the shade.

When the sun is low in the sky, all the children gather around as Nasser lights the mound and raises his arms up in the air. *Hariqa!*—Fire! I take Sham in my arms just as the whole pile goes up in flames reaching up toward the darkening sky, taller than the tallest among us. When the sun sinks below the horizon, faces that moments before were disappearing in the dusk now glow orange. As the fire engulfs the brush, its flames recede closer to the ground. The faces darken, but the fire still dances in everyone's eyes.

Canaan positions himself toward the edge of the fire, then makes a running leap and flies over the flames. I call out to him as he lands on the other side of the mound. "Be careful, Canaan!" Karmel decides to follow in his brother's footsteps and comes around to the same position. "You guys are crazy! Be careful!" My words are falling on deaf ears. Like his brother, Karmel takes off at full speed and flies over the fire, landing clear on the other side.

Now their older cousins follow suit, lining up at the same spot where Canaan and Karmel took flight. They stare into the fire as they brace themselves at the edge, then charge at it, their legs pushing off from the dry, rocky ground, sending them sailing over the flames in a single leap, their bodies glowing above the flames as they tuck their legs in flight. The younger ones cheer them on, their eyes wide open with each leap. By the time they each take several turns, the fire is low and tame. I can barely see their faces.

When we hear packs of wild dogs barking in the distance, Nasser declares it is time to go before they pay us a visit. He leads us down the wa'ra back to the dirt road, the white fluorescent lights visible from the windows of the houses at the edge of the village. Farther north in the distance are the faint, scattered lights of the village of Muqeibileh across the Green Line and a single green light at the top of the mosque's minaret. To the right of Muqeibileh is the yellow glow of streetlights from the settlement of Gan Ner in perfect rows. Besides the distant echoes of dogs barking, our voices are the only sound we hear in the still of the night.

Behind us, the freshly pruned olive trees bid us goodnight as they patiently await the olive harvest, still two months away, their branches reaching out with gratitude. Another generation of hands tends to them so that they may feed the next generation. I think of all the trees in the destroyed villages across the Green Line, wondering when the hands that cared for them will return to trim their branches and harvest their fruit. My heart is half broken for their loss, half glad that we can care for Nasser's Sidi's trees so they can feed us and future generations. *We are still here.*

39

Trials and Tribulations

Back in Madison, I complete my revisions for my dissertation and receive my doctorate in December 2004 while continuing to work at the university in diversity policy.[111] That same year, Nasser and I co-lead a roundtable discussion on a bi-national option in Palestine/Israel at the Middle Eastern Studies Association Conference in San Francisco, just after the death of Yasser Arafat. I want to do more work related to Palestine and try to get time off work after the new year to travel to Palestine for an academic exchange program, but hefty deadlines at work for our annual report on the status of diversity programs across the University of Wisconsin campuses force me to decline.

I want to be able to pursue both my passion for justice in Palestine and my commitment to the diversity agenda in the US, but when I discuss my interests at work or post a cartoon about the UN related to Palestine and Israel on my door, I am told it makes some colleagues uncomfortable, so I have to take it down. I feel silenced. If I cannot be myself at work, then maybe I don't belong there. But I need this job. It is our only income until the olive oil business takes off.

With a PhD, I receive a nominal raise, but the increase only bumps me just above the poverty line. Now, instead of qualifying for state health insurance, I have to pay for my own insurance through my employer. So much for the raise. I ought to be able to earn a decent living with a PhD, but salaries are below market across the board at the University of Wisconsin. I am the breadwinner of the family while Nasser is in school, so I swallow the terms of my employment, grateful to have a job at all that I at least enjoy and is related to the empowerment of marginalized communities.

Part of me wants to make a career in diversity work since there is greater recognition of the need and value of fostering diversity at all levels of education and employment. I try my hand at presenting a paper on the diversity divide in higher education at the Comparative and International Education Society conference at Stanford in the spring of 2005. I reserve my other commitments related to Palestine for another time and present my findings from my dissertation at the Association for the Study of Higher Education conference in Philadelphia just before Thanksgiving. Then, I dash to Washington, DC, to chair a second year of the roundtable discussion at the Middle Eastern Studies Association conference on the binational option in Israel-Palestine. In the midst of all these presentations, Nasser and I both apply for academic jobs across the country. Our lives could change at any moment if we pursue careers in academia.

In the fall, Nasser returns to Palestine for the olive harvest to oversee the collection of olives to press for our first olive oil shipment to the US. He also hosts the company's first olive harvest festival to celebrate the bounty of the harvest with employees and member farmers and their families. When he returns to Madison to finish his dissertation, we share in the festivities as we watch the gathering on videotape in our living room. Even though our hope for a bi-national state remains alive, it feels good to know that we are making a difference in people's lives on the ground right now through our company, Canaan Fair Trade.

In the midst of all these changes, I talk to my father on Sunday, December 5, 2005, about my application to Columbia University and the stress of all the uncertainty that lies ahead. I have no idea that will be the last time I speak to him. The following Friday, he falls and hits his head while at a concert in Munich, where he has been living since he retired. Instead of going to the hospital, he attends a second concert at intermission. By morning, he is unconscious; the next day, he is gone from internal bleeding to the brain. We usually talk on Sundays. My father was born on a Sunday—always said he was a *Sonntagskind*—a Sunday child—which has a connotation in German of being lucky. Now, he has also died on a Sunday. I drop everything and travel to Germany to see him one last time.

It is late afternoon when we arrive at the cemetery. The blistering cold wind and heavy cloud cover convince me that the Earth itself is mourning his death. When I see him and take his hand in mine, part of me believes that if I hold his hand long enough, the warmth of my body will bring him back to life. The winter chill that creeps under the door into the viewing room is a brutal reminder that he cannot be revived, and I let him go. I think of all the things I would still ask him if I could, about his childhood, his time in the war, what lies ahead for humanity. Now, I can only talk to him in my head, our weekly check-ins a thing of the past.

With the help of my father's inheritance, Nasser and I take our children to Hawaii in March 2006, one of many places in the world my father explored in his retirement. I am chairing a panel on Peace Education at the Comparative and International Education Society conference. Canaan is working on a school project on Hawaii, so we drive around the island of O'ahu to witness the discrepancy in land ownership between native Hawaiians and the big corporations and resorts. We also visit the Polynesian Cultural Center to learn about the other islands in the area. Everywhere we go, we hear the moving voice of the Hawaiian singer Israel Kamakawiwo'ole, otherwise known as IZ, who died years before but is so loved that everyone continues to play his music, particularly his version of "Somewhere Over the Rainbow."

My focus on Peace Education leads to a book proposal with Professor Jing Lin from the University of Maryland to bring together scholars on the subject. Over the summer, Nasser graduates with a PhD in anthropology and international development from the University of Wisconsin. We celebrate his graduation on May 14, which that year is also Canaan's 13th birthday, the 58th year of the Nakba, and Mother's Day in the US.[112] Nasser's sister Huda and brother Jamal travel to the US to celebrate with us. With a houseful of friends and family, we grill a whole lamb to honor the occasion, along with a spread of hummus, baba ghanouj, tabouleh, platters of rice covered with roasted almonds, plates of olives, and trays of Arabic pastries we ordered from Shatila in Dearborn, Michigan. So much to celebrate—there must be something new on the horizon.

Nasser returns to Palestine again in fall 2006 for the olive harvest, then I travel with Canaan, Karmel, and Sham over their winter break to visit him. Traveling with three kids, I don't get much sleep on the plane. When we arrive at Ben Gurion Airport, it is already afternoon, and we still have a two-hour taxi ride Nasser arranged for us to get to Jalameh. The airport security officials ask me the usual questions. *Where are we going? How long are we staying? Who packed our luggage?* The questions feel routine, until they tell me they need to talk to Canaan alone. My heart races at the thought of them taking Canaan out of my sight. And what for? He is 13 years old. I insist we come with him, but the officials make it clear they wish to interrogate him alone.

Here we are, just entering the country. In their eyes, we have no rights. After all, we are a Palestinian family. We are subjects of the State of Israel. We have no choice in the matter. I feel trapped, powerless. *What should I do?* Fear washes over me. If I push them harder, they may make more trouble for us. I just want to get through the questioning so we can go home to Jalameh. I am burning inside that I cannot keep my own child in my presence, that I cannot protect him from the unknown. I tell Canaan not to be afraid, assure him that he will be okay, as I accept to let them take him, knowing I am not the first, nor the last mother of Palestinians to be forced to succumb to their power.

My fear only increases when I watch them take Canaan out of my sight behind a curtain. All I can do is hope he remains calm and strong, does not let them intimidate him. He has nothing to offer them, nothing to hide. He is a child. The longest two hours of my life pass. We are all exhausted from the waiting, the wondering, the absurdity. When Canaan finally comes out okay, unharmed, unscathed by the relentless circle of questions, I breathe a deep sigh of relief, but cannot help but wonder at their motives. *Did they want to prepare him for a future of being Palestinian? Let him get used to the idea that his very identity makes him suspect, to wish he were someone else, or make him not want to come back here?* These questions are circling in my head as we make a beeline out front to find our taxi. The driver seems equally relieved when we appear. Like us, he has been waiting, wondering.

Finally, we are on our way.

The drive to Jalameh feels particularly long and our reunion with Nasser especially celebratory. We are home. We are safe. Nasser's sisters have prepared a feast for us of *mansaf*—slow-cooked lamb in yogurt soup over a platter of rice and roasted almonds sprinkled with fresh parsley. Sitti is delighted to have her three grandchildren, who live in America, in her company, as are all of their cousins, who are eager to try out their English, a subject in school they take more seriously so they can talk to their American cousins.

After dinner, Nasser can't wait to show us all the changes he has made to his family home in Jalameh, which he inherited when his father passed since he is the only brother who had not yet built his own house. The upgrades include a new front entrance made by enclosing the veranda, new aluminum windows, and a chimney in the center with a stone fireplace. In the old domed 'aqid, Nasser updated the wiring and added new lighting throughout the house. Later, we have gorgeous sconce lamps installed in the 'aqid that we find in the Old City in Jerusalem.

Nasser expands the kitchen to include an L-shaped counter made from a single piece of blue granite with snazzy steel barstools. The kitchen is outfitted with custom cabinets and a new ceramic double sink with a garbage disposal, likely the first in the village, as well as a new refrigerator, a modern five-burner gas stove with an oven, a washing machine that doubles as a dryer, and space for a dishwasher, though we don't buy one until years later.

Nasser completely redesigns the bathroom to include a full-size bathtub, a new toilet and countertop with a sink, wooden cabinets and shelves, and a large mirror. Last but not least, he refinishes the walls throughout the entire house with rich colors and installs AC units in the 'aqid and bedrooms that double as heaters. When Nasser orders shelving and desks for the company offices and showroom from a salvage wood company, he includes tables, dressers, and bed frames for the house. He also gets a hip, modern sofa set for the 'aqid with broad stripes that tie in perfectly to the orange, gold, and black design of the tile floor.

Outside the house, Nasser has the original well cleaned out and resealed to collect rainwater like in the old days, complete with a new pump and a tap at the kitchen sink. Now, we can make our own tea from *mayit as-sama'*—sky water. Those who don't already have their own well are not so fortunate. Any Palestinians caught digging a new well will be met with a "friendly" nighttime delivery of concrete to seal it up, as I have witnessed in the village of Burqin, where Israel sends helicopters to comb the landscape at night searching for violators.

Next to the lemon tree I planted, Nasser adds a carport, extends the privacy wall out front, adding iron bars at the top and flowerbeds at the base planted with sage and mint for tea, as well as jasmine that will one day climb the wall and cascade over the iron bars. By the front door, he mounts his father's plow freshly painted green and anchored in a slab of concrete as an honorable relic of the past. Last but not least, he has the old stone exterior sandblasted, transforming the weathered stone to its original creamy white. Unlike the houses that have been reduced to rubble in the hundreds of destroyed villages across Palestine, this house is still standing. Palestine is still here, just as it remains in the hearts and minds of those barred from returning.

Sitti is proud of her son putting such attention to the family home, but when he renovates the arched hamel in the 'aqid into a built-in bookshelf with space for a flat-screen TV, she throws her arms up in despair. *Wen bidna inhat il-farsh, yama?*—Where are we going to put the mats? With the house now fully furnished, not only is there nowhere to store the mats, but there is nowhere to put them out on the floor like in the old days. It is as if the house has been transformed to a new era and the days of sitting on mats has suddenly slipped through her fingers.

With time, her health deteriorates with dementia, so she moves in with Nasser's oldest brother, who has since remarried. His new wife Layla becomes her full-time caretaker. Little by little, Nasser's mother struggles to recognize the once familiar faces before her, though she easily recalls the old days, including that day of her wedding, when she first came to Jalameh on horseback.

Even though Nasser has completely renovated the old family home, he still plans someday to build a house on the plot of land his father left to him to fulfill his father's wish that he and his brothers all live in a row. For now, like his brother Jamal, whose date palms he planted years ago now tower over us, Nasser has filled the perimeter of his land with fruit trees—orange, pomegranate, apple, lemon—and, for the time being, leases the center of the land to a local farmer. In the meantime, we have our very own home in Palestine.

I realize he is lucky that he can renovate his family home. Palestinians in Israel who want to renovate their historic homes have to apply for permits, which are almost never approved. If they are caught modifying their homes in any way, the houses can be destroyed or seized by the state. Neither is new construction approved for Palestinians in the West Bank, particularly in Area C, since Israel drew a line around each Palestinian community when it took over the area during the Six-Day War in 1967, barring construction beyond it, while the state easily approves renovations and construction along with financial support for housing in Jewish settlements throughout the West Bank.

Jalameh is especially vulnerable in that village lands beyond the "borders" of the village specified by the circle are neither part of Israel proper, nor do they fall under the Palestinian Authority, which only has jurisdiction over Area A—the city centers of Ramallah, Nablus, Jenin, Tulkarem, Qalqilya, Bethlehem, Hebron, and Jericho—and Area B—the "inner circle" of most, but not all, Palestinian villages across the West Bank. According to the Oslo Accords, Area C is considered state land and falls under Israeli military control, even though it is Palestinian land where Palestinians live.

It seems absurd that Palestinians have to obtain a building permit from the military of the state that occupies their homeland. Not issuing building permits to Palestinians provides Israel with the legal framework for home demolitions, obliterating a family's life savings in seconds, not to mention that it blocks the natural growth of Palestinian towns and villages, and provides preferential treatment to Jews over Palestinians in their own homeland. It also forces Palestinians to build up, turning single family homes into apartment buildings.

The only time Jewish homes were demolished in Israel's history was for the removal of settlements in the Sinai Desert through peace agreements with Egypt in 1979 following the Camp David Accords and Ariel Sharon's Disengagement Plan in 2005.[113] The year I spent in Palestine with Canaan and Karmel in 1998–1999, I used to take the settlement road from Jalameh to bypass Jenin on my way to their school. Today, the settler road is just another route toward Jenin and the road to the hilltop a needless snake of asphalt.

The Israeli settlements of Ganim and Kadim are gone, dismantled in 2005 along with two other settlements in the West Bank and all 21 settlements in the Gaza Strip once the Israeli government found the costs too high to protect them.[114]

One afternoon, Nasser and I take the paved road to the hilltop that leads up the hillside to an open area scattered with trees and dried brush, where one of the settlements once stood. Unlike the destroyed Palestinian villages I have visited over the years, this settlement left virtually no trace of ever having been on the hill, with the exception of a few slabs of concrete that stick out like scars in the otherwise smooth hilltop. Most settlements begin with trailers as an outpost on a hilltop in the West Bank until the Israeli government authorizes and finances the building of permanent housing and structures that are offered to Jewish Israeli families at a subsidized rate. Like a thorn in their side, Palestinian resistance fighters in the area kept attacking their presence as the settlers made their way from the Jalameh checkpoint to the settlement road until Israel decided the settlements needed to be dismantled.

Standing on that hilltop, I can see how the winter rains have restored a softness to the landscape. No longer surrounded by fences and concrete barriers, the hilltop is now open to the sky and blends seamlessly into the surrounding hillsides. As I walk across the dried brush, I realize this hilltop almost became another place, renamed by residents who had the backing of God and the Israeli government. This hilltop settlement on Palestinian land, taken like a kidnapped child, would have been raised to forget her family, her language, her cultural heritage. She sits here with the trauma still visible somewhere deep in her steady gaze.

She is breathing softly now, the memory of the footsteps that tried to make her forget her family now fading into the past, the weight of the settlers' homes, guns, and ammunition no longer restricting her breath. The posts of fences no longer penetrate her flesh. No concrete barriers keep her from defending herself. No more strangers coming to her day and night, rejoicing in the victory of her capture. This piece of Palestine remains.

She welcomes us as we greet her. She smiles that we know of her capture and rejoice in her freedom. Our footsteps are light, and she carries us gladly as we take in the wide-open space and view she offers. She is the land again, no longer an Israeli watchtower over her relatives in neighboring Palestinian villages. Her long dress flows down the hilltop in all directions, a cloak of continuity that continues as far as the eye can see.

Her sisters in other areas of what was once Palestine were not so lucky. Those pieces of Palestine that have become Israel have new names, a new identity. *But don't they deserve to know who they are? Must one identity replace the other? Can't they be woven into one that acknowledges what has become of these spaces? Can't Israel exist with Palestine instead of replacing it?* The truth of Palestine will always linger restless in the shadows because everyone deserves their day in the sun. I know Palestine is real, and yet some Israelis believe they are restoring the Land of Israel to its former glory, that the Palestinians wandered into their homeland over the centuries and have no claim to *their* homeland. *How can both claims to the same land be reconciled?*

When it is time for the kids and me to go back to the US, our lives are also unsettled as we straddle the continents. After all, Nasser needs to be in Palestine for the olive harvest and tend to the growing business. Canaan ends up staying with Nasser to go to the same school he and Karmel attended the year we spent in Palestine back in 1998. It has more instruction in Arabic now, so it will be challenging for him, but we decide to give it a try.

I return to Madison with Karmel and Sham, back to my job at the university. It will be tough for me managing alone with my more-than-fulltime work schedule. I feel divided. I wish we could all stay together, not have to live separate lives, but we depend on my income, and Nasser needs to attend to the business overseas. It is not ideal, but this is our life. It will get better with time. At least that is what I tell myself.

We have only been back in Madison for 10 days when I feel a sudden pain in the back of my head. I am sitting in bed first thing in the morning. Luckily, the phone is in my hand since I just tried to call Nasser. I didn't reach him. Now, all I can think is to call 911. I feel my body shutting down. I summon all my strength to press the three digits—9-1-1. "Send someone right away," I muster when I hear a voice. "I am fading." I am bombarded with questions.

Am I alone? Is the door unlocked? I manage to call out to Sham, who is only five years old, to unlock the door. She doesn't come back to my room. I don't ask her to. I don't want to alarm her. I have called for help. Karmel has no idea what is happening, asleep downstairs with his friend Danny from down the street.

My body is becoming lifeless, my mind fuzzy, my limbs weak and tingling, my face unresponsive when I offer a word, now and then, to the voice on the phone. My job is to convince them that I am still here. When I fall silent, I hear, "Stay with me." I am disappearing from the inside. *What is happening? Is this the end?* The emergency crew arrives and arranges for Karmel and Sham to go to Danny's house. They carry my cell phone and me out on a stretcher. I don't even see the kids.

Next thing I know, I am in the ER. I can't open my right eye. They call my mother in Detroit and my sister in Chicago. My mother plans to fly out that night. My sister can be there in a few hours. In the meantime, they do a CAT Scan and an MRI. Nothing shows up. The nurse tells me it must be a migraine. I am lying perfectly still, but my chest is burning with frustration. *Seriously? A migraine?* I can hardly move and can't open my right eye.

I am relieved when my sister Erika and her husband show up. At least I am not alone. They admit me to the hospital and move me to a private room. It is then that I ask to go to the bathroom. I try to sit up and realize I can't. My mind is somehow disconnected from my body. The nurse helps me shift my legs off the edge of the bed, but they dangle lifelessly. I can feel them but I can't control them. "I can't get up."

"Here, let me help you." The nurse slides her arm under my left arm and tries to guide me to a standing position, but I cannot even step. All the power in my legs is gone. I can move them, but I cannot put any weight on them. I rest back against the bed and stare across the room toward the bathroom. It is right there, but I cannot get to it. "What is going on?" I am asking myself as much as I am asking the nurse. I don't expect an answer.

It is not until Monday that a new set of doctors comes by to take a look at me. A second MRI shows that I have had a stroke normally diagnosed through autopsy. I am lucky to be alive. The deadlines at work go through my mind, but it is clear I won't make them. Who knows when or if I will ever go back to work? My life has stopped.

Lying there in that hospital bed, I feel something shift deep within me. *What do I want to do with the rest of life now that I didn't die?* I think back to my childhood days sitting on the Detroit Boat Club balcony after swim practice, knowing I wanted to be a writer. Back then, I admired the writings of William Faulkner. *What is my story?*

At a recent student conference on access for marginalized groups that I helped organize through my office at the university, one of the students handed me a few blank sheets of paper from her notebook when I confided in her that I want to be a writer. "Go ahead. Write." I remember staring at that blank page like I am staring now at the rest of my life. Then, it comes to me. Even though I am committed to going back to my job at the university once I recover, in that moment, I realize what I need to do. *I need to write my story about Palestine.*

After two weeks of rehab with physical and occupational therapy in the hospital, it is almost time to go home. The doctors are confident that I will recover quickly. After all, I have no risk factors for a stroke, and I am young. They assure me I should be back on my feet in no time. Nasser offers to come home, but I insist he and Canaan stay in Palestine while I recover. We have already sacrificed so much to get to this point, and I know Nasser needs to focus on the business, now in its third year. My mother is here. She can take care of me for now. My sister Elisa and brother Dieter follow.

One of my last tasks before I leave the hospital is to practice preparing food in the kitchen. I choose to make tabouleh and give the nurse the list of ingredients I need to make it: bulgur, parsley, scallions, tomatoes, olive oil, lemons, salt and pepper. They have special utensils in the kitchen with extra wide handles so I can grip them more easily. I transfer from my wheelchair to a stool by the counter since I cannot stand. I slide the knife along the bunch of parsley I try my best to hold with the other hand, but I can only slice large chunks. When I try to slice it finer, my hands shake uncontrollably. I let the knife fall and feel the tears drip onto my hands. "It needs to be chopped fine." I feel like my recovery is dependent on this one task.

The occupational therapist tries to reassure me. "You're doing great." She takes the knife. "I can finish it for you. It will get easier. Don't worry!" She finishes chopping the parsley, then dices the tomatoes and slices the scallions, following my instructions, then sprinkles on some salt and pepper, drizzles olive oil, adds the bulgur soaking in lemon juice, and stirs it all up.

"Thank you. Please share it with the staff." It feels good to do something for all these people who have cared for me.

When they release me from the hospital, I don't feel ready. I still can't walk. They wheel me to the front door, the ice-cold air of the Wisconsin winter hitting my face. Getting in and out of the car is a challenge. My sister and mother grab me from each side to get me into the house and onto my wheelchair. Tears stream down my face. *How am I going to manage? How can I live like this?* I am exhausted just from getting into the house. They wheel me to my bedroom, the same room I left three weeks before on a stretcher.

Everything has changed. I am bound to a wheelchair. I can hardly lift a pound. I cannot even prepare food. There is no point in thinking about work. All I want to do is lie down. My mother wheels me over to my bed. I lock the wheels and transfer my body to the side of the bed, lie back, and take a deep breath, closing my eyes for a moment. *How did I get to this point?* The pain in my head. 911. The ambulance. The ER. Cat Scan. MRI. Migraine? Stroke. *Now what?*

The weeks of recovery turn into months. I can't go back to work. I am still committed to finishing the book on peace education I am editing with Jing Lin, but I can't write my chapter. I can hardly finish editing the articles others have submitted. I have double vision from the stroke. I can't look at a computer screen or television. My brain needs calm and quiet.

Nasser comes home for the summer with Canaan to a wife he doesn't even recognize. I have changed from a driven and capable workhorse to a broken spirit. When he has to leave again in the fall for the olive harvest, we hire a student to get Canaan, Karmel, and Sham to school and make meals. A physical therapist comes to the house. I have to start over from the ground up, literally. I graduate from floor exercises to pulling myself to my knees to standing and scooting back and forth along the counter. It is six months before I transition from a wheelchair to a walker, working on balance and speed so I can safely cross the street. It is another six months before I can walk with walking sticks. I practice walking with my eyes closed, following my hands along the wall. It is 18 months before I can walk unassisted. I thought I would never walk again. I recover, but will I ever be the same?

The following summer, in 2008, the book on peace education is released under the title *Transforming Education for Peace*.[115] It feels good to hold the book in my hand, but I feel the absence of my chapter on Palestine. Unable to travel, my spirits are lifted when I attend a performance at Edgewood College. The story of Rachel Corrie's tragic death in Rafah in 2003, when an Israeli bulldozer ran over her as she tried to stop it from destroying a Palestinian home, has been transformed into a one-person theatrical production, and her parents are in attendance. The entire play is Rachel's own words from emails she wrote to family and friends while she was in Gaza that year.

Hearing her words of what she witnessed in Palestine rips my heart to shreds. *How does one person's effort to do good end up in her untimely death and misery for her family?* I think about her passion for social justice even as a young child and her willingness to risk her own life so that others could live with dignity. I am honored to meet her parents, who carry on her legacy through the Rachel Corrie Foundation.

I encounter another personal testimony of life under Israeli occupation the following spring in 2009, when Jewish American activist Anna Baltzer comes to Madison after publishing her photo essay *Witness in Palestine*.[116] My desire to make a difference in Palestine still lingers, and yet I feel defeated, like a coward, a failure. *What can I possibly do?* I almost died of a stroke. *What have I even accomplished? What difference have I made?* I need to share my story, but I still don't know how.

At least I am able to help Nasser turn his dissertation on the Palestinian suicide missions into a book entitled *The Making of a Human Bomb: An Ethnography of Palestinian Resistance*.[117] I am so proud of him for going back to school, taking on a difficult and controversial topic that tells the story of what lengths people will go to if they are robbed of their dignity. And in the meantime, he is building a business to help Palestinian farmers stay on their land and protect their livelihood through the ancient agricultural traditions of those who came before them. At least he is making a difference. I always knew he would. *What will become of me?*

PART V

PERSISTENCE

60th Commemoration of the Nakba

2008-2011

40

Crossing

It is December 2008, nearly two years since my stroke and 60 years since the Nakba, when I travel to Palestine with our three children to visit Nasser and his family. I can finally walk unassisted. I can drive. In fact, no one would even know I had a stroke, though my vulnerability and the weight of a long recovery from wheelchair to walker stills hangs over our marriage. Our family business, Canaan Fair Trade, is in its fourth year. It is the second time we travel through Jordan. During the flight, my chest is bubbling with excitement.

When we arrive in Jordan, our checked luggage is missing. We are due to travel to Palestine the next morning. The airline assures us they will locate our luggage and deliver it to Nasser's sister Naziha's house in Amman or, if necessary, send it across the border. *How can they send our luggage across the border without us? Will the Israelis even allow unaccompanied luggage to cross?* I hope they find our luggage and get it to us quickly. The day after we arrive in Palestine, it will be 'Eid al-Adha. We will all need to dress up in our best clothes. I will be fine in the two-piece linen outfit I wore on the plane, but Canaan, Karmel, and Sham are wearing jeans and sweatshirts.

Nasser's nephew Abdullah has been waiting for us for over an hour when we finally leave the airport, the winter air chilly, the sun already setting. He greets us eagerly with excitement and relief. *Kifak, ya Kanaan?*—How are you, Canaan? *Kifak, ya Karmel?*—How are you, Karmel? He turns to Sham. *Shou, ya amoura?*—What about you, dear?

Canaan looks at me, then turns back. *Mabsout*—Fine. Karmel and Sham look at me, then Abdullah, a smile their only response.

When we arrive at Naziha's, I immediately acknowledge the sudden loss of her husband to a heart attack the year before. *Allah yirhamu*—May God have mercy on him. Her smile cannot hide her eyes, heavy with grief. Fortunately, her grown son Mohammed is living with her, so she is not alone in the house, but I feel the emptiness when she invites us into the same living room where her husband sat when we arrived on our last trip. The winter chill seeps into our bones, reminding me of when I went to Germany to see my father one last time after he died. We sit near the propane heater at the end of the coffee table, the front panel glowing red.

It is in this room that we will spend the night. The heater is not enough to take the chill out of the room, so I don't sleep well. I get up as soon as I hear Naziha in the kitchen. It is still dark. *Sabah al-khair*—Good morning.

Sabah an-nour!—Good morning! Naziha is heating milk to make Nescafé. I suggest she make Arabic coffee instead and mix it into the hot milk. *Ah, bijouz ahsan*—Yes, perhaps even better. We sit on a simple bench with cushions in front of a Formica coffee table in the back room, where we had dinner on the floor the night before.

Naziha is wearing a long flannel nightgown with a floral print, her shoulder-length, black hair tucked behind her ears. Her large brown eyes are simple and kind, her round cheeks warm and friendly. She is the eldest daughter, and yet she seems like a young girl. Like her mother, her life has been all about keeping house and motherhood, though she and all her sisters were educated, unlike their mother, who never had the chance to go to school. I wonder what Naziha's life would have been like had she gotten to stay in Palestine. She seems so isolated here, cut off from the extended family in the village and her only daughter. I ask her if she will ever get to visit Palestine again.

Ya rayt!—I wish! She raises her brow as she explains how she has tried repeatedly, but the Israelis won't give her a tasrih.

Jordan is one big desert and Amman one giant city. Besides Palestinians like her, who married outside and subsequently lost their residency following the 1967 War, Jordan is full of Palestinian refugees from 1948. Neither they nor their children nor their children's children can visit Palestine. It is only a memory for some, only a story for their descendants, a story so often told it has become their own memory. Today, there are more Palestinians in Jordan than Jordanians. No wonder Israel thought it could create a state of Palestine in Jordan. But for Palestinians, there is no comparison. The desert culture of Jordan, with its largely Bedouin population, is not home, even for those who were born there, who know nothing else. Even for the Bedouins of Palestine who fled to Jordan from the Naqab Desert to Palestine in 1948, Palestine will always be home. Palestinians need their land, the hills and valleys, the sea, the Naqab to feel whole. Palestinians swear the food tastes better grown on Palestinian soil.

After we have our coffee, I take a quick shower, get dressed, then wake up Canaan, Karmel, and Sham for a simple breakfast. Naziha sees my wet hair and offers, *Na'iman,* which is customary to say after someone takes a shower, to which I appropriately respond, *Allah yini'im 'aleiki.* It turns out this is the same expression when someone gets a haircut. Naziha offers us black tea with sage, which takes off the morning chill as we dip warm pita bread in olive oil, lebneh, and za'atar. She encourages us to try both the fried and boiled squares of cheese. I assure her we are eating and that the kids have had enough when they get up to wash their hands. We finish up to leave for the bridge, which closes early today because of the Eid.

Abdullah's wife Maysoun rides along dressed in a *niqab*, a black chiffon headdress that only shows her eyes, and a black chiffon *'abaya* that completely covers her long dress, her bright spirit radiating from her eyes. We all laugh when I tell her maybe next time, I will be dressed like her and perhaps also pregnant, though Nasser is neither fond of such Islamic traditions nor is he interested in having more children. I offer in jest, *Mumkin lazem ajawaz 'aleih*—Maybe I will have to "marry over him." We both laugh, knowing only men in Islam may take on a second wife.

Before long, we are at the bridge. Nasser assured us the crossing wouldn't be anything like last time, where we had to get on and off buses in the brutal summer heat. He has arranged for us to cross with VIP status. We follow Abdullah to a counter. The official asks us if we are going to the West Bank. *Duffeh?* He knows the answer. There is nowhere else to go from here. He calls out "VIP!" but when he looks at our passports, he explains that only Sham and I, as Americans, can cross VIP, not Canaan and Karmel, because they have Palestinian passports. I look at Abdullah, puzzled. I insist we travel together, but there is no way around it. The official promises someone will be with Canaan and Karmel the whole time.

I opt to forego the VIP status, but that is not an option since now, the only regular crossing for foreigners is the Sheikh Hussein Bridge farther north, which is off-limits to Palestinians. I feel cornered. *How can I let them take my sons?* Abdullah tells me they will be fine. I don't know whether to believe him, but I don't have a choice. One official takes Canaan and Karmel while another leads Sham and me to a large room with plush sofas like a living room, quiet and virtually empty. Sham sits on my lap, and someone offers us Arabic coffee in tiny plastic cups. All I can think about is Canaan and Karmel. *Are they okay?*

It feels like forever until we are summoned to board a large coach with tinted windows. Only a few other people get on before the bus pulls out. Moments later, we arrive at a large gate. The bus makes a couple of brief stops, but no one gets on or off. Only the driver speaks to the border guards through his window. In no time, we arrive at the other side. I am in disbelief. *How could we already be there?* Such a short distance that years before took us nearly as long to cross as it took us to fly from Chicago to Amman. When we get off the bus, we show our passports to Palestinian officials. Since our luggage is lost, all we have are our carry-on bags. It is not long before Canaan and Karmel appear, melting away my anxiety. The officials must have rushed them through, knowing I would be waiting for them.

Outside is a sea of taxis, the drivers calling out their destinations: *Ramallah! Khalil! Nablus!* Nasser told us to find a taxi to Nablus. From there, we will transfer to a taxi to Jenin. We climb into a van with several rows of seats, opting for the first bench, Sham on my lap, so we all fit. As soon as the van is full, the driver pulls out. It is almost noon. We head through the city of Jericho. The town is busy, with everyone doing their last shopping for the Eid. Street vendors wheel carts full of wares, one piled with bunches of tiny bananas. "Look, those are the famous Jericho bananas!" No time to stop now, but years later, Jericho bananas will become Canaan's favorite.

Once we reach the edge of the city, we are faced with an Israeli checkpoint, so our driver pulls to the side of the road. One soldier comes up to the driver's window, his eyes barely visible beneath his army-green helmet. He verifies we are headed to Nablus, then peers in the window and asks for everyone's ID. When he sees our American passports, he calls out in Hebrew to another soldier, who comes to the passenger side of the van, opens the sliding door, and scans the van from front to back to front again, resting his eyes on my three children and me.

"Where are you going?" His heavy Hebrew accent fills the van. I lift my chin, my voice clear and firm. "Jenin."

"Jenin?" He laughs in disbelief. "You going to Jenin?"

"Yes."

"Why?"

"To visit my husband and his family."

The laughter has left his voice. "You cannot enter from here."

I sit up straighter. "This is the way to Jenin."

"Yes, but you cannot enter from here. You must go from Tulkarem." He is referring to a Palestinian town farther north, on the western border of the West Bank. We are entering from Jericho, which is southeast near the Jordanian border.

"That doesn't make any sense. I would have to go all the way around south of Jerusalem, then up through Israel to enter from Tulkarem. This is the way to Jenin."

"You are American. You cannot enter from here."

"This is the way I came last time. Anyway, my sons cannot enter Israel. They are residents. I have to travel this way with them."

"They can come this way, but you must go to Tulkarem."

"No, I need to go this way. This is the way to Jenin, and I am not leaving my children."

"If you enter from here, we cannot guarantee your safety." The soldier tilts his chin down slightly so that I can just barely see his eyes below his helmet. The irony of this statement makes my blood boil. *Do these soldiers really think I am looking to them for protection?* Bordering on defiance, I tell them I do not need their protection, that I need to stay with my children. I will only enter from here. They seem genuinely shocked at my reaction. Out of frustration or perhaps amusement, they finally let us go.

I take in a deep breath, then stare out the window as we wind through the gray sandcastle-like formations west of Jericho that long ago lay beneath the sea. I take in the landscape as we gradually climb out of the lowest point on Earth and reach the dry, rocky hills farther north that await the imminent rains. No wonder this relatively small country feels so vast. The winding roads, the changing landscape, even the checkpoints all make it feel much larger. We use our last energy to hold our bodies in our seats as the van sways left, then right, then left again, following the curves of the hills.

We are high up in the mountains when we enter Nablus with its four- and five-story apartment buildings and wide streets lined with perfectly manicured trees with their white-painted trunks. The driver lets us out at the central taxi area. Drivers call out their destinations: *Tulkarem! Ramallah! Jenin!* All four of us walk toward one of the Jenin taxis as if drawn by a magnet, get in a yellow Mercedes limousine, filling the entire seat behind the driver. The car is full. We are on our way home.

41

Sidi's Grave

The day after Nasser and I arrive in Jalameh with our three children is 'Eid al-Adha—the Feast of the Sacrifice. Canaan is 15, Karmel is about to turn 13, and Sham is seven. This year, the Eid happens to fall during school vacation since it shifts by 10 days each year, so we can take part in the celebration. Because everyone is busy preparing for the festivities, we don't have the usual welcome of all the relatives coming by the house. We will see them soon enough when we visit each family over the next three days.

I shift my focus to preparing for the Eid. All I can think about is how I can still make ka'ak, the traditional Eid cookies shaped like a ring made with a thin firm crust filled with spiced date paste. I always make ka'ak at the Eid in the States. Now, I am in Palestine.

Nasser invites his brothers to join us to grill meat for breakfast, but first, we must sacrifice a lamb. Nasser's brother Faisal got a lamb for all of us to share and will slaughter it outside their house. At dawn, we walk down Tariq Burqin, a few houses away, the road that leads directly to Sitti's village of Burqin, the road by which she entered Jalameh on horseback on her wedding day, the road where three of the four brothers have built houses of their own all in a row.

When we arrive, Nasser's brothers Faisal and Jamal are out front trying to get the lamb down on its side to bind its feet. Jamal holds the lamb's body to the ground by leaning against it while Faisal bends one front and back foot toward each other at the joint to bind them together. The two free legs thrash about. Now, with only two legs to overpower, the task is much easier. With both sets of legs bound, the lamb vigorously jolts its legs in a vain attempt to free itself, but this process is a point of no return for the lamb.

Faisal whispers a verse from the Quran to himself, followed by *Bismillah ir-rahman ir-rahim*—In the name of God, the Almighty and Merciful. He holds a large knife just below the neck of the lamb and makes one deep, clean cut. I am usually squeamish with anything having to do with blood, but I find with deep breaths, I am able to observe this ritual sacrifice of the lamb. Canaan and Karmel watch in silence. Sham tucks her face into the nape of my neck as a pool of blood forms under the lamb's head.

Faisal cuts the rope to free the lamb's feet, which quiver rhythmically as life leaves its body. Just like that, a living, breathing being becomes still. The dry ground fills with blood as Faisal and his oldest son Fadi hoist the lamb up on a hook from the back legs. This process of making a clean cut and draining the blood is key to making the meat *halal* for Muslims. Having slaughtered our own lamb for previous Eids in the US, I am familiar with the process of neatly unpacking the perfect puzzle of its insides after sliding off its coat of fleece like an overcoat. We leave them to their work and return home to set up for breakfast.

Mid-morning, we begin to *liff*—do the rounds—by first visiting the eldest members of the family, then Nasser's brothers and sisters. We start at Nasser's aunt 'Amti Saymi's house. Canaan, Karmel, and Sham are thrilled to find Foufou is still there, the adorable tabby cat. Sham wants to take her home with us to Madison, but we remind her Foufou has a wonderful home here. Their formal diwan is lined with old brown sofas and several white plastic chairs arranged tightly around a large coffee table. The room is crowded, so we sit close while we sample Eid coffee and cookies.

Then we head to the home of Nasser's other aunt, 'Amti Ayshi. I look around the room, the sun streaming through high arched windows, casting a dreamy contrast to the stone walls of this otherwise tomblike space. Inset into one wall is the *hamel* stacked with several sitting mats like the indentation in the 'aqid of Nasser's family home that Nasser converted to shelves and a TV stand. Above the kitchen, I spot the khusheh, the elevated storage space traditionally used to store dry goods. Smaller windows illuminate the kitchen area. The house feels open and peaceful, as if we are protected from the contested space outside. I return my gaze to 'Amti Ayshi's stern brow and defined cheek bones and chin. The intensity of her gaze makes me wonder if anything escapes her. I am certain she can see right through to my soul. Her daughter serves us coffee, Eid cookies, and a platter of fruit and vegetables. 'Amti Ayshi's brow is stern when we rise to leave, then softens when she learns we are going to the maqbara to pay our respects to Nasser's father, her brother. I am honored to be a guest in her home, one of the original houses of the village, where time and history seem to stand still within its ancient walls.

On our way to the cemetery, we pass a pile of stones at a fork in the road. Nasser points to the remains of his grandfather's house. "This is Sidi Abdel Hadi's house." Only part of the far wall is still standing. I am crushed to see the house reduced to a pile of rubble. Once their daughters married, Nasser's father built his own house, and the brothers moved to Jordan, so when Nasser's grandparents passed away, the house was sold and crumbled in on itself. I stand there staring at the stones, stones that once formed the walls that contained the lives of Nasser's grandparents and his parents after they were first married, where Nasser's mother answered "Yes" to her mother-in-law's jarring questions about whether she could take on countless housekeeping tasks as a newlywed.

Sitti shared the challenges of those early years with me when I interviewed her and Sidi back in 1992. *Bit'arifi tikhbazi?*—Do you know how to bake? *Bit'arifi itghasli?*—Do you know how to wash clothes? She didn't dare say "No." It was within those stone walls that she struggled to measure up to her in-laws' expectations, where she became pregnant and miscarried her first child. She once told me she had *talatashir batan*—13 bellies—referring to 13 pregnancies, out of which 12 of 14 children survived, having had one miscarriage and losing one twin—Faisal's twin sister—and the youngest child Zahara, a short-lived little sister to Nasser, who died at the age of two. This period of hardship passed when Sidi and Sitti were able to build their own house in the village, where Nasser's mother no longer fell under the scrutiny of her in-laws, though raising 12 children and working the fields, in addition to cooking and cleaning, were no small task.

We enter the cemetery through an opening in the privacy wall of the mosque. I am pleased to see the minaret towering over the modest building below since the village mosque didn't use to have one. I had suggested starting a fund to build one the year I spent in Palestine with Canaan and Karmel, but others took on that task to raise the money to adorn their mosque with its very own minaret, which was completed the following year. A mosque without a minaret is like a mother without a voice. Now, when I awake in the middle of the night, I can hear the soothing call to prayer, one of the oldest forms of melodic spoken word.

In this part of the world, responding to the call to prayer knows no limits. I have seen men in the middle of the market bow down toward Mecca and pray while shoppers bustle by. Fulfilling this Muslim duty is between oneself and God, and yet I often hear Nasser's sisters ask their mother if she prayed at various times throughout the day. *Salayti yama?*—Did you pray, Mama?

Just inside the cemetery, Nasser points to the right and pauses. His father's grave. Somehow, the rectangle of concrete protruding above ground hits me with a finality I hadn't experienced from a distance. On the headstone, painted in black, is his name and the year of his birth and death in Arabic, below an inscription from the Quran. The rectangle is framed with the off-white stones used on the façade of houses, the center filled in with concrete. As a Muslim, Sidi was wrapped in a seamless, white muslin cloth and laid to rest on his side facing Mecca. I try to picture him there, but I can only feel the weight of the concrete. I look past the grave and realize there is no room on either side for Nasser's mother to be buried next to him. My chest tightens. *Where will they put Sitti when her time comes?*

Even though it is winter, the rains have yet to fall, so the ground is dry and dusty, prickly brush claiming the space between the graves. Farther ahead, Nasser points out a long grave of individual stones arranged in an oval with a large headstone at one end and bare earth in the middle. No name, only stones. "This is Sidi Abdel Hadi's grave," pointing to his father's father's grave.

I compare the longer arrangement of stones to nearby graves. "He really was tall, wasn't he?" Nasser walks a few more steps in silence, his movements slow as he points to a smaller grave of stones. "This is Khariyeh's grave." As his head hangs low, I immediately think of his sister Khariyeh's child, who died with her in her womb at seven months. And then I see it, next to

Khariyeh's grave, a tiny arrangement of stones, hardly big enough to form an oval, with a small headstone at one end. *The baby.*

Khariyeh was said to be the most beautiful of the sisters. I only know her through stories and the one photo I have of her that hangs in our home in Madison, along with photos of her children and Nasser's other siblings, and Sidi and Sitti in one multi-picture frame I put together to honor them all. At the cemetery, people are buried wherever there is room, so families are scattered, but at least they all lie undisturbed. I am reminded of graves in Germany that are only kept if the family maintains them. Otherwise, they are razed to make room for new ones. I wonder if my grandparents' graves are still there.

Later in the evening, Nasser's brother Jamal invites us to Jenin with his wife and children to get fresh juice from one of the local shops. The front case is filled with carrots, oranges, apples, and bananas. The streets are bustling with activity since all the shops and restaurants are open for the Eid, each storefront revealing an assortment of wares gleaming beneath the streetlights.

People of all ages are meandering along, their eyes sparkling from the lights, their faces all smiles and laughter, their clothes crisp and smooth, full of color and sheen. Shiny shoes, shimmering jewelry, an atmosphere of festivity and light. Young girls wearing frilly dresses. Boys in crisp dress shirts neatly tucked into dress pants with a belt. Teenage girls in fitted, long-sleeve shirts with jackets or sweaters over slim pants, their heads adorned with coordinated scarves tightly wrapped around their made-up faces as they walk close together in clusters. The older boys look chic in their slim pants and brightly colored button-down shirts with fitted jackets, walking arm in arm or holding hands, their hair shiny, slicked back with hair gel, full on top. They are clean shaven with dazzling smiles, like teenage pop stars parading down the sidewalks, their teeth gleaming in the light.

It is a delight to see Jenin so alive and full of cheer. No soldiers in sight to remind us of the occupation, no officials from the Palestinian Authority to give us a false sense of security. Tonight, Palestine is alive and free. It is a night to feel good, look good. No school, no work, except for the shopkeepers, who delight in the extra business. A time of connecting with family and friends, a time to reach out to those less fortunate, take pride in family and community, celebrate into the night. *Palestine is still there.*

While everyone is celebrating the Eid at home, those lucky enough to have the opportunity to travel to Mecca in Saudi Arabia—chosen by lottery—are participating in the Islamic ritual of the *hajj*.[118] I am reminded of our last visit, when Nasser's sister Huda and her husband Said were so fortunate to participate in the ritual of walking around the Kaaba seven times with millions of others, all dressed in seamless robes.[119] When they return with the honorary title of Hajji Huda and Hajj Said, they share holy water from the Zamzam Well with us and give us each a keychain with a photo of the Kaaba. *Is there another place on Earth where everyone walks as one?*

The following day, we drive to Burqin to see the Canaan Fair Trade facility for the first time. Until now, Nasser used olive presses in the area for the olives he purchased from local farmers and stored the oil in a rented warehouse in the village of Sanur, where we witnessed the fields flooded on our first trip to Palestine back in 1992, creating a temporary lake. The setup was cumbersome and disconnected, so Nasser sketched a factory on a piece of paper and reached out to socially conscious lenders in Europe to support his vision.

Now that vision is materializing before our eyes. The reinforced-concrete walls stand tall, with steel rods sticking out on the roof to build a second floor. The exterior of the building is *labis hajr*—literally "dressed in stone"—the same creamy-white stone façade of his family home. The framing for the arched walkway along the front wall is taking shape. Inside, we walk on floors painted brick-red and walkways bright green until we reach the state-of-the-art Italian olive press, which just had its first run during the olive harvest in November. It spans from one side of the room to the other, with several smaller stainless-steel tanks at the far end painted in a swirl of bright colors by local artists.

The walls of the olive press room are lined with tiles adorned with key words written in Arabic calligraphy to celebrate this communal effort. The inspiration came from a set of Arabic greeting cards Nasser and I had bought from the calligraphy artist Nihad Dukhan at the Arab World Festival in Dearborn, Michigan, years earlier.[120] The artist gladly designed dozens of tiles for the olive press room, including words that represent Palestinian culture and people's connection to the land: الجد (*al-jad*—perseverance), فخر (*fakhar*—pride), and شرف (*sharaf*—honor); شجرة (*shajara*—tree), الأرض (*al-ardh*—earth), and جذور (*jathour*—roots); and جاروعة (*jaru'ah*), the name of the celebration at the end of the olive harvest.

My heart swells with gratitude that these concepts are being brought to life through the entire project. Investing in people's lives and livelihoods by honoring the rich, age-old traditions of tending to the land is at the core of Nasser's vision. It is also the core of the story of Palestine, where people have tended the land for generations. Living on the land is what Palestinians live for, long for. It is their past, what they are fighting for in the present, and how they envision the future. It is also our future. *We are making a difference.*

I reflect on these realities as we walk past a simple bottling station, where employees hand-fill each bottle of olive oil and then glue labels on by hand before packing the finished bottles in custom cardboard boxes. The showroom, with reclaimed wood shelves and tables from Indonesia, houses an impressive display of bottles of Canaan olive oil for sale around the world. In the storage area, large plastic cubes in metal cages stand filled with olive oil, ready to be shipped for bulk orders. The entire operation is "insisting on life," as Nasser says, and our children are part of it.

Canaan gets a turn at driving the forklift to place the cubes against the wall. Karmel reaches his arms out wide between underground stainless-steel tanks that tower over him. Sham runs across a vast pit dug out to accommodate more underground stainless steel olive oil tanks in the future. We all laugh when she says she'd rather make it into a giant swimming pool. We climb up the still unfinished stairs to watch the sun set over a breathtaking view of the village of Burqin, the setting sun peeking from behind a sea of olive trees. That tiny sketch Nasser drew has become a reality. The entire operation of Canaan Fair Trade is under one roof, a legacy for the future of Palestine. How proud Nasser's father would be!

42

Naqab

It is Christmas Day. Nasser and I plan to take Canaan, Karmel, and Sham to visit our friends, Kathy and Ismael, who live in the Naqab Desert—what Israel calls the Negev. It has been four years since we attended the conference on marginalized peoples that Ismael organized at Ben-Gurion University of the Negev. Since then, they have visited us several times in Madison. Now, we get to visit them in their home. I am excited to experience their world, as I have read a great deal about the marginalization of Bedouins in Israel, including from Ismael's own work on the subject.

We drive two hours south through Ramallah to the Qalandia checkpoint. It is packed with cars, but we manage to find a crowded parking lot close to the checkpoint to leave Nasser's car while we enter East Jerusalem on foot. Vehicles from the West Bank and Gaza with white license plates are off-limits in East Jerusalem ever since it was annexed by Israel following the 1967 war. Makeshift concrete barriers demark dusty parking lots littered with trash. In the distance, Israeli soldiers peer down on the area from watchtowers while my eyes take in graffiti in protest of the gray concrete wall, including the famous CTRL+ALT+DEL mural. *If erasing this concrete wall were only that simple.*

We walk over to the entrance to the checkpoint, crowded with Palestinians. There are no lines. Ahead of the crowd is a wall of bars with a single entrance, a barred one-way swivel doorway. Above it is a buzzer and a red light that periodically turns green, prompting someone to push their way through. Some smaller-built people or women with small children squeeze themselves into the tiny space two at a time. I am nervous for my children. I want to squeeze Sham in with me so we don't get separated. Like the rest of the crowd, I am plotting my entry across this checkpoint. First, we have to show our passports at a counter with bulletproof glass between us and the guard, our gatekeeper. He decides who shall cross this border and who will be turned back. I feel like our whole family is on trial—the familiar gaze of scrutiny from behind the glass with repeated glances down at our passports, as if something in our eyes or papers will decide our fate. We can pass, but we have to wait for the light to turn green. Others are also waiting to pass from one sea of people to the sea beyond.

Finally, we squeeze our way through the narrow passageway, relieved to meet up with Ismael in East Jerusalem. It doesn't feel like Christmas. The streets are relatively quiet and dark. Karmel spots a chocolate Santa in the window of a candy shop just outside Damascus gate, and we go in to get him one. Sham is delighted by the fake Christmas tree in the corner and all the brightly colored candies displayed in the narrow shop. It is our island of Christmas.

I duck my face into the collar of my fur coat to shield myself from the cold and rain while Ismael leads us to a pleasant Arabic restaurant with stone walls and traditional décor of handwoven baskets, tatriz embroidery, and brass coffeepots. We have the place almost to ourselves. We feast on an array of grilled meats and roasted vegetables, as well as traditional favorites of hummus, baba ghanouj, a parsley dip called *baqdounisiyeh*, tabouleh and other salads, and a colorful display of pickled vegetables. Although we are all tired from traveling, we stay for a while after dinner to smoke *argileh*, the traditional water pipe with honey-soaked tobacco. The smoke creates a thick haze between us that is almost hypnotic as it changes shape before my eyes in mid-air like a ghost serpent. We spend the night at the Jerusalem Hotel, the owner a friend of Nasser's, with its distinctive stone walls and arched windows, as if we are distant travelers in an ancient palace, finding refuge at the end of a long day.

The next morning, we get a rental car with yellow license plates from Jerusalem so we can drive in Israel. Since Canaan, Karmel, and Sham now have a *hawiyeh*—an Israeli ID indicating their residency in the West Bank—they are technically not allowed to enter Israel without a tasrih permit. To circumvent this restriction, I have to pass through a checkpoint in West Jerusalem used primarily by Jews, where we will attract less attention as a mother with my three children. Since Nasser has a special tasrih permit to enter Israel as a businessman, he passes through a different checkpoint in East Jerusalem with Ismael, who, as an Israeli citizen, can enter Israel without any problem. We will meet them on the other side of the checkpoint in West Jerusalem.

I take a deep breath. *Will I find my way? Will I get through? What if we are stopped and turned back?* I wind through the city into West Jerusalem as Ismael instructed me. When I see modern apartment buildings, two or three stories tall, covered in the signature white Jerusalem stone, I know I must be getting close. The roads are new, and the median between them is lined with flowering bushes. Pristine, but deserted. I don't see anyone anywhere. *Like in Beisan.*

I finally reach the turn that leads us downhill to the checkpoint with several lanes, each separated by concrete islands and covered with an overhang like a tollbooth. I approach the area, slow down, and pick a lane in the middle. I need to look like I know what I am doing so I don't attract attention. I slow down, but not too much, and scan the area. I see soldiers off to the right, not at each lane as I had expected. I glance over at them, then smile and wave as I pass. I realize I am holding my breath. I look straight ahead and keep driving. I don't look back.

Once I am in the clear, I take a deep breath and call Ismael to let him know I got through. He says if I follow the Wall, I will find them. I drive along the Wall that separates Jerusalem from the West Bank. Israel constructed the Wall around Jerusalem, cutting deep into the belly of the West Bank so the city would fall within Israel. With the Wall immediately adjacent to the road, I feel trapped in its gloomy shadow. I don't see them anywhere. I keep driving, the shadow of the Wall looming over me like a thick storm cloud. Just ahead, the Wall turns sharply to the right. There they are, Ismael and Nasser, pulled to the side of the road, waiting for me in the bright sun. I pull up out of the shadow next to them, the weight of the Wall lifted for a moment.

Nasser rejoins us, and we follow Ismael, making our way out of

Jerusalem into 1948 Palestine, heading west toward the Mediterranean Sea. In the distance, I see how the Wall cuts across the land like a concrete snake, dividing communities in its path. We reach the highway and head south toward the city of Beersheba. The sign is in Hebrew, English, and Arabic. The Hebrew reads באר שבע, the English Be'er Sheva, the Arabic بئير شيبع which, like the signs to Beisan, is only an Arabic transliteration of the Hebrew instead of the Arabic name for the city, بئر السبع (pronounced *Bi'r es-Saba'*). Before Israel, this city was called Beersheba in English, derived from the Arabic. Now, there is no acknowledgment of the Arabic name even though Palestinians still live there.

As I look around, the land becomes noticeably drier, less populated, empty. Vegetation becomes sparse with open spans of flat desert, where we occasionally see a herd of camels off the side of the road. I almost don't see them since they are the same color as the ground.

After an hour or so, we exit the highway and head east until we reach the entrance to the town of Lakiya, one of a number of townships the State of Israel built in an attempt to sedentarize the Bedouin community in the Naqab.[121] The entire town has the look and feel of a suburb, consisting of mostly two-story, single-family homes neatly arranged next to each other on paved streets with curbs. Some homes are still under construction—no open spaces, no shops, no larger buildings. It is a town of houses, one after the other. The streets are straight and end at right angles. In order to live in these townships, Bedouins must relinquish their claim to their ancestral land, which Israel has claimed as "state land." *Dispossession disguised as development.*[122]

Ismael explains that it was not long ago that all these families lived traditional Bedouin lives in tents out in the open landscape of the Naqab Desert. The state is determined to have them settle, to live in houses, to abandon their traditional way of life of raising animals and moving from place to place to graze and grow seasonal crops. By barring the Bedouin from grazing their animals, a central part of their semi-nomadic lifestyle, the state has transformed the legal claim of entire Bedouin communities to their land into the criminalization of individuals.[123]

Ismael adds that there are still at least 40 Bedouin communities in the area known as the "unrecognized villages," who refuse to settle in the townships. They live difficult lives because the State of Israel does not provide them access to water, electricity, or other municipal services, including schools and clinics. They are there but invisible on the map. Roads go past them, and powerlines skip over them. They are the last outposts of Bedouin resistance to a state that wants to sever their connection to the land and their capacity to live free, unbound lives.[124]

Since its founding, Israel has sought to settle the Naqab in the south and the Galilee in the north with Jews, two regions heavily populated by Palestinians. Since its founding, Israel has sought to settle the Naqab in the south and the Galilee in the north with Jews to Judaize these areas with larger concentrations of Palestinians. In the Naqab, Israel claims to "make the desert bloom" but restricts Bedouins from cultivating their land. Viewing Bedouins in the unrecognized villages as squatters on their own land, the state repeatedly demolishes their homes or tents, destroys their crops, and uproots their trees while fully backing Jewish settlement in the area with ample resources and services for a comfortable lifestyle.[125]

We settle in at Ismael's house, see his wife Kathy and their children, and meet Ismael's brother and mother, who shows us the traditional weavings she made of sheep's wool hand-spun into yarn and dyed in bright colors that stretch along the top of the wall as decoration. She fears soon no one will know how to make these prized crafts. Most Bedouins have resorted to plastic or burlap tents instead of the traditional black goat-hair tents since grazing herds of black goats has long since been outlawed by the State of Israel's Green Patrol, a police force that criminalizes grazing or building structures on "state" land, to allegedly protect the environment from desecration. Those who still have goat-hair tents reserve them for special occasions. Ismael's mother also points out that all the richest areas of land, where they used to grow lentils and other crops during the winter months, are off-limits to them now. They have all become Israeli farms.

Kathy is doing her doctoral research on health problems among Bedouin communities in Israel. Completely isolated in the township, out in the middle of the desert with no center of commerce, no local industry, their change in lifestyle has been detrimental to their health. To make matters worse, Israel has declared surrounding areas "firing zones," or built petrochemical factories, landfills, and nuclear facilities nearby, which threaten both their safety and their health. Pushed into less fertile areas of the Naqab and forced to abandon their traditional way of life, Bedouins live in a food desert, now mostly dependent on store-bought foods. With severe restrictions on land access and land use, fresh produce is limited, resulting in high rates of diabetes and malnutrition.[126]

Later in the afternoon, we head to a simple, one-story building that serves as the extended family's gathering space for hosting guests. It is a poor equivalent to the traditional diwan, where guests passing through are received, and mostly men gather to exchange the news of the day. We sit on mats along the wall across from an iron wood-burning stove. One of the family elders serves us the signature slow-brewed Bedouin coffee in tiny porcelain cups, ready and waiting over the glowing fire in a traditional brass *ghalai* topped with an ornamental crescent moon. The rich aroma of coffee and cardamom fills the cool air. The tradition of honoring guests with a cup of coffee persists, only within four walls instead of under a tent. *Not all is lost.*

The next day, Nasser and I drive out with Ismael and Kathy and our five children to visit the nature reserve of Ein Avdat, situated in a canyon with a spring, waterfalls, and ancient caves. It used to be a vital water source for the Bedouin community, but its national park status means access is now restricted to tourism. On the way, we see some of the unrecognized villages strewn on the hillsides, their black tents visible from the road. Electrical wires cross over them like bridges. Not a single line of electricity runs to them. They are faced with either succumbing to the state and giving up their way of life or being further marginalized. In their current standoff, they remain invisible to the state, neither counted nor named, but I see them and know who they are.

We drive farther south to an overlook of a giant crater not far from the grave of David Ben-Gurion, the first prime minister of Israel. While we stand in the hot sun, trying to imagine the massive impact from space that transformed this landscape, we hear F16 fighter jets roar in the distance. I am accustomed to hearing F16s in the West Bank, but their distinctive roar always makes me nervous. I know it is the Israeli army either practicing to attack or on the attack. From where we are, I assume they are on a practice run.

Moments later, I notice Ismael standing next to his car with the door open, listening intently to the car radio. His face is long, his eyes intense, staring at the ground without seeing. He tells us Israel has just launched an attack on Gaza with air strikes. It is December 27, 2008.

A surge of disbelief and fear races through my body. Unable to exhale, my stomach tightens. The familiar roar in the distance is no practice mission. It is the beginning of Operation Cast Lead, only two years after Hamas came to power in Gaza through contentious parliamentary elections that ousted Fatah's authority from the Gaza Strip. I am stunned, standing there in the hot sun, staring toward the Mediterranean Sea. I cannot see the sea, and I cannot see Gaza, but I know it is no more than 40 miles away. Here we are at a tourist site, a giant crater caused by bombardment of the Earth from space, while people in Gaza face Israeli bombing from the sky. My throat tightens as I ponder this madness.

The operation drags on for three weeks, leaving over 1,400 Palestinians and 13 Israeli soldiers dead. This attack will not be the last. In 2014, Gaza will again be under attack with the launching of Operation Protective Edge, where more than 2,200 Palestinians are killed and 71 Israelis. More madness. More killing. More destruction. Subsequent attacks on Gaza in accordance with Israel's "mowing the grass" policy follow, allegedly to debilitate Hamas' military capabilities and serve as a deterrent to create "periods of calm." Sidi's words ring in my ears. *The war is not over.*

Back in Lakiya, we visit Ismael's cousin, who still has camels, sheep, and goats, though they are confined to an outdoor, covered pen at the perimeter of the township. Grazing is only allowed by the State of Israel for a select few with permits and only during a few months of the year. Anyone else caught grazing in the open desert will have their animals confiscated by the Green Patrol. Violators are fined and have to also pay for the feed given to their animals during confiscation. I try to wrap my mind around this twisted reality that Bedouins are deemed an environmental hazard. Under the pretext of protecting the landscape, the State of Israel forbids the indigenous people of the area from living their traditional way of life on their own land.[127]

A group of female camels stands with a young calf in a tent-covered area. The one and only male is tied to a rope in a separate pen off to the side, angry at being confined and separated from the females. He calls out to them in frustration, digging his soft, round feet into the dry sandy ground, raising and lowering his head in defiance of his captivity. We get to touch the females and the baby, scratching the bony bridge of their noses and patting their warm dusty necks, but we are told to keep our distance from the male, as he could be dangerous.

There are also goats and sheep all organized in a line next to each other, the feed at their heads in a long narrow trough. Buying feed for them from Israel instead of grazing as they have done for centuries is not financially viable, but they have no choice. At least they have access to fresh milk and can make cheese.

Ismael's cousin's setup is rare here. Nearly all the Bedouins in the townships gave up their animals long ago because there is virtually no extra land to keep them. Instead, they compete for limited job opportunities as day laborers in neighboring towns or in the only nearby city of Be'er Sheva. For most Bedouins, there is little work. But there is no going back.

Ismael uses his position as a professor at Ben-Gurion University of the Negev to increase opportunities for Bedouins to pursue degrees in higher education, but options are limited. He sends his children to a Jewish school with instruction in Hebrew in the hope that they will have a greater chance to fulfill their own dreams than if they stay in the local Arab schools, with the highest school dropout rates in the country. Either way, they are immersed in Jewish history and culture, their own identity and background not even in the curriculum. But they stick it out. They are strong kids. They know who they are. They know their history, their land, their language, and their culture. Now, they also know those of their oppressor. Maybe that knowledge will give them some edge, some way of making sense of the context in which they live, some understanding of how to make room for themselves in what has become of their land and their way of life.

I wonder about the future of the Bedouins, given the State of Israel's targeted policies to disrupt their lives and undermine their livelihood. I wonder what will become of the residents of the unrecognized villages throughout the Naqab, determined to stay on their land rather than be corralled like animals into the confined and unviable spaces of Israeli-built and Israeli-designed townships. These neatly packaged townships hide the bitter realities of life there, the renaming of places, the rewriting of history, forcing these people to live completely different lives than their ancestors. *How will their memories guide them and future generations? Will they find a way back to the land? Or are the old ways lost forever?*

43

Persistence of Palestine

In the summer of 2011, Nasser gets Sham a tasrih, a permit, so Sham and I can once again travel to Palestine through Tel Aviv. I do not know in that moment that this will be my last trip for some time.

The Ben Gurion Airport has been rebuilt. It is no longer the modest, crowded building of the past. I gaze up at the high ceilings, stone walls, and multi-story panes of glass. It feels like quite a walk to get from the gate where I land to the baggage claim area. I enter an immense hallway with floor-to-ceiling glass panes on one side and a smooth stone wall on the other, lined with posters of stark, hand-drawn images with messages in bold letters.

I look more closely and realize each poster is from a different year, beginning in 1921. I pause to read the messages, some in Hebrew with translation, such as "Jews! The Key to Zion is in Your Hands! Open the Gates!" Others call on Jews to send money or come to Palestine to settle Erez Israel—The Land of Israel. Posters after 1948 celebrate the "Conquest of the Desert," the unity of the Jewish people with "One People, A Common Destiny," the immigration of Jews from the former Soviet Union, and the final poster, "Shaping Our Future. Together." These annual pleas for support to establish a Jewish homeland in Palestine with images of men and women working the land served as invitations to Jews from all around the world to come to Palestine.

With each poster I take in, my heart sinks deeper into my stomach. Year after year, poster after poster, this fund was running a campaign to reconfigure Palestine into the Land of Israel.[128] Of course, Zionists believe they are restoring the Land of Israel to its former glory, that the Palestinians wandered in over the centuries but have no claim to the land. *How can both truths, both claims to the same land, be reconciled?* And yet, Palestine is still there. There is more to the story. Maybe I can fill in the missing pieces, the rest of the narrative, the unnamed truths that have reduced Palestinians to living in Israel's shadow.

In 2009, Nasser's brother Jamal built a new house on the land his father left him, the land with the date palms. His eldest son is planning to get married and will renovate their old house next to Nasser's family home. I see Jamal has kept some of the mature date palms he planted years ago that now tower over his stately, two-story villa. I recall Nasser and I weighing in on the final plans of his house on our last trip. Now, I get to see the real thing!

I climb up the stone steps of the prominent entranceway and enter through the oversized wooden door, as if entering a palace. The foyer is an open two-story space with a round formal dining table in the center adjacent to a round family room with a built-in sofa that lines the entire perimeter. The adjacent kitchen gleams with black granite countertops and custom wood cabinets.

The wide-open staircase winds up to a landing that overlooks the foyer and leads to the bedrooms, each with high ceilings and built-in cabinets. A veranda off the kitchen opens to the backyard with surely the first and only lawn in the village with a large gazebo in the center. Nasser has spent years renovating his family home, but someday he will live right next door to Jamal. Year after year, seed by seed, stone by stone, things fall into place.

During that summer, I am fully engaged in our company, working with an American volunteer and the current group of Canaan university scholarship recipients to document the impact of Canaan Fair Trade from its inception in 2004 to the present. The company has grown considerably, now housing a bottling line for the olive oil, a jarring line for pickled olives and tapenades, a laboratory, and a completed second floor of office space. Working with the children of Palestinian farmers—most of them the first in their families to attend college—is a delight and feels like a natural progression from my previous work at the university. I build the data collection process into an Action Research Summer Program, so each student can take on a piece of the project to learn hands-on how to collect meaningful data that can directly benefit the communities under study.

With our guidance, the students conduct interviews with farmers to learn about how their life as farmers has been transformed through their affiliation with Canaan Fair Trade. Their testimonies are inspirational, expressing their love for their land and how, through Canaan's training programs, they have learned to take better care of their land with increased production. One farmer shares how farming alone supports his livelihood. He used to take his truck to Israel for work before the Wall. Now, he can rely on the company to purchase his harvest. The Canaan project has also benefited women through the establishment of women's cooperatives, which add income and value to their families.

It is an honor for me to tell the company's story. The interviews with farmers, women producers, and key people at the Palestine Fair Trade Association, as well as suppliers and financial supporters around the world, provide rich material to illustrate how Nasser's vision has reinvigorated the farming sector in Palestine. The annual celebration of the olive harvest in November, known as *al-jaru'a*, brings farmers together with the international guests who sell or distribute their products or use them as ingredients in their own products like Dr. Bronner's Magic Soaps—all companies that have a social commitment to supporting Palestinian livelihood as part of their business model.

Working with the students sends my heart soaring as I witness their dedication to their communities, bright creative minds carving out a place for themselves in their homeland. Many travel great distances by taxi to come to the company to participate in the training and research, eager to be part of something larger than themselves. The way they embrace the opportunity to go to college and use their skills to empower small-scale farmers—their families—to stay on their land and carry on their rich agricultural traditions, energizes me to pull all the stories and data together to document Canaan's story of "insisting on life" so we can more easily share it with the world.[129]

There are more stories in the making. Canaan Fair Trade is partnering with an organization to support a five-day ultramarathon Run Across Palestine in February 2012. Nasser and I travel to Jerusalem to finalize the runners' route. The thought of coming back to Palestine in a matter of months to witness the event fills my body with joy. I am overcome with a sense of promise that I am part of making a difference on the ground, creating stories of hope, where Palestine shines through Israel's shadow.

One afternoon, Nasser and I visit a cherry farmer in a nearby village to explore the possibility of adding cherry jam to the Canaan product line. We walk through the cherry orchard nestled down a steep slope behind the farmer's modest home, the gleaming red cherries reflecting the open blue sky. We arrive at a spring at the bottom of the hill. Clinging to the back wall of this oasis is a cloak of grape vines extending in all directions.

By mid-summer, most of the Palestinian landscape is dry and thirsty, the winter rains long over, but the grape leaves at this spring are a brilliant light green. The sun shines through them, proclaiming their youth and tenderness. My eyes open wide as my heart begins to sing a song of absolute joy and disbelief. The farmer hears my song. He calls out to me from the speckled shade of one of his vibrant cherry trees. *Lukuti qadesh ma biddik!*—Pick as many as you want!

I look at Nasser, wondering if we have time. "Go ahead." Thrill and anticipation race through my body as I approach the tender leaves sprouting toward the sun, fed by the cool, clear water of the spring. Carefully bending the stem back at the base of each leaf, I snap it and arrange the leaves in my other hand, one on top of the other, like a stack of fresh linen, the crown of the leaves mirroring the extension of my fingers. When I have accumulated a healthy stack of green velvet, I set it aside and continue gathering until I have several piles resting like freshly folded laundry.

The farmer's wife appears with a white plastic bucket, her slender face illuminated by her wide smile, the sun glistening in her gracious eyes. She and I pick leaves until we have gathered enough for a generous meal of dawali. My eyes meet hers with gratitude. *Yislamu ideiki*—Bless your hands.

U ideiki—And your hands. *Lukuti keman*—Pick more. She extends her arms out, as if welcoming the world to pick from her vines.

La, bekeffi—No, it's enough. After all, I have all I need to feed my family. My heart warms with this simple gift from the land, blessed with the sun and spring water that offers this family both life and livelihood. I realize these leaves, this practice, this place are all part of the story of the persistence of Palestine, a story that has become my story.

One evening, while visiting Nasser's sister Suhaila in the village of Rummaneh, we take a walk through what is left of their olive grove. Suhaila reminds me that Israel confiscated some of their land with over 150 olive trees just inside the Green Line when it began construction of the Separation Barrier back in 2002. Like in Jalameh, the barrier here is a fence constructed on Palestinian land inside the Green Line. I can't help but think of the land with the olive and almond trees Israel seized from Nasser's family to build the fence in Jalameh. Suhaila adds that others in the village also lost hundreds of olive trees. At the time, Suhaila's husband Riyadh tried to challenge the decision, but since village lands are located in Area C, as designated through the Oslo Accords, giving the Israeli army jurisdiction over what it considers state land, there was no reversing the decision.

Local residents cannot help but feel the decision is part of the same collective punishment they have experienced over the years for resisting Israeli occupation. They were denied access to water and electricity up until 2007, forced to truck in water and depend on generators for power that would often fail because they could not handle the demand. When Israel widened the main road—Highway 66 or Haifa Street that used to run from Jenin to

Haifa—they lost even more trees, some thousands of years old that were right along the road.

Not long after residents widened the main road into the village at their own expense, the Palestinian Authority expanded a different road into the village, likely under Israel's direction to provide the army with another access point into the village, resulting in the loss of even more trees. Suhaila's eyes sharpen as she tells me how their annual olive oil supply is shrinking with the loss of yet more land.

I remind her how years ago we picked zamatot—the cyclamen leaves to roll like stuffed grape leaves—in their hilly wa'ra close to the border. She smiles for a moment, then her eyes are heavy with sadness since they no longer walk deep into the wa'ra the way they used to—only to tend to their olive trees—because the Israeli army has dumped wild boar just inside the Green Line. I wince at the thought of wild boar roaming the hillside. She describes how these new residents near Palestinian villages and farmland run and rub and snort and dig, damaging trees and destroying crops, often roaming in groups with younger ones trailing behind them. Her eyes widen as she tells me how they sometimes charge at people, making it dangerous to tend to the trees and crops in these border areas. Like restless dogs let loose in a pristine garden, wild boar now trample crops with their sharp hooves, rub or chew the bark off trees, and roam the borderlands, as if the farmers are the intruders. Wild and aggressive, it is a challenge for farmers to safely navigate their land that offers them both life and livelihood.

Wild boar let loose on Palestinian lands, where most of the population is Muslim, only adds insult to injury since observing Muslims—and Jews, for that matter—don't eat pork. Unlike Jewish Israeli citizens who must serve in the Israeli army and have the right to bear arms, Palestinian civilians are not allowed to own weapons, so these creatures roam their lands under protected status. With so many offspring, the numbers of wild boar are increasing, making it even more challenging to safely care for their trees and crops. I wonder at this obscure form of animal terrorism. *How are Palestinians supposed to defend themselves from these invaders? How are they supposed to protect their livelihood?*

We linger in an open field, from where Suhaila says wild boar are sometimes visible in the distance at dusk. The sun is low in the sky, casting an orange glow on the faces of our children, the next generation of Palestinians. Once the glow fades, it is time to go home. It is no longer safe to be out here in the dark. I don't get to see the beasts that are wreaking havoc on the village. The very thought of them lurking out there is terrifying enough. *How will this family, this village, Palestinians the world over, protect their homeland?*

It is mid-July, and the days are getting hotter. Our visit is coming to a close, but I don't want to leave without making kras za'atar—flat loaves of bread laced with fresh thyme leaves. I have seen thick bunches of za'atar growing in the fields and right outside Nasser's brother Faisal's house. His wife, Feriyal, invites me to make it at their house with their za'atar. It is her mother, Mart Khali Isma'ayn, whom we have visited often in the village of Burqin, who makes the best *kras* za'atar I know. Now, I will get to learn this delicacy from her daughter.

I arrive at their house and ring the doorbell. *Min?*—Who's there? The voice of their youngest son, Firas, now 15, flows through the intercom.

Ana, Christa—It's me, Christa. The door buzzes and I open it, slide off my sandals, and make my way up the tile-covered stairwell. Feriyal invites me through the open door at the landing. *Ahleen, Im Kana'an*—Welcome Mother of Canaan.

Ahleen, Im Fadi—Hello, Mother of Fadi, I respond in kind in honor of her eldest son.

Tafaddali—Come in. Feriyal's right arm is outstretched toward the family room behind her. My eyes travel across the room to the view of the mountains from the western window. Just beyond them is the Mediterranean Sea.

We enter the kitchen, where large trays and a steel tub rest on a white plastic kitchen table next to the refrigerator and a four-burner gas oven range. Beneath white wooden cupboards is a black granite countertop that extends the entire length of the wall, the sink in the middle beneath another western-facing window. *Another window to the Mediterranean Sea.*

Khallina na'mal al-'ajin awal—Let's make the dough first. *Mish bithabi itstakhdami tahin qamih?* Don't you like to use whole wheat flour? She knows my trademark.

Ah, bas khallina inhut nus nus—Yes, but let's do half of each.

Mashi—Okay. I watch her scoop white and whole wheat flour into the steel tub and sprinkle yeast and water. She scoops the flour from the edge of the tub into the moist center, then kneads it to form a lumpy glob of dough.

Hati al-malih—Hand me the salt. I hand her a small bowl of loose salt, which she sprinkles with her dough-covered fingers, then continues kneading until it becomes a smooth elastic mass. She sets it aside and covers it with a large cloth.

While the dough rises, we head outside to harvest the za'atar planted in neat rows alongside their two-story house. Feriyal cuts an entire cluster of thyme off at the base and hands it to me, then moves from cluster to cluster until my arms are full. Back at the house, we sit across from each other and carefully slide our fingers down to the base of each stem until we are left with a bare stem in one hand and a bunch of loose leaves in the other, which we toss onto an empty tray.

Mish biddik tishtaghli?—Don't you want to go back to work?

La, wallah. Bekeffi shou ba'mal ma'a shughal Nasser wal-awlad—No, it's enough helping Nasser with the business and taking care of the kids. *Inshallah baktib 'an Falastin fil-mustaqbal*—Hopefully, I will write about Palestine someday.

Esh biddik tiktabi?—What do you want to write?

'Ankum—About all of you.

Helu—Beautiful.

Feriyal's whole face smiles like her mother's as she methodically strips the stems of their leaves, the fine black line of her eyebrows resting perfectly on her brow bone, the delicate lines in the corners of her eyes more pronounced when she smiles. I see her and she sees me, a growing pile of za'atar leaves between us.

Chatting about our children, school, and their upholstery business in Jenin to make cushions and pillows for floor mats, the time passes quickly. Before I know it, we have a mountain of thyme leaves on the tray and a pile of stems on the floor. Feriyal fills the sink below the window that faces the sea, the warm afternoon breeze brushing past my cheeks. She slides all the leaves into the sink, pressing them under the water to loosen the soil. They float magically to the top, agile swimmers, while the soil settles below. What a perfect system.

After a few minutes, I join her as she lifts out the za'atar, shaking the leaves as she lifts them, then sets them aside. We catch the stragglers by making our hands into a sieve until we have removed all the leaves, leaving a dark layer of soil at the bottom. Feriyal rinses out the sink, and we repeat the process two more times until she declares, *Bekefi, inthif*—That's enough, they're clean.

Feriyal uncovers the dough, now double in size, then pushes it down with her strong hands. We form balls the size of oranges, which we set aside on a steel tray. *Like Jaffa oranges.* Feriyal rolls each ball flat with a rolling pin, dribbles olive oil across with her hand, then sprinkles a handful of za'atar on half the dough before folding it over the leaves. She presses it down with her hands, then rolls it out gently, repeating this process several times to create layers of leaves poking out the sides, others completely embedded in the dough.

The rich and spicy aroma of the za'atar baking in the oven permeates the kitchen, the stationary fan softening the edge of the hot afternoon sun. Feriyal sprinkles water on each loaf as she pulls it out of the oven, then covers it with a cloth before sliding the next loaf into the oven. The pale-green leaves are now dark green and shiny from the olive oil. The stiff, golden loaves laced with thyme soften as they cool. She tears off a corner of one of the loaves.

Dukki—Try it. The soft bread laced with za'atar warms my heart and tantalizes my taste buds. Feriyal takes another bite. *Zaki*—Delicious.

Ah, zaki kitir—Yes, very delicious. I savor the flavor with each bite. Feriyal's smile is full of pride. *'Atik al-'afiyeh*—Nice work.

Allah 'afiki—May God also give you strength. My eyes move from hers to the golden stack of freshly baked loaves.

Khuthi ma'aki 'a Amrika—Take them with you to America.

Inshallah—God willing. *Yislamu ideiki*—Bless your hands.

U ideiki—And your hands.

Later that evening, my friend 'Aida and I *inkazdar*—take a slow walk—through the village. She lives next door and is the daughter-in-law of the former mayor, who organized a *yom tanthif*—day of cleaning—after I expressed concern about the garbage in the village streets on our first trip to Jalameh back in 1992. As we walk, I admire the creeping branches of jasmine atop the privacy walls. Hibiscus flowers close for the night. 'Aida reaches over to a lush green bush speckled with white flowers peeking through a privacy wall. Unlike the thin, delicate jasmine flowers, these are more substantial, though about the same size, with five or six rounded petals.

'Aida carefully holds one of the flowers up to my nose. *Shimmi*—Smell. So sweet and fragrant is the flower that I breathe in deeply to savor its scent.

Shou hatha?—What's that?

'Aida's gracious eyes meet mine. *Fulla*. She motions for me to tuck it away in my top to enjoy its sweet scent into the night, but I decline. I want to keep it in my hand, feel its soft, hearty petals between my fingertips, and hold it up to my nose so I breathe in its fragrance with every breath. I am delighted that I can rub my fingers on its rounded petals without destroying the flower. So aromatic is the fragrance that I now understand how perfumeries attempt to capture the essence of a scent so that women and men can experience these nightly walks or seaside soirées through ornate bottles, like magic potions that become more dazzling with each breath. By the time we reach home, the once-firm petals are crimped from my incessant handling. I let the flower fall to the ground, wishing I had some way of preserving its enchanting scent.

In earlier times, it was the orange trees that filled the night air with their sweet blossoms. I never got to experience the beauty and scent of their flowers as I only saw the orange trees in the heat of summer, when their blossoms had already transformed into succulent fruit covered with the pervasive dust of the dry summer heat.

Years later, when I experienced winter or spring in Palestine and could have seen their deep green leaves washed clean by the winter rains or the delicate white buds blossom into fragrant white flowers of spring, the orange trees of Jalameh were long gone. The groves were all cleared, one by one, due to the exorbitant price of water only Palestinians had to pay. The groves fell like dominoes, turning the thick green perimeter of orange trees around the village and the magnificent songbirds that nested in their branches into a silent, barren wasteland. In time, the groves were replaced with rows of the plastic hamamot greenhouses. They popped up like mushrooms. First a few, then the village was surrounded by them until all the former groves and much of the farmland transformed into a sea of white plastic ripples.

When I look at the greenhouses today, I still see the trees where they once stood. I recall the deep grooves in the rich, brown soil that channeled the water from one tree to another. I feel the cool shade they offered and hear the birds that I hardly saw; so thick and lush were the branches. I cannot help but mourn the loss of the trees and, at the same time, lament the larger loss of Palestine and the world-renowned Jaffa oranges, once the livelihood of Palestinian farmers, now a product of the State of Israel. I am reminded of Palestinian author Ghassan Kanafani's story, *The Land of Sad Oranges,* where a Palestinian family is forced to leave Jaffa and flee to Lebanon:

> *...rounding the bends in the roads and putting more and more distance between themselves and the land of the oranges, I too burst into a storm of weeping. Your mother was still looking silently at the orange. And all the orange trees that your father had abandoned to the Jews shone in his eyes, all the well-tended orange trees that he had bought one by one were printed on his face and reflected in the tears that he could not control in front of the officer at the police post. In the afternoon when we reached Sidon, we had become refugees.*[130]

What will become of the oranges? What will become of the birds? The sweetness of the *fulla* flower softens the hard edge of history. Its scent provides hope amid hardship. How grateful I am to take in that scent, to experience a sense of peace that sometimes only a flower can provide. I take the memory of this scent and all the other experiences of my travels with me as Sham and I head back to the US. Little do I know they will become the foundation of the story I have been waiting to tell my whole life about the persistence of Palestine.

PART VI

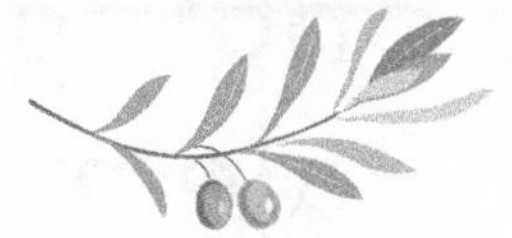

PATIENCE

Longing for Palestine

2012-2017

44

Longing for Palestine

That summer of 2011, when I worked so closely with the Canaan scholarship students to conduct research for the Impact Study, made za'atar pies with Feriyal, and carried the scent of the *fulla* flower home with me in my muscle memory, I had no idea it would be another seven years before I would return to Palestine. As Nasser and I sat at the Jerusalem hotel that summer to finalize the route of the Run Across Palestine through East Jerusalem, I knew there was nowhere else I would rather be. Palestine was home.

Unfortunately, the distance between us takes its toll and brings our marriage to an end, leaving me in a sea of uncertainty. I am heartbroken that I do not get to witness the event in February 2012, in which six Ultra Marathon runners from the US sponsored by On the Ground Coffee from Traverse City, Michigan, run over 100 miles in five days right through Palestinian communities most affected by the Wall. Besides, Canaan, Karmel, and Sham have school, so we stay home.

The run raises money to build schools and contribute to community projects. Sitting in Madison in the middle of winter, I feel helpless when I find out the first day that the Israeli army arrests Nasser for allegedly organizing a demonstration without a permit, though they shortly after release him on bail with the help of the American Consulate in Jerusalem. I tune in every day to watch video footage of the Run on Facebook, which later that year, is released as the documentary *The People & The Olive*.[131] In my mind and spirit, I am right there with them, and yet I wonder when I will get to see the olive trees Nasser dedicated to each runner on the grounds of Canaan Fair Trade. As I look out the window at the bare corkscrew willow during another Wisconsin winter, my heart aches to return to my homeland.

That summer, Canaan, Karmel, and Sham—now 18, 16, and 10—travel to Palestine for the first time without me, the seeds of their own future involvement in the family business being planted, while I attend a writer's retreat in the south of France and retrace the footsteps of famous writers like Ernest Hemingway and Simone de Beauvoir in Paris. My hope was to join the kids after, but I end up returning straight to Wisconsin.

Later that summer, Sitti passes away—*Allah yirhamha*—May God have mercy on her. It turns out to be the exact same day that Sidi passed away—*Allah yirhamu*—15 years earlier: July 22. Their souls were truly united. Now, it is up to those of us who remain to keep their memories alive.

Back in Madison, I meet up with Palestinian writer Lilas Taha, who is just finishing her first novel. As I sit by one of the fountains amidst an abundance of flowers in full bloom at Olbrich Gardens—a nationally recognized botanical garden in its own right and one of my favorite places in Madison with Lake Monona in the distance—the pivotal events from my years of experiences in Israel and Palestine flash before my eyes like scenes in a film I have seen a thousand times. Walking through the Old City in Jerusalem. Arriving at Salem's family in Gaza. Seeing the soldiers in army Jeeps outside my window. Meeting Nasser's family. Standing up to Israeli soldiers. Combing the landscape for destroyed villages.

Soon after the writer's retreat, on Nov 14, 2012, the Israeli army attacks Gaza in an offensive known as Operation Pillar of Defense. As my words pour onto the page, bombs are falling on Gaza. If only I could write fast enough to keep the bombs from falling. I wonder how long it will take me to finish, if my book will open some window of possibility to keep this senseless suffering in check.

In fall 2013, while Nasser is visiting the kids and me in the US, we take a family road trip, for old time's sake, all the way to Yellowstone in our RV. I am homeschooling Karmel and Sham, so it is a great opportunity to allow their interests and passion to drive their learning.

Along the way, I am reminded of the legacy of suffering and injustice in the US. As we drive through the Badlands and past Mount Rushmore, the white stone faces carved into Native land are visible from the road, a bitter reminder of the darker side of American history.

I recall t-shirts I have seen at powwows with the four images of Indian leaders Chief Joseph, Sitting Bull, Geronimo, and Red Cloud arranged like the American faces of George Washington, Thomas Jefferson, Theodore Roosevelt, and Abraham Lincoln on Mount Rushmore with the words "The Original Founding Fathers."

We boycott this memorial and instead travel to the Crazy Horse Memorial nearby, where we spend hours taking in the immensity of the monument, its construction, and the history and culture on display throughout the museum. Crazy Horse's message to the world is universal:

I see a time of Seven Generations
when all the colors of mankind
will gather under the Sacred Tree of Life
and the whole Earth
will become one circle again.

As we explore the natural wonders of Yellowstone Park and listen to the wolves calling out to one another at night, I think of all the places that have been robbed of their natural beauty, redefined by the force of progress and civilization. New lines form skyscrapers and bridges, roads and railways, nightclubs and neighborhoods. The glistening stars give way to neon lights. The hum of cars and trucks washes out the rustle of trees and grasses. And the multitude of calls among creatures, day and night, gives way to cityscapes overrun with sirens. *What has become of the land?*

It has been 27 years since I first met Nasser at the 5th Commemoration of the Sabra and Shatila massacre at Wayne State University in Detroit back in 1987. In spite of all the years building our life together, and our shared commitment to making a difference in Palestine, I can't help but feel that my homeland is slipping through my fingers with the loss of our marriage.

Beginning on July 8, 2014, Israel bombs Gaza yet again with Operation Protective Edge. As I witness the smoke, flames, and leveling of homes from my TV in Madison, my life feels in shatters. I wonder when I will go back to Palestine. Nasser, back overseas, is immersed in the business, and after spending most of his adult life in North America, he is once again living in his homeland.

I sink into sadness, wondering how a lifetime of personal and professional commitment to a place that has become home and a people that have become family, can suddenly feel so far away, so out of reach. As my body attempts to make sense of this despair, my hair falls out, first in patches, then before I know it, I don't even recognize myself as my battle with alopecia transforms the woman in the mirror, ultimately leaving me hairless.

After nearly three decades of traveling to Palestine, I cover my head with the gorgeous scarves I have collected over the years. Previously, if someone asked me why I don't cover my hair, I would say, in jest, *Ana imghati bi sha'ri*—I am covered by my hair. Now, the sting of such jokes comes full circle. In my mind, I don't know how to make sense of these layers of loss, but my body has clearly stepped in to grieve in full force. Somehow, I need to find inner peace even if *the war is not over.*

I hear a report that it will take 20 years to rebuild Gaza. To receive building materials, any new homes must register their GPS coordinates with the State of Israel. That way—from Israel's perspective—any misstep can be dealt with efficiently. People in Gaza live under the most desperate conditions of all Palestinians, held captive in an open-air prison in their homeland. They had already lost their homes, their land, their livelihood in 1948. Now, they are faced with a second round of homelessness. *How will they go on?*

After a childhood of moving from place to place with nowhere to call home, my connection to Palestine has formed deep roots that won't release me, like the images in Salem's paintings. I turn to writing, making Palestinian food, and occasional phone calls to Nasser's extended family. With each Palestinian dish I prepare, I assert my connection to a lost homeland, cling to it. After all, Palestine has been central to my life longer than any other place or memory. It has become part of everything I do. I fall back on pen and palate. I sink into my writing, as if memory is my only remaining connection to this far-off land.

My longing for Palestine and the loss of a lifetime of connection to a homeland fuels my writing, flooding the page with memories of the only place I have ever felt at home. I relive every memory like it was yesterday. Fresh as the newly picked romaine from 'Amti Saymi's farm, crisp and green, glowing in the sun. Not like Ghassan Kanafani's sad oranges, dried up and shriveled on the nightstand:

> *You were huddled there, as far from your childhood as you were from the land of the sad oranges—oranges that, according to a peasant who used to cultivate them until he left, would shrivel up if a change occurred and they were watered by a strange hand.*[132]

Even though the memories are fresh and powerful, I am not sure what story I am telling. *How can I share my words with the world when the story of my own life has become so uncertain?*

45

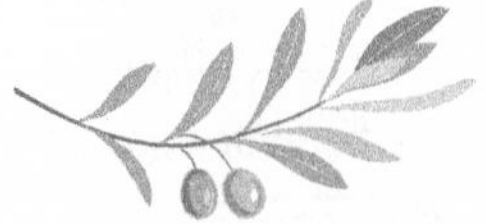

Standing Rock

The week before Thanksgiving in 2016, a friend who is Native American invites me to a rally in Madison in support of the Water Protectors at Standing Rock Indian Reservation in North Dakota. The rally is calling for an end to the construction of the Dakota Access Pipeline (DAPL) that would run under the Missouri River and threaten the water supply of the Lakota Sioux Nation. The $3.8 billion pipeline was originally planned to run farther north past the town of Bismarck, but its mostly white residents rejected having a pipeline run through their town for fear of water contamination, so the path was shifted south, putting the Lakota's water supply in danger.

Jewish Voice for Peace (JVP) is one of the event sponsors, a group committed to social justice, the environment, and peace and justice in Palestine. Member Fran Zell asks me to read a prayer for Phyllis Young, a Water Protector at Standing Rock known as "Woman Who Stands by the Water." Her words become my words: *"You'll never displace me again. You'll never put me somewhere where I don't belong."*

We march to the State Capitol building in Madison, chanting, "Water is life!" I recall marching for Palestine so many years ago, wondering what difference it made then and what difference we can make now. My doubts are softened by the bright faces of the children among us—the next generation—reminding me there are still battles to fight so that justice is served. There is no giving up, no surrender. And yet I wonder if I belong here. *Is this my battle?*

When we reach the Capitol Square, all eyes and ears are on a medic who just returned from Standing Rock. My heart pounds in my chest as she recounts tales of Water Protectors being met with tear gas and rubber bullets. *Like Palestine.* When she mentions that the camp needs chefs, a seed sprouts in my soul, takes root in my heart, and grows. Her story blossoms into a road trip to Standing Rock in South Dakota with my brother, Dieter, 30 years since we first traveled to Palestine. Nasser is coming from Palestine for Thanksgiving to spend time with Canaan, Karmel, and Sham, so I can just pick up and go.

Sacred Stone is the original Water Protector camp LaDonna Brave Bull Allard established on her property earlier that year. It is named after the Sacred Stones that used to form from the strong current of the Cannonball River and gave the river its name. When the Army Corps of Engineers seized land under eminent domain to build a hydroelectric dam in 1958, the river was forever changed and stopped producing Sacred Stones. Dieter and I will join the Water Protectors just south of the Oceti Sakowin Camp (see Map 13).

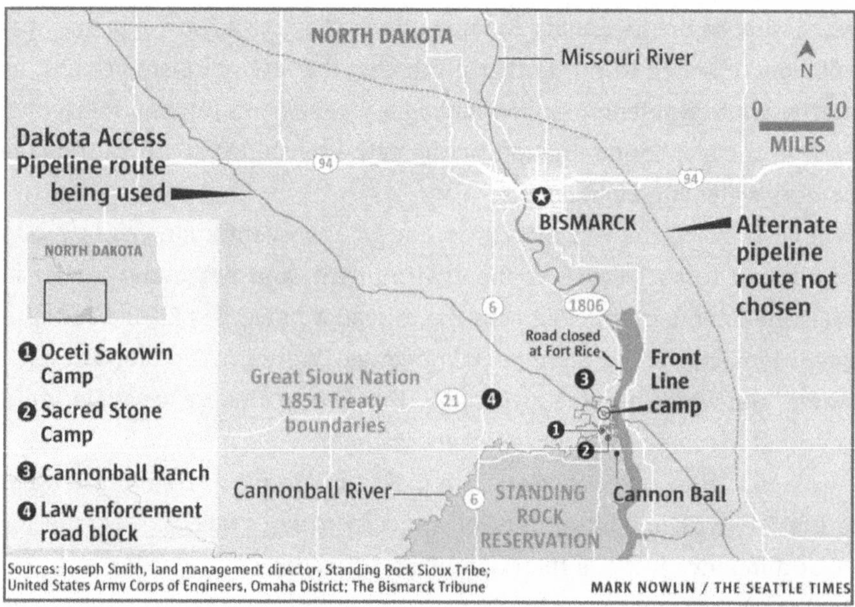

Map 13: Standing Rock Indian Reservation with Water Protector Camps, 2016 (Source: *The Seattle Times*)

Before I leave for Standing Rock, I hear reports of a standoff at the Backwater Bridge, where concrete barriers topped with barbed wire block the only access point to supplies and medical facilities in the nearby town of Bismarck. *Like road closures in Palestine.* Despite the freezing temperatures of a South Dakota winter, the heavy police presence blasts the Water Protectors—their bodies their only weapons—with water cannons, resulting in over 300 people injured, half suffering from hypothermia. Police also use pepper spray and beanbag rounds, as well as a high-pitched sound device, to disperse the crowd. Rather than evoke fear in me, the news of the standoff makes me more determined than ever to stand with Standing Rock.

Dieter drives with a couple of friends from Boulder, Colorado, his car packed with donations of thermal sleeping bags, jackets, stoves, propane, and flashlights. I travel from Madison with Monika, a Hungarian woman I met after the rally, who has been to Standing Rock before. Karmel helps me load my car with donations of down coats, blankets, tarps, rope, lighters, and storage bins, along with 200 pounds of cheese from a local cheesemaker and a jar of honey from a local beekeeper. I personally bring over a hundred pounds of grains, a case of onions, a hundred heads of garlic, and plenty of Canaan Fair Trade olive oil to make several Palestinian specialties I can easily cook in a pot over the fire from one indigenous culture to another. I plan to make *freekeh* soup using our company's own fire-roasted landrace wheat, *mujadara* with green lentils and brown rice, and the Palestinian crushed lentil soup *shoribut adas* we used to serve in our restaurant, the Shish Café, adding a Native American twist of wild rice.

The miles pass quickly. Dieter and I meet up just south of the camp. We follow the road over a hill, then cross the Cannonball River until we see a line of cars pulling into the main entrance next to a prominent banner that reads "Palestine Stands With Standing Rock." *Palestine is welcome here. Now, I know I am welcome, too.* We walk down the hill into the camp past flags fluttering softly in the wind that line both sides of the road as far as the eye can see, representing over 300 First Nations who traveled here in solidarity with Standing Rock. Ahead of us are several men on horseback. I have crossed into a whole new world.

The people of Standing Rock asked others to gather here from all over the world to raise awareness about indigenous rights and environmental protection, and they came (see Map 14). Hundreds have become thousands, with more people pouring in each day. As dusk sets in, the line of cars by the entrance to the camp grows longer, their headlights glowing in the darkening sky.

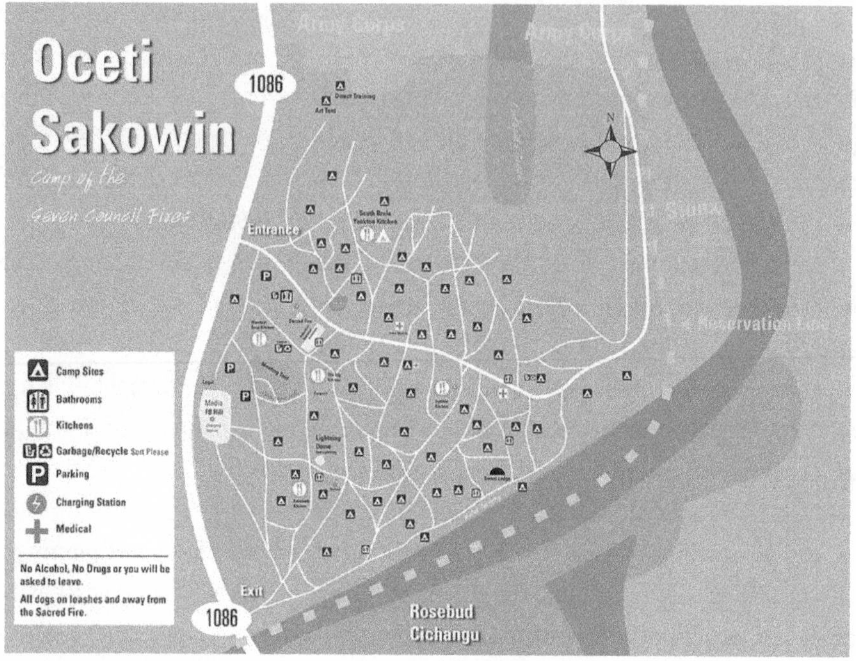

Map 14: Oceti Sakowin Camp at Standing Rock Reservation, 2016 (Source: Wix Images)

We pass by the main kitchen to say hello to Chef Brian Yazzie from the Sioux Chef restaurant in Minneapolis, who welcomes me to cook there anytime. We end up setting up camp at the Hoopa Nation, where we meet Patty and BeaVi, who run the California Kitchen named after Patty's restaurant in California. With time, we learn everyone calls it "Grandma's Kitchen." When I tell them about the food I brought, a young man in the kitchen walks over to me. "So, you want to make Palestinian food? Sounds great!" He has spent time in Hebron and loves Arabic food. It turns out he is Israeli. "I am from the other side, but I feel closer to the Palestinians." I am honored to be welcomed into this kitchen. I feel right at home.

After dinner, we meet Wonase, a tall elder from Standing Rock, who calls the gathering at the camp the real United Nations. "We must welcome all, even the enemy. They are all in need of healing." He says that is why they want to hurt us. Their hearts are full of greed, full of fear, full of pain. We can help them heal by remembering what it means to be human. "We all need healing. We are all the same. We need water. We need safety. We need to trust that it is time." He speaks slowly and quietly, his message clear and strong. *Israelis and Palestinians need healing, too.*

I hang on every word. We thank him for his words. Later in the evening, we visit the Sacred Fire in the center of camp, where several elders are gathered. Different nations take turns holding a Drumming Circle and singing. Now and then, someone shares words from a microphone. As the evening progresses, we join hands and dance the Circle Dance, stepping clockwise to the rhythm of the drums. *Like dancing dabkeh.* Facing each other around the fire, my heart acknowledges we are all one. Occasionally, someone kneels to pray, offering cedar, sage, or tobacco to the fire to honor the ancestors, Mother Earth, the Great Spirit.

A young woman from Red Warrior Camp across the river steps up to the microphone. "Tomorrow is Thanksgiving. You all know what that means." Her voice is stern and serious. She talks about what her people have suffered and how we must defeat the Black Snake, referring to the oil pipeline. "Our message for this day is no thanks, no giving, no pilgrims, no promises, no pipelines, no prisons, no problems!" Her voice is strong and loud now. I hear Wonase's words in my head. *We all need healing.*

As we head back toward the camp, I notice a glow coming from the north. Monika points in the distance. "Those are the floodlights from the police." The eerie glow backlights the camp, the tops of teepees illuminated from behind. *Like the Israeli army's flares that lit up the Jenin night sky on my first visit to Jalameh.*

That night as I lie in my tent taking in our first evening at Standing Rock, I hear drumming and singing in the distance. Then a hum emerges overhead, louder, then softer, then louder again, possibly a helicopter or a plane. *They are watching us.* The sound drowns out the peaceful drumming and singing. *What are you looking for? We want to sleep.* I drift in and out of sleep, waking to the hum circling overhead. My eyes close again. I think again of Wonase's words. *They need healing.*

I awake on Thanksgiving to a sheer dusting of snow, blending all the colors and textures of the camp into whiteness. Grandma's Kitchen has already made macaroni and cheese for breakfast from the cheese I brought from Wisconsin. After breakfast, I wrap a red shawl around my waist that my brother brought me from one of his teacher-training assignments in Pakistan to cover my legs, as his friend explains is customary among Lakota women.

Dieter and I walk with our friends to the river and spot a wooden post covered with signs made of scraps of wood, noting places where people came from and how far they traveled.

Tascarona Skarure. Detroit 1,607 mi. Port Huron. Santa Fe. Thunder Bay. Onondaga Nation 1,572 mi. Akwesasne 1,664 mi. Phoenix. White Earth Nation. Six Nations 2,165 km. Hiaki. Teh Luh Lah Center in Chimayo, NM 1,400 km. Haudenosaunee. Grand River.

The call to come here has touched so many. And here we are. I feel hopeful that our presence can make a difference and shake off the Black Snake that threatens this community, though I have my doubts, given the decades of injustice I have witnessed in Palestine.

On our way back, I spot a red triangle anchored in green, white, and black stripes dancing in the wind. *The Palestinian flag*. The words of Gaza writer Israa Suliman come to mind: *We know what you know: that our land is sacred*. Land, water, way of life, burial sites—the story of Palestine has much in common with the story of Standing Rock, and where they intersect. I begin to see more clearly the power of coming together.

We pass people sorting donations, a tent filled with boots and jackets for those who need them, people chopping firewood, and others placing hay bales around the base of teepees to insulate them for winter. I realize we are all here simply being human, doing what needs to be done, and taking a stand with our very presence. This is what it means to stand with Standing Rock. Lend a hand, cook a meal, be present in body on the ground. It occurs to me that all the years I went to Palestine, I was standing with Palestine by simply being there, joining in on food and festivities, bearing witness to people's celebrations and struggle for survival. *Insisting on life.*

The calm of the camp is broken when a car drives by urging all women and children to get to the round white tent known as the Dome right away. Men are asked to go to the North Gate. The police are going to raid the camp. *Like the night raids of the Israeli army on Palestinians.*

Dieter and I look at each other. *Are we going to split up?* Then someone else announces that the elders want everyone to stay in the camp. After all, we did not come here to be driven out. Besides, it is Thanksgiving, and dinner is nearly ready.

We head back to Grandma's Kitchen, where a couple of guys dig turkeys out of a deep fire pit that have been slow cooking all night and all morning. The kitchen is bustling with activity. I help carry various dishes and desserts out to the Dome, filled with a feast arranged on tables along the perimeter from all the camp kitchens.

Before dinner, the leader of the Hoopa Nation leads the prayer with words of gratitude, hope, peace, and resilience. We stand around him like penguins, huddling to keep warm. He announces two babies were born today at the Sacred Stone Camp. Standing Rock has become a village.

People are called to dinner in succession, first the Native elders, then Native women and children, followed by Native men, then non-Native women and children, and finally, non-Native men. Hours go by as each group is called to enter the Dome. Even though the Dome holds no more than 200 people, there is enough room for people to eat, then move on to make space for those who come after.

It is late afternoon, and the sun peeks out from behind the clouds, casting a warm glow over the teepees and tents that have become our village. I feel hope as the sun softens the biting chill of the winter wind. We find out later that evening that Water Protectors built a bridge across the river to Turtle Island to protect the sacred remains of their ancestors buried there. Three hundred people crossed the river before the police dismantled the bridge, blocking access to Turtle Island.[133] Now, reinforcements and snipers are positioned up on the hills. Planes and helicopters fly overhead. My eyes follow as they circle the area. *They need healing.*

The next morning, I bring an offering to Grandma's Kitchen. "Here, Grandma, a beekeeper in Wisconsin donated this jar of honey. I want you to have it but promise me you will share it with Wonase. I know he loves honey in his coffee."

"Oh, that's wonderful! Thank you, I will! Wonase is a good guy."

I head back outside, the sun just coming up over the horizon, illuminating the teepee tops. I head to the river, the edges frozen into stunning crystals, gleaming in the sun. Back at the kitchen, we spot Jane Fonda arriving in her burnt orange SUV. We heard she cooked Thanksgiving dinner in town at the high school. Dieter calls out to her. "Are you cooking today?"

She laughs through her open window. "No, not today!"

Maybe today is my day to cook. I go check in with Grandma. "Hey, Grandma, I brought all this Palestinian food to make. I was wondering if you want me to make something today."

"Sure! What do you got?"

I tell her about the freekeh but that I need meat for the soup. "I've got plenty of meat I can give you."

"And then I have a lentil and rice dish called *mujadara* I serve with roasted onions."

"That sounds wonderful. We have a lot of vegans here."

"I also have a vegan soup made with crushed lentils and wild rice."

"Oh, that sounds perfect."

"So, what do you want me to make?"

"Make everything! We will have a lot of people. They'll eat it!"

"Everything? Ok, I can do that. Are you sure?"

"Oh, yes! Of course!"

"Okay, I will get started. Thank you!"

Someone is already in the kitchen preparing a southwestern meal with enchiladas, spicy chili with meat, baked vegetables, and salads. I need the stovetop. He is using the ovens, so we work together seamlessly. My voice is full of gratitude. "Our dishes will complement each other perfectly!"

I am honored that Grandma has handed her kitchen over to us. My heart opens at the thought of being trusted to feed hundreds of people without her having to lift a finger. She is also full of gratitude. "Let's plan dinner at 6:00. Can you do that?"

"No problem, Grandma." It is early afternoon.

I set the meat on the stove for the freekeh, which Dieter helps me unload from the car, along with the lentils, rice, onions, garlic, and olive oil. Several women offer to help prep, including a woman who introduces herself as a rabbi. I thank her for helping prep this meal and let her know I am making Palestinian food.

"Oh, I've been to Palestine. I take interfaith delegations there."

"Really? You've probably been to Canaan Fair Trade, the olive oil company in Burqin."

"Yes, we've been there!"

"That's our family business. I'm using our olive oil in the dishes I am making today!"

"That's wonderful! I'm honored to be part of this meal."

By the time Patty announces that the prayer has started, everything is ready. We arrange the food on the front tables of Grandma's Kitchen. I am tasting the freekeh when a young woman comes running up to me from the serving area. "Where is she? Who made the freekeh?" I hear her Palestinian accent before I see her.

"I did! How is it?"

"I can't believe it! Freekeh at Standing Rock?"

"I made all Palestinian food in solidarity with Standing Rock. From one people dispossessed of their land to another!"

"This is so incredible! Thank you so much!"

A few minutes later, a man with an Arabic accent comes up to the line. "Please, no meat. I am a vegetarian." When he hears about the mujadara, his eyes open wide.

"Mujadara? This is my mom's food! I can't believe it! I've been starving for four days."

I serve him an extra helping of mujadara and put a hefty serving of roasted onions on top. "Have some *adas* soup, too. It has wild rice in it and sage from my garden."

"I'm going to call my mom. She won't believe it!"

"Where are you from?"

"Syria."

"Really? Then you will love my daughter's name, Sham. We named her after *Bilad ish-Sham*."

"That's where I'm from. Sham!"

"You're from Damascus?"

"Yes. Oh, I'm so happy!"

"Come by anytime. We always have vegetarian dishes."

"I will. Thank you so much!"

I am not the only one here making connections between the Middle East and Standing Rock.

On Saturday, I wake up before dawn to take a walk. To the east, a sliver of moon hangs in the brightening sky. *Like the hilal moon marking the beginning of Ramadan and the Eid.* A thick fog still hovers over the Cannonball River. Tufts of smoke billow up from the teepees, the horizon reddening in the distance. I walk up to two white horses taking in the stillness, our eyes meeting in the morning calm.

I want to help make breakfast, but there is already a crew of people from an organization called French Toast and Hugs cutting up bananas and strawberries, filling bowls with blueberries and orange slices. They travel around the world to different causes and make French toast. Before long, there is a line out the door, people coming out of the kitchen with a plate of French toast piled with fresh fruit topped with syrup, whipped cream, and powdered sugar. We get in line and watch three stations of people making French toast to order, then handing it to a couple of women who add the toppings. What an operation!

After breakfast, we all help Grandma clear the space since musicians Jackson Browne and Bonnie Raitt, as well as Dennis Banks, the leader of the American Indian Movement, just arrived for a press conference at Grandma's Kitchen. We escape the commotion to take a walk along the main road onto the bridge that we crossed when we first arrived at the camp. I gaze down at the Cannonball River, smooth as glass, the thin sheet of ice from the day before melted. I try to imagine the river before the dam, its rapid current spinning Sacred Stones.

We pass signs along the road nestled in wild sage. NO DAPL. DAPL + WATER = DEATH. DAPL = GENOCIDE. From the top of the hill, I see the Dome, Grandma's Kitchen, and Cell Phone Hill—the only place to get reception. It has only been a few days, but I feel a deep connection to this place and its cause.

We visit the art tent, where people are handing out silkscreen prints designed by Native artists from across the country to pin on jackets during actions. Dieter and his friends want to get one before they head back to Colorado later that day. Monika and I help make tobacco prayer necklaces for the Jackson Browne and Bonnie Raitt concert tomorrow evening at the Standing Rock Casino. We place a large pinch of tobacco in the center of tiny squares of black, red, yellow, or white fabric to symbolize the four directions, then gather the corners and tie a string around them until there are four tobacco satchels—one of each color—tied onto one string as a necklace.

When the chill sets in as the sun moves lower in the sky, Monika places one of the prayer necklaces around my neck, just as someone put one around her neck. A volunteer from the art tent offers us each one of the silkscreen prints, a beautiful image of a woman with the familiar message "Water is life" written at the top.

In the evening, we drive to the casino to watch spray-paint artists, Native dancers and singers perform, then hear Dennis Banks share stories from his childhood and his optimism for the future. Taboo from the group the Black Eyed Peas comes on stage urging support for young, up-and-coming artists before singing several songs, including a new song he wrote for Standing Rock called "Stand Up."

To all my Native people,
to all the original people,
to all my indigenous people,
recognize yourself,
keep your head up,
Stand up...for Standing Rock.

Such a hopeful atmosphere, the spirit of Standing Rock and the future right here in this room.

Out in the lobby, I connect with artist Gilbert Kills Pretty Enemy III standing next to his work, a huge, framed piece filled with hand-drawn images entitled "Stand With Standing Rock!" Seven teepees arranged around a sacred fire. Policemen and riot police, pepper spray, attack dogs baring their bloody teeth. Barbed wire. Barricade at the Backwater Bridge. Floodlights. Bulldozers desecrating Indian remains. Planes and helicopters. Documents representing treaties and eminent domain that claimed Indian land. Money bags surrounding the town of Bismarck. Two vicious black snakes, their heads reared at the Missouri River—the unfinished pipeline. The more I look, the more I see images that depict the reality people are facing here. Just as an artist can paint a people's truth, so can words. The story of Standing Rock has become part of my story.

On Sunday, I wake up to glorious sunshine. It is my last day. I don't know how to leave. In the distance, the heartbeat rhythm of a Drumming Circle calls out to me to come to the Sacred Fire. I take a few pieces of sage and cedar in my hand, then approach the fire, reflecting on how many days and nights this fire has been burning—a flame of hope, intention, and purpose. I kneel at the edge, my eyes locked in its flames, my mind still, my body calm with gratitude for this place that has set up camp in my heart. *Just like Palestine.* I let the sage fall through my fingers into the fire, then the cedar. They glow as the flames envelop them, then transform to ash.

Back at Grandma's Kitchen, I give Patty and BeaVi a hug.

"Are you leaving today?" Grandma's eyes meet mine, heavy with sadness.

"I don't want to, but I have to. My daughter has school tomorrow. Thank you all so much for letting me cook with you!"

"Thank you, Christa."

I find Wonase seated at a table in the warming tent. My eyes meet his with a heavy heart. "I'm leaving today. I don't know how to leave, though."

"Yeah, you and a lot of others. It's okay, though. You need to take what's here with you, share it out there."

"That's what I've been working on all morning, preparing myself to do that."

Outside, I meet a woman who is one of the cooks for the Sacred Stone

Camp and has a restaurant in Boulder. I tell her that's why I came here, to cook, that I used to have a restaurant and made Palestinian food while I was here. She asks me if I'm going to the Women's March. "I would go, but I need to get back to the kitchen." She tells me it will be a silent prayer march, that non-Native women will surround Native women to escort them to the bridge so they can pray for the river.

Even though I came here to cook, I realize I can use my privilege to protect the Native women in the march. My mind is made up. I am not going to leave now. I find Monika, and we walk up to the procession, where rows of women linking arms are organized by numbers. Large, blue and white silk tunnel-shaped banners with the motto of this movement, "Water is Life," are flying overhead. I join other women at the front of the line, where I spot the Palestinian woman whom I met the day before and smile. *We are in this together. From Palestine to Standing Rock.*

When they call out "One," I link arms with her.

"Do you know what a 'One' is?" Her voice is slow and steady.

"Yes." I look into her eyes, linking my arm tighter to hers. *"One" means we are the frontline.*

An elder woman followed by other Native women leads us through the entire camp. When we get to the Oceti Sakowin Sacred Fire surrounded by the seven teepees to symbolize the Seven Fires Council, she explains we are walking in silence and prayer because women have great power when they stand together. "Remaining silent takes great discipline." Her tone is calm and serious, her words deliberate. "We will walk to the frontline so that the Native elders can pray and do ceremony for the river." She explains that if the police interfere with them praying on the north side of the river, the elders will simply pray on the south side of the river, then we'll all return to camp.

We follow their lead in silence, row after row of six to eight women linking arms, eyes forward, until we reach the Backwater Bridge, where we are met by a group of veterans facing off the police and armored vehicles on the bridge. They scramble toward us. "What are you doing here? We're in the middle of an action. You can't be here. Their guns are loaded."

The elder women continue forward without speaking.

The veterans form a line in front of the women. "We can't let you pass."

The elder women proceed, briefly breaking their silence to insist our action is approved by the Camp Council.

The veterans' eyes cannot hide their concern. "To do what?"

"To go onto the bridge."

The veterans' eyes turn toward the lines of riot police halfway across the bridge. "How far?"

The elder women stand tall. "All the way to the frontline."

One of the vets calls out to his fellow veterans. "We have to stop them."

The elder women motion for us to proceed. The veterans realize we are not going back and reluctantly let us pass. We walk past two sets of concrete barriers before the elders motion for us to stop. Elder women, Native and non-Native, stand at the barricade and proceed with prayer and ceremony, the smoke of sage rising from the gathering. Sage is also passed among us as we patiently sit behind them in solidarity.

One of the policemen instructs the riot police at the barbed wire to move back. The elders continue with their ceremony and sing for the river beneath our blue and red tube banners fluttering overhead in the strong wind. The floodlights get brighter as dusk sets in. When I blink, I can see the four lights of each post arranged in a square in my eyelids. I close my eyes in prayer.

As I kneel in stillness, eyes closed, I see a drop of water fall into a smooth sheet of water, forming a circle that becomes larger and larger. Then I see water moving, spinning, swirling. The four spotlights before me become glowing hearts. I reflect on the meaning of the images, one after the other. The drop of water with the circle showing the impact of one act rippling outward—*We can each make a difference.* The swirling water—*The Cannonball River restored to her former glory of fast-moving water that spins the Sacred Stones.* The lights become hearts as fear and aggression melt into love and kindness—*Love brings peace.*

I open my eyes. The elders have finished their ceremony on the bridge. We wait in silence. Then, suddenly, the police let the elders through the barricade down to the north side of the river. My eyes follow the miracle of their footsteps all the way to the water's edge. *We can make a difference.*

After the ceremony, the elders return up the riverbank through the barricade and face us on the bridge. We rise to our feet as one of the elders takes a megaphone and addresses us. "We have done what we were told was not possible. Today we prayed with our brothers." She is referring to the line of police officers behind the barricade. She commends us on our courage to come to the frontline, our strength as we stand together, and our commitment to the water. She then instructs us to turn around and silently walk back to camp. We walk, arms locked, heads held high. Mission accomplished. We are safe. We are grateful. We are proud. No attacks. No arrests. No injuries. Only gratitude. Somehow on that bridge, we met each other halfway. *If we can meet each other halfway in Standing Rock, there must be a way for people to meet each other halfway in Israel and Palestine.* I think of my parting conversation with Wonase. *I can take the story of Standing Rock out into the world, and I will.*

46

Northern Ireland

When I return from Standing Rock after that Thanksgiving weekend in 2016, I reach out to local groups in Madison committed to the environment and social justice which leads me to a number of opportunities to draw connections between my unfolding memoir on Palestine and my experiences at Standing Rock. I meet Art and Dawn Shegonee from Call for Peace who invite me to hold Talking Circles on current events.[134] Our connection runs deep through our mutual friend Nick Hockings of the Ojibwe Nation I knew from presentations on how to make fire he gave at my sons' elementary school years ago and his outdoor museum up north in Lac de Flambeau, Wisconsin. The last time I saw him before he passed away was at Indianfest in Milwaukee, Wisconsin. This networking extends beyond Standing Rock and Palestine when Dawn invites me to co-present with Call for Peace at an international peace conference in Northern Ireland the following spring.

I also reach out to Salem, since my memoir begins with his family, and decide to visit him in Switzerland on the way to Northern Ireland. Here we are after a lifetime of living separate lives, standing face to face, both with three grown children. I recognize his dark eyes, but the soft curls of his youth are only to be found on his toddler son from a recent marriage, who appears as a mini version of himself. It is as if I am meeting Salem's father, with his short, graying hair and neatly cropped beard. Both father and son, and the next generation, are still barred from returning to their hometown of Jaffa. Salem's entire extended family is held in limbo in the outdoor prison of Gaza.

I hadn't been to Basel, Switzerland, since 1986, when I was a student in Freiburg and went there to celebrate *Fasching* when local residents parade through the streets wearing oversized masks to scare away evil spirits. It happens to be exactly 120 years since Theodor Herzl presented his pamphlet *Der Judenstaat*—The Jewish State—at the First Zionist Congress at the Stadtcasino in Basel in 1897 to declare his desire to establish a Jewish homeland in Palestine, and 100 years since the British formally backed his vision with the Balfour Declaration of 1917.[135] I look for some commemoration of this historic moment—the launching of Zionism. I find nothing. Still, I want to see this place where history was set in motion that would affect the lives of Jews and Palestinians, the entire world, for years to come.

I go to the Stadtcasino, where the meeting was held, and find an archeological dig currently underway. I look for some sign of what once took place here, but there is no plaque reminding passersby of that moment in history. No tours of the building. I stand outside on the sidewalk in the cool spring air, wondering at the power of men to have a vision and then go after it. I think of the forces of history then and now, what players were brought into this game of reconfiguring Palestine. Herzl himself said in his diary:

> *Wenn ich den Baseler Kongress in einem Wort zusammenfassen müßte...es wäre das: In Basel habe ich den Judenstaat gegründet... Wenn ich das heute laut sagte, würde mir ein universelles Gelächter antworten...In fünf Jahren vielleicht und sicher in 50 Jahren wird es jeder einsehen.*
>
> *If I had to summarize the Basel Congress in one word...it would be this: I founded the Jewish State in Basel...If I said this out loud today, there would be universal laughter...Maybe in five years and for sure in 50 years, everyone will know.*

Herzl was right. Fifty years later, in 1947, the UN recommended the partition of Palestine into a Jewish and Palestinian state with Resolution 181. Herzl died in 1904, so he did not live to witness his vision become a reality, but he did get to observe several waves of Jewish immigration to Palestine to establish the first Zionist colonies there with the support of the World Zionist Organization founded at the First Congress and the organization Keren Kayemeth in London, which came to be known as the Jewish National Fund and was instrumental in acquiring land in Palestine.[136]

In his utopian novel *Altneuland (Old New Land)*, Herzl did not envision any bloodshed over the establishment of a Jewish homeland. In fact, he thought the existing population would welcome Jewish influence in their land with open arms. In that regard, he was naïve. I wonder if he is resting easy now that he lies with his family in Jerusalem after being moved from their final resting place in Hungary in 1949, knowing how the State of Israel formed, what it has become, to find his vision of model coexistence in ruins.

Certainly, I don't think Herzl would be surprised that the question of Palestine will not go away, that it has simply gotten pushed aside for seven decades and counting while Israel gains more power and control over what was once Palestine. What would Herzl say about Israel's relentless program to build settlements on Palestinian land to create "facts on the ground" that make it impossible to honor Palestinians' own dream of self-determination?

Given his high moral standards for his vision of a Jewish homeland that would grant all people equal rights, including women, what would Herzl say about Israel's extensive discriminatory legal system that puts Jewish interests above those of the non-Jewish population, including the Law of Return that welcomes Jews from all around the world to become citizens of the State of Israel while it bars Palestinians who were born there and their descendants from returning home? Wouldn't he balk at Israel's claim of being the only democracy in the Middle East?

I don't know if Herzl would agree with international law that recognizes Palestinians' right to resist the occupation of their homeland. Given how he heralded the intellectual rigor of German *Bildung*, what would he think of how Israel has reframed Palestinian resistance as terrorism so that Palestinians can be legitimate targets of state violence? Israel's privilege as a nation among nations? What would he think that Israel considers any criticism of its policies and practices toward the Palestinians anti-Semitic?

Would he, as a Jew, remain silent today at how his people, with their long history of persecution, are holding another people in the crosshairs?

As the daughter of a German whose grandparents were born two years after the First Zionist Congress, the very generation that rallied behind Hitler, I wonder why Palestinians are asked to pay the price for the persecution of Jews in Europe, particularly the Holocaust. Was it guilt or a desire to rid themselves of the "Jewish problem" that led the victors of WWII to solve one problem by creating another?

As an American, I feel personally responsible for this domino effect on Palestinian lives, given the blanket support the United States continues to give the State of Israel and its failure to hold Israel accountable for transgressions against the Palestinians. Can the United States only be the nation of conquerors and genocide, or can it live up to the ideals of freedom, democracy, and dignity it professes as a nation? I wonder why the American people, whose taxes and corporations directly support discrimination against Palestinians, do not demand an equitable sharing of land and power in Palestine and Israel as they did for South Africa. Perhaps because in South Africa, the issue was literally Black and White, a story Americans knew too well.

As I stand there in front of that place where Herzl created the State of Israel, the afternoon sun making it feel like a summer rather than a spring day, I wonder what I am doing here retracing the footsteps of history. I turn my head back toward the building for one last look. I want to acknowledge this place, the time, and the outcome. Things don't just happen. People make things happen. The year 2017 marks the 50th anniversary of the occupation of the West Bank and Gaza during the Six-Day War. This is a big year. And only a year away from the 70th anniversary of the founding of the State of Israel, the day Palestine was wiped off the map. It started in this town, on this very spot where I am standing. And yet I wonder if Herzl's vision is still possible. Maybe Israelis can reclaim it, and Palestinians can come to support one state where Jews and Palestinians live in harmony, a true "light unto nations."

In Northern Ireland, I come face to face with a place where people are still dealing with the legacy of The Troubles—the period of intense conflict between Catholic Irish Nationalist Republicans resisting discrimination in their own homeland and Protestant Union Loyalists aligned with Britain, a struggle rooted in the division of Ireland into the mostly Catholic Irish Free State and mostly Protestant Northern Ireland in 1921 following centuries of British control over all of Ireland.

In conjunction with the conference, Dawn and I sign up for the Belfast Peace Trail Walk organized by INNATE (Irish Network for Nonviolent Action, Training, and Education), a local organization that promotes peace, justice, inclusion, and sustainability. We tour Protestant East Belfast, where, in addition to C.S. Lewis' childhood home,[137] we see militaristic murals commemorating the defiance of the UVF (the Ulster Volunteer Force)—the loyalists paramilitary wing—showing young men covered in black face masks holding rifles. One reads, "We seek nothing but the elementary right implanted in every man: The right if you are attacked, to defend yourself." The Republicans have their share of murals speaking to their own resistance and suffering, including the mural of Bobby Sands of the IRA (the Irish Republican Army), who led a hunger strike in 1981 and died in prison.

I am intrigued that both sides of this conflict can tell their story in plain view within the shared—albeit segregated—space of Belfast. I can imagine how each side must have difficulty viewing the murals of the other, though some non-sectarian murals are scattered throughout town. One person's victory is often the other's demise, and here the wounds of history have yet to fully heal. *Israeli statehood is the Palestinians' Nakba.*

The tour includes a visit to an especially powerful exhibit of political posters called "Troubled Images from the Northern Ireland Conflict" at The Linen Hall Library that includes evocative images such as "REMEMBER DERRY" written in red letters on a black background with a pile of 13 skulls in reference to Bloody Sunday, and another with a black swastika over the British flag. Some posters offer universal words of wisdom such as "War is not a game," with blood splattered on a white background. Another poster with a soldier pointing a gun at an unarmed civilian reminds me of Palestine: "Plastic bullets kill. Ban them."

We also visit a section of the Peace Wall, one of numerous stretches of "Peace Lines"—walls constructed in Northern Ireland separating Protestant and Catholic communities within the city. The first wall was built by the

British in 1969, and nearly 100 walls followed that persist to this day, 50 years later. One part of the Peace Wall bears an inscription quoting Lebanese poet Gibran Khalil Gibran, whose poetry Nasser and I cited at our wedding. It reads, "Your neighbor is your other self, dwelling behind a wall." In West Belfast, signs for the nationalist party Sinn Féin call for "BRITS OUT, NOT SELL OUT," "WEST BELFAST STANDS AGAINST BREXIT," and "Equality, Integrity, Respect for All."

In the cobblestone pedestrian zone of the Cathedral Quarter off Donegall Street, I find elaborate murals celebrating Irish labor and literary traditions, some three-dimensional, as if the mural had come to life and was then frozen in time. Perhaps the most powerful mural I come upon is a young man crouching down holding a dead dove that has been struck by two arrows, one with the symbol of the Church of Ireland and the other with a Protestant cross.

Dawn and I attend an evening reception at parliament in Stormont—currently empty due to policy disputes—where I meet Mairead Maguire, a Nobel Peace Prize Laureate from Belfast, who has done nonviolent peace work in Northern Ireland and around the world. It is her Palestinian tatriz jacket over a t-shirt with the colors of the Palestinian flag that draws me to her. I study the image, the face of a woman created from a swirl of red, black, and green with the inscription "Women's Boat to Gaza" underneath. She is one of 26 women who set sail from Barcelona to Gaza in 2016 as part of a Freedom Flotilla Coalition initiative to raise awareness about the contributions of women in the Palestinian struggle. I have heard of other such expeditions to deliver needed supplies to Gaza to offset the hardships of the Israeli blockade, efforts that exhibit both bravery and creativity in drawing attention to the plight of Palestinians.[138]

The last day of the conference, Dawn and I take an excursion to the northern shore of Ireland and stop in the town of Derry on the way. A number of prominent murals emphasize the challenges during The Troubles, making connections to other contexts, such as South Africa. From the top of the 30-foot-wide 17th-century wall of the Old City, I see several murals with messages. "End British Internment. End the Torture." One mural has an image of Nelson Mandela and Bobby Sands with the South African and Irish flags behind them. My heavy heart softens when I see the mural of a peace dove made of a swirling white line over colorful squares. Another mural depicts a demonstration calling for "Civil Rights for All" with the message "ONE MAN ONE VOTE."

We visit the Bloody Sunday Memorial, where a local guide explains that 13 unarmed protesters engaged in a civil rights march were gunned down by British forces in 1972. Victims' families are still demanding justice from the British government. Decades later, in 2010, Prime Minister David Cameron issues an apology, followed by further investigations that finally lead to the prosecution of one of the soldiers. *Will Israeli soldiers one day be held accountable for the slaughter and assassination of Palestinians calling out for freedom and justice?*

Bloody Sunday takes on a more personal aspect once we are inside the newly opened Museum of Free Derry. We are greeted by a gentleman who lost his brother on Bloody Sunday. The woman behind the counter points out a photo of her father, who attended the demonstration that day. The museum is an invitation to honor Northern Ireland's resistance to oppression and the victims of Bloody Sunday as "part of a wider struggle in Ireland and internationally for freedom and equality for all." Outside we view an installation of a steel wall with the sound wave of "We Shall Overcome" etched into the metal. All these intersections of injustice are part of the same fight for freedom and dignity.

Conflict does not always end in resolution. The American national narrative is still grounded in fear in spite of tales of bravery laced throughout the American story—fear of admitting to the conscious destruction of Native peoples, their property, their culture, their languages, their livelihood, and the systematic discrimination against Black Americans long after the Emancipation Proclamation of 1862. I recently read an essay my father wrote as part of his application to transfer from his home university in Kiel to Switzerland after World War II. He reflects on post-war Germany:

> *Es liegt an uns zu entscheiden, wer uns Vorbild, wer abschreckendes Beispiel sein soll. An dieser unserer Wahl wird es sich dann zeigen, ob wir in der Lage sind, aus der Vergangenheit für die Zukunft zu lernen.*

> *It is up to us to decide, who will be our role model, and who our villain. And when we choose, it will be clear whether we are able to learn from the past for the future.*

Outside the museum, I reflect on my father's words, fresh from the complete destruction of his homeland and the defeat of the Nazi era in which he grew up in Germany. The stories and struggles of South Africa, Standing Rock, and Northern Ireland offer me hope and inspiration that there is more to conflict than loss and victory. When people come together and share their truth, stories can truly transform the future. In presence and in story, power is being shared. People are being heard. Histories are being remembered. And only then can new futures be imagined. My hope for Palestine and Israel is that they can come to appreciate the shared context—and suffering—from which they both come and integrate their respective truths into a common future.

I return to Madison with the historic and current struggle for peace and justice front and center in my mind. I think of my own journey that has cut across contexts to make a difference: Marching in Washington, DC, engaging with others on a bi-national state, writing this memoir. I'm not sure what impact I have had, but I see how people have come together around South Africa, Northern Ireland, and Standing Rock. Taking action and sharing personal stories of resistance and resilience has touched the hearts and minds of so many around the world, including governments that have been forced to change their policy and even reimagine the state. I simply must add my voice to the mix. I resume my writing, inspired by what I have seen at Standing Rock and in Northern Ireland, determined to use the power of story to open people's hearts and minds to bring about positive change. I also don't give up hope on returning to Palestine. Neither do the Palestinians.

PART VII

RETURN

70th Commemoration of the Nakba

2018

47

March of Return

The following spring in 2018, leading up to the 70th commemoration of the Nakba, I hear reports in the news of Palestinians in Gaza holding a weekly march on Fridays to the border fence—what Israel uses to keep Palestinians in Gaza locked in a cage.[139] They are demanding the Right of Return for Palestinian refugees and an end to the blockade—now in its 11th year—which Israel, in collaboration with Egypt, imposed on the Gaza Strip in 2007 following the Hamas victory through democratic elections (see Map 15).

It is such a simple idea for Palestinians in Gaza to walk to the border fence to demand their rights and their dignity. *Why shouldn't Palestinians be free of the confines of these borders?* My heart fills with admiration for their bravery and *sumoud*—steadfastness—as men, women, and children face off against Israeli snipers with their bodies. Three-quarters of the population of the Gaza Strip are refugees, like Salem's family, displaced from areas swallowed by the State of Israel.

Over the course of the first year of the March of Return, protesters are met with rubber bullets and live ammunition from the Israeli army, leaving hundreds dead and tens of thousands maimed or injured, including women and children. They are standing up to one of the strongest armies in the world, backed by the most powerful nation in the world, reasserting the memory of their homeland.[140]

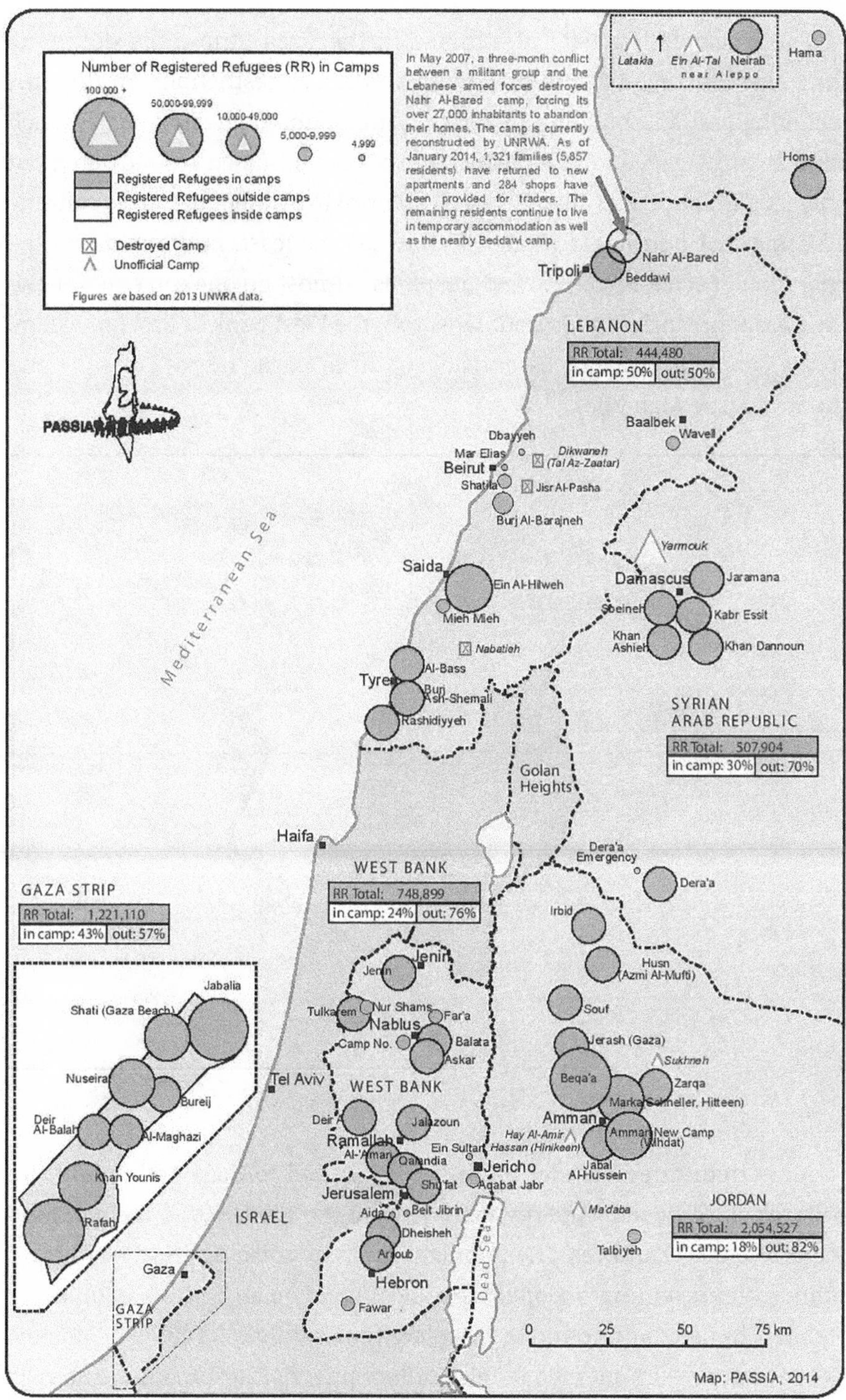
Number of Registered Refugees (RR) in Camps
100 000 +
50,000-99,999
10,000-49,000
5,000-9,999
4,999
Registered Refugees in camps
Registered Refugees outside camps
Registered Refugees inside camps
Destroyed Camp
Unofficial Camp
Figures are based on 2013 UNWRA data.
In May 2007, a three-month conflict between a militant group and the Lebanese armed forces destroyed Nahr Al-Bared camp, forcing its over 27,000 inhabitants to abandon their homes. The camp is currently reconstructed by UNRWA. As of January 2014, 1,321 families (5,857 residents) have returned to new apartments and 284 shops have been provided for traders. The remaining residents continue to live in temporary accommodation as well as the nearby Beddawi camp.
Latakia
Ein Al-Tal
Neirab
near Aleppo
Hama
Homs
Nahr Al-Bared
Tripoli
Beddawi
LEBANON
RR Total: 444,480
in camp: 50%
out: 50%
PASSIA
Baalbek
Wavell
Dbayyeh
Mar Elias
Dikwaneh (Tal Az-Zaatar)
Beirut
Shatila
Jisr Al-Pasha
Burj Al-Barajneh
Mediterranean Sea
Yarmouk
Saida
Ein Al-Hilweh
Mieh Mieh
Damascus
Jaramana
Sbeineh
Kabr Essit
Khan Ashieh
Khan Dannoun
Nabatieh
Al-Bass
Tyre
Burj Ash-Shemali
Rashidiyyeh
SYRIAN ARAB REPUBLIC
RR Total: 507,904
in camp: 30%
out: 70%
Golan Heights
Haifa
WEST BANK
RR Total: 748,899
in camp: 24%
out: 76%
GAZA STRIP
RR Total: 1,221,110
in camp: 43%
out: 57%
Dera'a Emergency
Dera'a
Irbid
Husn (Azmi Al-Mufti)
Jenin
Jabalia
Shati (Gaza Beach)
Tulkarem
Nur Shams
Far'a
Nablus
Camp No.
Balata
Askar
Souf
Jerash (Gaza)
Sukhneh
Nuseirat
Bureij
Deir Al-Balah
Al-Maghazi
Khan Younis
Rafah
Tel Aviv
WEST BANK
Deir
Jalazoun
Ramallah
Al-'Amari
Qalandia
Ein Sultan
Jericho
Shu'fat
Aqabat Jabr
Jerusalem
Aida
Beit Jibrin
Dheisheh
Arroub
Hebron
Fawar
ISRAEL
Dead Sea
Beqa'a
Zarqa
Marka (Schneller, Hitteen)
Amman
Hay Al-Amir
Hassan (Hinikeen)
Amman New Camp (Wihdat)
Jabal Al-Hussein
Ma'daba
Talbiyeh
JORDAN
RR Total: 2,054,527
in camp: 18%
out: 82%
Gaza
GAZA STRIP
0 25 50 75 km
Map: PASSIA, 2014

Map 15: Palestinian Refugees, 2014 (Source: PASSIA)

The blockade has left Palestinians in the Gaza Strip more desperate than ever with the barring of exports and heavy restrictions on imports, including fuel and building materials. Limitations on basic services, such as electricity needed for the purification of contaminated groundwater, not only jeopardizes the availability of clean drinking water but makes running a business or household challenging, to say the least, not to mention the operation of schools, clinics, and hospitals. Almost no one can enter or exit the Gaza Strip, including Palestinians from the West Bank or East Jerusalem, so the people in Gaza are essentially cut off from the rest of Palestine and the world (see Map 16).

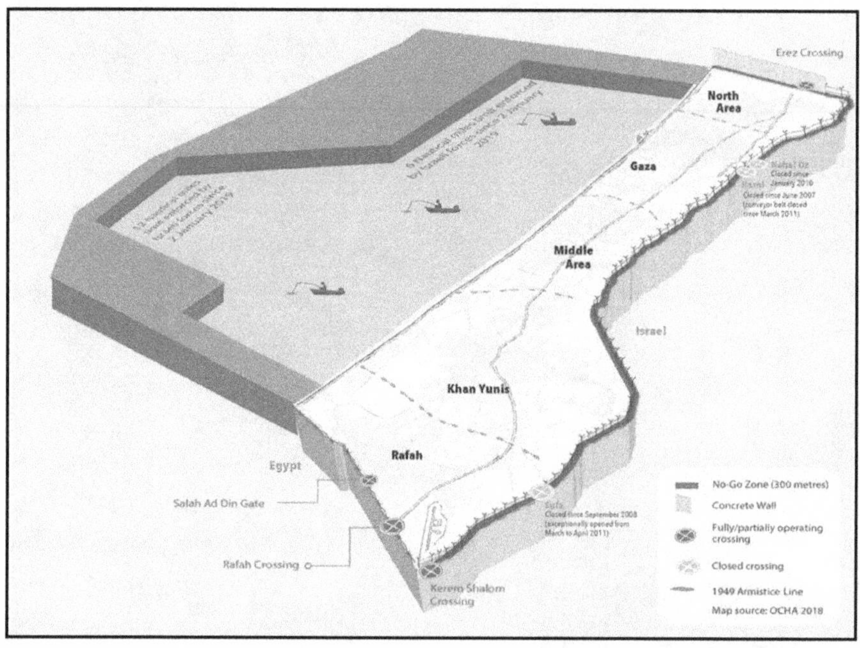

Map 16: Gaza Blockade, 2018 (Source: UNRWA)

More than three decades since I first traveled to Gaza and nearly two decades since I conducted my interviews at the universities, the situation there is worse than ever. The population has doubled again to nearly two million, representing a population density of nearly 5,000 people per square kilometer and counting in a place that is only 365 square kilometers (141 square miles). Squeezed in this outdoor prison, Palestinians are literally dying to get out.

On one of my video calls with Salem's sister Salwa—with only a few hours of electricity a day—she speaks to me through her cell phone screen at night, her face illuminated only by flashlight, as if she and her grandchildren are on a camping trip. She shares with me how, miraculously, everyone in her family is okay, but the streets are filled with young men who are either missing an eye or a limb, or hobble through the streets, their bodies testimony to the battle between the Israeli army and the persistence of Palestine. I wonder when the people of Gaza will be free of this madness. *How do I erase these borders that stand in the way of their return and living a life of dignity?*

48

Return to Palestine

It is summer 2018 when I finally get to return to Palestine, seven years since I experienced the intense beauty of the *fulla* flower, 70 years since the Nakba of 1948. Although Nasser and I live separate lives, he asks me to come with Sham to Palestine for 'Eid al-Fitr. The prospect of going back instigates both fear and excitement. I have been going to Palestine for more than three decades, nearly half of Israel's existence as a state. Much has changed since I was last there, and yet I have waited for this day, never sure when or if it would come. My heart is overflowing with gratitude to be welcomed back into a space that has filled my life with such meaning and joy and inspired me to write these lines.

Canaan, now a grown man, decides to stay in the US, working remotely for the family business, but Karmel, Sham, and I travel together through Jordan to visit Nasser in Palestine. Like years ago, Naziha's eldest son Abdullah picks us up from the airport, then takes us to his brother's house outside Amman, also named Nasser. It is a wide-open area with few buildings. All four of Naziha's sons plan to build next to each other—just like "my Nasser" and his brothers in Jalameh have done. So far, two of her sons' houses are completed. Two down, two to go.

It is nearly the end of the holy month of Ramadan, so everyone is fasting until sunset. First, we walk around the house and look at all their fruit trees—avocado, pomegranate, pomelo, almond, and peach, among others. In the corner of the garden is a barn with two majestic horses peeking out, a mother and daughter. Sham and I walk up to them, and I place my hand on the front of the mother's head. Her daughter, who backed away as we approached them, now joins her mother by her side.

Inside, we help Naziha's son Nasser with the final touches on the *mansaf* by spreading large circles of nearly transparent bread on two large round platters topped with yellow rice and chunks of lamb followed by yogurt soup drizzled over the entire arrangement with a final touch of parsley and roasted almonds—truly a work of art. Naziha and I help his wife with dessert by filling rounds of spongey *kitayef* dough with cheese, then folding them over and pressing them closed. The moment the sun falls below the horizon, it is time to break the fast for today's Ramadan feast. *Fatour* is served.

While we eat, Naziha recounts the story of giving birth to Abdullah in a cave in 1967 during the Six-Day War and how she lost her residency in Palestine after she returned to Saudi Arabia with her husband and their newborn son. After fatour, we have tea and watermelon beneath the dark sky by a simple fire suspended in the *muqadeh*, a three-footed ceramic firepit, with coals in the bottom and topped with scraps of wood. I watch the shadows shift on Nasser's glowing face while we engage in conversation and enjoy coffee with dessert. The kitayef has the perfect mix of savory cheese with sweet syrup. Such a lovely evening beneath the stars.

Back at Naziha's, I hear the call to prayer echo in the silence of twilight as a cool breeze comes through the window. The muezzin calls out into the night: *Allahu akbar! La ilaha ilallah*—God is the greatest. There is no God but Allah! The call is both beautiful and soothing as I take in every moment of this warm welcome in Jordan, the familiar sound alerting me I am one step closer to Palestine.

When I awake, a jolt of panic races through my body to find that it's already noon. We were supposed to leave for the bridge first thing in the morning. I guess we needed the rest, but will we still be able to cross the bridge? Even though it is Ramadan and Naziha is fasting, she makes us tea and serves us a delicious Palestinian spread for breakfast, reminding us that those who are ill or traveling are exempt from fasting for Ramadan. We savor fried squares of traditional jibneh cheese, lebneh balls made from strained yogurt, tangy za'atar, green olives, and baby eggplant stuffed with garlic, almonds, and hot peppers preserved in olive oil known as *makdous,* which her daughter Nadia brought from Jalameh so that her mother can enjoy the delicacies of her homeland.

At the border crossing, when the van reaches the Israeli guards, the driver tells us "The Jews" have lightened up a little, so it is easier to cross than in the old days. I realize he is Palestinian when he explains that he doesn't resent the Jews because they are Jewish—everyone has a right to choose their religion—but because they took his land. It feels absurd to think this man drives people back and forth across the bridge between Jordan and his homeland but cannot visit or live there himself.

At the Israeli checkpoint, while our bags go through a security check, a security guard invites me to a window with bulletproof glass, then guides Karmel and Sham to a different area to be processed as Palestinians, now that Sham also has residency in the West Bank. I catch my breath when I notice the border security attendant behind the window has a gold map of Palestine hanging from her neck, like the pendant I had made when Nasser and I got married, but hers is different. "Are you Israeli?"

"Yes." She briefly glances up at me while thumbing through our passports.

"It's the first time I see that necklace on an Israeli."

"One time, there was a Palestinian girl with the same necklace. Well, almost the same."

"Yours has the Golan Heights." I spot an extra bit of gold at the top right corner.

"Ah, so you know."

"Yes, I know."

I know that Israel occupied and annexed the Golan Heights after the Six-Day War in 1967. I know that the Golan Heights is part of Syria, not Palestine. I don't have the Golan Heights on my necklace. *Two maps, two narratives, the same space.*

The attendant smiles. "Not many know the difference." She changes the subject. "Do you know your husband's full name, his father's and grandfather's names?"

I list off Nasser's first name and the first name of his father, grandfather, and great-grandfather, followed by his family name.

She seems impressed. "You really do know."

Yes, I know that my husband's family in Palestine goes back for generations. She inserts a piece of paper the size of a business card in my passport and hands it back to me.

"Thank you." I take a final look at her necklace that represents the reconfiguration of Palestine and the Golan Heights into Israel, then sit down to wait for Sham and Karmel to come through with the other Palestinian residents of the West Bank. I open my passport, surprised to find the flimsy piece of paper the size of a business card with my photo in black and white is my visa. I remember the days when the Israelis stamped the visa directly into the passport. We had to ask them to stamp it on a separate piece of paper since Arab countries would not accept anyone to enter if their passport had a stamp from Israel. We didn't want to jeopardize our chances to travel to Egypt, Iraq, Lebanon, or Syria, dreams unfulfilled with subsequent wars in Iraq, the unrest of Arab Spring, and the civil war in Syria.

Once Sham and Karmel appear, a van takes us to our final stop in Jericho, where one of our employees from Canaan Fair Trade is waiting for us. I recognize him from photos on the company's Facebook page. There he is, right in front of me, with his soft smile and gracious manner to take us to Jalameh. He drives us in Karmel's Ford pickup truck as we wind our way out of the familiar dry Jericho landscape into the rocky hills of central Palestine. We follow a new road that leads to Qabatiya through Sahil Al-Fara until we reach the village of Burqin. He drops himself off at home, just down the road from our company, to join his family before sundown for fatour. I greet his mother, who bakes bread at the company's annual Olive Harvest Festival. She insists we come visit. *Inshallah*—God willing.

Karmel takes the wheel as we pass through Jenin on our way to Jalameh, the light fading in the wide-open sky. The area is so much more built up than on my last visit. Now, there are houses and buildings all the way from Jenin to Jalameh, with new traffic circles and speed bumps. As we approach the village, a center barricade has been added, dividing the road to prevent head-on collisions.

We enter Jalameh just before sunset via Tariq Burqin, the same road

Nasser's mother traveled on horseback from Burqin to Jalameh for her wedding, once a dirt road, now paved. Nasser has since built a house on his land, where he planted fruit trees years ago. I am delighted that he fulfilled his father's dream to have all four sons next to each other.

When we arrive, Sham runs up to her father at the top of the front staircase. We enter the foyer flooded with natural light and proceed toward the kitchen. Nasser invites us to the dining table off the kitchen for fatour to break the fast for Ramadan. We are right on time. We feast on chicken biriani, rice with peppers, raisins, almonds, and Arabic salad. Sham, Karmel, and I recount our visit to Naziha and her son Nasser in Jordan, my tongue easily switching between Arabic and English.

After dinner, Nasser takes us to a house he built in the wa'ra he calls the *azbeh*. We follow the same path when we picked saber on our first trip to Jalameh after we got married. Nasser has upgraded the natural saber fencing to a high metal fence and chain-link gate since the house stands alone, not far from the Israeli border fence.

Nestled among the olive trees is a modern, two-story house covered in smooth black stone like the old Palestinian houses of the Galilee. Inside is an open space with sleek furniture and floor-to-ceiling panes of glass. Nasser makes us each a cappuccino with his built-in German coffee machine and invites us to have *halawat ij-jibin* on an open veranda lined with a chrome railing. I have only eaten this Syrian specialty from Shatila Bakery in Dearborn, Michigan, which we enjoyed with Nasser's parents when we visited my mother back in 1996. What a treat to eat it in Palestine! I savor its characteristic cheese dough filled with creamy *qushta* topped with rose-water syrup.

As the sun sets in the distance, the sky fades from brilliant yellow to fiery orange to smoldering red over Mount Carmel—Karmel's mountain in Haifa—and a pleasant breeze brushes over my face from the Mediterranean Sea just beyond it. After dessert, we take a walk between the olive trees. What used to be an ancient olive press is now a fountain with running water that cascades down the same path where olive oil used to flow, the water glistening from flood lights. Off to the side is a chicken coop in a large fenced-in area, but there are no chickens to be seen. They have already retired for the night. As the last glimpses of light disappear, the stars twinkle overhead like the lights of Nazareth to the north.

Before we head to Nasser's original family home—still my home in Palestine—we stop by Nasser's brother Faisal's house to have coffee, tea, and traditional ma'moul cookies filled with nuts or dates. Nasser's brothers' wives stop by with their daughters and grandchildren—a whole new generation of children! Faisal's son excuses himself for just coming from the field in his work clothes, but his father praises him instead. *Ma fi 'ayb bi-shughl*—There is no shame in work. For Palestinians, working the land is an honor.

At the end of the night at home, Karmel, Sham, and I have a midnight snack of lebneh and za'atar, pickled eggplant known as *makbous*, and apricots called *mishmish*, which reminds me of the Arabic tongue twister: *Hath al-mishmish mish min mishmishna*—These apricots are not from our apricots.[141] It makes me think of the English tongue twister: "Sally sells seashells down by the seashore."

By the time we go to bed, the night sky gives way to the faint glow of sunrise. What a full first day back in Palestine. So much to celebrate. So good to be home again. And yet I cannot help but think of the injustice of those who cannot return home. Whereas I can cross through borders, come home to the Palestine I love and cherish, all the refugees in Gaza being shot for simply walking to the fence in their March of Return, remain confined in their own homeland, and still others are barred from returning in refugee camps in Jordan, Syria, Lebanon, and across refugee camps throughout the West Bank, including right in Jenin, and from exile around the world. My heart aches with this twisted reality that has been dragging on for decades. *When will all Palestinians be free to go home?*

The next morning, I realize it is the day before the 'Eid al-Fitr marking the end of Ramadan. I can't imagine not making ka'ak. Nasser thinks it's too much trouble, but I disagree. Once I mention I could use the landrace wheat—the heirloom varieties Nasser recently reintroduced to the local market through our family business—he pauses, and his eyes, first fixed in thought, brighten. "I can bring you the wheat from the new harvest. It will be a lot of work, though. You'll have to clean it first."

"That's okay. I can do that. They will be the best ever!"

Nasser is back in no time with a large container of wheat kernels. "I have to go to the company for a meeting. I'll get the rest of the stuff on my way back. What do you need?"

I ask him for date paste and spices. "Bring *'ajweh* and whole and ground anise, and ground cardamom. We have olive oil, right?"

"You have plenty." He points to the glass door cupboards filled with narrow bottles of Rumi and Nabali olive oil neatly lined up under spotlights, as if appearing on stage, along with smaller bottles of infused olive oil in each of the five flavors—Lemon, Thyme, Basil, Garlic, and Chili.

I set up my workstation in the entranceway by the front window, where there is good natural light. I pour some of the reddish-brown kernels onto a baking pan and carefully shake it back and forth until the pale straw-like husks work their way to the surface, appearing as if crawling out from between the kernels on their own. I pick them off, then re-shake the pan until more husks appear, repeating the process over and over. When I pour the cleaned wheat into a steel bowl, the sound echoes across the room.

Nasser stops by with the date paste and spices. "How far are you?"

"I'm getting there—not quite done." I show him the container with the rest of the wheat. "I'll call you when I finish so you can grind it."

It is early afternoon by the time I finish the last round. Nasser takes the wheat to grind it. At first, when I add olive oil to the wheat, the dough has a sandy consistency like semolina, but when I add water and knead it, the dough holds together in a moist ball. In another bowl, I mix the date paste with the spices and a little olive oil until the deep, reddish-brown mass is smooth and shiny. I am ready to begin.

While Sham rolls the date paste into uniform balls, I make slightly larger balls of dough that I press onto the granite countertop. I roll the date ball between my hands to make a short snake to place onto the dough before folding it up around the snake until it is completely covered. I roll it with both hands until the short, dough-covered snake lengthens and is smooth and uniform. I curve it into a circle, overlapping the ends, and press into them with the tips of two fingers like a staple to lock them together. I place the perfect circle on a baking sheet and repeat the whole process until we have several trays of circles in neat rows.

Nasser stops by with a baby goat he bought from the local Bedouins for the Eid. We take a break from our work and peer into the truck bed to find an adorable baby goat with sandy brown fur huddled in the corner behind the cab, its legs bound. Sham winces when she finds out Nasser and Karmel will slaughter it at the azbeh to share with the family and those in need. "He is so cute!"

Nasser's brother Ghazi and his wife Layla stop by to greet us after our safe arrival. *Alhamdillah 'ala salamitkum!*—Praise be to God for your safety!

I respond in kind. *Allah yisalamkum!*—May God bless you!

I place the first trays of ka'ak in the oven while Layla and I finish the last tray. When we are all done, I set some aside to give to Nasser. Now, we are ready for the Eid!

That evening, Nasser prepares the *'alak* of the goat for the final fatour of Ramadan at the azbeh—the pancreas, heart, lungs, kidney, and liver—sautéed in olive oil with salt and pepper. The next morning, I put on one of my traditional Palestinian dresses with tatriz panels down the front and along the sleeves before heading to Nasser's for Eid breakfast.

It is the first time we have goat for the Eid. Baked on low fire, the chunks of meat glisten in their juices. The meat is so tender it simply falls off the bone. Nasser passes out some traditional taboun bread made with landrace wheat and invites us to start eating. *Tafaddalou*—Enjoy!

After breakfast, Nasser's brothers stop by with their wives, children, and grandchildren to wish us Happy Eid. *Kul 'am wa antum bikhair*—May you be well every year. The response echoes through the room. Wa antum bikhair—And may you be well. I am thrilled to see everyone and offer them ka'ak in person after all these years of sending photos, noting that I made them with landrace wheat. They each take one, singing a chorus of *Zaki*—Delicious, and *Yislamu ideiki*—Bless your hands.

I respond in kind. *Wa ideikum*—And your hands.

Now it is our turn to do the rounds. I am heartbroken to visit 'Amti Saymi's house since she just passed away in December. Her daughters welcome us, but their eyes well up with tears when they tell us how happy their mother would have been to see me. Had she not fallen and broken her hip, she would still be alive, having died from complications from surgery. In my mind, she is still standing strong, harvesting *khas*—the fresh, crisp romaine lettuce she planted herself years ago. Soon we are surrounded by her sons, their wives, and children. The house is full but feels empty without 'Amti Saymi. The generation that lived through the Nakba is returning to the land. At least she was laid to rest in her homeland. What about all the refugees who never made it back home?[142]

We visit Nasser's sisters and brothers. Now, Nasser's sisters Nawal and Maha, having each lost her husband, have their own apartments in Jenin. I feel the passage of time when we visit several of Nasser's nieces and nephews, who live close by, have finished college, and are married with children of their own. When we visit Nasser's uncle Khali Mahmoud in Burqin, he is thrilled to be able to converse with Karmel in Arabic. I see Karmel is also right at home in Palestine. At Khali Khalid's next door, Sham is delighted when he cuts us plump, green grapes from his grape vines overhead. Our last stop is Nasser's sister Kifah in Nablus. I am relieved to hear that one of her sons, who suffered internal injuries during the Second Intifada when shrapnel pierced his body through the window of their home, has finally healed. *Alhamdillah*—Praise Allah.

At the end of the night, my heart is full after being welcomed by Nasser's entire extended family. My head is spinning with the whirlwind of visits, familiar and new faces of the next generation. I am back in Palestine. Not all is lost.

In the morning, Karmel gives me a tour of the company, renamed Canaan Palestine, where he has been working with his father since 2013. I finally get to see the olive trees dedicated to the Run Across Palestine runners that stand out like honorable islands. Familiar smiling faces greet me as we walk through the facility to admire the showroom, the expansion of olive oil tanks, the olive press waiting for the next harvest, the jarring and bottling lines, and the laboratory for product testing. Karmel walks me through the new almond line that shells and sorts almonds, as well as new storage areas for the finished products: freekeh—the roasted green landrace wheat I cooked at Standing Rock known as freekeh, the cracked wheat hand-rolled by women's cooperatives with landrace wheat flour like I made with Sitti so many years ago called maftoul, the za'atar spice mix, and almonds, as well as cases of olive and almond oil ready to ship. Canaan Palestine has become quite an operation!

I have been working with Fida', one of Canaan Palestine's employees, remotely to develop new promotional materials for the business. Fida' invites me to look at what she's put together so far for the brochure. This is our chance to fine-tune the language and incorporate appropriate photos face to face. We sift through images of olive trees, the farms in springtime bursting with various shades of green, and close-ups of farmers and their crops. Every photo tells a story even more than the words, so we select them carefully.

Nasser is shifting the company's core message from empowerment to the human legacy of agriculture in the Land of Canaan. This emphasis will ultimately include regenerative agriculture to underscore how the people of Palestine and the land are part of the same ecosystem. It is the traditional farming culture of the fellahin that safeguard this treasured inheritance that has sustained life and livelihood for millennia.

It is nearly noon when a tour group arrives, our cue to head out back to the company wood-burning oven, where the baker is preparing an assortment of freshly baked bread made with landrace wheat topped with olive oil and za'atar, cheese, or eggs for the guests. Typically, he bakes them in the morning, a reward for any employees who show up early to work. He makes a few extra for Fida', Karmel, and me.

I feel so grateful to taste these freshly baked treats. *Masha' allah!*—Wow! *'Atik al-'afiyeh*—May you have strength.

The baker smiles with pride. *Allah 'afiki*—May God grant you strength.

Karmel points out the giant mural painted on the back wall of the company, depicting a traditional festive scene with musicians and dabkeh dancing among the olive trees. He also shows me the brand-new cafeteria outfitted with a commercial kitchen and second-floor seating with panoramic windows overlooking the facility. It is astounding how an idea, a sketch, a vision can become an entire operation that is making such a difference in the lives of farmers and allowing the world to taste what Palestine has to offer.

We head back into the office and share some of the freshly baked treats with the rest of the staff, have a cup of tea, then get back to work to finalize the text and photos. I congratulate Fida' with a high five. "See? We did it! And look how beautiful!" Fida' is all smiles and takes a sigh of relief. It will not be long before we share these new brochures with the world just in time for this year's Olive Harvest Festival in the fall.

After work, Karmel and I give Fida' a ride home to the Christian village of Zababdeh. She shows us the apartment she shares with her sister, then introduces us to her mother and father, who live one level down, and her brother with whom Karmel shared an apartment at Birzeit University when he was studying Arabic one summer. It is late, and her father is already dozing on the couch, her mother still fully alert in spite of just finishing a full day's work as a travel agent.

I can't help but think about the fact that they are among the few Christian families remaining in Palestine. Even though 20 percent of Palestinians are Christian, at least half of them live outside Palestine. I have always admired how Palestinians take pride in the religious diversity in Palestine, boasting how Christians, Jews, and Muslims have lived together for centuries. It was only when European Jews planned to take over Palestine with their Zionist ideology to redefine it as a Jewish state that Palestinians took issue with the Jews in Palestine and the State of Israel.

We sit on the veranda and talk into the night. These two sisters are lucky to have each other and their parents right there with them. No one here is on their own. I much prefer this way of life over the emphasis in the US on the individual, being independent, and paying your way at the age of 18. Somehow, this sense of community in Palestine feels kinder. Less lonely. Less scary. There is always family to fall back on, depend on, and look to for guidance and support. Even though I was raised in the US, I am drawn to this social network of extended family. I like the idea of being part of something larger than myself. It feels familiar, like I have known it my whole life, even before I experienced it. I feel fortunate to be part of such a welcoming family and share their joy and sorrow.

Another day, I get to share in the joy of one of Nasser's nieces, who has delivered her first baby. We wind through olive trees as a caravan of aunts and cousins until we reach a dirt road in the village of Kufr Qud, not far from our company where her husband works, until we spot her one-story, burnt-orange house glowing in the afternoon sun. What a beautiful setting to live and raise a family! The new mother welcomes us into her living room, where her baby girl is asleep in her car seat. She looks like a doll with her delicate fingers resting on her chest and a lovely lace headband with a bow across her forehead.

I lean over the tiny sleeping angel. *Fi ahla minha?*—Is there anyone more beautiful?

Her proud mother smiles, tilting her head down in modesty. *Tislami*—Thank you. She presents us with a tray of tiny glass cups of *qanar*, a traditional drink of chopped roasted almonds steeped with cinnamon sticks served when a woman delivers a baby.

Some of the women ask about her delivery, so she recounts her long labor, which prompts others to tell their own stories of childbirth. Sharing seems to calm this new mother as she reaps the wisdom of her female relatives. Holding her head high and shoulders back, she plays down the pain and challenges. My heart swells with admiration at the support this young mother enjoys from her fellow sisters. She is not alone. She will always have many women to turn to for advice, who are behind her 100 percent.

We sit there for well over an hour. I sneak into the kitchen and quickly wash up all the tiny cups despite her attempts to stop me. My heart swells with gratitude to see happiness in her eyes, having known her since she was a young girl playing in the streets of Jalameh with her cousins. Now she is a grown woman, married with a baby of her own, the next generation coming to life before my eyes. Just as the farmers pass on their knowledge of cultivating the land, the women pass down their knowledge of caring for their children. Everyone knows what to do, what their role is, and where they are needed. Such clarity makes it all seem so easy.

The Germans have a saying: *Wer die Wahl hat, hat die Qual*—Those with choice have agony. Not that people are not making choices here, but tradition and social norms make choosing more straightforward. People are encouraged to follow in the path of their ancestors, and most people do just that. There is no going it alone or having to figure it all out. The smoothness of this young mother's brow expresses confidence intertwined with relief. Life goes on and on here, guided by the rich traditions that have allowed this community to thrive. My heart swells with gratitude that I can sit among them and share in this moment. No wonder I feel at home in Palestine.

49

Hidden Treasures

Karmel has an appointment for his truck at the dealer in Ramallah, so Sham and I ride along, taking the old road through the Palestinian villages for old time's sake even though we have to keep slowing down for speed bumps. After we check the car at the dealer, Karmel takes us to one of his favorite restaurants, Snowbar, pronounced *snober* in Arabic, which means "pine nuts," a catchy play on words across the two languages. We are, in fact, surrounded by pine nut trees that tower over the expansive outdoor seating. A cat wanders by our table, seemingly right at home, across old tiles like those in Nasser's family home. These relics of the past stand in stark contrast to the Western pop music playing on loudspeakers and women dressed in bikinis hanging out at the pool. I tell Karmel I am in culture shock. I saw hip cafés in Ramallah, years ago, when I did my fieldwork for my dissertation in 2000, but never this degree of Western culture. The atmosphere feels loose and relaxed, as if no one—not simply the cat—has a care in the world. Ramallah has changed.

After dinner, we visit one of Nasser's nephews and a couple of nieces who are all married with young families of their own. We hear how expensive life is in Ramallah with private schools, food, and household items costing more than in Jenin. They all visit their families on the weekends when they can and stock up on produce and other items to carry over until the next visit.

Besides the cost of living being higher, they are also no longer surrounded by the support and social life of the extended family, so except for each other, they are on their own. I ask them why they don't live in Jenin, which seems economically stronger than ever, especially with all the Palestinians shopping in Jenin from 1948 Palestine, but they claim their particular work opportunities are better in Ramallah, even with the added expenses. To lighten the heaviness of making ends meet, we have a sampling of the infamous Ruqab ice cream. Sham is excited to taste this local favorite made right in Ramallah with its signature bright colors and creamy consistency. *A taste of Palestine to remember.*

For all the years we traveled to Palestine, Nasser and I have never taken the kids to Sakhne, which means "hot" in Arabic. Sakhne is the natural spring near Beisan that Nasser's nephew showed me 20 years earlier, what Israelis have renamed Gan Hashlosha National Park. I never realized several Palestinian villages once stood nearby, including Al-Sakhina, which Jewish militias destroyed on May 12, 1948, just two days before Israel declared statehood.[143]

We take the scenic route via the mountain road on top of the Gilboa Mountains. The winding road carries us higher and higher until we can see in every direction. We stop a few times to get out to enjoy the view. Along the way, we spot the Herb Garden, a restaurant Nasser would like to try on the way back.

I don't know then that just farther south of the Herb Garden once stood the Palestinian village of Al-Mazar, and farther north along the main road, the village of Nuris.[144] In 1950, Israel established an agricultural cooperative nearby called a *moshav* in Hebrew that today has become an ecovillage. *How can people care about the well-being of the land but not those who call it home? Has Israel so successfully buried the past of those who once lived here, who, to this day, are barred from returning?*

Nasser's brother once told me the story of his great-uncle's brother, who fell in love with a girl from the destroyed village of Nuris, but her father would not approve of their marriage. When she married someone else, he died of a broken heart. Now, the entire village of Nuris is heartbroken, uprooted from their homes. I had no idea all these years when I looked over at the settlement of Gan Ner from Jalameh that those trees on the mountainside were planted—with collections from the Jewish National Fund—to hide the remains of Palestinian villages. How fortunate are those who managed to remain on their land rather than have their villages buried beneath a forest.[145]

Toward the end of the mountain pass, we wind our way down to Sakhne. I don't recognize the entrance with its grand palm trees. Mahmoud and I must have come in another way those many years ago. We pay the hefty entrance fee that feels unaffordable by local standards. We walk onto the grass-covered grounds, past the first deep aqua pool, and find a place to sit under a young olive tree. The depth of the water is intimidating to Nasser, who is not the best swimmer, but he joins us once we scout out the far end with a waterfall by an ancient Roman bathhouse and a shallow river, where we find pottery shards, perhaps as ancient as these pools. Nasser walks up onto the bank, thrilled to find *kharoub*. We chew on the carob pods, delighting in their nutty sweetness. Nasser also shares a few almost ripe green *tin* with us, delicious figs of Palestine.

This spring is the perfect destination on a hot day. Here we are 20 minutes from Jalameh, but no one from the village can come here. Such beauty simply out of reach. It feels criminal to me to deprive people of their own treasures. The older generations know the spring, but for the younger generations, it is like a dream when they hear stories of a gorgeous spring with crystal-clear water, as if there is another dimension through which they cannot pass.

The sun is still high in the sky as we pack up our things, take a quick shower, and leave this magical place, taking the same mountain pass back toward Jalameh. Unfortunately, the Herb Garden is closed, so we decide to keep driving and eat dinner at the azbeh back in the village instead. We grill the rest of the goat meat from the Eid with eggplant, onions, tomatoes, and peppers, along with leftover baba ghanouj—everything so fresh and delicious. As we enjoy a cappuccino and a sampling of chocolate on the veranda after dinner, the evening breeze greets us from the west, the sun's glow emanating like a crown of light.

As I look into the fading sunset, my eyes cross right through these borders, my mind aware of what is beyond them. Even those who cannot cross know what is beyond, the land etched in their minds. Nothing can eliminate that longing to see what is just beyond the next hill, especially when it is your homeland. I have the privilege of seeing it for myself, bearing witness to past and present, where the future is just around the bend.

By the end of June, Nasser and Sham leave to celebrate Sham's 17th birthday in Newfoundland and Quebec—a promised father-daughter trip—so it's just Karmel and me in Palestine. It is evening, and we are sitting in the 'aqid with its lovely domed ceiling when Karmel says we could watch a movie. I am surprised by his suggestion. We haven't turned on the TV at all this whole trip. He explains we have Netflix and starts bringing up options. *Netflix in Palestine?*

We sift through the choices, watch a few trailers. One movie stands out among the rest: *Sara's Notebook*. The movie takes place in the Congo. Sara is there trying to make a difference, journaling about her experiences in her notebook. Her sister is worried about her, so she makes the difficult trip to the Congo to find Sara and bring her home, but she doesn't want to leave.

The Congo is one of many places in the world where some people live at the expense of others. People's lives are at stake, caught in the crosshairs of history. At the end, Sara dies there trying to make a difference. Her sister turns her notebook into a book and brings it to her grave. I feel a lump in my throat. It feels too familiar. I think of Rachel Corrie, who died trying to keep the Israeli army from destroying Palestinian homes in Rafah. She left behind her words, which her parents turned into their life's work. Her story became a play, a foundation, a cause.

Rachel's story is also part of my story. Unlike her, I am not standing in front of a bulldozer or putting myself in the crosshairs of history. I am simply sharing what I have witnessed in Palestine. I have been writing this story since 2012. It is the past, but it is also the present. I am still living my story. *This book is my notebook. I hope I get to finish it before I die.* I want people to see life in Palestine. I want others to care enough to demand peace and justice, to see that if there is no dignity for some, then there cannot be dignity for all. There is always more to tell. The story will keep unfolding, and I know I will keep telling it, even after the book itself is frozen in time.

The next morning, Karmel and I get up at dawn to hike the Din Mountain just beyond the wa'ra. Karmel sets his bare feet onto the dry, sandy earth, the air still cool. We begin our hike along the base of the Din Mountain, the Israeli security fence just past the farmlands of Jalameh. The land is still, no Israeli army Jeeps patrolling. Beyond the fence, we see the settlement of Gan Ner beyond Sidi's land and the pine tree-covered hills of the Gilboa Mountains.

After we have walked halfway around the base of the Din, we head up the mountain, making our way between the dry brush. I see the familiar bushes with thorns like hexagons and shtella, the plant Samira used to brush the fine thorns off the saber on our first trip here back in 1992. Large boulders are scattered throughout the mountain, some nestled in the earth, others protruding out like cliffs.

We walk from boulder to boulder to stay clear of the brush, occasionally descending to the ground when the boulders are farther apart. Some areas with olive trees were recently plowed and cleared of stones, revealing the rich, chunky, brown soil the color of raw cacao gleaming in the early morning sunlight. With Jalameh in full view, I see the new mosque at the southern end of the village with its gold dome and minaret and the original mosque farther north. Framing the village are the dome-shaped hamamot greenhouses.

We continue around the crown of the mountain until we see Mount Carmel in the distance. "See, just beyond your mountain is Haifa and the Mediterranean Sea." I wonder how people here feel when they gaze into the distance and see the rest of their homeland, knowing they cannot go there. Their eyes look past the border, but if they follow their eyes with their feet, they will be stopped in their tracks and only let through depending on their Israeli ID or permits. In my lifetime, I have seen the full range of open borders to total lockdown and everything in between. And yet the people who live here—Israelis and Palestinians—live in the same place but have yet to truly share the same space.

The soft glow of an impending sunrise brings several hot air balloons into focus, floating magically toward the Gilboa Mountains from Afula in a perfect line. This tourist attraction in Afula takes Israelis over the Gilboa mountain range for a bird's-eye view of the scenery, all visible from Jalameh, but out of reach for the people who live here. The sky is open to their eyes, but the border is closed to their legs to explore the forbidden landscape of their homeland across the Green Line.

For Nasser's father, the rift between what his one good eye could see—his own farmland—and the reality of the loss of his land meant a lifetime of heartbreak. What artistry it must take to carry that bitterness and still find a way to live with laughter. I can't think of anyone with a greater smile than Nasser's father.

We make our way back down the mountain. When we reach the bottom, I, too, walk barefoot, eager to feel the warm, smooth soil beneath my feet. Now, I carry the geography of the Din Mountain in my body. The mountain seemed so massive, but we walked all the way around it and even climbed to the top. If I walked it often as Karmel does, I would begin to know every tree, boulder, and bend in the landscape as previous generations did, who used to travel everywhere on foot, horse, or donkey over the hilltops and across the valleys.

Back at the azbeh, we make a simple breakfast of eggs fried in the *makleh*—a clay pot with two handles the size of a small frying pan, along with taboun bread, lebneh, za'atar, sliced tomatoes, and olives. I make a scoop with the bread and dip it into the creamy lebneh covered in rich green olive oil, then the tangy za'atar, before popping the perfectly prepared bite into my mouth. "I love it here! I never have to think what to eat for breakfast! In the US, we always have to decide what to have. There are too many choices."

"I know, right?" Karmel sprinkles some salt on the juicy wedges of tomatoes, then picks one up and puts it in his mouth. "I never get tired of eating this stuff."

"It really is the perfect food. I don't know why I make things so complicated when I'm in the US. Lebneh is like an occasional thing when it could be every day like here." The perfect ending to a perfect morning!

The sky is clear and bright, the air still cool and fresh as we walk between the olive trees. We admire all the special plants Nasser has arranged between the islands of ancient boulders protruding from beneath the earth. Flowering vines grow along the fence line that will soon create a wall of blossoms as a buffer from the packs of wild dogs that roam the hillsides. I recall how, years ago, we walked among these trees, the boulders islands of safety from the thorny brush. The only fences were the saber that marked the borders between each family's share of the wa'ra. Now, just beyond Nasser's wall of flowers, the Israeli border fence cuts the landscape between us and them. *What will it take to erase these borders?*

Later that week, we are invited for dinner at Nasser's sister Suhaila's in the village of Rummaneh. They tell us about a guy named Benjamin Ladraa from Sweden, who walked all the way from Sweden to Palestine to draw attention to the situation here. Apparently, he was just denied entry at the bridge by the Israeli border security.[146]

Like Rachel Corrie, those who take a stand for Palestine pay the price. It is ironic that on the very day that a man from Sweden arrives at the border to walk through Palestine, Karmel and I hiked the Din Mountain. We are the fortunate ones, still free to walk here, keeping our connection to Palestine alive through our very footsteps.

Back at Nasser's family home, Karmel and I walk from room to room, studying the original floor tiles, admiring the rich colors, intricate patterns, and impressive durability, wondering how and where they were made. When we find out the factory that made the tiles still exists in Nablus, we make an excursion to check it out, along with a soap factory that still makes soap like *zaman*—the old days.

We stop in Jenin on the way for breakfast at a famous place where the entire menu is based on hummus. We sit down at a table and order a plate of hummus topped with lamb and another dish with hummus topped with the spicy daqa sauce made with garlic, hot peppers, lemon, and olive oil I first ate in Gaza back in 1986. A young man brings us our food along with a basket of warm pita bread, a plate of pickled vegetables, and a bottle of water. The hummus is so smooth and creamy. It's absolutely delicious!

Hummus is truly a dish from the land—chickpeas, tahini ground from sesame seeds, and lemon juice—all local, nutrient-dense ingredients that have sustained people here for generations. To know the land is to know what to eat and how to prepare it. The cultural traditions of the fellahin are the backbone of Palestinian society. They know the land, cultivate the food, and supply the market. Masters of food preparation and preservation, they still make the most time-tested dishes that nourish the body and the soul.

No wonder Palestinians remain rooted in the land, even those who lost their land, because it is their culture, survival, and legacy. Pickled olives and other vegetables, dried grains and legumes, nuts and seeds, and seasonal harvests of fresh produce offer a pleasing array of culinary masterpieces year-round. The soil, the seasons, the seeds are like a secret shared among those who serve the land. Sitting there with Karmel, I feel privy to that secret.

When we arrive in Nablus, we visit the soap factory first. We enter the stone building and find an older man willing to show us around. He directs us to a huge vat with a mechanical rotating arm dragging itself through a thick yellowish liquid composed of olive oil, caustic soda, water, and salt. This simple mixture cooks until it thickens, then they pour it into metal buckets to carry upstairs. As we follow the man up a narrow stone staircase, he warns us to step carefully as it can be slippery from the soap.

Across the floor in front of us is wall-to-wall soap, sectioned off with pieces of wood. He explains how they pour the soap into the sections on the floor, let it cool, then cut it and press the company stamp into each cake of soap. Once it fully cools and hardens, they stack the cakes of soap into towers to let it dry out for about a month before packaging it for sale.

I am in disbelief that the whole process is still done by hand on such a massive scale. We walk over to the stacks of individual bars of soap arranged in circles staggered neatly on top of each other along the entire wall, each level of soap forming a slightly smaller circle that narrows toward the top of the tower, the dim light passing through like tiny windows between each brick of soap. A man sitting on a wooden stool with a small wooden platform in front of him takes a bar of soap from a stack next to him, sets it on a white square of paper, then folds it neatly in and flips it over, the name of the factory printed on the front. He looks up at me, smiling, and hands it to me. I ask him if he really wraps each one by hand. He nods and wraps another one, his hands quick and methodical. I offer words of praise: *Masha' allah*.

The bars of soap sell for five shekels—handmade olive oil soap for just over a dollar. I buy a few to take home, and he tucks them into a black plastic bag. On our way back to the stairs, a man ahead of us is carrying four boxes of soap on his back, with his hands cupped behind him to support the load. I turn to Karmel. "They don't even have an elevator. This is crazy!" I think of these men, carrying buckets of liquid soap up these narrow stone stairs, then boxes of soap back down once it has been dried, cut, stacked, and packaged. Every step in this process makes me feel like we are going back in time. They have been making soap here this way for over 150 years.

Our next stop is the signature tile factory, unmistakable because the outer walls are covered with tiles in various colors and patterns, some appearing three-dimensional. We find a young man seated in an outdoor area behind a wooden table surrounded by racks of tiles lined up on their sides in neat rows. I gasp when I see one of the racks has the exact same tile design as the original entranceway of Nasser's family home, its creamy white squares and deep red and mustard-yellow pattern ingrained in my memory. The brand-new tiles look perfect.

The young man appears to be in the middle of making tiles. A thrill swells up in my chest to witness the tiles being made before our eyes. He sets a square metal frame the size of one tile onto a square base and carefully pours a trickle of cream paint into sections of the design using a tiny copper ghalai, briefly interrupting his pouring to move to a new area. He repeats the process with light blue, then carefully lifts the design out of the base. He sprinkles white powder over it to set the paint, then spreads a layer of thick, gray concrete-like paste into the outer frame. He finishes off the tile by pressing down on the filled surface with a square block, then sets the finished tile on a rack to dry in the sun. He places the frame with the design back in the base to start the whole process over again.

An older man comes over to welcome us to the factory. His eyes light up when I tell him how the tiles in our house in Jenin were made here. He offers to show us around the factory. We walk through a narrow doorway filled with metal tile designs hanging on the walls in no particular order, others stacked haphazardly on shelves. He tells us how there are hundreds of designs, mostly made in France long ago. Here and there are tile samples, their geometric designs and muted colors brightening up the otherwise dusty and chaotic space.

His eyes are heavy as he tells us he is the only one who really knows how to make the tiles. He has two sons, but they have not learned the trade. *Itha bamut, biruh kul ishi*—If I die, everything goes.

I cringe, unable to imagine this whole operation shutting down. These tiles are a Palestinian legacy found in every old home. *Like the Kanafani villa in Haifa*. He laments the stiff competition with cheaper manufactured tiles flooding the market, noting it's mostly Palestinians in 1948 Palestine who buy them.

As we walk back through the narrow passageway, my heart races with delight when I see tiles on the wall just like the ones in the domed 'aqid in Nasser's family home. He says that pattern is called *Shamiyeh*—the Damascus design—literally the adjective of Sham. I laugh and tell him how perfect since our daughter's name is Sham. His smile widens as he tells us his mother was from Sham, referring to Syria, and his father from Turkey.

I think about the tiles and the soap factory that persist to this day, hoping these traditions will carry on from generation to generation. So far, this man is running the tile factory much the way his father did before him, *zay zaman*—like the old days. Perhaps it is this appreciation for tradition and memory of the past coupled with living here and now that keeps Palestine alive and serves as testimony that Palestine was here and still exists. I feel more driven than ever to share these stories, anchored in the past. Stories that will carry Palestinians into the future.

50

Return to Haifa and 'Akka

It has been nearly 20 years since I took Karmel to see his mountain in Haifa. Then, he was three years old, his only memory of that day was the stories and photos I have shared with him. I want him to see his mountain as an adult and also take him to the beach in Haifa. We drive to the Jalameh checkpoint to find only the left lane open. I hand the security personnel our American passports.

"What are you doing in Jenin?" The Israeli army that used to oversee the Jalameh checkpoint has been replaced by a security firm, their personnel outfitted with Tavor rifles, an upgrade from the M16s of the past. The border guard has a heavy Hebrew accent, her eyes hidden behind mirrored sunglasses. When we tell her we are visiting, she sends us to the right, where there are two lanes under a carport-like covering. We get out of the car and open all the doors and the back hatch, then proceed into the security building. Another security guard. More questions.

"Where is your luggage?"

"We are just going to the beach."

The border guard raises her eyebrows. "To the beach!" I suppose that is not what they typically hear from someone coming from Jenin.

"Where is your visa?" She is looking at Karmel.

"I don't have one." Karmel hands her his *hawiyeh*—Palestinian ID—and tasrih permit that piggybacks off his father's businessman's tasrih. *Like when I had a* Mehrfachvisum—*multiple entry visa—to East Germany that piggybacked off my father's visa before the fall of the Berlin Wall.*

Her eyes open wide as she examines Karmel's ID. "Oh, so you live here!"

"No, I don't live here, but my father works here, and I come and visit him."

The border guard stiffens, staring at his hawiyeh. "No, you have this, then you live here. You don't live in the US."

There is no point in arguing with her. In her eyes, he is not an American if he carries a Palestinian ID. He will be dealt with as a Palestinian. There is no getting around it. For the first time, they take the car to a shed in another area farther back for inspection.

We proceed into the building to pass through the metal detector, several border guards eyeing us, gripping their Tavor rifles. Two of them approach after we pass through to ask questions, then one makes a phone call, holding up Karmel's hawiyeh as he speaks in Hebrew. I decipher he is reading off his ID number, as the words resemble Arabic.

They come back over, looking at Karmel as if he is a specimen in a lab. "Are you Muslim?" Karmel has a full beard and long strawberry-blonde hair. Perhaps they are worried he is affiliated with the Muslim Brotherhood or Hamas.

"No, I'm not religious." They peer at him further and discuss amongst themselves. Without any evidence for alarm, they say we can go. A deep breath calms my racing heart.

Once we pass through the checkpoint, we head west on Highway 66, which is Haifa Street, the same road that once led directly from Jenin to Haifa, still blocked by a military outpost on the Green Line between the Palestinian villages of Rummaneh and Salem. On our way, we spot the ruins of stone houses up on the hills to our left near the kibbutz of Mishmar HaEmek. When I spot thorny clusters of saber in the distance, my senses tell me we are passing destroyed villages.

I later look at the map to discover that just north of the kibbutz we passed are the remains of the Palestinian village of Abu Shousha.[147] Nearby are several other destroyed Palestinian villages: Al-Ghubayya Al-Tahta,

Al-Ghubayya Al-Fawka, and Naghnaghiya.[148] Like Nasser's village of Jalameh and the nearby villages of Muqeibileh and Sandala across the Green Line, these three villages used to share the same elementary school. Although the Armistice Line of 1949 ended up cutting off Jalameh from the other two, the three villages of Al-Ghubayyat were completely destroyed, and their residents forbidden to return.

We follow the road north toward Afula, then veer off to Mount Carmel. First, I want to take Karmel to his mountain. We pass open countryside or farmland, then a huge settlement under construction, where the entire mountainside has been cleared. Several rows of white townhouses glow in the bright sun, some already outfitted with red Spanish-tile rooftops. We stop to get gas, but I can't read the machine—everything is written in Hebrew—so I ask inside if anyone knows English. As one woman approaches me, I hear some of the employees behind the counter speaking Arabic. My body softens with relief. *Ana bahki 'arabi*—I speak Arabic. One of the employees comes out to help me, asking where we are from. When we tell him we are from Jenin and on our way to visit Daliyat al-Karmel, the town on top of Mount Carmel, he blurts out he is from Daliyat al-Karmel. His smile only widens when I tell him my son's name is Karmel.

Karmel and I stop at a lookout point at Mount Carmel National Park. We walk over to a huge stone archway with a sea of pine trees beyond it, extending out into the distant hills that roll downward to the Mediterranean Sea. Karmel stands under the archway, then climbs on it.

I call him by his nickname. "Mouli on Mouli's Mountain!"[149]

"This is so cool!" Karmel reaches his arms up and out, his smile as wide as the sea. He was only three years old the last time Nasser and I brought him to his mountain. Now, he is all grown up.

By the time we reach Daliyat al-Karmel, we simply drive through, saving the time we have left for Haifa. First, we head to the Bahá'i Gardens to enjoy the view from the upper terrace of the meticulously maintained gardens that extend down to the gold-domed temple, the harbor just beyond it where the pale-blue sky merges into the deep-blue sea in the distance.

A young guy with a heavy Arabic accent wearing a black Diesel t-shirt walks up to Karmel. "Can I take a picture with you?"

Karmel smiles. "Sure."

The guy holds up his phone to frame the photo. "Where are you from?"

"Jenin."

His eyes open wide. "Jenin!" He continues in Arabic. *Ana min Khalil*—I am from Hebron. We all laugh.

I chime in, explaining that Nasser's family is originally from Hebron. *Ma'na antu qaraybna!*—So, we are relatives! He laughs because he thought he was getting a picture with a foreigner, and it turns out both he and Karmel are Palestinian.

We are starving, but time is running out—we only have until 7:00 p.m. to make it back to the checkpoint—and we still want to go to Wadi Salib and the beach. We quickly eat some nuts and apples in the car.

Wadi Salib and neighboring Wadi Nisnas were the heart of the Palestinian neighborhoods in Haifa before 1948. All but 3,000 of the original 75,000 residents of Haifa were driven out, and those remaining were forced to settle in Wadi Nisnas.[150] Wadi Salib is the same neighborhood I visited back in 1999.

I explain to Karmel how the Kanafani villa stood prominently on the ridge, but I read recently that it was slated for demolition. I was hoping it was still standing, that someone had found a way to save it, even if it meant turning it into an office building like so many of the other villas along the ridge.

We circle around the area still filled with older stone buildings, but I cannot find the landmark staircase that leads up the steep slope to the house. I keep looking back down at the harbor as a reference point, but I can't find it. My heart sinks when I realize most of the older crumbling homes I saw then are gone, replaced by newer buildings as part of a redevelopment of the area into an art haven that has yet to materialize. It reminds me of Jaffa, where so many of the homes in the Old City were converted into art galleries and antique shops.

I give up my search. "Forget it. It's okay. I don't have to find it today. Let's just go to the beach."

We drive down the mountain to the beachside promenade lined with grass-covered hills and parking lots. All I want is to go to the sea, but Karmel is hungry, so we walk to a seaside restaurant and sit down at one of the sofa seating areas by the water. The sand is creamy white, almost blinding in the bright sun, people swimming and body surfing amidst the waves crashing onto shore.

It is already after 5:00 p.m. when we finish our delicious spread of beet and goat cheese salad, roasted eggplant with tahini, a black rice salad, and fresh carrot juice. We need at least half an hour to drive back to the Jalameh checkpoint.

As we walk over to the water, my feet sink into the hot sand. We proceed into the waves though the water remains shallow, only up to our hips. Karmel joins in with the others to body surf, pushing off with the next wave and letting it pull him toward shore, then makes his way back to me. He positions himself for the next wave. "This is so awesome!" I wish Sham and Canaan were with us.

The water is warm and magical. I swim a little farther out, then let myself float onto my back as I did in Gaza. I look up at the open sky, my body suspended by the wave as it carries me gently up and down. Now, all I can think is how no one from Nasser's village can come here, only 45 minutes from Jalameh. Of course, they can apply for a tasrih permit, but they are not allowed to drive their own cars—only yellow license plates can enter—so most people lucky enough to get a tasrih come with a tour group by bus with a set itinerary. And the tasrih is only for the day, which means getting back to the checkpoint before it closes.

It is 5:30 p.m. when we get out of the water to rinse off in the showers. By the time we get back to the car, it is almost 6:00. We put Afula in our navigation since it won't register destinations in the West Bank. It says 45 minutes. We should just make it. We pass through the new Carmel Tunnels for a hefty fee of 125 shekels but decide it's worth it to save time. Unfortunately, we make a wrong turn, missing the road to Nazareth. By some miracle or act of kindness, the attendant stops all six lanes of traffic at rush hour to guide us to the other side of the road to turn around. We should make it just before 7:00 p.m. as long as we don't make any more wrong turns.

When we arrive at the border, it's 6:50 p.m. We made it! But something's not right. Across the checkpoint, there is a line of cars with yellow license plates coming from Jenin—Palestinians with Israeli citizenship headed home after a day of shopping—but no cars are headed in the other direction. We approach the gate, but a security guard waves his hands that we cannot enter. I roll down my window only to hear, "The border is closed."

I gasp in desperation. "It's before 7:00—it doesn't close until 7:00."

"No, it's closed. This side closes at 6:45."

A blast of pressure fills my head. "We live right over there—I have to get through."

"Sorry, it is closed. You have to go back."

"Back where? This is the road to Jenin."

"I cannot open the gate. It is closed. You will have to go to another gate." I plead with him to call someone to open the gate, but he says he already talked to his supervisor. There is nothing he can do. I insist to talk to his supervisor myself. He walks away, and we sit there in front of the wide barrier of steel bars, a tire spike strip an ominous warning not to drive any closer.

A few minutes later, his supervisor appears. I show him my American passport and insist he opens the gate. He tells us it is electronically programmed, and once it's closed, he can't open it.

"What am I supposed to do?" I plead with him in desperation. "I have to enter."

He tells us we have two choices: to go to the Tulkarem border crossing to the southwest, or back toward Beisan and head south from there past Bardala. I am not familiar with these options, but I am certain either route will take hours. He insists it's only a 45-minute drive. The village is literally before our eyes, just beyond the gate, but we cannot get through. I recall when I demanded they open the road on my way to the school years ago. This time, I am not so lucky. We have no choice but to go back. We decide to head toward Beisan, a little worried Karmel will not be able to cross at Balada with his Palestinian ID, but we take the risk.

We return to the Yizre'el Junction. I can't help but notice the sign to Beisan still does not bear the name Beisan in Arabic, only a transliteration of the Hebrew. We follow the same scenic route up the Gilboa Mountains that we took with Nasser when we went to the Sakhne Springs. After we cross the mountain, we follow along a smooth, two-lane road that winds around the curves of the desolate mountainside overlooking farms in the Jordan Valley. Lower in the valley, we see Bedouin camps and deep gorges carved into the earth, where water flows in the spring like I saw back in 1986 in the Naqab Desert at Salim's family. I realize that it will be at least 45 minutes to reach the border crossing and probably another 45 minutes to get back to Jalameh.

We stop worrying about the time and just take in the scenery, grateful to see another part of Palestine.

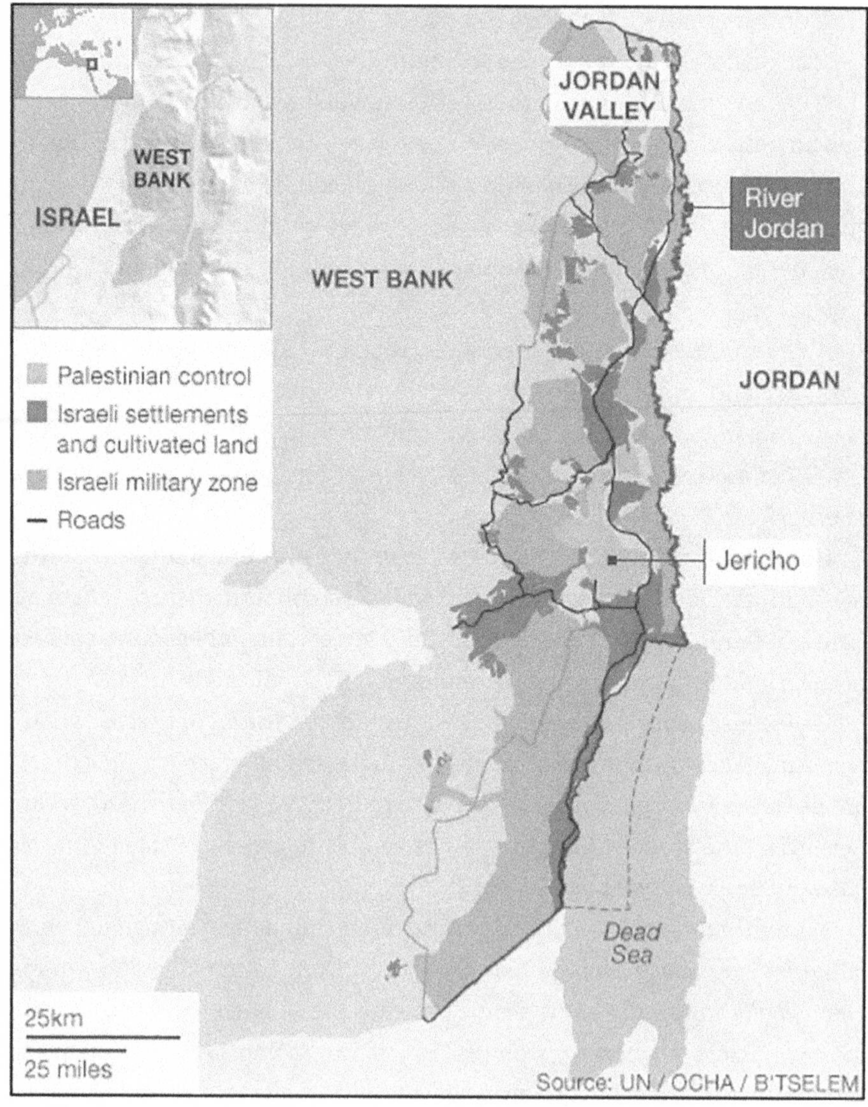

Map 17: Restricted Areas in the Jordan Valley (Source: UN / OCHA / B'Tselem)

I think of all the land in this area that roughly 10,000 Israeli settlers are farming (see Map 17). Even though more than 60,000 Palestinians live in the Jordan Valley, primarily in the city of Jericho, most of the area is off limits to Palestinians, designated as a closed security area or nature reserve, even though it lies within the West Bank.[151] Israel declared most of the area a buffer zone with neighboring Jordan, and yet Israelis are allowed to settle there and farm the land. Palestinians in the West Bank are contained in their cities and villages, leaving most of the West Bank under Israeli control.[152]

When we get to the border crossing, no one is monitoring it. Relieved, we pass through without stopping and head toward the Palestinian village of Tubas in the West Bank, making our way north through the hills until we reach Jalameh. It is 9:30 p.m. when we arrive. This senseless detour took us over two hours. At least we made it safely back home.

Karmel and I take another day trip, this time farther up the Mediterranean coast to the city of 'Akka. When we arrive, we drive along the ancient wall not far from the marina I explored with Salem so many years ago. We walk into one of the nearby stone passageways that branches off in different directions like a maze to explore the Old City. We are delighted to find a local vendor selling juice, just what we need on a hot summer day. He tells us we should see the Templar Tunnel, which once connected the Templar Fortress to the Mediterranean Sea in the 12th century when the Crusaders ruled the city. It was only discovered in 1994 while repairing a backed-up toilet.

As we meander through the stone passageways, I look up at the walls at the intersections. "Hey, they have signs now in Hebrew, Arabic, and English. This way to Templar Tunnel!" Inside, the tunnel glows from lights strategically placed along gutters, where water runs on either side of the walkway. The farther we walk, the lower the rounded ceiling, forcing us to bend over.

Near the marina, we find an inviting seaside restaurant with a perfect view of the next generation of Palestinian youth diving off the ancient walls, then swimming to a stone staircase that leads back up to the top of the wall. At one point, two men at the next table take off their shoes and shirts and jump into the water right from the restaurant, and then swim over to the stairway. I imagine being able to jump off the walls of 'Akka is a rite of passage for those who grow up in this ancient city. We eat a delicious fish dinner to the sound of crashing waves, then climb on the ancient walls for a view of the coastline and the city.

I can't believe it has been over 30 years since Dieter and I first came here with Salem. Unlike then, when we could explore the city into the evening, Karmel and I must leave before sunset to get back to the checkpoint before 6:45 p.m. At least Palestinians here get to experience the sea and the sunset and live among Palestinians. No wonder when Palestinians in the West Bank apply for a tasrih to enter Israel, 'Akka is a favorite destination. Here, they are among Palestinians. Here they are not strangers in their own homeland. I, too, hold this city dear to my heart. I, too, am no stranger here.

But what does the future hold? Israel is forcing a Jewish presence in the West Bank with the continual establishment and expansion of settlements, a seeping annexation of Palestinian land. *Will Israel simply swallow the rest of Palestine whole, thereby completing its mission to reconfigure Palestine into Israel? Or will Israelis realize their own security is dependent on stopping and reversing the ongoing Nakba?*

51

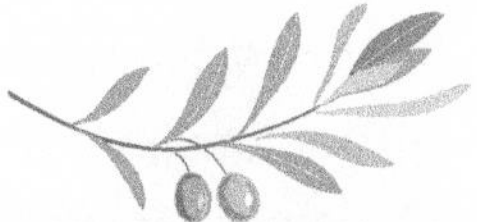

Last Generation

At the end of our trip, Karmel and I pay a visit to 'Amti Ayshi, Nasser's father's eldest sister, who is in her 90s. No longer does she live in the old stone house in the center of Jalameh. Her sons and daughter moved her to Jenin, where they live as neighbors. When we enter the house, she is sitting on a daybed against the wall. Her eyes brighten when she sees us, her wide smile filling the room as her arms stretch out to welcome us. After I greet her with kisses on both cheeks, I wish her good health since she recently broke her knee. *Salamtik, ya 'Amti!*

'Amti Ayshi's daughter stops by from next door, her eyes sparkling with delight as she welcomes us with her raspy voice. She is thrilled when I remind her how much I loved the dessert she made with *halbeh*—fenugreek—when we visited her mother in the old stone house in the village. She promptly tells me how to make it, listing off semolina, whole wheat flour, fenugreek soaked overnight, black seed, and sesame topped with the sugar syrup known as *qatr*. She even promises to make me some to bring home to the US and faithfully delivers the next morning.

Her face becomes long when I ask about the old house that stands empty since no one in the family lives there right now. I encourage them to maintain the house, lest it crumble like Nasser's grandfather's house after they sold it. These old homes with their gorgeous domed 'aqid ceilings are a national treasure. They must be protected.

Eager to hear stories from long ago, I ask 'Amti Ayshi how she used to bake bread. When her weathered hands animate her description of grinding whole wheat beneath a large stone disk by rotating it over another stone disk with a wooden handle, I notice one of her fingers is much shorter than the others. *Shou sar bi-yidik, ya 'Amti?*—What happened to your hand?

She looks down at her hand and breaks out in laughter, explaining that when she was in her 20s, she was carrying water in a *jarra*—clay jug—and it fell from her shoulder onto her left hand and broke the end of her finger, which had to be amputated. I am surprised how candidly she speaks, so accepting of the loss, brushing it off like it was nothing. Perhaps this personal loss is nothing compared to the lifelong occupation of one's homeland. Here she sits, the last one of her generation in the family to witness the Nakba.

Not long after that visit to Palestine, 'Amti Ayshi returns to the Earth. I wonder what the current and future generations will witness. More loss, or will there be peace, resolution, justice?

It is mid-morning. I walk over to 'Amti Ayshi's sister's house, 'Amti Saymi's, near the entrance to the village to check in with her daughters Intisar and Fawziya if they will take Karmel and me to see their mother's grave this evening. 'Amti Saymi passed away in December, so I just missed the chance to see her again. The last time I saw her was 2011. Even though it is customary, Intisar asks me why I slip off my sandals before entering the house. I tell her I don't want to make more work for her. Sure enough, she has already washed the floor and is still dressed in the clothes she wears when she tends to the goats. I tell her what Faisal told me, that there is no shame in work. Her cheeks lift as she laughs in agreement, insisting it's better to keep moving. I encourage her to take care of the goats and her health so she can continue to make cheese and grow her own food, basic life skills lost by the younger generations.

She complements me on my health. *Bas anti mniha*—But you look good.

Lazem adiri bal 'ala hali—I have to take care of myself. I add how most people don't bother to take care of themselves until something goes wrong, but I have always taken care of myself, now more than ever, alluding to my stroke.

The two sisters serve me fresh lemonade and *kharoub*. I take a bite of one of the stiff, dark brown carob pods and chew, delighting in its nutty sweetness. How I enjoy it as a drink when the pods are soaked in water with just the right amount of sugar. I always tell people here, who needs Coca-Cola when you have tamar *hindi* and kharoub!

I tell them I have to return the rental car tomorrow. *Ya rayt okhuthkum rahleh juwa!*—How I wish I could take you on a trip inside! I am surprised to learn that Palestinians over 50, who are residents of the West Bank—those who have a hawiyeh—don't need a tasrih to enter Israel. I wish I had known! I would have taken them. Unfortunately, I won't get a next time. Israel changes its policy yet again, requiring anyone who wants to travel inside to apply for a *maghneta*—a magnetic card that not only stores their personal information but comes at a hefty price.

It doesn't matter since Fawziya and Intisar don't want to go anywhere anyway. *Wen bidna inruh!*—Where would we even go? They insist they have everything they need at home and don't like the idea of eating out in restaurants, claiming they would just get sick.

Ah, bas lazem itshufu Falastin. 'Akka, Haifa, Yaffa. Kul hatha baladkum—Yes, but you have to see Palestine: 'Akka, Haifa, Jaffa. It's all your homeland.

Intisar gathers the lemonade cups, with her eyes focused on the tray in front of her. Fawziya smiles at me. *Yumkin*—Maybe.

Why should Palestinians ever think that their homeland is out of reach? Why can't all these restrictions on access to all of Palestine become a thing of the past?

It is late afternoon when Karmel and I pick up Fawziya and Intisar to go to the cemetery. We park on the side of the road and follow their lead. As they point to their father's grave, a long circle of stones and a white headstone with black lettering in Arabic, images of him grazing the goats come to mind, his long white scarf held in place by the 'iqal, like Nasser's father wore, his wooden cane in hand. Farther ahead lies their mother's grave, also outlined in stones with a white headstone.

Intisar's voice is quiet and low. *Hayaha Mama*—Here is Mama.

I bow my head. *Allah yirhamha*—May God bless her soul.

Intisar and Fawziya echo in unison. *Ta'ish*—May you live.

The sisters stand at their mother's headstone and recite the *Fatiha*, the first verses of the Quran.[153]

Bismillah ir-rahman ir-rahim—In the name of Allah, the Merciful
Alhamdillahi—All praise is [due] to Allah,
Rabb il-'alamin—Lord of the worlds
Ar-rahman ir-rahim—The Entirely Merciful, the Especially Merciful
Maliki yawm id-din—Sovereign of the Day of Recompense
Iyyaka na'budu—It is You we worship
wa liyaka nasta'im —and You we ask for help.
Ihdinas-siratal mustaqim—Guide us to the straight path
Siratal-lazina—The path of those upon whom
an'amta 'alaihim—You have bestowed favor,
ghayr il-maghdoubi 'alaihim—Not of those who have evoked [Your] anger
wa la id-dallin—or those who are astray.

Their palms are open, cradled in front of them, their faces long, eyes cast down on their mother's final resting place. I have them pause between each line so Karmel and I can repeat after them. Then they recite another verse known as *Surah Al-Ikhlas*—The Surah of Sincerity:[154]

Bismillah ir-rahman ir-rahim—In the name of Allah, the Merciful
Qul huwa Allahu ahad—Say he is Allah, the One
Allahu as-samad—Allah, the eternal refuge
Lam yalid wa lam yulad—He neither begets nor is born
Wa lam yakul-lahu kufuwan ahad—Nor is there to him any equivalent.

As they finish the last verse, they touch their hands to their faces and slide them down before letting them fall to their sides. My eyes are on the grave, but all I can see is 'Amti Saymi's smiling face, her bright eyes, the curls of her white hair peeking out from beneath her white scarf. I think of all she witnessed in her lifetime, how many crops she sowed and harvested. Now, the very land that she so loved has reclaimed her. It is up to those of us who remain to honor her memory by celebrating her life, her love of the land, and a future that was out of her reach.

52

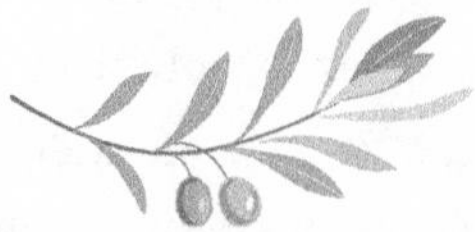

Time to Go

With my visit coming to a close, I need to return the rental car to Afula, so I drive to the Jalameh checkpoint. When I hand the security guard my passport, he puts a blue slip under my windshield and has me pull to the right. I thought maybe just this once, since I am alone, I could cross through as an American without inspection, but I am coming from Jenin, so I am suspect, my punishment for being affiliated with Palestinians. Before I move forward, I ask him how to cross the checkpoint without a car on my way back. The guard tells me only Palestinians can walk across. I have to take a taxi, but only an Arab Israeli taxi, not a Jewish one. *Arab taxi. Jewish taxi. Why so complicated?*

I drive to the right, open all the car doors, then proceed to the building to walk through the metal detector. I watch the border guards have the man ahead of me empty his cooler of drinks he just purchased in Jenin to inspect them. Every Palestinian, every day. *Is this really how the Israelis want to live?* Certainly, the Palestinians are tired of this "special treatment."

Outside, the border guards check a large white Mercedes van with a police dog—a German Shepherd—which sniffs the tires, then inside the van. It reminds me of when I took the train from East to West Germany, and the border guards would run German Shepherds along the train to find East Germans trying to escape from behind the Iron Curtain. The Israeli border guards take another car into a steel shed and close two large metal doors behind it.

What burden the Israelis carry, living in fear. I suppose subjecting a people to occupation in their own homeland is cause to be afraid. What human being wouldn't defy subjugation? And yet these Palestinians are just coming back from shopping in Jenin. They simply want to go home. Even as Israeli citizens, these Palestinians are worthy of "special treatment" because they, too, are subjugated to being strangers in their own homeland. After all, Israel is, first and foremost, a country for the Jewish people, not those who have lived here for generations, long before Israel became a state. In case anyone had any doubt about the exclusive Jewish character of the state, Israel passes the Nation-State Law that same year declaring as much.[155]

I head north on Highway 60—the old road that runs all the way from Nazareth in the north to Beersheba in the south. I arrive at the rental car place in 20 minutes. I ask the car rental staff to call me a taxi that can pass through the checkpoint. It takes some phoning around to find someone willing to take me. The taxi arrives, and I ask again to make sure he can take me through. He assures me he is the right kind of taxi driver, even though he speaks English with a heavy Hebrew accent. I take his word for it, and we head south toward Jenin. When we approach the checkpoint, he veers off to the right to a large parking lot.

My blood races through my body. "Where are you going?"

"This is where I drop you off."

"What do you mean? I told you I am going to Jalameh. They said you could take me across the checkpoint."

"No one can do that."

"That's not true. I specifically asked for a taxi that can cross. You assured me you could."

"No, I cannot pass through there. This is where I drop off."

"How am I supposed to get across? The guards told me I can't walk across."

He throws up his arms and shakes his head. "I can't help you."

"You can't just leave me here. How will I cross?"

"You have to find someone who can take you."

I look at the line of cars, trying to get a glimpse of faces, but we are too far away. *I can't believe this. What am I supposed to do?* I pay the taxi driver 50 shekels and walk over to the line of cars, wondering if the Israeli guards are watching me. I must look suspicious wandering around the checkpoint by myself on foot. I take a deep breath and look at the passengers of each car, hoping to find a Palestinian family I can ask. I am not sure who is more nervous, them or me. Why should anyone trust me to ride with them? I see a van with a man driving and a woman next to him in the passenger seat. I walk up to their open window.

Biddi aruh 'a Jalameh, mumkin aji ma'akum? Bas hunak b'ad al-hajiz—I want to go to Jalameh. Can I ride with you? It's just past the checkpoint. I explain what happened with the taxi and that I have family in Jalameh. They look at each other, then welcome me into the van. After all, we speak the same language. *I am no stranger.*

I take another deep breath, this time of gratitude. *Alf shukran*—A thousand thanks. I open the sliding door to find a young boy sitting behind the driver and take a seat behind the woman. I cast my eyes toward the checkpoint. *Shou hath al-ghalabeh!*—What a nuisance!

They nod their heads, then shift their attention to the border crossing as we approach. When it is our turn, I hand the driver my passport. He hands it to the border guard. The guard looks at their IDs and peers in the back at the small boy, then at my passport and me. He hands the passports back to the driver and waves us through. I take yet another deep breath, relieved that there are no questions. I thank the driver again and have him drop me near the road that leads to Jalameh. I walk through the line of cars waiting to cross the checkpoint in the other direction, then up the familiar road past 'Amti Saymi's house. *How many more checkpoints must I cross until there are no borders?*

My last morning before I travel back to the US, Karmel and I have jibneh, lebneh, za'atar, and grapes for breakfast with tea. The taxi arrives. It is time to say goodbye since Karmel is staying through the summer and fall to help with the almond and olive harvest. As I give him a final hug, my heart is heavy but also full of gratitude that I finally got to come back to Palestine. Soon, Sham will be returning to Madison from her trip to Canada with Nasser, so I have to leave so I get there before them.

We head out of the village, past 'Amti Saymi's house, then south toward Jericho. On the way, I learn that the driver is from the nearby village of Faqu'a but lives in Jalameh. His eyes light up when I tell him I have been to Faqu'a, high up in the hills. Such a beautiful setting! How lucky he is that his village was not destroyed in 1948! I cannot help but think of the other villages in the area that were not so fortunate, now hidden under the forests of the Gilboa Mountains.

The driver is even more thrilled when I tell him I am writing a book about my experiences in Palestine, noting there is nothing like living in one's homeland. He shares his impressions of America, though he has never visited, proclaiming that everyone lives their own life, whereas, in Palestine, people are there for each other. He mentions a German who once came to Palestine and was astonished that funerals don't cost anything here and that the grieving family feeds everyone who comes to pay their respects. He can't imagine that there is the same level of generosity in America. Here in Palestine, in spite of all the difficulties, people go on living their lives, celebrating their successes, and mourning their losses as a community.

As the landscape changes from rocky, rolling hills to the desolate, dry landscape of the Dead Sea Basin, I think about the tremendous gap between American values of freedom and democracy and a US policy that perpetrates Jewish privilege over Palestinians in their own homeland.

I pay the taxi driver 250 shekels, then another 150 dollars at the entrance to the bridge for VIP service to travel across the border by van instead of bus. When we reach the Israeli authorities, I have to pay 190 shekels for the Israeli exit tax. All these fees! Fortunately, Nasser flew to Canada with Sham from Ben Gurion Airport, so we will no longer have to travel to Palestine through Jordan. Whichever airport you leave from as a Palestinian resident is how you must return.

We spend one final night at Nasser's sister Naziha's. When she offers us a platter of grapes, I remind her of the story her parents told me about Nasser hiding under the bed where their mother had placed a platter of freshly picked grapes, his cheeks bulging, and we all laugh. Sham is also fond of grapes. How I wish she were with us to enjoy this delicious summer treat!

As we arrive at the airport, I reflect on the seven years away. I have reconnected with every member of the family and have been welcomed by all. In my heart, I hope there are many visits to come. *How can I not return to my homeland?* When my eyes connect with Abdullah's wife Maysoun as we say goodbye, she shares a proverb with me: *Ruba akhin laka lam talidhu umak*—Best friends are the siblings Allah didn't give us.[156]

And it's true. We are sisters of the heart.

53

Living in Palestine

Back in Madison, Sham is in her last year of high school. That fall of 2018, Sham and I decide to return to Palestine so she can spend a semester abroad at a bilingual high school in Ramallah while Canaan and Karmel remain in the US for the time being. It is late October, and we were just there in summer. Sham and I pack a mix of summer and winter clothes since soon the warm weather will turn to the cool chill of the rainy season. We even bring our two cats since we don't know how long we will be staying.

My heart sings with gratitude that we are headed back to Palestine again in the same year! This time, we travel to Ben Gurion Airport in Tel Aviv. I am dreading the airport security, but everything goes smoothly. I have not been to Ben Gurion Airport since 2011. Even with two cats, they simply wave us through, something I have never experienced in my entire life. This is as it should be—we can freely travel to our homeland without fear, without shame.

The entire first week in the village, it keeps hitting me. *I am in Palestine, and this time not to visit, but to live, like when I came here with Canaan and Karmel in 1998.* The heat of summer persists, the hills dry and dusty, the fields still full of summer crops of romaine, eggplant, tomatoes, potatoes, cabbage, cauliflower, and onions. I am surprised to find a few guavas hanging on Sitti's tree behind the old house. The lemon tree I planted has more lemons than we could ever eat, some green in their youth, others bright yellow, calling to me to pick them in their prime.

My heart beats faster with anticipation that soon the winter rains will awaken the wildflowers of Palestine. With the initial rains, clusters of the bright green *khobezeh* leaves gather along the side of the road. I can't wait to make it into a delicious meal sautéed with olive oil and topped with lemon juice. Young grasses peek out of the earth, softening the rugged landscape one blade at a time. The trees are washed of the dust of summer, and the air is clearer and cooler. *Palestine is outside my window.*

For the first time since the founding of our family business 14 years ago, Sham and I are in Palestine for *Al-Jaru'a*, the Olive Harvest Festival Nasser has hosted at Canaan Fair Trade each November since its beginnings in 2004. Canaan, Karmel, and Sham had school that time of year, so we always missed it. After only seeing photos and watching video footage of the event year after year, I will finally get to join in on the celebration of the olive harvest. The tradition of caring for trees that live for thousands of years passed down from generation to generation is reflected in a proverb. *Gharasou fa akalna wa nighrasu fa ya'kalouna*—They planted so we eat, and we plant so they eat. It is the next generations who eat from the olive trees planted by the previous generations, the ultimate act of planning ahead to secure their food supply and livelihood. It reminds me of my time at Standing Rock, I learned that Native communities think of the next seven generations when making decisions with lasting impact. If only everyone thought of future generations in this way!

The day before the festival, Canaan staff are busy preparing the grounds, including prepping food for the next day's festivities. The lambs have already been slaughtered, and the kitchen staff sauté the organ meats in olive oil for the staff as a special treat as they prepare for this year's festivities. The grounds are more polished than ever, with stone walkways behind the factory and lush grass beneath the olive trees lined with picnic tables. Sham and I gather with a group of employees to share in the 'alak delicacy with freshly baked taboun bread made from landrace wheat baked in the company oven. Spirits are high in anticipation of the next day.

The olive press runs around the clock, pressing olives from this year's harvest. Not only does Nasser offer the most advanced facilities in Palestine, but he also guarantees the farmers affiliated with Canaan Palestine that he will buy their olive oil and protect the quality by storing the oil on site in temperature-controlled stainless-steel tanks infused with nitrogen. Farmers know they will get more olive oil from their olives with such a sophisticated olive press, some of which they will keep for their own family's consumption.

Out front, several farmers wait their turn to channel this year's harvest into the feeder. I watch how the olives are first cleaned of sticks and leaves, washed, then pressed, resulting in opaque green olive oil glistening under the bright industrial spotlights as it is released into the first tank to be tested for quality and determine the quantity in liters.

Karmel, Sham, and I come early the next day to help set up for the festival. Along the front wall of the company is a photography exhibit of farmers from around the world. The sheer diversity in faces and landscapes warms my heart. So many different contexts, but everyone honoring the Earth and committed to growing food for their families and communities. We are truly all connected by this labor of love and life.

We walk through the showroom displaying Canaan products: various varieties of olive oil in dark green bottles, packets of za'atar, maftoul, and jars of olive tapenades. The walls are decorated with ancient farming equipment: a thresher known as *loh ad-dras*, which consists of a wooden board with wooden knobs to wedge stones used to drag over the wheat with a donkey to separate the wheat from the chaff; a wooden pitchfork called a *mithreh* used to throw the wheat up in the air so the wind carries away the chaff, leaving the wheat kernels behind; and high up on shelves is an extensive collection of huge clay jugs once used to store olive oil, each *batta* unique in size and shape with its narrow spout and round belly like Nasser's grandmother used to store olive oil until the next harvest.

On one of the display tables is a wheat grinder called *jarusheh*, like 'Amti Ayshi used to grind the wheat by grabbing the wooden peg handle and rotating the upper stone disk over the lower one. Stalks of sesame are also on display to showcase one of the ingredients for za'atar, which reminds me of Sidi's last sesame harvest in 1948. Now that Nasser is also selling almonds and almond oil, a plexiglass case displays the varieties of almonds that grow in Palestine, famous for their sweet flavor and satisfying crunch. I wonder which variety grew on Nasser's family's land that Israel confiscated to build the Separation Fence.

Canaan employees are bustling about, making the final touches on the displays and arranging the literature that includes the brochure Fida‘ and I worked on together earlier this year. An entire wall is lined with olive oil bottled right here in the facility, as well as brands that buy olive oil from Canaan to sell under their own label. Palestine may not be on the map, but it is certainly on the shelf all around the world.

In the cafeteria, Sham and I fill paper cups with samples of freekeh and maftoul salad made with landrace wheat that we arrange on three-tiered towers on a cafeteria cart. Across the room is a display of fresh lemons with their leaves still intact, fresh thyme, red chilis, heads of garlic, and purple basil in woven olive branch baskets, representing the ingredients pressed with the olives to create the line-up of "fused" olive oils. A sampling bowl of each variety is next to its corresponding bottle so attendees can dip the fresh-baked taboun bread to savor their delicate flavor. As a gift, each attendee will receive a bottle of Basil Fused Olive Oil for joining in the festivities.

Another table displays a bowl of landrace wheat kernels used to grow the wheat for freekeh and maftoul, as well as a bowl of olive pits, the trees of future generations. I am reminded of the Palestinian prisoners during the First Intifada, who made necklaces out of olive pits that were on display at events on campus when I first met Nasser back in 1987. New olive trees are planted every year, in part with the support of the Palestine Fair Trade Association's Trees for Life Program, which gives seedlings to new farmers or farmers whose trees have been uprooted by the Israeli army. Already tens of thousands of olive trees have been distributed through this program since the start of the company in 2004, which now includes almond seedlings as well.

I go on the factory tour with some of the international guests, including the consul general of the American Embassy and his wife, who have attended the festival in the past. We wind our way through the factory to admire the processing and storage facilities for the olive oil and other products. Nasser leads the way, sharing how the company's close relationship with farmers has enabled them to stay on their land and share their bounty with the world. At the olive press, guests eagerly taste samples of freshly pressed olive oil by dipping taboun bread into shallow white bowls at sampling tables.

The fresh olive oil leaves a slight prickle on my tongue that reminds me of when Ibtisam and I visited an old olive press in Kabul back in 1998. Then, we got to taste a farmer's freshly pressed olive oil seeping out of large disks of rope covered in crushed olives pressed together to release the olive oil into a steel vat below. I think of how people must have gathered around that ancient olive press carved into the stone of the wa'ra Nasser made into a fountain. This tradition goes back thousands of years, and here we are contributing to making sure it continues for generations to come.

After the tour, I head to the festival grounds, where the musicians are setting up their equipment and arriving guests claim their seats. The light breeze carries the scent of lamb stew across the grounds. Outside the cafeteria, I spot a man dressed in a white blouse and traditional wide-legged *sirwal* pants, like we saw in Majdal Shams on our tour with Johnny back in 1992, wearing a red *tarboush* hat—a relic from the Ottoman Empire. He is serving tamar hindi juice made from fresh tamarinds from an ornate brass pot strapped to his back. I join Sham, who is already in line. We watch the man tip the pot to pour each cup of juice from a long narrow spout, lowering the cup farther and farther away as he pours without spilling a drop. My taste buds are bedazzled by the cool sweet-and-sour juice—a refreshing local treat on this sunny afternoon!

My eyes scan the grounds and find Nasser's sisters and nieces claiming a long table not far from the bandstand, some wearing traditional dresses adorned with tatriz designs down the front panel and along the sleeves and hemline. I also welcome Nasser's uncles and their wives from Burqin. Soon, the program begins as several speakers share their thoughts on the company, including Nasser himself, the consul general, as well as farmers and employees from the company. A team of employees distributes bottles of water and plates of maftoul with lamb, carrots, and potatoes to the delightful sound of musicians playing traditional songs about the land and the bounty of the harvest, weaving Canaan into the lyrics. The musicians invite everyone up to join hands to dance the traditional line dance dabkeh, so I join in the circle, syncing my steps to theirs. It reminds me of our days as students at events on campus when everyone would dance dabkeh at the end. I am smiling so much that my cheeks ache. How I have waited for this day!

At one point, Nasser dances in the center, and some of the farmers lift him up on their shoulders and parade him around as if he were the groom. As the circle thins, the Palestinian men who remain dance rhythmically hand in hand in a line, the leader holding one hand high above his head as he adds in a few more complicated steps. The men behind him follow his lead, sometimes squatting down and standing back up in perfect rhythm.

I look around at all the international guests, relatives, farmers, employees, and families, their faces filled with smiles as they delve into this cross-cultural exchange over food and festivities. I think of all the work throughout the year and over the years that culminates in this event. This day is a celebration of history, of life, of community. It is beautiful when people come together, share a common purpose, show respect, and delight in each other's company. I can only hope that one day Palestinians and Israelis find a way to join hands and dance to the rhythm of a shared future, one that honors their unique traditions so they can each feel whole, safe, and respected.

Life in Ramallah is a different world than village life. Our apartment is not far from Sham's school and offers a gorgeous view of the valley and a panorama to the north from our kitchen veranda. Soon, we buy a Subaru Outback with yellow plates from Jerusalem, the same car I have in Madison. Until then, I walk Sham to school each day, and we take a taxi everywhere else. Ramallah is higher in elevation than Jenin, so there is often a breeze, if not outright wind, making it at least a few degrees cooler. Sometimes it even snows.

Since the city is spread across the hilltops, roads follow the curves of the hillside or cut steeply up or down the hills with smaller roads connecting valleys. The city feels more cosmopolitan than Jenin, with unique boutiques and brightly lit glass storefronts. Clothing and household items are tastefully displayed, with plenty of room to walk around. Like Jenin, Ramallah has an outdoor market or *hisbeh* with local produce vendors and smaller local shops.

Near the center of town is the *Muqata'a*, a complex built like a fortress with smooth high stone walls and a grand front entranceway with wide open staircases where the main offices of the Palestinian Authority (PA) are located, and Yasser Arafat was laid to rest after he passed away in 2004. Every now and then, when President Mahmoud Abbas travels somewhere, all the roads around the complex are closed to escort him to his destination in a line of black Suburbans.

Most of the time, I forget the Palestinian Authority is right there. I have mixed feelings about this quasi-Palestinian government created after the Oslo Accords were signed back in 1993 that essentially replaced the Israeli Civil Administration in the Palestinian city centers across the West Bank. Israel still controls all borders and natural resources, and the Israeli army maintains control over all areas in between these city centers. Regardless of the distinctions between Areas A, B, or C, the army enters Palestinian areas without warning whenever they see fit.

Karmel can't wait to show Sham and me around all his favorite places from when he spent time in Ramallah while studying Arabic at Birzeit University several summers ago. He takes us to the King of Dates shop that sells numerous varieties of prized dates from Palestine, as well as all kinds of spices, dried fruits, and nuts beautifully displayed in baskets. I feel like a kid in a candy shop, only this shop is even better since everything is natural food. Karmel also shows us a high-end grocery store called Max Mar that sells specialty food items from Palestine and around the world. Sham is delighted to find Asian sauces, tortillas to make quesadillas, salsa and chips, spaghetti and tomato sauce, and Western cheeses.

Sham settles into her classes at school, but the Arabic class is too advanced, so we have to find a tutor in town. Even though my Arabic is strong, I sign up to polish my use of colloquial expressions. Sham's school agrees to let her shadow her father at the company on Saturdays, a three-day weekend to spend in Jalameh Friday through Sunday since school is already closed Fridays and Sundays for Muslims and Christians. If Israel and Palestine were one country, everyone would have a three-day weekend since the Jewish Sabbath is on Saturday. Now, we have two homes in Palestine!

Being away from the US, Sham is upset that she missed Halloween and doesn't want to miss Thanksgiving, too, so we invite Nasser's brother Jamal and family to join us at the azbeh for a traditional Thanksgiving dinner: turkey, mashed potatoes, stuffing, gravy, macaroni and cheese, greens, corn bread, and pumpkin pie. Nasser will get the turkey. At Max Mar in Ramallah, Sham and I find noodles and cheese from Wisconsin for the macaroni and cheese and even discover they sell fresh pumpkins and whipping cream for pumpkin pie. We load up the car with our Thanksgiving groceries and head to Jalameh.

Nasser, Sham, and I spend the day cooking at the azbeh. When we arrive, the turkey is already cooking in a smoker out back among the olive trees. I am slicing oranges while Sham peels pomegranates when Nasser calls Sham to come with him to check the turkey. No sooner does she wash her hands than she lets out a scream. I dash over and find a sizeable brownish-black creature on the stone floor. *'Aqrabeh* is the first thing that pops in my mind. "Sham, that's a scorpion!"

Nasser dashes over. "No way! Where the heck did he come from? Maybe it was hiding in one of the apron pockets." Sham shudders with the thought that this dangerous creature was crawling on her. It must have stung her through her jeans but only nicked her, or the pain would be much worse. Luckily it wasn't a red one, as they can be lethal. I put some ice on her leg to help with the swelling.

The scorpion puts a dent in Sham's enthusiasm for Thanksgiving, but little by little, she manages to take her mind off the pain so she can get back to preparing her dream dinner. Moving around turns out to be a good distraction. Nasser leaves at one point to get some greens and comes back in no time with a huge bunch of *'ilich*—dandelion leaves—like a bouquet of flowers he got from the village.

Dinner is basically ready when Jamal arrives with Samira and two of their children. I share the story behind this tradition, that it represents friendship and cooperation between the European settlers and the American Indians. I emphasize how the true story is not exactly one of friendship since American Indians were ultimately pushed off their lands, and their way of life was virtually obliterated. It is the official story of American history that has been embraced by the European writers of history, the one that fails to acknowledge the loss and suffering experienced by Native communities in what became the United States.

What happened to Native Americans feels ominously similar to the loss of land and livelihood for Palestinians, especially with Sidi's lost land within view outside the panoramic window. I mention how I traveled two years before, over Thanksgiving weekend, to Standing Rock to share food from one indigenous people who lost their land to another. Now, I am making an American Thanksgiving dinner for Palestinians in Palestine. Sham is all smiles to have a real Thanksgiving dinner in Palestine. It is what she knows and longs for each year, though she loves both worlds, two places she calls home.

As winter sets in, I can hear the cars drive over the wet roads, glistening from the cool rain. *I still can't believe Palestine is outside my window.* A lifetime of longing, and there she is. She has changed over time, grown, suffered, bled—oh, how she has bled—but she is still there, maturing in her voice, transfigured but resilient, still full of fire and life.

One weekend in early December, Sham and I visit Nasser's sister Kifah in Nablus for dinner instead of driving all the way to Jalameh for the weekend. The traffic is terrible coming back from Nablus. It is solid cars both ways. What should have taken us 45 minutes becomes hours. Finally, we make it back to our apartment in Ramallah.

The next day, I take Sham to school, then go out to do some errands in town. I come to an intersection where several Palestinian youth are standing on the corner, one of them propelling rocks using strips of cloth tied into a sling. I watch him spin it around and around until he stops abruptly, and the rock flies off into the distance. I drive toward a group of them and roll down my passenger window. *Shou fi?*—What's going on?

Sakri ash-shubbak wa itla'i!—Close the window and get out of here!

Lesh?—Why?

The young man points down the road behind him. *Fi jeysh wa bitukhu*—The army is over there, and they're shooting.

I look where he is pointing, and sure enough, there are several army Jeeps parked down the road. Soldiers are standing there in various positions, pointing their rifles our way.

Tislam, Allah ma'akum—Thank you, may God be with you.

I close my window and pull past them, making my way through the neighborhood and back to the main road so I can get home. My heart is racing. I could have been shot for simply being in the wrong place at the wrong time.

I call Nasser and tell him what happened. He says he heard there was an operation the day before near the Israeli settlement Ofra, which is located about halfway between Nablus and Ramallah. Now, I understand the backup on the road to Ramallah on our way home from Nablus.

I plead with him. "Why didn't you tell me? You really should let us know if something happens." Apparently, a Palestinian youth shot at Israeli settlers at the bus stop, killing two soldiers and injuring seven.

The Israeli army seals off Ramallah to try to find who shot at the settlers. Sham and I won't be able to leave the city, much less drive to Jalameh on the weekend. Tensions are high, and there are reports of settlers throwing stones at Palestinian cars north of Ramallah. Even if we could leave the city, it wouldn't be safe to drive. Just like what happened to me yesterday, we could end up in the wrong place at the wrong time.

Clashes break out with the army in Ramallah, especially in the adjacent town of Al-Bireh. From our balcony, we can see black smoke filling the sky. I turn on the news, and Palestinian youth are confronting Israeli soldiers with burning tires and stones. My mind is racing, knowing the images on TV are right outside my window. Sham calls me from school and says many of the students are going home early due to the unrest. I pick her up, and we sit at home, waiting for the tensions to subside.

For now, we are stuck in Ramallah. The Israeli army finds the perpetrator's car and his brother, who helped him carry out the attack. The soldiers kill the brother on the spot. It turns out an Israeli woman, who was seven months pregnant, was injured in the attack. She had to deliver her baby prematurely, and it died four days later. It is not until after the new year that they apprehend the young man who carried out the shooting. As is customary after an operation, the Israeli army destroys his home. I learn later that he was released from prison earlier that year after spending 11 years in prison. It will be three years later that he receives four life sentences.

It is unsettling to think that Sham and I just happened to be driving by not long after the incident, not knowing people had just lost their lives or been injured. I don't know why the young man was in prison in the first place, but clearly, he did not waste any time planning an attack after his release.

For decades, I have witnessed Palestinian calls for justice through both violent and nonviolent means—demonstrations, negotiations, operations, uprisings, peace conferences, and peace plans. And where are we now? Perhaps the furthest we have ever been from finding a way to live together. Palestinians have become a thorn in the side of Israelis, or what some Israeli leaders call a virus, cancer, or territorial terror. Both sides blame the other for the lack of progress. Both declare the other side is not interested in peace, that it simply wants to make the other side disappear so they can have the land all for themselves. Mistrust abounds with heartbreaking stories laden with suffering. And yet one side is a recognized state that controls the borders and the natural resources and enjoys the full backing of the US, whereas those on the other side have lived at the mercy of that state and watched their homeland slip through their fingers for decades.

Regardless of how we got to this point, I can't help but think that the only way out of this vicious cycle of resistance and punishment is to follow our company Canaan's motto by "insisting on life," find a way to live together. And like the principles of fair trade and organic farming, any solution must be sustainable so communities can thrive and live with dignity.

Days of closure keep Sham and me in Ramallah. We finally take our chances and head to Jalameh for a long weekend. My eyes comb the landscape more than usual, especially as I pass by the settlements between Ramallah and Nablus (see Map 18). I feel like I am driving through a war zone, wondering if a rock, or worse, will hit my car and break the windshield. *What if something happens and I lose control of the car?* Fortunately, the roads are open and calm, except for a heavy Israeli army presence near Za'tara Junction north of Ofra. It seems like it has been months since we've seen Nasser and his family. It feels good to be home.

Sham is angry that we will not be in the US for Christmas, convinced Santa will never find us in Palestine. And how will we have a Christmas tree?

And what about snow? I remind her that Christmas is actually a Christian celebration of Jesus' birth in Bethlehem. We are in the Holy Land. *What better place to be than in Palestine?*

When we return to Ramallah after Thanksgiving, we begin to see signs of Christmas appearing in store windows. Fake Christmas trees with flashing lights, giant bulbs hanging from storefront awnings, and multi-colored lights framing windows. We discover the bookstore on the way to town is selling Christmas trees. We even stumble into a shop that only sells Christmas decorations.

Sham wants to celebrate Christmas at our apartment in Ramallah and go to Jalameh after Christmas for the rest of her winter break. We find a fake Christmas tree that looks like it is covered with snow, as well as Christmas decorations and ornaments, including multi-colored lights and a giant star for the top of the tree, and even a tree skirt to put underneath. We also find adorable little candles in the shape of snowmen, Santa boots, and pinecones. At the Christmas shop, we find stockings and stocking caps, including an extra-long red cap with a white ball on the end for Nasser. Back at the apartment, we decorate the tree and hang the stockings on the radiator behind it, our mock fireplace. When I plug in the tree lights, Sham's smile fills the room. We are ready to celebrate Christmas in Ramallah.

The week before Christmas, I take Sham to Bethlehem. I was only at the university in 2000 when I was doing my fieldwork for my dissertation. I want Sham to see the place that is also mythical in its magnitude—the place where Jesus was born. I have heard that the decorations for Christmas are enchanting. There is also a museum about the Wall I want to see.

It turns out that driving to Bethlehem is not straightforward since it is partially surrounded by the Wall. The main road to Jerusalem is backed up into town in Ramallah. Perhaps some are headed to the Al-Aqsa Mosque for Friday prayers. I think I find an alternate route on the map and head that way. I am relieved to discover an opening in the Wall like a tunnel. I drive through, surprised there are no Israeli soldiers, no checkpoint.

The road leads into a Palestinian town. The streets by the mosque are already lined with cars for Friday prayers. I ask some men in the street how to get to Bethlehem. They laugh and tell me I have to go back. There is no way to get through here. It turns out I have entered through an underpass to the town of Bir Nabala which is now completely surrounded by the Wall, cutting off access to neighboring villages and Jerusalem (see Map 12, page 283).

We turn back the way we came, back to the line of cars waiting to get through the Kalandia checkpoint. Once we actually reach the border guards, I am relieved we pass through quickly with my American passport and Sham's

Map 18: Israeli Settlements and Outposts in the West Bank by Population, 2016
(Source: Vox.com and Vox Media, LLC)[157]

hawiyeh and tasrih, her ID and permit to enter Israel. We drive through Jerusalem right past Damascus Gate. My eyes shift from the Old City walls on my right to the opening in the wall on my left that leads to the Browns' old house that was once my home. *Has it really been more than three decades since I first came here?* I pull my eyes back to the road and continue south to Bethlehem.

My heart sinks into my stomach when I see that the entrance to Bethlehem is an opening in the Wall, as if we are entering a high-security prison. I slow down to take in the sight of the Wall and the Israeli army towers on either side of the entrance. Just inside the Wall is the Wall Museum, but we decide to keep driving to find the center of town first. Bethlehem is high up on the mountain, so the road takes us along one of the hillsides, past shops and restaurants, until we see signs to Manger Square, where the Church of the Nativity was built above Jesus' birthplace.

I am surprised we can drive right up to the square, a wide-open area all paved in stone with a giant Christmas tree at one end next to the church. The other three sides of the square are lined with shops and restaurants. There are not many people. Here we are in Manger Square just before Christmas, and it is desolate. The atmosphere feels sad and heavy to me. I suppose without the complications with Israel, this city would be full of international visitors this time of year. I am not surprised, when I think about how difficult it is to get here. What could have been an hour's drive from Ramallah took us hours because of all the traffic at the checkpoint.

We walk into some of the shops lined with olive wood crafts, scarves, embroidery, pottery, tiles, and glass. Past the square are the narrow passageways of the Old City. My eyes light up when we find a man selling fresh juice from a pushcart. We watch as he passes carrots through a juicer and hand-presses pomegranate seeds. One sip, and I feel revived from the car ride.

Even Christian towns like Bethlehem have a majority Muslim population, so most of the shops are closed for Friday prayers. Still, it is intriguing to simply take in these ancient corridors, where people have been living for thousands of years. I imagine the city now mostly survives on tourism. The few shopkeepers we encounter welcome us with smiles. They are more subdued than the pushy shopkeepers of Jerusalem. I find some elegant scarves in rich colors and a sheen finish to add to my collection. When we reach a residential area, we turn around and go back the way we came. It is late afternoon, and we still want to go to the museum.

Before going to the car, we duck our heads to enter the Church of the Nativity through a small doorway on the side. In the sanctuary, a few people are sitting in the pews praying or reveling in the space. Several tour groups are gathered along the sides. I try to imagine this sacred place under siege back in 2002 during the Second Intifada after hearing eyewitness testimony from Reverend Dr. Mitri Raheb, who spoke in Madison over the summer of 2018 while Sham and I were back in the US. After hearing his riveting account and later reading his book *Bethlehem Besieged: Stories of Hope in Times of Trouble,* he is lucky to be alive. Sham and I walk toward the front to find a crowd of people waiting to go underground. *Perhaps that is where Jesus was born.* Too bad we didn't come here years ago with Johnny during our tour of Palestine back in 1992. We leave the crowd and head back to the car. Because the roads are one-way, it takes a little trial and error to make our way back to the Wall area where we originally entered the city.

The museum is part of The Walled Off Hotel, recently opened with the support of the world-renowned street artist Banksy. They have very few guest rooms, each one unique with a close-up view of the Wall, guaranteeing guests the worst view from the rooms. We enter the main lobby, which is also a restaurant, where we grab a bite to eat. One wall of books turns out to be a door that leads to the private rooms. A player piano takes the spotlight on a stage in the center of the room. Sham is delighted with the old-world flair of drinking tea in antique teacups, each one unique, and eating soup and hummus on elegant, mismatched antique dishes.

On the walls of the restaurant is a collection of devices related to the occupation: old surveillance cameras used by the Israeli army, slingshots, and sledgehammers. Upstairs is a gallery with a private collection of local Palestinian artwork—paintings and sculptures beautifully displayed under spotlights, as well as an exhibit on the history of the Wall. There is also a bookshop with books about Palestine.

We head outside to walk along the actual Wall. I have seen the Wall from a distance, I have seen the Wall at Kalandia, I have even seen the Wall under construction in the middle of the street near the town of Al-Ram, but I have never walked along the Wall the way you can in Bethlehem. Artists and visitors have painted images and messages all along it. Being able to touch it and view it up close rips my heart out of my chest

I feel like I am back in West Berlin, where people could get close to the Wall and add their own artwork and messages to that blatant symbol of division and animosity between two worlds. The colorful expression of artwork and messages stood in stark contrast to the gray concrete in the East buried deep behind a security perimeter. As Sham and I walk along the Wall, noting Banksy's own stenciled images and taking in the many pleas to tear it down, I remember that the Berlin Wall no longer stands and find hope in this madness of separation and isolation.

One of the messages jumps out at me. I stop in my tracks to read it and reread it. "The Berlin Wall came down, so will this." I know it is inevitable. I don't know when or how it will happen, but I am hopeful all the same. Other messages catch my attention, like the Nike symbol with "JUST REMOVE IT," a play on their motto of "JUST DO IT," and my favorite, "MAKE HUMMUS, NOT WALLS." Artist stencils of children and barbed wire have a sharp edge of how it feels to be the one caged in. Other images bring a bitter smile to my face, like one with an Israeli soldier checking a donkey's ID.

I think of the murals I witnessed in Northern Ireland in 2017 with images of IRA fighters holding their machine guns, guns that killed British citizens. I also recall reading years ago that even 20 years after the barbed wire came down between East Germany and Czechoslovakia with the fall of the Berlin Wall in 1989, the deer in the area still would not cross where the barbed wire used to be such that the deer populations on either side of the previous border fence still live separate lives.[158] A more recent report confirms that the red deer continue to stay clear of the border area.[159] Apparently, the next generation follows the routes of the mothers, and the mothers are still teaching their offspring to stay clear of a border that no longer exists. In fact, the once heavily fortified border between East Germany and what is now the Czech Republic has been turned into a cross-national nature preserve. *How long will it take for the Israeli Wall to be a thing of the past?*

54

New Year's in Aqaba

Nasser plans a company outing for all his employees each year, and this year, it will be New Year's in Aqaba. He invites Sham and me to come along. We cross into Jordan to meet up with the rest of the group to begin the five-hour bus ride south to Aqaba, the flat dry landscape racing past us. Part of the way, someone plays Arabic music from their phone on a portable speaker. Others sing and dance along with the music, clapping their hands to the rhythm. When the cell phone battery is depleted, the group switches to singing in unison. Nasser joins in at one point, standing in the narrow aisle between the seats, clapping his hands high in front of him. Faces are all smiles and laughter as they cheer him on, singing and clapping their hands. It seems in no time, we are pulling up in front of our hotel in Aqaba.

Some people in the group have never been out of the village or traveled outside of Palestine, so getting to explore Aqaba and play by the sea is a real treat. I encourage everyone to take off their shoes, professing that if Karmel were here, he would insist they all walk barefoot. Their faces become a sea of laughter as most comply by sinking their bare feet into the warm sand. Some of the men in the group go jet skiing. Others swim or bask in the sun.

A few hang out on the pier, watching the fishermen, while the women gather on the beach in a semi-circle of chairs, some wearing full-length coat dresses and *hijab*, others in Western clothes. Sham wants to go tubing, so she and I walk over to one of the speed boats and sign up for a turn.

In the evening, we venture out into the desert to a Bedouin camp in Wadi Rum for dinner. The dry, rocky landscape gives way to smooth red sand and rocky cliffs. At one point, our bus turns off the road into what feels like the middle of nowhere. Up ahead, between the cliffs, we spot large goat-hair tents and an array of concrete buildings. We have arrived at the camp. Some of the group gather around a bonfire to offset the evening chill as dusk sets in.

Before it is completely dark, Sham and I join a few others to explore one of the bluffs, stepping carefully to higher and higher elevations until we reach a rocky plateau with a gorgeous view of the wide-open desert, other islands of bluffs barely visible in the distance. The darker it gets, the more stars emerge across the wide-open sky. I take a deep breath, in awe of the vastness overhead. It feels like we are on another planet far out in space, free of borders.

We join the others at the center of the camp, where a DJ is playing traditional Bedouin music. We find a seat along the perimeter, lined with a continuous cushioned bench that encircles an open-air dance floor illuminated by strings of lights overhead. The blasting music and bright lights seem like an odd feature of a desert Bedouin camp. I find myself longing for the plateau under the stars.

Now that the sun has set, a chill sets in like in the Naqab Desert I experienced years ago. Sham and I get some hot tea from a stand off to the side to keep warm, wishing we had on our winter coats. Some of the men in our group get up to join hands to dance dabkeh as we cheer them on. I join some of the women, who form a second line around the men, two circles inside each other dancing in unison. Our Bedouin hosts welcome us into a massive goat-hair tent for a delicious spread of platters of rice, juicy chunks of lamb, colorful salad, and roasted mixed vegetables. When it is time to call it a night, our bus driver retraces our steps through the dark, cold desert to our hotel. This time, everyone on the bus is silent, exhausted from a full day of activities and a full belly.

The next day, Nasser hosts a companywide meeting at the hotel before our New Year's Eve celebration. The group sits in a circle as Nasser praises them for a prosperous year and the many years of hard work. Each person offers an eloquent mix of humility and gratitude as they share how the company has changed their lives, cultivated community at work, and encouraged them to push themselves harder than they ever thought possible. I witness pride at being part of something bigger, something global, something that connects people all around the world to Palestine. I do not speak. I choose to listen. If I spoke, I would remind them that many have been with the company for years, if not since the beginning. They are all the roots of what has become a thriving tree grounded in the earth, giving its bounty to the world.

After the meeting, everyone heads back to their rooms to get dressed up in their best attire for a New Year's celebration on the Red Sea. We head upstairs to an open-air area arranged with small tables. The whole boat is decked out for New Year's with lights suspended overhead and shimmering decorations, including a giant 2019 over the stage where a band is playing upbeat Arabic music. Everyone's smile is gleaming. The weather is perfect, warm with clear skies overhead.

When the boat takes off, I scan the Red Sea in front of me, dotted with the lights of other boats. I point out the lights of Eilat glowing in the distance to Sham. "That is the tip of Palestine." I explain that no Palestinians are allowed there.[160] Israel has claimed it for itself as an exclusive resort area. To the left, I see the lights of Taba in Egypt and imagine the lights of the resort town Sharm El-Sheikh in the far distance. As we head out to sea, we look back on the lights of Aqaba. Three countries adjacent to each other around the Red Sea—Israel/Palestine, Jordan, and Egypt—each with its own tourist destination on the sea (see Map 19). It is harder to draw lines in the water, but there are borders. Among the boats are patrol boats making sure no one crosses into foreign territory. Our boat heads toward Eilat, then turns and circles back toward Aqaba.

It is a couple of hours before our group is called down to the main level for a delicious dinner of chicken and lamb, rice, vegetables, and salad. We sit down with other members of the team in roomy booths lined with windows that look out onto the Red Sea. When we head back upstairs, the air is much cooler. I pull my shoulders into my neck to shield myself from the breeze.

Some of the men in our group get up to dance dabkeh along the outer ring of the tables, holding hands and stepping in unison.

As the New Year approaches, the sea is a bed of lights from so many boats. When the clock strikes midnight, a siren goes off, and then fireworks are visible in all directions. The faces around me light up with the glow of red, blue, yellow, green, and white, their eyes sparkling as they gaze up at the flickering sky. At least in this moment, everyone on the Red Sea is celebrating together.

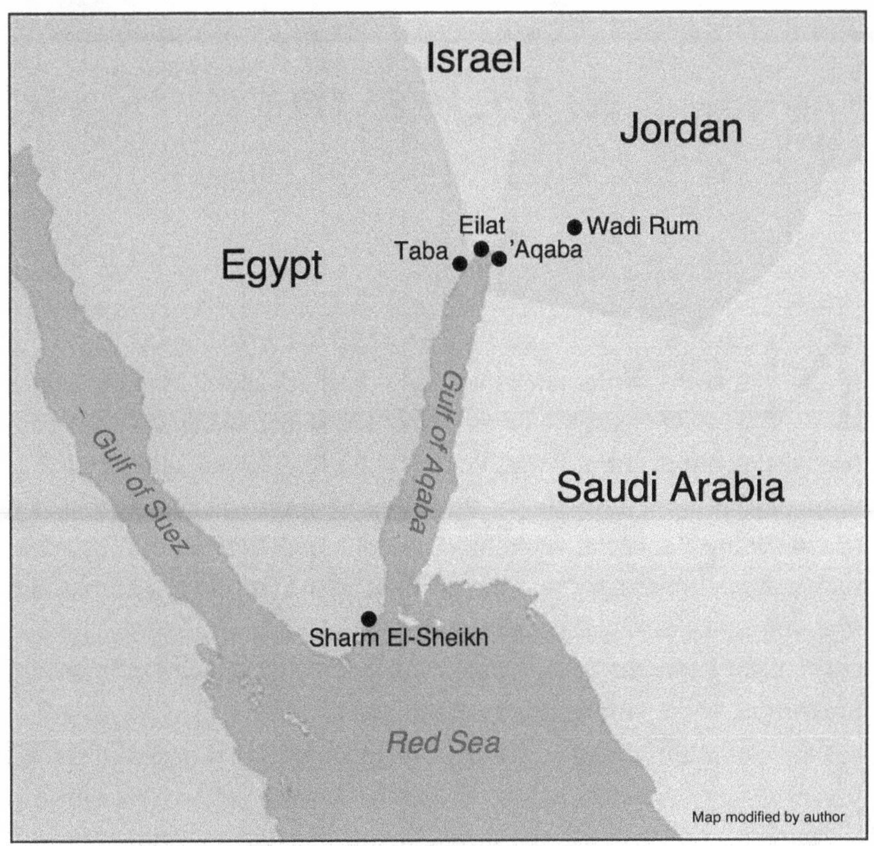

Map 19: The Red Sea (Source: Phys.org)

55

Farewell to Palestine

Nasser wants me to take photos of Palestine for the company now that the winter rains have once again transformed the hills into a sea of green. We drive out mid-afternoon along dirt roads past the wa'ra, continue around the Din Mountain that Karmel and I hiked up on my last visit, then up the mountain on the southern side, making our way to the top across rough terrain laden with boulders. We get out of the truck and walk through the olive trees. Jalameh is in full view, and just beyond it in the distance, we can see Jenin spanning across three hilltops and stretching into the valley below. How the city has grown, spilling over into the flat, fertile farmland at the foothills!

Nasser and I head back down the Din and continue along the dirt road toward the next village of Deir Ghazaleh, the Separation Fence in the background, and beyond it, the Gilboa Mountains scattered with destroyed villages hidden in the forest.

I look in the distance toward the mountains. "Which village is that?"

"'Arraneh."

"That's where your parents fled in 1948, right?"

"Yes, then they fled to 'Ajja. You can't see it from here."

"Where Ghazi was born." He nods as he maneuvers the dirt road through the farmland. I try to imagine Sidi and Sitti making their way across these hills in their 1940s truck, running for their lives with Khariyeh and Naziha, who is now barred from visiting her homeland, Sitti, nine months pregnant, delivering her first son in a cave.

We continue south. The hills are bursting with various shades of bright green from the winter rains. We pass young crops of wheat, their tufts of hair gleaming in the afternoon sunlight. Now and then, we stop to take pictures of the landscape, admiring the crops poking through the rich brown soil.

I look off to the side as we pass Deir Ghazaleh and spot a village high up in the hills. "Is that Faqu'a?" I recall that my taxi driver is from that village.

"Yes, of course."

"I thought so." That's where Nasser's ancestors first settled after coming to this area from Hebron many generations ago.

We continue farther south but then realize the sun is sinking lower in the sky, so we head over to the former settlement road I used to take to drive to Canaan and Karmel's school 20 years ago. We head north, passing by his brother Jamal's grove of young olive trees he recently purchased, their leaves a rich olive green after the cleansing winter rains. We make it back to Jalameh just before sunset. As we enter the village, we drive past the landrace wheat field Nasser recently planted, the tufts of wheat glowing in the last light of the sun. *The same field that once held the last orange trees of the village.*

Images of the young crops covering the hillsides and valleys swirl in my head. It has been 20 years since I saw spring in Palestine. The transformation from what seems like arid land to a lush green landscape is breathtaking. The rains are magical, bringing the land each winter to life to feed the people who cultivate it year after year after year. The land seems to reward them for passing down this knowledge for generations. I want to know every hill, every valley, every village. I repeat the names of the villages we passed in my head, committing the path we traveled to memory. I wish there was more daylight left in the day.

Nasser reassures me. "We can always come back another time."

I think of the German phrase, *Was man hat, hat man*—Whatever you have, you have. At least I got to see spring again in Palestine.

The next morning, Sham and I pick lemons out back behind Nasser's family home to take with us to Ramallah. "Can you believe I planted this lemon tree 20 years ago? Look at it now!" It's the lemon tree I got from Nasser's brother Ghazi's nursery and planted the year I spent in Palestine with Canaan and Karmel so there would be a lemon tree behind their Sitti's house. I examine the broad trunk firmly anchored in the ground and recall how narrow it was when I first planted it, its delicate branches so fragile and sparse. I look up at the sturdy branches extending in all directions, covered with lush green leaves and more lemons than we could ever eat. The shiny green leaves and bright yellow lemons are glowing in the afternoon sun and attest to the life surging forth in this well-established tree.

I spot a few lemons with a blush of green. "Be sure to pick the yellow ones." I extend my arms as high as I can reach so Sham can pick from the lower branches. "I think that's enough for today. Don't forget we can pick more next time we come."

Sham comes out from under the tree with a few more lemons cradled in her hands. "Look at this one!" She proudly holds up her largest find, her smile as bright as the lemon.

We pack up our things and load the car, hoping to arrive before dark. No matter where we are, we remain anchored in the soil like the lemon tree. *Its roots have become our roots.*

Even though we are settled into a good routine in Ramallah during the week and in Jalameh on the weekends, Sham's school in Ramallah is becoming more and more disappointing. By the end of the term, we find out the director is going back to England, the English classes have been discontinued, and her business classes are focused solely on preparing for the British exams. No more vibrant discussions of current events. No more group projects. Sham is bored and frustrated.

"This isn't school," she pleads. "Why can't I just go back to my school?"

We check in with her high school in the US, and sure enough, she could resume her schedule and still graduate this year. We agree to go back toward the end of January in time for the second semester. In the meantime, Sham makes the best of school, spending as much time as she can with her new circle of friends in Ramallah.

I have mixed feelings about leaving Palestine. Sham has enjoyed the chic boutiques that line the main streets in Ramallah. She will miss exploring restaurants and coffee shops with her new friends, where they serve unique variations on Arabic and Western cuisine and delicious coffee drinks. For now, her study of Arabic will be interrupted, and I will have to finish writing my book in the US. I know going back to the US is what is best for Sham, but still, my heart is heavy as we pack up our things for the last time and drive to Jalameh to spend our final days.

There is hardly time to say goodbye to everyone. We will leave as suddenly as we came. But before I go, I have to see zamatot growing in the wild. The winter rains have awakened the earth and zamatot is one of the first flowers to poke out of the rich brown soil. Nasser says there are tons of it growing behind the company, so we drive to Burqin. I can't wait to show Sham these delicate flowers. We walk among the olive trees, making our way across the chunky, chocolate-colored earth.

"Here are some!" Nasser finds a cluster of exquisite deep-pink flowers reaching for the sky, their two-tone leaves poking out of the grassy brush. He points out some other patches of zamatot, explaining how they grow where there is shade on one side. I know I don't have time to roll the leaves into a meal, so we don't pick any. As we walk deeper into the land, the valley comes into view. It is full sun, but the breeze high up over the valley cools the air. Every few steps, Nasser points out another cluster of zamatot.

"I can't believe I haven't seen them in 20 years!" I walk among the zamatot, greeting them like old friends. "Look at them! They're so beautiful!"

It is our last full day in Palestine. Somehow, it feels perfect to be spending it among these resilient flowers that magically reappear each spring to brighten the rocky hills following the winter rains. I have been wondering all these years when I would ever see them again. My heart is swelling with gratitude. Here I am with Nasser and Sham, walking among the olive trees, from cluster to cluster of zamatot, like it's the Eid when we go from house to house to visit family. They all look so happy to see me, peeking out of their protected spaces, dancing to the rhythm of the soft breeze. They seem as excited to see me as I am to see them. Yes, it has been a while. I wish I had more time to visit, to catch up. But like the Eid, we have to keep moving to be able to see everyone.

Nasser combs the land with his eyes as we walk, meandering through the olive trees until we have come full circle at the gate. It is time to go. I bid the beautiful zamatot farewell, my eyes filling with tears of joy. *So good to see you again.*

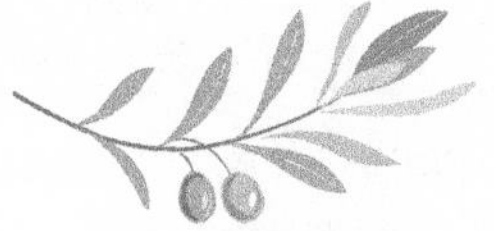

Epilogue

As I bring this memoir to a close, we are on the eve of the 75th anniversary of Israel's founding on May 14, 2023, which marks the 75th Commemoration of the Nakba.[161] In order for my words to reach others and touch their hearts and minds, I must interrupt my story since the story of my life is not over. I have to release this part of it like a grown child who needs to find their way in the world, but who I, as their mother, wish to protect. I know that without letting go, the message of this story—dignity—cannot become a drop in the sea of change toward a brighter future for Israel and Palestine.

For me, it is painful to end the story with no ending. I wish I could write that the Question of Palestine has finally been answered, that both Israelis and Palestinians have found the courage to swallow the bitter pill of an arranged marriage, where there is no Israel without Palestine, and no Palestine without Israel. I wish I could write that enough Jews have come to acknowledge the shortcomings of a Zionism that sought to make Palestine into Israel, initially parcel by parcel, then, once the Zionist agenda led to all-out war, city by city, town by town, village by village, hill by hill, and even neighborhood by neighborhood or house by house, right up to the present. *The ongoing Nakba.*

I wish I could write that the Jews of Israel now welcome Palestinians *wen makan*—wherever they may be—to return to their homes *wen makan*—wherever they may be. That instead of entertaining the idea of transferring Palestinians across the border as a final act of ethnic cleansing to secure a Jewish state—what some call the unfinished business of 1948—they are transferring titles of land ownership back to Palestinians so they can finally come home to their cities, towns, and villages, and issuing compensation for the loss of their property and livelihood so Palestinians can rebuild their communities, their lives, in their homeland (see Map 20).

I wish I could write that the bloodshed has stopped, the siege on Gaza lifted, the Israeli army's shoot-to-kill policy shot down, administrative detainees and political prisoners freed, house demolition orders revoked, the confiscation of homes and land banned, new settlements throughout the West Bank outlawed, checkpoints dismantled, and the Wall destroyed. Someday, I will. Not today. Maybe not even tomorrow. But someday. When depends on me, you, them, us—all of us. *Persistence.*

Today, the Question of Palestine is simple: Do the Jews of the world have the courage to come out of the shadow of persecution they inherited from their ancestors, particularly the Holocaust, that has both blinded and justified their takeover of Palestine and brought suffering on the Palestinian people? Do Jewish Israelis have the courage to redefine their presence in Palestine from this legacy of victimhood—that drove them to become conquerors—to copilots, or do they wish to remain in a vicious cycle of trying to erase a Palestine that, like saber, only grows back more resilient than ever? *Sumoud*—steadfastness.

I wish I could write that Israelis and Palestinians, rather than stew in frustration or denial, have come to embrace a shared future where neither Jews nor Palestinians are forced to live in each other's shadow. Just as the trees left unattended for decades in the hundreds of destroyed Palestinian villages of 1948 and 1967 still await the hands of the next generations to tend to them, so do the village lands await dynamic development plans from the descendants of those Palestinians whom Israel has barred from returning so their voices can fill the streets of their hometowns with ululations of their return. *Al-Awda.*[162]

I am not naïve. I know that wishing is not enough to deliver dignity to Palestine. Such a hopeful shift would mean that the United States, Great Britain, and Europe—Israel's staunchest allies—in partnership with Israelis and Palestinians, demonstrate bold leadership to launch a powerful plan that backs both Palestine and Israel, not Israel at the expense of Palestine as we have witnessed for the last 100 years, one that provides a framework for rebuilding lives with guarantees of support, safety, and security for both sides to flourish.

Then, I could write that American policy truly reflects the American values of freedom and democracy the United States professes to promote—at home and abroad. These are the same values that have led to global outrage at the murder of George Floyd in May 2020 and Palestinian journalist Shireen Abu Akleh in May 2021, and the Russian invasion of Ukraine in February 2022.

But where is the American outrage for the blatant threats to freedom and democracy in an Israel whose entire *raison d'état* and legal system holds the well-being of its Jewish citizens above the people of Palestine, whether they be citizens, imprisoned, detained, occupied, refugees, or in exile, or those simply tending to their crops, going to work, to school, to pray, to rest, celebrating a new birth, mourning another death?

Where is the line between the terrorists and freedom fighters for the rock-throwing Palestinian youth confronting tanks and Israeli snipers, to mothers facing off Israeli soldiers so their children can walk safely to school, to farmers guarding their land with their bodies, to those who target Israeli soldiers and settlers with their cars, kitchen knives, or whatever weapons they can find on the black market or make themselves? And where is the line between crimes against humanity and Israel's exclusive right to state violence in the name of self-defense with its formidable military and the entire backing of the free world? Just as the world condemns the indiscriminate killing of civilians, what citizens of any privileged nation would withstand the humiliation of Israeli occupation? Of apartheid?

I wonder about the Fourth Geneva Convention that honors the right of occupied peoples to protect and defend themselves. Is the backing of the entire Ukrainian resistance—heralded as brave and deserving of the moral and military support of the international community—then blatant hypocrisy?

As a human being, I can only ask: are Americans, Europeans, and Jewish Israelis really at peace with Israel's subjugation of the entire Palestinian people, of my own children and extended family in Palestine? Where is the dignity in that? Are they really asking Palestinians to sacrifice their right to self-determination in their own homeland?

I also wonder about the Christian Zionists who seem to care more for prophecy than the values in the scripture Jesus gave his life to uphold. What twisted stories are these that grant Jews exclusive rights to the Holy Land, the homeland of the Palestinians? As human beings, are we not all children of God? Where is the righteousness in that? Can't the deep connection to both peoples to the same land be upheld?

If the United States, the United Kingdom, European nations, and Israel did step up—as conscience-driven individuals and organizations within these nations have—to back freedom and democracy in Palestine and Israel, I could write that the call for upholding human rights and international law around the globe is finally being answered. That policies of exclusion and privilege are a thing of the past. That Palestinians' right to self-determination will no longer be ignored.

Bringing Palestine out of Israel's shadow requires the courage among Israelis and Palestinians to take risks, perhaps even a leap of faith. In spite of all I have witnessed and experienced, rather than becoming bitter and disillusioned, I remain hopeful that these two peoples—with genuine support from the international community, grounded in democratic principles of equality and justice for all—can construct a shared future that honors the suffering and loss, as well as the wisdom and promise of both communities. Peace with justice may be just around the next bend.

Map 20: Feasibility of Palestinian Return to Cities, Towns, and Villages by Region
(Source: Palestine Land Society)

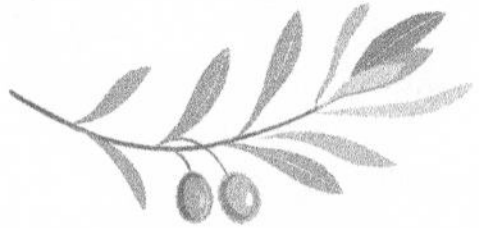

Acknowledgments

Crossing Borders came into being over a lifetime of curiosity and experience, celebration and heartache. First, I wish to express my deepest gratitude for the generosity and openness of Salem's family in Gaza and Nasser's family in Jalameh, two families who filled me with passion and inspiration to transform Palestine from a place of study and exploration to understand geopolitical challenges, to a personal space I came to call home.

Traveling to Palestine would not have been possible without the encouragement and support of my father Joachim Bruhn to engage with different cultures, who himself never hesitated to explore the world even after finding a second home in the United States, and the trust of my mother Marsha Bruhn to follow my gut to life's next adventure. I appreciate the encouragement of my siblings, Elisa, Dieter, and Erika, and other family and friends who have rallied behind me to see this project through over the 10 years I spent bringing my stories onto the page. I also thank my children, Canaan, Karmel, and Sham, and their father, Nasser, for their patience in allowing me to carve out the time, space, and emotional energy life stories take to become memoir.

I am eternally grateful to novelist Lilas Taha for encouraging me to transform my key memories about Palestine into a memoir, author Ghada Karmi for illustrating the power of personal stories to teach others about Palestine, and historian Ilan Pappé for demonstrating how the principles of truth and justice far outweigh the personal risk of speaking out.

For those who appear in my memoir and have read my work, I extend my deepest appreciation to your generosity in allowing me to share my stories inspired by you in this book, including Ismael and Kathy Abu-Saad, John Hallak, Ibtisam Ibrahim, and Tony Sarrouh, and their families.

I thank the many institutions of higher education I attended or connected with through research for the depth and breadth of knowledge I learned about the history, politics, and cultures of the Middle East and North Africa and beyond, the Arabic language, and the impact of historical context and global power on people's lives. I particularly thank numerous professors under whom I studied who expanded my thinking about the Middle East and the power of ideas and actions to make a difference in our world, including Elias Baumgarten, Mimi Bloch, Sidney Bolkosky, Juan Cole, Clifton Conrad, Thomas Popkewitz, Anton Shammas, Amy Stambach, Jacob Stampen, Ronald Stockton, and Andreas Kazamiaz. No knowledge, however, can replace the privilege of the lived experience on the ground in connecting with people in Palestine to understand the critical role insisting on a life of dignity plays in the persistence of Palestine.

As for the process of writing this book, I wish to thank Miriam Hall for her leadership in creating a contemplative writing community through numerous classes and retreats that has given me not only honest and heartfelt feedback over the years but has served as a welcoming and safe space in which to release the stories of my life that have found their way into this memoir. Besides Miriam herself, fellow writers include Rebecca Krantz and Karen Milstein, who provided me with regular writing dates and extensive feedback and support right up to the end, as well as Kristina Amelong, Linda Balisle, Wendy Miller, Eileen Rosensteel, Barbara Samuel, Janet Swain, and Sara Williams. I am also grateful to Miriam Hall's mentor, Natalie Goldberg, for providing a framework for understanding writing as a life practice through retreats and her extensive repertoire of books on writing.

I extend my gratitude to Julie Tallard-Johnson, whom I met through the University of Wisconsin's Write by the Lake writers' conference, for her numerous programs, retreats, and books that have inspired me to live the writer's life. Others I met through her writing community who have contributed to the integrity of my work include Rebecca Cecchini, Suzan McVicker, and

Richard Wilberg. I am also grateful to Kristin Oakley, whom I met through the University of Wisconsin Writers' Institute, for her ongoing support with our writing dates at Barrique's coffee shop in Fitchburg, Wisconsin, and for introducing me to a supportive circle of women in Writers Must Eat, as well as the Chicago Writers Association, which has provided excellent programming through its annual conference and online. I greatly appreciate Laurie Scheer, whom I also met through the University of Wisconsin Writers' Institute, as well as Valerie Biel and Molly Sturdevant for their commitment to my work and guidance throughout the editing and publication process.

Finally, I wish to extend my sincerest appreciation to Kristin Mitchell at Little Creek Press and Book Design and her amazing editing and design team, including Mimi Bark and Shannon Booth, for their enthusiasm for my work in seeing my manuscript through to publication so I can share my stories with the world.

Works Cited

Abu-Farha, Christa Bruhn. 1993. *The Palestinian Dialect of Al-Jalameh: A Phonemic Study*. Ann Arbor: University of Michigan.

Abufarha, Nasser. 2009. *The Making of a Human Bomb: An Ethnography of Palestinian Resistance*. Chapel Hill: Duke University Press.

Abu-Saad, Ismael, and Amara, Ahmad, and Yiftachel, Oren, eds. 2012. *Indigenous (In)Justice: Human Rights Law and Bedouin Arabs in the Naqab/Negev*. Cambridge: Human Rights Program at Harvard Law School.

Abu-Saad, Ismael, and Sa'di, Ahmad, eds. 2023. "The Unfinished Zionist Settler-Colonial Conquest of its Elusive 'Last Frontier,' and Indigenous Palestinian Bedouin Arab Resistance." *Decolonizing the Study of Palestine Indigenous Perspectives and Settler Colonialism after Elia Zureik*. London: I.B. Tauris-Bloomsbury Publishing.

Abu Sitta, Salman. June 20, 2020. "Massacres as a weapon of ethnic cleansing during the Nakba." *Mondoweiss*, https://mondoweiss.net/2020/06/massacres-as-a-weapon-of-ethnic-cleansing-during-the-nakba/ (last viewed April 7, 2023).

Abu Sitta, Salman. June 2003. "Beer Sheba: The Forgotten Half of Palestine." Palestine Land Society, https://www.plands.org/en/articles-speeches/articles/2003/beer-sheba-the-forgotten-half-of-palestine (last viewed April 7, 2023).

"Al-Nakba and Return: The Aftermath." n.d. Palestine Land Society, https://www.plands.org/en/maps-atlases/maps/al-nakba-return/slide11. (last viewed April 7, 2023).

Alter, Robert. July 1973. "The Masada Complex." *Commentary*, https://www.commentary.org/articles/robert-alter-2/the-masada-complex/. (last viewed April 7, 2023).

Anderson, Per-Olow. 1957. *They Are Human Too: A Photographic Essay on the Palestine Arab Refugees.* Chicago: Henry Regnery Company.

"Annual Operational Report 2021." United Nations Relief and Works Agency for Refugees in the Near East, (https://www.unrwa.org/sites/default/files/content/resources/2021_aor_eng_-_sept_20-2022_1.pdf (last viewed April 7, 2023).

"A Threshold Crossed: Israeli Authorities and Crimes of Apartheid and Persecution." April 27, 2021. Human Rights Watch, https://www.hrw.org/report/2021/04/27/threshold-crossed/israeli-authorities-and-crimes-apartheid-and-persecution (last viewed April 7, 2023).

Avnery, Uri. 1986. *My Friend the Enemy.* Westport, Connecticut: Lawrence Hill & Company.

BADIL. December 2020. "Creeping Annexation: A Pillar of the Zionist-Israeli Colonization of Mandatory Palestine," https://badil.org/cached_uploads/view/2021/04/19/wp25-creepingannexation-1618823962.pdf (last viewed April 7, 2023).

BADIL (Resource Center for Palestinian Residency and Refugee Rights). October 2022. "Israeli Colonial-Apartheid Policies and Practices that Deny the Right of Self-Determination of the Palestinian People." BADIL's Submission to the UN Human Rights Council's Universal Periodic Review – 4th Cycle, https://www.badil.org/cached_uploads/view/2022/10/11/badil-sub2hrc-upr-oct2022-1665491012.pdf (last viewed April 7, 2023).

BADIL. *Survey of Palestinian Refugees and Internally Displaced Persons 2010–2012, Volume VII.* BADIL Resource Center for Palestinian Refugees and Refugee Rights. Bethlehem, Palestine.

Baltzer, Anna. 2006. *Witness in Palestine.* Boulder: Paradigm Publishers.

Bernstein, Ellie. 2016. *Ghost Town – Hebron,* documentary film.

Binur, Yoram. 1990. *Mein Bruder, Mein Feind: Ein Israeli als Palästinenser.* Schweizer Verlagshaus, (originally published in English 1989).

Bruhn, Christa. *The Power of the University: Palestinian Universities as Vehicles of Social and Political Change.* Doctoral dissertation. Madison: University of Wisconsin, 2004.

B'Tselem. January 12, 2021. "A Regime of Jewish Supremacy from the Jordan River to the Mediterranean Sea: This is Apartheid," https://www.btselem.org/publications/fulltext/202101_this_is_apartheid (last viewed April 7, 2023).

B'Tselem. May 2011. "Dispossession and Exploitation: Israel's Policy in the Jordan Valley and the Northern Dead Sea," https://www.btselem.org/sites/default/files/sites/default/files2/201105_dispossession_and_exploitation_eng.pdf (last viewed April 7, 2023).

Budanovic, Nikola. June 8, 2018. "Are you lost? The deer that still won't cross the German border." *The Vintage News*, https://www.thevintagenews.com/2018/06/08/iron-curtain-fence/ (last viewed April 7, 2023).

Canaan Impact Study 2005–2011. 2012, https://blog.canaanpalestine.com/impact-study-2012/ (last viewed April 7, 2023).

Call for Peace, http://www.callforpeace.org/aboutcfp/admin.html.

Carter, Jimmy. 2006. *Palestine: Peace Not Apartheid.* New York: Simon & Schuster.

"Convention (IV) Relative to the Protection of Civilian Persons in Time of War. Geneva, 12 August 1949." International Committee of the Red Cross (ICRC), International Humanitarian Law Databases, https://ihl-databases.icrc.org/en/ihl-treaties/gciv-1949 (last viewed April 7, 2023).

Dajani, Lubna. 2013. *My Ramleh,* documentary film.

Darwish, Abu Al-Rish. 2020. *Haifawi* (حيفاوي), documentary film.

Dirbas, Sahera. 2018. *On the Doorstep,* documentary film.

Dirbas, Sahera. 2012. *Deir Yassin Village and Massacre,* documentary film.

El-Funoun Palestinian Popular Dance Troupe (فرقة الفنون الشعبية الفلسطينية): https://el-funoun.org/ (last viewed April 7, 2023).

"Family Unification Bill Meant to Stop Palestinian 'Creeping Right of Return,' Israel's Shaked Says." February 9, 2022. *Haaretz*, https://www.haaretz.com/israel-news/2022-02-09/ty-article/shaked-family-unification-bill-meant-to-stop-palestinian-creeping-right-of-return/0000017f-e4f1-df2c-a1ff-fef118710000 (last viewed April 7, 2023).

Freedom Flotilla, https://freedomflotilla.org/ (last viewed April 7, 2023).

The Freedom Theater, https://thefreedomtheatre.org/who-we-are/. last viewed April 7, 2023).

Grorud, Mots. 2018. *The Tower.* documentary film.

Giles, Frank. June 15, 1969. Interview with Golda Meir. *The Sunday Times.*

Grossman, David. Translated by Haim Watzman. 1988. *The Yellow Wind.* New York: Farrar, Straus and Giroux.

Handala.org, http://handala.org/handala/ (last viewed April 7, 2023).

Herzl, Theodor. 1896. *Der Judenstaat: Versuch einer modernen Lösung der Judenfrage.* Leipzig & Vienna: M. Breitenstein Verlags-Buchhandlung.

Herzl, Theodor. 2015. *AltNeuLand: Ein utopischer Roman.* Berlin: Karl-Maria Guth, (first published in Leipzig, 1902).

"Instead of Planting Trees, the Jewish National Fund's Negev Project Starts a Fire." January 13, 2022. *Haaretz* Editorial. https://www.haaretz.com/opinion/editorial/2022-01-13/ty-article-opinion/instead-of-planting-trees-the-jewish-national-funds-negev-project-starts-a-fire/0000017f-e812-df5f-a17f-fbdeee980000 (last viewed April 7, 2023).

International TD-24. Wikimedia Foundation, http://tractors.wikia.com/wiki/International_TD-24 (last viewed April 7, 2023).

"Israel's System of Apartheid." February 1, 2022. Amnesty International, https://www.amnesty.org/en/latest/campaigns/2022/02/israels-system-of-apartheid/ (last viewed April 7, 2023).

Jbara-Tibi, Marwah. 2021. *Bread and Butter,* documentary film.

"Judaization of Jerusalem: Could it get any worse?" July 24, 2019. International Movement for a Just World, https://just-international.org/articles/judaization-of-jerusalem-could-it-get-any-worse/ (last viewed April 7, 2023).

Kadman, Noga. December 23, 2015. "Palestinian Villages, Israeli Parks: How the Past Echoes the Present ." Palestine Square . Institute for Palestine Studies, https://www .palestine-studies .org/en/node/232332 (last viewed April 7, 2023).

Kanafani, Ghassan. 1999. "The Land of Sad Oranges," *Men in the Sun and Other Palestinian Stories.* London: Lynne Rienner Publishers.

Keren Hayesod – United Israel Appeal, https://www.kh-uia.org.il/ (last viewed April 7, 2023).

Khalidi, Rashid. 2020. *The Hundred Years' War on Palestine: A History of Settler Colonialism and Resistance, 1917–2017.* New York: Metropolitan Books.

Khalidi, Walid. 1992. *All That Remains: The Palestinian Villages Occupied and Depopulated by Israel in 1948.* Institute for Palestine Studies: Washington, DC.

Khalidi, Walid. 1984. *Before Their Diaspora: A Photographic History of the Palestinians 1876–1948.* Institute for Palestine Studies: Washington, DC.

Light Unto the Nations. Wikimedia Foundation. Last Updated March 19, 2023, https://en.wikipedia.org/wiki/Light_unto_the_nations (last viewed April 7, 2023).

Lin, Jing, and Brantmeier, Edward J., and Bruhn, Christa, eds. 2008. *Transforming Education for Peace: A Volume in Peace Education.* Charlotte, SC: Information Age Publishing, Inc.

Mandewo, Alexandra. n.d. "A Brief History on the Trail of Tears." The Indigenous Foundation, https://www.theindigenousfoundation.org/articles/a-brief-history-on-the-trail-of-tears (last viewed April 7, 2023).

Morris, Benny. 2004. *The Birth of the Palestinian Refugee Problem Revisited.* Cambridge: Cambridge University Press.

Nihad Dukhan Modern & Traditional Calligraphy, https://ndukhan.com/ (last viewed April 7, 2023).

Nofal, Aziza. May 10, 2016. "Why More and More Israeli Druze Prefer Prison to Military Service." *Al-Monitor*, http://www.al-monitor.com/pulse/originals/2016/05/israel-druze-reject-military-service.html#ixzz4VO3wjf3r (last viewed April 7, 2023).

Palestine Land Society, https://www.plands.org/en/home (last viewed April 7, 2023).

Palestine Remembered, https://www.palestineremembered.com/index.html.

"Palestinians Wage Nonviolent Campaign During First Intifada, 1987–1988." May 1, 2010. Global Nonviolent Action Database, https://nvdatabase.swarthmore.edu/content/palestinians-wage-nonviolent-campaign-during-first-intifada-1987-1988 (last viewed April 7, 2023).

Pappé, Ilan. 2006. *The Ethnic Cleansing of Palestine.* London: Oneworld Publications.

Portman, Joshua. November 20, 2015. "An Introduction to Understanding Land Registration and Ownership in Israel." Buy it in Israel, https://www.buyitinisrael.com/news/land-registration-ownership-israel/ (last viewed April 7, 2023).

Rachel Corrie Foundation: https://rachelcorriefoundation.org/rachel/emails (last viewed April 7, 2023).

"Report of the Palestine Royal Commission," July 1937. League of Nations, https://digital.nls.uk/league-of-nations/archive/194669198#?c=0&m=0&s=0&cv=404&xywh=-1681%2C-209%2C5626%2C4171 (last viewed April 7, 2023).

Eliana Riva. 2023. *The Sabra and Chatila Sky.* documentary film.

Rohwedder, Cecilie. November 4, 2009. "Deep in the Forest, Bambi Remains the Cold War's Last Prisoner. *The Wall Street Journal*, https://www.wsj.com/articles/SB125729481234926717 (last viewed April 7, 2023).

Said, Edward. 1979. *Orientalism*. New York: Vintage Books.

Salah, Rajaa. March 1, 2023. "A Life Interrupted at 18 Begins Again." The Electronic Intifada, https://electronicintifada.net/content/life-interrupted-18-begins-again/37266 (last viewed April 7, 2023).

Satha-Anand, Chaiwat, and Urbain, Olivier, eds. 2013. *Protecting the Sacred: Creating Peace in Asia-Pacific*. Herndon: Transaction Publishers.

Schwartz, Alon. 2022. *Tantura,* documentary film.

Shipler, David. 1986. *Arab and Jew: Wounded Spirits in a Promised Land*. New York: Times Books.

Stop the Wall, Palestinian Grassroots Anti-Apartheid Wall Campaign, https://www.stopthewall.org/the-wall/ (last viewed April 7, 2023).

Surah Al-Fatiha—The Opening Verse (1). My Islam, https://myislam.org/surah-fatiha/ (last viewed April 7, 2023).

Surah Al-Ikhlas—The Surah of Sincerity (112). My Islam, https://myislam .org/surah-ikhlas/ (last viewed April 7, 2023).

"Swedish Pro-Palestinian Activist Ladraa Barred from Entering Israel." July 6, 2018. Middle East Monitor, https://www.middleeastmonitor.com/20180706-swedish-pro-palestine-activist-ladraa-barred-from-entering-israel/ (last viewed April 7, 2023).

Sweidan, Ruqyah. November 1, 2021. "Israel's Greenwashing Campaign." The Jerusalem Fund, https://thejerusalemfund.org/2021/11/israels-green-washing-campaign/ (last viewed April 7, 2023).

The People and the Olive: The Story of the Run Across Palestine. 2012. Stone Hut Studios, https://www.imdb.com/title/tt2330286/ (last viewed April 7, 2023).

"Thirteenth Grade." Wikimedia Foundation, https://en.wikipedia.org/wiki/Thirteenth_grade (last viewed April 7, 2023).

Tolan, Sandy. 2007. *The Lemon Tree: An Arab, A Jew and the Heart of the Middle East*. New York: Bloomsbury.

Tolkien, J.R.R. *The Lord of the Rings*. First published by George Allen and Unwin in England in three volumes due to paper shortages as The Fellowship of the Ring (1954), The Two Towers (1954), and The Return of the King (1955).

Turki, Fawaz. 1988. *Soul in Exile: Lives of a Palestinian Revolutionary*. New York: Monthly Review Press.

Abu-Saad, Ismael, and Turner, M., and Shweiki, O., eds. 2014. "State-directed 'Development' as a Tool for Dispossessing the Indigenous Bedouin Palestinian Arabs in the Naqab," in *Decolonizing Palestinian Political Economy*. London: Palgrave Macmillan.

United Nations Relief and Works Agency for Palestine Refugees in the Near East. *Food Assistance*, https://www.unrwa.org/food-assistance (last viewed April 7, 2023).

UNRWA Statistics 2010. November 2011. United Nations Relief and Works Agency for Palestine Refugees in the Near East, Program Coordination and Support Unit, http://www.unrwa.org/userfiles/2011120434013.pdf (last viewed April 7, 2023).

Weits, Michal. 2021. *Blue Box*, documentary film.

Williams, Jennifer and Zarracina, Javier. December 30, 2016. "The Growth of Israeli Settlements, Explained in 5 Charts." *Vox*. https://www.vox.com/world/2016/12/30/14088842/israeli-settlements-explained-in-5-charts.

World License Plates, http://www.worldlicenseplates.com/world/AS_PALE.html (last viewed April 7, 2023).

Endnotes

PART I: HOMELAND

Chapter 1: Homecoming

1 'Akka (عكا) is the Arabic name for the Palestinian city on the Mediterranean Sea known in English as Acre and in Hebrew as Akko (עכו).

Chapter 2: Jerusalem

2 At the time, I didn't yet fully understand that the desert refers to the Naqab Desert in the south, which Palestinian Bedouins cultivated seasonally for generations. Images of dedicated Zionists working the land in the Naqab to "make the desert bloom" were used for promotional purposes to make it seem like Palestine was a barren wasteland in need of the Jews from around the world to transform the land into a thriving haven of agriculture.

Chapter 3: Arrival

3 In 1986, there were 12 Israeli settlements in the Gaza Strip, one at the north end of the Gaza Strip by the sea, one in the center, and 10 in the Gush Katif settlement block located close to the Egyptian border. By 2005, there were a total of 21 settlements in the Gaza Strip built on land confiscated from Palestinians who were already squeezed in this tiny strip of land, and that further restricted Palestinian access to the coastline. All 21 Israeli settlements were dismantled through the Disengagement Plan in 2005. It was originally the Labor Party that advocated for the establishment of Jewish settlements in the West Bank and Gaza soon after Israel's victory in the Six-Day War in 1967, though settlement policy was inspired by the Allon Plan calling for the annexation of East Jerusalem, the Jordan Valley to provide a buffer zone on the eastern front, and the Etzion Bloc of settlements in the West Bank south of Jerusalem.

Chapter 5: Gaza

4 Al-Shati is one of eight refugee camps in the Gaza Strip established to accommodate Palestinians who fled their homes during Israel's 1948 War of Independence. Others include Bureij, Deir El-Balah, Jabaliya, Khan Younis, Maghazi, Nuseirat, and Rafah. Shelters started out as tents supplied by the United Nations which were gradually replaced by mud brick buildings, then cement block structures. As the population grew, conditions became increasingly crowded, forcing families to build additional floors to accommodate more family members. For a visual depiction of life and hope in Palestinian refugee camps in spite of the increasingly crowded conditions, see Mats Grorud, *The Tower*, documentary film, 2018.

5 As of 2022, UNRWA (United Nations Relief and Works Agency) still provides emergency food assistance to over a million Palestinian refugees—what amounts to three-quarters of Palestinian refugees in the Gaza Strip—because their income falls below the abject and absolute poverty line of $1.74 (62%) and $3.87 (38%) per person per day, respectively. See https://www.unrwa.org/food-assistance.

Chapter 6: Ein Gedi

6 Israeli forces took over the Palestinian town of al-Majdal Asqalan on November 5, 1948, with the majority of its roughly 10,000 Palestinian residents and those of neighboring villages becoming refugees in Gaza. Israel renamed the town Ashqelon.

Chapter 7: Point of No Return

7 Salim is referring to the fortress mindset of Israeli politics, of which Golda Meir was accused during her reign as prime minister. For more on the Masada Complex, see Robert Alter, "The Masada Complex," *Commentary*, July 1973, https://www.commentary.org/articles/robert-alter-2/the-masada-complex/.

Chapter 9: Storm

8 By 1991, Israel required Palestinians to have a permit to leave the Gaza Strip. Restrictions on travel to Gaza only increased over time until it became virtually impossible to enter or leave, which is why Gaza is often referred to as an open-air prison. Over the years, Israel has issued a limited number of work permits.

PART II: RESISTANCE

Chapter 10: Sabra and Shatila

9 The PLO fighters agreed to leave Lebanon as long as Palestinian civilians in the Sabra and Shatila camps would be protected. For personal testimonies of survivors of the Sabra and Shatila massacre as well as the current living conditions of the camps, see Eliana Riva, *The Sabra and Chatila Sky*, documentary film, 2023. Unfortunately, the ensuing Sabra and Shatila massacre was not the first massacre of Palestinians in Lebanon. Similarly, in 1976 during the Lebanese Civil War, Lebanese militias under the direction of the Israeli army imposed a siege on the Tel Al-Zaatar Refugee Camp in Beirut in an effort to drive Palestinian fighters out of Beirut. In spite of an agreement for the Palestinian fighters and civilians to leave the camp, the Lebanese militias attacked them as they left, killing thousands. See Rashid Khalidi, *The Hundred Years' War on Palestine: A History of Settler Colonialism and Resistance, 1917–2017*, New York: Metropolitan Books, 2020, 57–61.

10 In 1980, Israel incorporated the newer part of the village, Beit Hanina al-Jadida, into the municipality of Jerusalem, including village lands while excluding the older part of the village, Beit Hanina al-Balad. Israel confiscated more than 30 percent of village lands to build six settlements in the area. Israel ultimately built the Wall between these two parts of Beit Hanina, formally dividing the city in two.

11 The United Nations established the International Day of Solidarity with the Palestinian people beginning in 1978 as an annual reminder to recognize that Palestinians have yet to realize their inalienable rights to self-determination and independence as well as the Right of Return. November 29 was chosen since it was on that day the UN recommended the partition of Palestine with the dissolution of the British Mandate in Palestine in 1948.

12 The commemoration of Land Day honors Palestinian citizens of Israel who were killed by the IDF and Israeli police in the Galilee on March 30, 1976, after Israel issued land confiscation orders in a number of Palestinian villages there and instituted a curfew about which villagers returning from work were not aware.

13 The practice of administration detention continues to this day. For example, Ahmed Abu Jazar was released from administrative detention on February 3, 2023, after nearly two decades of harassment and torture, allegedly for being affiliated with Islamic Jihad. See Rajaa Salah, "A Life Interrupted at 18 Begins Again," The *Electronic Intifada*, March 1, 2023, https://electronicintifada.net/content/life-interrupted-18-begins-again/37266.

14 Handala.org, http://handala.org/handala/.

15 When Ibrahim Abu-Lughod passed away in 2001, the State of Israel allowed him to be buried next to his father in his family plot in Jaffa.

16 For the cultural significance of tatriz—the cross-stitch of Palestine—see Carol Mansour, *Stitching Palestine*, documentary film, 2017.

17 The First Intifada, which began following a traffic accident at a military checkpoint in Gaza on December 8, 1987, quicky transformed into a campaign of nonviolent resistance coordinated by popular committees that issued daily leaflets with instructions for General Strikes, boycott of Israeli products, refusal to pay Israeli taxes, coordinated demonstrations and acts of civil disobedience, the organization of underground education and social services, as well as a renaissance of music, theater, and art illustrating Palestinians' resolve to be free of Israeli occupation. Participation cut across all age groups, and both men and women fully participated in the struggle. In response, Israel incarcerated thousands of Palestinians, imposed curfews, blocked the flow of goods between towns and villages, and even called for breaking the bones of protestors. As more and more leaders were either thrown in jail or deported, the PLO seized control of the intifada, returning its tactics to armed struggle for the remainder of the uprising until it was brought to an end through peace negotiations in Oslo in 1993. See Global Nonviolent Database at https://nvdatabase.swarthmore.edu/content/palestinians-wage-nonviolent-campaign-during-first-intifada-1987-1988.

18 David Grossman, Translated by Haim Watzman, *The Yellow Wind*, New York: Farrar, Straus and Giroux, 1988.

19 Uri Avnery, *My Friend, the Enemy,* Westport, Connecticut: Lawrence Hill & Company, 1986.

20 Yoram Binur, *Mein Bruder, Mein Feind: Ein Israeli als Palästinenser,* Schweizer Verlagshaus, 1990 (originally published in English 1989).

21 Per-Olow Anderson, *They Are Human Too: A Photographic Essay on the Palestine Arab Refugees*, Chicago: Henry Regnery Company, 1957.

Chapter 11: Jalameh

22 The British Mandate of Palestine was formally approved by the League of Nations on August 12, 1922.

23 Sidi is used in spoken Arabic to denote "grandfather" or "grandpa" but is also used to address to an elderly man to show respect.

24 The formal instruction of Levantine Arabic is typically based on the spoken Lebanese dialect of Beirut, though it is close to Palestinian urban dialects. Rural dialects can vary from region to region within Palestine and even from village to village, which is true as well for the entire Arab world. The Arabic dialect of Gaza is influenced by both neighboring Egypt and Bedouin dialects in the area.

25 In Modern Standard Arabic, there is no letter in Arabic to write *chaf* for the sound "ch" as in the English word "much." However, in the colloquial village dialect, the letter *kaf* (ك), similar to "k" in English, becomes *chaf* in certain cases. The sound "ch" as in English "much" is only written out in Arabic with the two Arabic letters *ta* (ت) and *shin* (ش) with foreign words such as Czechoslovakia (تسيكوسلوفاكيا). Incidentally, there is also no letter "v" as in the English "very" in Arabic, so the letter *fa* (ف) is used instead as in Czechoslovakia above.

Chapter 12: Jenin

26 Britain's all-out repression of the Palestinian Arab Revolt of 1936 and Britain's growing partnership with Jewish militias to take on the role of policing Palestinians subject to collective punishment but were also barred from carrying or acquiring weapons. This policy stood in sharp contrast to the British arming Jewish militias as police forces such that by the time Britain attempted to curb Jewish immigration in an effort to appease Palestinian demands, Zionist militias resorted to attacking the British in Palestine in 1945–1947, forcing Britain to pull out of Palestine and throw the Palestine Question to the UN in 1948. See Rashid Khalidi, *The Hundred Years' War on Palestine,* 44–47.

Chapter 13: Johnny

27 Ontario, Canada, originally had five years of secondary education through 1988 when grade 13 became the Ontario Academic Credit (OAC) until it was phased out in 2003, https://en.wikipedia.org/wiki/Thirteenth_grade.

28 For personal testimonies on life in Ramleh before the Nakba and the subsequent loss of this city, see Lubna Dajani, *My Ramleh,* documentary film, 2013.

29 Haganah and Irgun militias occupied the Palestinian towns of Lydd July 11, 1948, and Ramleh on July 12, 1948, using bombs, grenades, and live ammunition to carry out Yitzhak Rabin's orders to expel Palestinian residents. Whereas residents of Ramleh were bussed out, residents of Lydd were stripped of their belongings and property, then forced to walk for three days to the Arab front lines in the extreme summer heat, leading to many deaths from dehydration and exhaustion. See Ilan Pappé, *The Ethnic Cleansing of Palestine,* London: Oneworld Publications, 2006, 166–170. Also see Benny Morris, *The Birth of the Palestinian Refugee Problem Revisited*, Cambridge: Cambridge University Press, 2004, 423–436.

30 Israel also occupied the Sinai Peninsula during the Six-Day War but gave it back as part of the peace treaty between Egypt and Israel in 1979. Israel formally annexed the Golan Heights in 1981. UN Resolution 242 from November 22, 1967, called on Israel to withdraw from areas it occupied in 1967 which became the basis for many failed negotiations regarding a final settlement between Israel and the Palestinians.

31 License plates for private vehicles in the West Bank were blue with black numbers from 1967 through 1994, whereas in Gaza they were white with black numbers. In 1994 following the Oslo Accords, license plates in the West Bank were also white with black numbers. Taxis, however, have green license plates. Until 2005, Israeli settlers had white plates with green numbers. Since then, Israeli cars, including settlers, have yellow plates. See http://www.worldlicenseplates.com/world/AS_PALE.html.

32 See http://tractors.wikia.com/wiki/International_TD-24.

33 Israeli forces occupied Nazareth in July 1948, but residents were spared the same treatment as other Palestinian cities and towns, largely due to its sizeable Christian population. Many Palestinians fled to Nazareth from Tiberias, Haifa, and Beisan and neighboring villages. Like other Palestinians in what became Israel, residents of Nazareth were under martial law until 1966.

34 Prior to the establishment of the State of Israel in 1948, Jews owned only seven percent of the land. With the expulsion of nearly 80 percent of the Palestinian population in what became Israel, the new state was in control of 78 percent of Mandatory Palestine. Through various legal frameworks, 93 percent of the land in what became Israel is now owned by either the State of Israel, the Jewish National Fund (13 percent), or the Israel Development Authority. This land is managed by the Israel Land Authority Land Registry Bureau, which is typically leased to individuals for a period of 45 or 99 years, so it feels like it is privately owned for the leasee, though ownership is never transferred. Land is only leased to citizens of the State of Israel or foreign nationals who can proved they are eligible for citizenship under the Law of Return. This scheme essentially blocks private ownership of land and keeps what was once Palestinian land in Israeli hands. See Joshua Portman, "An Introduction to Understanding Land Registration and Ownership in Israel," Buy It In Israel, November 20, 2015, https://www.buyitinisrael.com/news/land-registration-ownership-israel/.

35 Al-Omari Mosque, Tiberias.

36 After the war in 1948, Israel gave Christians access to most of their holy sites, but most Muslim properties were confiscated.

37 Tiberias was the first of 12 Palestinian cities to be taken over by Jewish forces on April 16–17, 1948, shortly after the Deir Yassin massacre on April 9. Under the British Mandate, Tiberias had a majority Jewish population and was allocated to the Jewish state under the 1947 UN Partition Plan. The Jewish militia Haganah engaged in a bombing campaign, seizing the city, while British forces evacuated the entire Palestinian population (nearly 6,000 residents). By 1949, the Israeli army bulldozed or blew up 500 Palestinian residences in the Old City of Tiberias. See Ilan Pappé, *The Ethnic Cleansing of Palestine,* 92, 216. Also see Benny Morris, *The Birth of the Palestinian Refugee Problem Revisited,* 181–186.

38 Israel occupied the Golan Heights during the Six-Day War in 1967. Only four Syrian villages were allowed to remain, though cut off from Syria, separating families and isolating these communities. Israel promptly took control of land and water resources to build settlements in the area, making it more difficult for local residents to continue farming. Israel annexed the Golan Heights in 1981, though the annexation was only formally recognized by the US in 2020. Syria still considers residents Syrian citizens, though Israel refers to them as "residents of the Golan Heights" and has issued laissez passé documents for travel purposes. In 2011, Israel offered Syrians in the Golan Heights citizenship, though few have opted to become Israeli citizens. Travel to Syria remains restricted.

39 The Druze are a small sect of Islam that split off in the 11th century when the Egyptian leader Al-Hakim Bi-Amr Allah was declared divine. Members are loyal and close knit, living mostly in Lebanon but also Syria, Jordan, and Israel/ Palestine. Druze in Israeli-controlled areas have been required to serve in the Israeli army beginning in 1956 as part of a "divide and conquer" strategy against Palestinian resistance. Druze who refuse military service are imprisoned for two years—the full length of required military service. Serving in the Israeli military provides a number of benefits that Christian and Muslim Palestinians are not eligible for, namely preferential housing, loans, employment in state institutions, and financial benefits in higher education. Aziza Nofal, "Why More and More Israeli Druze Prefer Prison to Military Service," *Al-Monitor,* May 10, 2016, http://www.al-monitor.com/pulse/originals/2016/05/israel-druze-reject-military-service.html#ixzz4VO3wjf3r.

40 Majdal Shams is Aramaic for "Tower of Sun."

41 Monument to the Martyrs of the Great Syrian Revolt of 1925 acknowledges a general uprising across Mandatory Syria and Lebanon from 1925 to 1927 to end French control.

42 Even though the Jewish population of Safad was consistently around 30 percent from the early days of the British Mandate through 1948, Safad was allocated to the Jewish state in the 1947 UN Partition Plan. The seizure of Safad by Jewish militias followed the ethnic cleansing of surrounding Palestinian villages and fell on May 11, 1948, with all of the more than 9,000–12,000 Palestinian residents (depending on the source) driven out. For a full account of the seizure of Safad, see Ilan Pappé, *The Ethnic Cleansing of Palestine*, 97–98, and Benny Morris, *The Birth of the Palestinian Refugee Problem*, 221–226.

43 Though there has historically been a Jewish presence in Safad due to its religious significance, the artist quarter of present-day Safad was the Arab section of town prior to 1948.

44 Kufr Bir'im is a Palestinian Christian village that Haganah forces captured on October 31, 1948, subsequently driving out all inhabitants on November 4, 1948. Israel established Kibbutz Bir'im on village lands in 1949. As with the villages of Iqrit and Ghabisiyya, residents of Kufr Bir'im appealed to the Israeli Supreme Court in 1953 to return to their village, but the state razed the village and expropriated all village lands. In 1977, Menachem Begin promised the villagers they could return to their village but did not follow through with his promise. In the summer of 1972, internally displaced descendants returned to their church to repair it but were forced out by the Israeli government. The operational name of the massacre at the 1972 Olympics in Munich was named after Kufr Bir'im and the village of Iqrit, another Christian village that was emptied of its inhabitants by Israeli forces in November 1948. Today, only the Church of Kufr Bir'im remains. See Benny Morris, *The Birth of the Palestinian Refugee Problem Revisited*, 507–509; Illan Pappé, *The Ethnic Cleansing of Palestine,* London: Oneworld Publications, 2006, 187; and Walid

Khalidi, *All That Remains: The Palestinian Villages Occupied and Depopulated by Israel in 1948,* Institute for Palestine Studies: Washington, 1992, 13–17, 460–461.

45 Israel established the Law of Return in 1950 to enable any Jew anywhere in the world with one or more Jewish grandparent and their spouse, or those who converted to Judaism, to come to Israel and be granted full Israeli citizenship.

46 Toward the end of WWI in 1916, Britain and France signed a secret agreement between British and French diplomats Mark Sykes and Francois Georges-Picot, respectively, to carve up areas under Ottoman control between them whereby Turkey, Kurdistan, Syria, and Lebanon would fall under France, and Palestine, Jordan, and Iraq under Britain. At the conclusion of the war, these countries felt double-crossed because they were promised independence after the war if they fought alongside Britain and France against the Ottoman Empire.

47 Caesarea is an ancient port city along the Mediterranean Sea as well as the location of the Palestinian-destroyed village of Qisariya, a village dating back to the Phoenicians, which was the first village to fall under the watch of the British. Palmach forces led by Yitzhak Rabin drove out the residents and destroyed the village on February 15, 1948. The State of Israel transformed the ancient ruins into a tourist attraction. See Benny Morris, *The Birth of the Palestinian Refugee Problem Revisited,* 130; llan Pappé, *The Ethnic Cleansing of Palestine*, 75; and *All That Remains: The Palestinian Villages Occupied and Depopulated by Israel in 1948,* 182–184.

48 *Yallah* is a colloquial expression with contextual meaning of setting something in motion or conveying a sense of urgency. For example, *Yallah, qoum!*—Come on, get up! or *Yallah?*—Shall we (leave)?

49 Mosques according to Islamic tradition are held by the *waqf*, which is a religious trust that protects the sanctity of Islamic sites. When Israel declared statehood in 1948, it confiscated waqf properties to be held in "guardianship" of the newly formed state. Subsequently, numerous holy sites were desecrated or destroyed. Such acts continue to this day, threatening the sanctity of holy sites in Palestine. See Chaiwat Satha-Anand and Olivier Urbain, eds., *Protecting the Sacred: Creating Peace in Asia-Pacific,* Herndon: Transaction Publishers: 2013, 78.

50 "There were no such thing as Palestinians. When was there an independent Palestinian people with a Palestinian state? It was either southern Syria before the First World War, and then it was a Palestine including Jordan. It was not as though there was a Palestinian people in Palestine considering itself as a Palestinian people and we came and threw them out and took their country away from them. They did not exist." See Frank Giles, Interview with Golda Meir, *Sunday Times,* June 15, 1969. This interview also appeared in *The Washington Post*, June 16, 1969.

Chapter 14: Next Generation

51 This building in Ramleh contains the Church of Saint George and the El-Khidr Mosque.

52 Edward Said, *Orientalism*, New York: Vintage Books, 1979.

53 Al-Bahr Mosque—The Sea Mosque—is the oldest mosque in Jaffa built in the 16th century during the Ottoman Empire. Palestinians have been forbidden from entering or caring for the mosque since 1948.

54 About 25 percent of the population of Jaffa was Jewish toward the end of the British Mandate. Jewish militias attacked the city on April 25, 1948, even though, according to the UN Partition Plan of 1947, Jaffa was designated as part of the Palestinian state. By the time Israel declared statehood on May 14, 1948, less than 4,000 out of nearly 70,000 Palestinians remained in the city, confined to a single neighborhood ('Ajami). Israel destroyed roughly 75 percent of Jaffa following the takeover on May 15, 1948, as well as nearly all neighboring Palestinian villages. See Palestine Remembered, https://www.palestineremembered.com/Jaffa/Jaffa/index.html.

For a thorough exposition of life in Palestine before the establishment of the State of Israel, see Walid Khalidi, *Before Their Diaspora: A Photographic History of the Palestinians 1876–1948,* Institute for Palestine Studies: Washington, DC, 1984.

55 Back in the 1980s and during the First Intifada, not only was it illegal to wear the colors of the Palestinian flag, but artists' work was confiscated by the Israeli army if they included the colors of the Palestinian flag or symbols of occupation or connection to the land such as barbed wire, oranges, or olive trees. Artist Suleiman Mansour, for example, recalls an exchange with an Israeli soldier where he was told that even painting a watermelon would be grounds to seize his work since it included red, black, green, and white. Palestine Art Week at the Palestine Museum, US, May 16, 2021.

56 In Islam, men are allowed to marry up to four wives, as long as they can treat them equally as written in *Surah An-Nisa'* —The Surah of Women—in the Quran (4:3):

وَإِنْ خِفْتُمْ أَلاَّ تُقْسِطُوا فِي الْيَتَامَىٰ
فَانكِحُوا مَا طَابَ لَكُم مِّنَ النِّسَاءِ مَثْنَىٰ وَثُلَاثَ وَرُبَاعَ
فَإِنْ خِفْتُمْ أَلاَّ تَعْدِلُوا فَوَاحِدَةً أَوْ مَا مَلَكَتْ أَيْمَانُكُمْ
ذَٰلِكَ أَدْنَىٰ أَلاَّ تَعُولُوا

And if you fear that you will not deal justly with the orphan girls,
Then marry those that please you of [other] women, two or three or four.
But if you fear that you will not be just,
Then [marry only] one or those your right hand possesses.
That is more suitable that you may not include [to injustice].

Even though it is deemed impossible to treat two or more women the same, Islamic law allows for men to marry up to four wives. See My Islam, https://myislam.org/surah-an-nisa/.

Chapter 15: Nablus

57 The placement of Jewish settlements on hilltops is no coincidence. Britain formally took over the administration of Palestine in 1920 after the fall of the Ottoman Empire. Once Britain declared support for a Jewish homeland in Palestine with the Balfour Declaration in 1917, early Zionists developed plans for the new British Mandate in Palestine to plant pine nut forests on hilltops that would become future Jewish settlements as strategic outposts to overlook Palestinian cities and villages. This forestation ordinance was among the first established under British Mandate Palestine.

Chapter 18: Rummaneh

58 International Committee of the Red Cross (ICRC), Geneva Convention Relative to the Protection of Civilian Persons in Time of War (Fourth Geneva Convention), August 12, 1949.

Chapter 19: Nakba and Naksa

59 Christa Bruhn Abu-Farha, *The Palestinian Dialect of Al-Jalameh: A Phonemic Study,* Ann Arbor: University of Michigan, 1993.

60 A UN truce, which came to be known as the First Truce, was called on June 11 to July 9, 1948 (the 28-day truce Nasser's father mentions), but fighting broke out again immediately at the end of the truce.

61 Nasser's father must have returned to the village at the end of the ceasefire on July 9, 1948, when fighting resumed.

62 The Arab Liberation Army was formed by the Arab League, consisting of only a few thousand volunteers from Syria in the north, Egypt in the south, and Jordan from the east. Lebanon only sent volunteers to the Lebanese border. The largely volunteer army proved ineffective compared to the well-armed and trained Jewish forces numbering well over 100,000 soldiers.

63 Nasser's parents returned to the village 40 days after their eldest son Ghazi's birth on July 17, 1948, which would mean toward the end of August—when they would have harvested their wheat—making their time away from home nearly three months.

64 The UN General Assembly Partition Plan of 1947 is also known as Resolution 181. By 1947, after successive waves of Jewish immigration to Palestine, Jews made up 33 percent of the population of Palestine—up from 7 percent at the start of the

British Mandate but were allocated 62 percent of the land under the UN Partition Plan. The area allocated to the Jewish state would have had a roughly equal population of Jews and Palestinians had Jewish forces not expelled 80 percent of the Palestinian population there.

65 Even before the dissolution of the British Mandate on May 14, 1948, Jewish militias began driving Palestinians out of their villages immediately following the 1947 UN Partition Plan. The British did not interfere with the Jewish militias driving out Palestinians from their homes in areas designated for a Jewish state, even though the plan did not call for or sanction the ethnic cleansing of Palestinians in these areas. For a nearly daily account of the unfolding of events following the 1947 Partition Plan, see Walid Khalidi, *All That Remains,* 576–579. Also see Benny Morris, *The Birth of the Palestinian Refugee Problem Revisited* and Ilan Pappé, *The Ethnic Cleansing of Palestine.*

66 Haganah received its first shipment of arms from Czechoslovakia in Haifa on April 1, 1948, and subsequent shipments on May 12–14, 1948. Clearly, these shipments gave Jewish militias a huge advantage in clearing Haifa and other cities, towns, and villages of their Palestinian residents.

67 On March 10, 1948, Haganah finalized Plan Dalet to conquer areas designated for the Jewish state in the 1947 UN Partition Plan, including additional areas that were to become a Palestinian state according to the plan. Haganah formally launched Plan D—as it came to be called—on April 4, 1948, though they carried out initial clearing operations on villages in the coastal plain north of Tel Aviv, the coastal area of Haifa and Jaffa, and near Lake al-Hula, as well as Bedouins in the Naqab (Negev). This ethnic cleansing operation in cities, towns, and villages was systematically implented by Jewish militias consisting of 120,000 soldiers organized in nine brigades carrying out 31 military operations. Villages were surrounded and men were separated from women and children. Men were either killed or sent to concentration camps or labor camps, while women and children were expelled in the one direction left open, toward Syria and Lebanon in the Galilee, the West Bank and Jordan in the center, and Gaza and Egypt in the south. In over 150 villages, Jewish militias committed massacres. See Salman Abu Sitta, "A Palestinian Address to Balfour: In Honor of Truth, Memory, and Justice," Palestine Land Society, November 30, 2022, https://www.plands.org/en/articles-speeches/speeches/2022/a-palestinian-address-to-balfour. For a thorough treatment of the Tantura massacre, see Alon Schwartz, *Tantura*, documentary film, 2022. Moreover, the creation of "Village Files" on every village in Palestine following the Arab Revolt of 1936–1939 proved critical information in the implementation of Plan Dalet. See Ilan Pappé, *The Ethnic Cleansing of Palestine,* 17–22.

68 Deir Yassin was one of dozens of massacres carried out by Jewish militias and the Israeli army during the establishment of the State of Israel. For a thorough discussion of such massacres, including maps of their location. See "Al-Nakba and

Return: The Aftermath," Palestine Land Society, https://www.plands.org/en/maps-atlases/maps/al-nakba-return/slide11. For personal testimonies from survivors of the Deir Yassin massacre, see Sahera Dirbas, *Deir Yassin Village and Massacre*, documentary film, 2012.

69 For a riveting personal account of what it's like to go back to one's ancestral house and confront those who now live there, see Sahera Dirbas, *On the Doorstep*, documentary film, 2018. Also see Sandy Tolan, *The Lemon Tree: An Arab, A Jew and the Heart of the Middle East,* New York: Bloomsbury, 2007.

70 Roughly 30,000 Palestinians fled from West Jerusalem in April 1948, which was the wealthiest area of Jerusalem, when the city came under the attack of Jewish militias. Jordan expelled about 1,500 Jews from the Old City when it took control of East Jerusalem in 1949, but the Jewish population of the Old City has since recovered after Israel's seizure and annexation of East Jerusalem following the Six-Day War in 1967.

71 In response to the white migration westward under the direction of Thomas Jefferson's presidency, some 4,000 American soldiers carried out the expulsion and forced migration of the Cherokee Nation from their ancestral lands in what is now North Carolina, South Carolina, Georgia, Alabama, and Tennessee, to territories west of the Mississippi River. A quarter of the Cherokee Nation perished on this forced journey during the fall and winter of 1838–1839. Today the majority of the Cherokee Nation lives in Oklahoma. This Native American Nakba was carried out in spite of efforts to assimilate into the culture of the encroaching settler communities and their own formal government and constitution. Other Indian Nations experienced similar displacement and dispossession of their lands, including the Muscogee, Seminole, Chickasaw, Choctaw, Ponca, and Ho-Chunk and Winnebago Nations. The forcible removal and cultural genocide of indigenous peoples happened not only throughout the Americas but around the world. See Alexandra Mandewo, "A Brief History on the Trail of Tears," The Indigenous Foundation, https://www.theindigenousfoundation.org/articles/a-brief-history-on-the-trail-of-tears.

72 The State of Israel or Zionist agencies are known to offer Palestinian homeowners a blank check in East Jerusalem in an effort to Judaize the city. Israel also advances its policy of Judaization of Jerusalem by building settlements, demolishing homes, restricting building for Palestinians, and stripping Palestinians of their residency. West Jerusalem was cleansed of Palestinians in 1948. See "Judaization of Jerusalem: Could it get any worse?" International Movement for a Just World, July 24, 2019, https://just-international.org/articles/judaization-of-jerusalem-could-it-get-any-worse/.

73 This secret agreement between Israel and King Abdullah of Jordan was reached on March 23, 1949, in conjunction with the 1949 Armistice Agreements in Rhodes, Greece.

74 Whereas the official Zionist narrative of Israel claims that Palestinians left due to calls by Arab governments to leave their homes, the vast majority of Palestinians fled for their lives due to military assault by Jewish forces. Other reasons for leaving their homes include psychological warfare (whispering campaign) or fear of Jewish attack, in part due to news of the fall of a neighboring town or village or outright massacres. See Salman Abu Sitta, "Massacres as a weapon of ethnic cleansing during the Nakba," *Mondoweiss,* June 20, 2020, https://mondoweiss.net/2020/06/massacres-as-a-weapon-of-ethnic-cleansing-during-the-nakba/.

75 The Balfour Project seeks to hold Britain accountable for its failure to protect the interests of the Palestinians under the British Mandate and secure equal rights for Palestinians and Israelis. See Balfour Project, https://balfourproject.org/.

76 United Nations General Assembly Resolution 194 passed on Dec 11, 1948, stating that "refugees wishing to return to their homes and live at peace with their neighbours should be permitted to do so at the earliest practicable date, and that compensation should be paid for the property of those choosing not to return and for loss of or damage to property which, under principles of international law or equity, should be made good by the governments or authorities responsible." There are currently 58 official Palestinian refugee camps in the Middle East: Jordan (10), Syria (9), Lebanon (12), the West Bank (19), and in Gaza (8). *UNRWA Statistics 2010,* United Nations Relief and Works Agency for Palestine Refugees in the Near East, Program Coordination and Support Unit, November 2011, http://www.unrwa.org/userfiles/2011120434013.pdf.

77 At the end of 2011, there were 7.4 million displaced Palestinians, representing 66 percent of the entire Palestinian population (11.2 million) worldwide. Among them were 5.8 million 1948 Palestinian refugees of whom 4.8 million are registered with and assisted by the UN Relief and Works Agency for Palestine Refugees (UNRWA) and one million unregistered refugees; more than one million 1967 refugees; and 519,000 internally displaced persons (IDPs) on both sides of the Green Line (1949 Armistice Line). See *Survey of Palestinian Refugees and Internally Displaced Persons 2010–2012, Volume VII,* BADIL Resource Center for Palestinian Refugees and Refugee Rights, Bethlehem, Palestine.

78 The United Nations General Assembly asserted the Palestinian Right of Return with resolution 194 in 1949, stating that "refugees wishing to return to their homes and live at peace with their neighbours should be permitted to do so at the earliest practicable date, and that compensation should be paid for the property of those choosing not to return and for loss of or damage to property which, under principles of international law or equity, should be made good by the Governments or authorities responsible."

Chapter 20: Canaan (كنعان)

79   See Sabreen, https://www.sabreen.org/sabreen-band and George Kirmiz https://www.palestinechronicle.com the-disappearance-of-george-kirmiz-unravelling-a-palestinian-musical-mystery/.

80   At 4:00 p.m. local time in Tel Aviv, David Ben-Gurion, the first prime minister of Israel, declared that Israel would become a state at midnight on May 14, 1948, which is 4:00 p.m. EST in the US. Canaan was born at 3:40 p.m. EST.

Chapter 21: Back to Jalameh

81   *Surat Al-Ahqaf*—The Surah of the Wind-curved Cranes—in the Quran (46:15), My Islam, https://myislam.org/surah-ahqaf/.

$$\text{وَوَصَّيْنَا ٱلْإِنسَٰنَ بِوَٰلِدَيْهِ إِحْسَٰنًا}$$
$$\text{أُمُّهُ كُرْهًا وَوَضَعَتْهُ كُرْهًا}$$
$$\text{وَحَمْلُهُ وَفِصَٰلُهُ ثَلَٰثُونَ شَهْرًا}$$

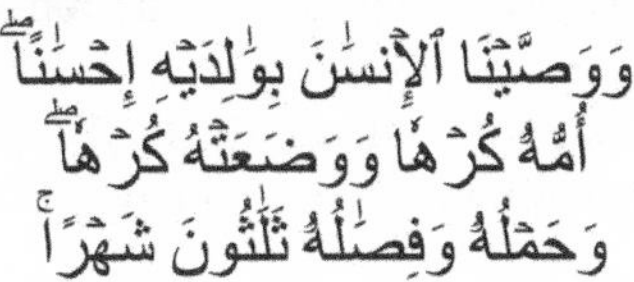

And we have enjoined upon man, to his parents, good treatment.
His mother carried him with hardship and gave birth to him with hardship,
and his gestation and weaning [period] is 30 months.

82   El-Funoun Palestinian Popular Dance Troupe
(فرقة الفنون الشعبية الفلسطينية), https://el-funoun.org/.

Chapter 22: Karmel (كرمل)

83   It is traditional in spoken Arabic to call children by how they are to address the person speaking to them. So, Nasser's mother addresses her grandson Sitti rather than by his name. Parents address their children as Mama and Baba, paternal aunts and uncles address their nieces and nephews as 'Amti and 'Ami (the same words to address one's mother- and father-in-law), and maternal aunts and uncles as Khalti and Khali, and so on. Relationships within the family are emphasized in Arab culture, so these distinctions are learned early and, of course, evolve as children grow up, get married, and start families of their own.

84   *Wallah* is from the Arabic Wallahi (والله), which means "I swear to God" and is used to convey confidence or certainty.

85   *Akh* is from *akhi* (أخي)—my brother, so as to call out to one's brother for help.

PART III: ROOTEDNESS

Chapter 25: Villages

86 Jewish forces destroyed the Palestinian village of Zir'in on May 28, 1948, just two weeks after the establishment of the State of Israel. Today, the moshav of Avital (established in 1953) and the kibbutz of Yizre'el (established August 20, 1948)—each with a population of just over 500—are located on Zir'in village lands. See Benny Morris, *The Birth of the Palestinian Refugee Problem Revisited,* 346; and Walid Khalidi, *All That Remains,* 339–340.

87 The Palestinian village of Hawsha was occupied and destroyed on April 16, 1948, along with the village of Khirbet Kayasir. See Walid Khalidi, *All That Remains,* 162–163.

88 Internally displaced Palestinians—those who remained in what became Israel but whose villages were destroyed—are also known as "present absentees" because their lands were confiscated under the 1950 Absentee Property Law for temporarily leaving their homes, property, and lands, even though they remained present in Israel.

89 The Palestinian village of Indur was occupied by Israeli forces on May 16, 1948, and depopulated on May 24, 1048. See Benny Morris, *The Birth of the Palestinian Refugee Problem Revisited,* 260; and Walid Khalidi, *All That Remains,* 344–346.

90 The Israeli army partially destroyed the village of Deir Ayyub in March 1948, and the adjacent villages of Imwas, Yalo, and Beit Nuba following the 1967 war to clear the Jerusalem corridor. Between 7,000 to 10,000 Palestinian residents were driven out of these three villages. Once cleared, the villages were completely destroyed. After the war, Israel annexed the area, which is located in the West Bank. The State of Israel subsequently declared that the area would be developed as a recreational park in 1969. Residents of Imwas, Yalo, and Beit Nuba requested to return to their lands and rebuild their homes in 1975 but were rejected due to security concerns. That same year, Canada Park was established on the village sites of Imwas and Yalo with funding from the Jewish National Fund of Canada, hence the name Canada Park.

As Benny Morris clearly outlines, The creation of parks where Palestinian villages once stood is nothing new in Israel. Of the more than 500 Palestinian villages Jewish forces and the Israel Defense Forces destroyed, Israel established 186 Jewish communities by 1949 with Hebrew names on or near the original village. Of the destroyed Palestinian village sites that have not been developed as Israeli settlements, 182 of the sites were designated as Israeli national parks showcasing ancient ruins that have been excavated from beneath the ruins of Palestinian villages. See Noga Kadman, "Palestinian Villages, Israeli Parks: How the Past Echoes in the Present," Palestine Square, Institute for Palestine Studies, December 23, 2015.

Other village sites have become nature reserves and recreation areas that highlight the natural features of the land, such as springs or orchards. Only in rare cases is there any mention of the former Palestinian inhabitants, with no indication of why they are no longer present. Some areas, such as the Carmel Coast Forest south of Haifa and the Biria Forest near Safad in the Galilee, are covered with trees as part of the Jewish National Fund's Plant a Tree in Israel campaign, in part "to obscure the remains of destroyed Palestinian villages." The Carmel Coast Forest has 2,470 acres of trees over the remains of the destroyed Palestinian villages of 'Ayn Ghazal, Jaba,' and Sawamir. The Biria Forest contains 5,000 acres over the destroyed Palestinian villages of 'Amuqa, 'Ayn al-Zaytun, Fir'im, Mughr al-Khayt, and Qaba'a.

Chapter 27: Beisan

91 By 1991, at the height of the First Intifada, Israel required permits to leave the West Bank and Gaza. This permit system was formalized under the Oslo Accords in 1993. Movement in and out of Gaza became increasingly restricted over time, which is why Gaza is often referred to as an open-air prison.

92 David Ben-Gurion, the first prime minister of Israel, established a commission to rename Palestinian places into Hebrew names in July 1949.

Chapter 29: Haifa

93 The city of Haifa was one of the few cities in Palestine where there was roughly an equal number of Jews (70,000) and Palestinians (65,000) prior to 1948. However, once Jewish militias attacked the city on April 21–22, 1948, with a combination of arms they had just received from Czechoslovakia and psychological warfare to drive out Palestinian residents in collaboration with the British authorities, who planned to depart by May 1948, only 4,000 of the original 65,000 Palestinian residents of Haifa remained, mostly Christian. Martial law was imposed on Palestinians who remained in the newly established State of Israel until 1966. See Benny Morris, *The Birth of the Palestinian Refugee Problem Revisited,* 186–211; and Illan Pappé, *The Ethnic Cleansing of Palestine*, 92–96. For personal testimonies from those who remained in Haifa after the Nakba in 1948, see Abu Al-Rish Darwish, *Haifawi* (حيفاوي), documentary film, 2020.

94 See Benny Morris, *The Birth of the Palestinian Refugee Problem Revisited,* 207–209; Ilan Pappé, *The Ethnic Cleansing of Palestine,* 160–161; and Walid Khalidi, *All That Remains,* 195–198.

95 As reported by Golda Meir on May 6, 1948, as acting head of the Jewish Agency Political Department a few days after the Jewish conquest of Haifa. See Benny Morris, *The Birth of the Palestinian Refugee Problem Revisited,* 310.

96 Reference to "a light unto nations" appears in the Old Testament in Isaiah 49:6 where God states, "It is too light a thing for you to be My servant, to establish the tribes of Jacob, and to restore the scions of Israel, and I shall submit you as a light unto the nations, to be My salvation until the end of the Earth." This

phrase was also used by religious leaders of the Zionist movement such as Rabbi Abraham Isaac Kook, who looked to Israel to be a "light unto nations." David Ben-Gurion, the first prime minister of Israel, designated the Menorah as the emblem of Israel as a symbol of Israel as a "light unto the nations." See "Light Unto the Nations," Wikimedia Foundation, Last Updated March 19, 2023, https://en.wikipedia.org/wiki/Light_unto_the_nations.

Chapter 30: Encounter

97 "Making Aliyah" is specified under the Law of Return of 1950. Israeli citizens, with some exceptions, are required to serve in the Israeli army.

98 Here in the village dialect, the letter *kaf* (ك) becomes *chaf* in this case, so *Allah yubarik fiki* becomes *Allah yubarich fich*.

PART IV: STEADFASTNESS

Chapter 31: Fieldwork

99 Historically, Palestinian primary and secondary education were administered by whatever occupying power was in control of the area, such as the Ottomans during the Ottoman Empire and the British during the British Mandate. After Israel was established in 1948, the Jordanians administered education in the West Bank and Egypt in the Gaza Strip, but once Israel took over these areas during the Six-Day War in 1967, primary and secondary education in the West Bank and Gaza fell under the Israeli Occupation Authorities. Palestinian universities emerged beginning in the 1970s and operated fairly independently in spite of being under Israeli occupation. Previously, Palestinians had to travel outside of Palestine for higher education. The Oslo Accords of 1993 gave Palestinians the opportunity to define their primary and secondary education for the first time in history with the establishment of the Ministry of Education and also provided some oversight for institutions of higher education through the Ministry of Higher Education.

100 Ultimately, the Arab American University in Jenin also served Palestinian students from within Israel as a place where they could study and be among other Palestinians from the West Bank.

101 For an in-depth account of the history of tensions in Hebron and the impact on the lives of Palestinians, see Ellie Bernstein, Ghost Town: Hebron, documentary film, 2016.

102 Jewish Israelis consider the Temple Mount the site of the First Temple believed to have been built by King Solomon in 957 BC. The Western Wall of the temple still stands and is the site where Jews gather to pray. A Second Temple built in 516 BC was destroyed by the Romans. Orthodox Jews believe the Third Temple will be built on the same location when the Messiah returns. The Temple Mount is the holiest site in Judaism.

Muslims refer to this same site as the Noble Sanctuary, where both the Al-Aqsa Mosque and the Dome of the Rock are located. It is the third holiest site in Islam after Mecca and Medina. The site has been managed by the Jerusalem Islamic Waqf since the Crusades, which currently falls under the protection of the Hashemite Kingdom of Jordan. Visits and prayer by non-Muslims are highly regulated and sometimes banned to keep the peace at this highly contested space.

Chapter 32: Sham (شام)

103 The Peel Commission recommended granting Jews 40 percent of Palestine even though they only owned 5.5 percent of the land and included a provision for the forcible transfer of Palestinians—"Arabs"—from areas allotted to the Jewish state: "If Partition is to be effective in promoting a final settlement, it must mean more than drawing a frontier and establishing two States. Sooner or later, there should be a transfer of land and, as far as possible, an exchange of population...voluntar[il]y or otherwise." See League of Nations, "Report of the Palestine Royal Commission," July 1937, 389 & 392. The subsequent British White Paper of 1939 rescinded on its recommendation for two states, opting for a single independent state of Palestine for two peoples comprised of Jews, and Muslims and Christians. Zionist leaders, including Ben-Gurion, and thousands of American Jews gathered in New York in 1942 for the Biltmore Conference to formally reject this recommendation, demanding the fulfillment of a national home in Palestine according to the Balfour Declaration.

Chapter 33: Rachel Corrie

104 See Rachel's own words at Rachel Corrie Foundation, https://rachelcorriefoundation.org/rachel/emails.

105 At the publication of this memoir in 2023, it has been 20 years since Rachel Corrie's death.

Chapter 34: Opportunities

106 Over the years, Israel has issued work permits to Palestinians living in the West Bank or Gaza which allows Palestinians to enter Israel for employment, but they are not allowed to stay overnight, so Palestinians have to line up at checkpoints at 3:00 a.m. to be transported to that day's work opportunities, then return late into the night. Some stay overnight illegally to avoid this impossible work schedule. Though financially lucrative compared to most work opportunities in the West Bank and Gaza, such work is taxing on workers and their families, and work permits—which come at a hefty price—can be revoked at any time. See Marwah Jbara-Tibi, *Bread and Butter*, documentary film, 2021.

Chapter 35: The Wall

107 In the construction of the Separation Barrier, Israel has effectively annexed 13 villages in the northern region of the West Bank since they are located on the Israeli side of the Wall. Dozens of villages have lost access to village lands along the Wall's path, some as much as 50 percent, like the village of Sulfit. In some areas, the Wall either partially or completely surrounds Palestinian villages, whereby residents only have access to the rest of the West Bank via tunnels.

108 The Freedom Theater, https://thefreedomtheatre.org/who-we-are/.

109 The Wall ultimately surrounds Jerusalem, further restricting Palestinian access to surrounding villages, and leads to the construction of more Israeli settlements on Palestinian land. See Stop the Wall, https://www.stopthewall.org/the-wall/.

Chapter 36: Conference

110 بروح بدم نفديك يا فلسطين

Biruh, bidam, nifdiki, ya Falastin!

With our souls, with our blood, we will redeem you, Palestine!

Chapter 39: Trials and Tribulations

111 Christa Bruhn, The Power of the University: Palestinian Universities as Vehicles of Social and Political Change, Doctoral dissertation, Madison: University of Wisconsin, 2004.

112 Mother's Day in Palestine is on March 21.

113 In 2023, the Knesset subsequently passed an amendment to repeal part of the Disengagement Plan of 2005 that dismantled four Israeli settlements in the northern West Bank (Homesh, Sa-Nur, Ganim, and Kadim). See Hagar Shezaf and Jonathan Lis, "Explained: The Amended Law Allowing Israelis to Return to West Bank Sites Vacated During 2005 Disengagement," Haaretz, March 23, 2023, https://www.haaretz.com/israel-news/2023-03-23/ty-article/.premium/explained-the-new-law-allowing-israelis-to-return-to-evacuated-2005-settlements/00000187-08ff-d4dd-a1c7-2dff651c0000.

114 The last Israeli soldier left the Gaza Strip on September 12, 2005, my 38th birthday.

115 Jing Lin, Edward J. Brantmeier, and Christa Bruhn, eds., *Transforming Education for Peace: A Volume in Peace Education,* Charlotte, SC: Information Age Publishing, Inc, 2008.

116 Anna Baltzer, Witness in Palestine. Boulder: Paradigm Publishers, 2006.

117 Nasser Abufarha, *The Making of a Human Bomb: An Ethnography of Palestinian Resistance,* Chapel Hill: Duke University Press, 2009.

PART V: PERSISTENCE

Chapter 41: Sidi's Grave

118 The *hajj* is the fifth pillar of Islam where Muslims make a pilgrimage to Mecca at least once in their lifetime during 'Eid al-Adha if they are physically and financially able. Traveling to Mecca any other time of year is referred to as *omra.* The other pillars of Islam are *ash-shahadah*—declaring there is one God and Mohammed is his messenger, *as-salah*—praying five times a day, *al-zakat*—giving alms to the needy, and *as-sawm*—fasting from sunrise to sunset during the month of Ramadan.

119 The Kaaba is the large black stone cube in the center of the Great Mosque in Mecca all Muslims face when they pray, no matter where they are in the world, and which they will face when laid to rest.

120 For more information on Nihad Dukhan's artwork, see https://ndukhan.com/.

Chapter 42: Naqab

121 In 1948, Israel seized the entire Beersheba district through a number of legal ordinances left over from the Ottoman Empire, the British Mandate, and their own legal frameworks to declare the entire district "state land." During this military assault on their homeland, nearly 90 percent of Bedouins in the Naqab Desert fled, mostly to Jordan. Those who remained, like other Palestinians in Israel, were subject to military rule until 1966. After the founding of Israel, Bedouins of the Naqab were forced into a fenced-in area of 1,100 km^2 known as *siyaj,* which only constitutes about 10 percent of the area they used to inhabit.

As early as the 1960s, Israel sought to settle the Bedouins in order to create a pool of wage-laborers for the state. These development efforts were framed as a way to modernize the Bedouin communities, and yet such projects did not proceed on terms compatible with the communities who were supposed to "benefit" from them. Given the strong traditions of living off the land among the Bedouins, Israel could have fostered the establishment of agriculture-based communities like the Jewish moshavim and kibbutzim if the state were genuinely interested in meeting their needs but established suburban-style townships instead.

See Ismael Abu-Saad, "State-Directed 'Development' as a Tool for Dispossessing the Indigenous Palestinian Bedouin-Arabs in the Naqab" in M. Turner et al. eds., *Decolonizing Palestinian Political Economy: De-development and Beyond,* London: Palgrave Macmillan, 2014. Also see Ismael Abu-Saad, "The Unfinished Zionist

Settler-Colonial Conquest of its Elusive 'Last Frontier,' and Indigenous Palestinian Bedouin Arab Resistance" in Ahmad Sa'di and Nur Masalha eds., *Decolonizing the Study of Palestine: Indigenous Perspectives and Settler Colonialism after Elia Zureik*. London: I.B. Tauris-Bloomsbury Publishing, 2023; Ahmad Amara, Ismael Abu-Saad, and Oren Yiftachel, eds., *Indigenous (In)Justice: Human Rights Law and Bedouin Arabs in the Naqab/Negev*, Cambridge: Human Rights Program at Harvard Law School, 2012; Salman Abu Sitta, "Beer Sheba: The Forgotten Half of Palestine," Palestine Land Society, https://www.plands.org/en/articles-speeches/articles/2003/beer-sheba-the-forgotten-half-of-palestine.

122 Ismael Abu-Saad, "State-Directed 'Development' as a Tool for Dispossessing the Indigenous Palestinian Bedouin-Arabs in the Naqab."

123 Ismael Abu-Saad, "State-Directed 'Development' as a Tool for Dispossessing the Indigenous Palestinian Bedouin-Arabs in the Naqab."

124 The Bedouin community in the Naqab engages in several forms of resistance to Israeli policies of discrimination and dispossession. First and foremost is refusing to move to the planned towns so they can expand naturally with the population growth of their communities. This practice is comparable to the building of homes or additions on homes for Palestinians in cities, towns, and villages in 1948 Palestine for Palestinian citizens of Israel as well as Palestinian residents of East Jerusalem who have Israeli ID cards, and Palestinian residents of the West Bank, particularly those living in Area C, which Israel has mostly declared "state land." When Israel demolishes Palestinians' homes, people choose to rebuild both in defiance and out of necessity to accommodate their growing families.

For the Bedouins, resisting settlement in planned Israeli towns allows them to protect their agriculturally based way of life. Another form of resistance is through legal channels by challenging the outright discrimination due to the lack of services to Bedouin communities in education, healthcare, electricity, water, and trash removal. Other cases challenge the confiscation of Bedouin lands for nearby Jewish settlements in the Naqab, which are part of the larger effort to Judaize the Naqab. A third level of resistance among Bedouin communities in the Naqab include forming alliances with Jewish-Arab non-governmental organizations such as Forum Together for Equality and Growth for greater voice and representation in advocating for the needs of their communities. See Ismael Abu-Saad, "State-Directed 'Development' as a Tool for Dispossessing the Indigenous Palestinian Bedouin-Arabs in the Naqab," 152–154.

125 More recently, the State of Israel gave the green light to land-grab projects intended exclusively for the Jewish community, such as the Jewish National Fund's forestation plans in the area. See editorial, "Instead of Planting Trees, the Jewish National Fund's Negev Project Starts a Fire," *Haaretz,* January 13, 2022, https://www.haaretz.com/opinion/editorial/2022-01-13/ty-article-opinion/instead-of-planting-trees-the-jewish-national-funds-negev-project-starts-a-fire/0000017f-e812-df5f-a17f-fbdeee980000.

126 Ismael Abu-Saad and Cosette Creamer, "Socio-Political Upheaval and Current Conditions of the Naqab Bedouin Arabs," 50–52.

127 Such environmental protective measures are, in fact, greenwashing and only seek to hide past transgressions against Palestinians or seize more Palestinian land. See Ruqyah Sweidan, "Israel's Greenwashing Campaign," The Jerusalem Fund, November 1, 2021, https://thejerusalemfund.org/2021/11/israels-greenwashing-campaign/.

Chapter 43: Persistence of Palestine

128 The exhibit is comprised of posters created by the organization Keren Hayesod: United Israel Appeal to raise funds for the Zionist Movement following the Balfour Declaration in 1917. It still operates today. See https://www.kh-uia.org.il/.

129 *Canaan Impact Study 2005–2011, 2012,* https://blog.canaanpalestine.com/impact-study-2012/.

130 Ghassan Kanafani, "The Land of Sad Oranges" in *Men in the Sun and Other Palestinian Stories,* London: Lynne Rienner Publishers, 1999, 76.

PART VI: PATIENCE

Chapter 44: Longing for Palestine

131 *The People and the Olive: The Story of the Run Across Palestine* was produced by Stone Hut Studios and can be accessed at https://www.imdb.com/title/tt2330286/.

132 Ghassan Kanafani, "The Land of Sad Oranges," 80.

Chapter 45: Standing Rock

133 Turtle Island is a small island at Standing Rock, not to be confused with the various creation stories among the indigenous peoples of North America that refer to the entire continent as Turtle Island. The turtle in these traditions carries life on its back and thus symbolizes the sanctity of life, autonomy, and identity, and a deep respect for the Earth.

Chapter 46: Northern Ireland

134 Call for Peace, http://www.callforpeace.org/aboutcfp/admin.html.

135 Theodor Herzl, *Der Judenstaat: Versuch einer modernen Lösung der Judenfrage.* Leipzig & Vienna, M. Breitenstein Verlags-Buchhandlung, 1896.

136 A key strategy to solicit donations to the Jewish National Fund's efforts to acquire land in Palestine was the *Blue Box* campaign. Blue Boxes were present in virtually every Jewish home in the Diaspora until the establishment of the state of Israel in 1948 where Jews would contribute their spare change to what they believed was the noble mission of reclaiming the State of Israel. See Michal Weits, *Blue Box,* documentary film, 2021.

137 C.S. Lewis is best known for his children's book series, *The Chronicles of Narnia*, and was close friends with J.R.R. Tolkien, author of *The Lord of the Rings*, whom he met when they both served on the faculty at Oxford University. My father, incidentally, studied under Tolkien in the 1950s before coming to the US.

138 Although a total of 31 ships sailed to Gaza in defiance of the Israeli blockade against Gaza instituted in 2007, including one ship named after Rachel Corrie, only the first five voyages were successful in reaching Gaza. These voyages provided humanitarian relief as well as safe travel to Palestinians accepted to foreign universities or in need of medical treatment abroad. Following the 2014 siege on Gaza, subsequent voyages were intercepted by the Israeli Navy, outright attacked, or seized, whereby passengers were kidnapped, imprisoned, interrogated, deported, wounded, or even killed. One more voyage attempt was made in 2018. Following the COVID-19 pandemic, plans are underway to once again set sail in an effort to secure "full human rights for all Palestinians, and in particular, freedom of movement within historic Palestine and the right of return." See Freedom Flotilla, https://freedomflotilla.org/.

PART VII: RETURN

Chapter 47: March of Return

139 The Great March of Return in Gaza became a recurring event on Fridays to demand a lift of the siege on Gaza and the Right of Return for Palestinian refugees. Palestinian refugees and supporters in Jordan and Lebanon have also marched on occasion to the border fences in those areas. Similarly, internally displaced Palestinians—those living in Israel who carry Israeli citizenship—regularly visit their home villages destroyed by Jewish militias or the Israeli army in 1948–1949 or 1967 to draw attention to their Right of Return.

140 For an artistic representation of the March of Return, see the photographic collage by Palestinian artist Steve Sabella entitled The Great March of Return: https://stevesabella.space/pages/the-great-march-of-return. Steve Sabella was one of the few official photographers allowed into the Gaza Strip to document the March of Return in 2018.

Chapter 48: Return to Palestine

141 هذا المشمش مش من مشمشنا

Hath al-mishmish mish min mishmishna

These apricots are not from our apricots.

142 As of 2021, there were six million Palestinian refugees: 1.5 million in the Gaza Strip, nearly 900,000 in the West Bank, nearly 500,000 in Syria, nearly 900,000 in Lebanon, and 2.3 million in Jordan. These figures do not account for internally displaced Palestinians or other Palestinians living in exile. See United Nations Relief and Works Agency for Refugees in the Near East, Annual Operational Report 2021, https://www.unrwa.org/sites/default/files/content/resources/2021_aor_eng_-_sept_20-2022_1.pdf.

Chapter 49: Hidden Treasures

143 The village site of Al-Sakhina has become farmland for the nearby Israeli settlement of Nir David established in 1936. Two other nearby villages were destroyed the same day, the villages of Tall Al-Shawk and Khirbat Al-Jawfa.

144 Israeli forces destroyed the Palestinian village of Nuris on May 29, 1948, and the Palestinian village of Al-Mazal on May 30, 1948. See Benny Morris, *The Birth of the Palestinian Refugee Problem Revisited*, 346 and Walid Khalidi, *All That Remains*, 337–338.

145 For an example of how Israel systematically buried the remains of Palestinian villages beneath the forest, see Mark J. Kaplan, *The Village Under the Forest*, documentary film, 2013.

146 "Swedish Pro-Palestinian Activist Ladraa Barred from Entering Israel," *Middle East Monitor*, 2018, https://www.middleeastmonitor.com/20180706-swedish-pro-palestine-activist-ladraa-barred-from-entering-israel/.

Chapter 50: Return to Haifa and 'Akka

147 In response to an attack by the Arab Liberation Army on the kibbutz Mishmar HaEmek, Haganah militants, in collaboration with kibbutz leaders, occupied and destroyed the surrounding 10 Palestinian villages in the Battle of Mishmar HaEmek, including Abu Shousha on April 9, 1948, such that by April 15, all the villages in the area had been evacuated. These attacks marked the first time Palestinian villages were systematically occupied and destroyed by Haganah militants under Ben-Gurion's direction in order to cleanse the area of Palestinians between Jenin and Haifa. The British called for a ceasefire, but Ben-Gurion rejected it, insisting the destruction of the nearby villages was necessary to prevent any further attacks on the kibbutz. Most residents fled to Jenin, while those who remained were killed or taken hostage and expelled. See Benny Morris, *The Birth*

of the Palestinian Refugee Problem Revisited, 240–244; Illan Pappé, *The Ethnic Cleansing of Palestine,* 107–109; and Walid Khalidi, *All That Remains,* 142–143.

148 The three villages of Al-Ghubayya Al-Tahta, Al-Ghubayya Al-Fawka, and Naghnaghiya, known as Al-Ghubayyat, were destroyed by the Haganah on April 8 and 9, 1948. See Benny Morris, *The Birth of the Palestinian Refugee Problem Revisited,* 242; Illan Pappé, *The Ethnic Cleansing of Palestine,* 107; and Walid Khalidi, *All That Remains,* 159–161 and 179–180.

149 Mouli is a shortened version of the Arabic diminutive for Karmel: Karmouli.

150 Benny Morris, *The Birth of the Palestinian Refugee Problem Revisited,* 210.

151 For a brief but thorough discussion of restrictions on Palestinians in the Jordan Valley, see The Jordan Valley, B'Tselem, November 11, 2017, https://www.btselem.org/jordan_valley. For a more in-depth discussion, see B'Tselem Report, "Dispossession and Exploitation: Israel's Policy in the Jordan Valley and the Northern B'Tselem Report, "Dispossession and Exploitation: Israel's Policy in the Jordan Valley and the Northern Dead Sea," May 2011, https://www.btselem.org/sites/default/files/sites/default/files2/201105_dispossession_and_exploitation_eng.pdf.

152 After the 1948 war, the West Bank and Gaza constituted 22 percent of historic Palestine. Under current conditions, the nearly five million Palestinians in the West Bank were left with less than half the land there. In 2022, Israeli-controlled areas in the West Bank include over 200 settlements with a population nearing one million. Settlers enjoy full Israeli citizenship rights and privileges whereas less than a third of the nearly seven million Palestinians living between the river and the sea are citizens of the state that controls their lives. Even those with Israeli citizenship are subject to discrimination. Those without it live in a precarious status as refugees in the West Bank or Gaza, or under the quasi-state structure of the Palestinian Authority. That said, nearly half of Palestinians live in exile—the legacy of the Nakba—and remain subject to the State of Israel to determine access to their homeland.

Chapter 51: Last Generation

153 *Surah Al-Ikhlas*—The Opening Verse—in the Quran, My Islam, https://myislam.org/surah-fatiha/.

بِسۡمِ ٱللَّهِ ٱلرَّحۡمَٰنِ ٱلرَّحِيمِ
ٱلۡحَمۡدُ لِلَّهِ رَبِّ ٱلۡعَٰلَمِينَ
ٱلرَّحۡمَٰنِ ٱلرَّحِيمِ
مَٰلِكِ يَوۡمِ ٱلدِّينِ
إِيَّاكَ نَعۡبُدُ وَإِيَّاكَ نَسۡتَعِينُ
ٱهۡدِنَا ٱلصِّرَٰطَ ٱلۡمُسۡتَقِيمَ
صِرَٰطَ ٱلَّذِينَ أَنۡعَمۡتَ عَلَيۡهِمۡ
غَيۡرِ ٱلۡمَغۡضُوبِ عَلَيۡهِمۡ وَلَا ٱلضَّآلِّينَ

154 *Surah Al-Fatiha*—The Surah of the Opener—in the Quran (1), My Islam, https://myislam.org/surah-fatiha/.

بِسْمِ ٱللَّهِ ٱلرَّحْمَٰنِ ٱلرَّحِيمِ
قُلْ هُوَ ٱللَّهُ أَحَدٌ
ٱللَّهُ ٱلصَّمَدُ
لَمْ يَلِدْ وَلَمْ يُولَدْ
وَلَمْ يَكُن لَّهُۥ كُفُوًا أَحَدٌۢ

155 Even though the original Proclamation of the State of Israel in 1948 sought to "ensure complete equality of social and political rights to all its inhabitants irrespective of religion, race or sex," the Knesset adopted a new Basic Law: Israel: The Nation-State of the Jewish People on July 19, 2018, known as the Nation-State Law which defines Israel as the nation-state of the Jewish people with its Jewish symbols, anthem, and holidays and Hebrew as the only official language (previously Hebrew, Arabic, and English were recognized as official languages of Israel).

This law was proposed and passed in response to increased efforts to question the legitimacy of Israel as a Jewish state, including by some members of the Knesset, who proposed changing Israel to a state of its citizens, as well as by activists such as the Boycott, Divestment, Sanctions (BDS) movement, and more recently the human rights organizations Amnesty International, BADIL, B'Tselem, and Human Rights Watch, which compare Israel to the Apartheid regime in South Africa.

See Human Rights Watch, "A Threshold Crossed: Israeli Authorities and the Crimes of Apartheid and Persecution," April 27, 2021, https://www.hrw.org/report/2021/04/27/threshold-crossed/israeli-authorities-and-crimes-apartheid-and-persecution; B'Tselem, "A Regime of Jewish Supremacy from the Jordan River to the Mediterranean Sea: This Is Apartheid" January 12, 2021, https://www.btselem.org/publications/fulltext/202101_this_is_apartheid; Amnesty International, "Israel's Apartheid Against Palestinians, February 7, 2022, https://www.amnesty.org/en/latest/campaigns/2022/02/israels-system-of-apartheid/, and BADIL (Resource Center for Palestinian Residency and Refugee Rights), "Israeli Colonial-Apartheid Policies and Practices that Deny the Right of Self-Determination of the Palestinian People," BADIL's Submission to the UN Human Rights Council's Universal Periodic Review: 4th Cycle, October 2022, https://www.badil.org/cached_uploads/view/2022/10/11/badil-sub2hrc-upr-oct2022-1665491012.pdf. For a much earlier denotation of apartheid in Palestine and Israel, see Jimmy Carter, *Palestine: Peace Not Apartheid,* New York: Simon & Schuster, 2006.

That said, this shift in the Basic Law from its original emphasis on human dignity and liberty to the Jewish character of the state is regarded as a blow to Israel's non-Jewish citizens, particularly the Palestinians who essentially are made invisible in their own homeland, never to be considered equal under the law as citizens of the state.

Another document that may be relevant to these considerations includes the Declaration of Independence from 1948, which recognizes the right to self-determination for the Jewish people without recognizing an equal right to self-determination for the Palestinian people. This failure to recognize the legitimacy of Palestinians is hugely problematic given that the historic space of Palestine that has become Israel is the homeland of the Palestinian people. Moreover, as outlined in the B'Tselem and Human Rights Watch reports, Palestinians do not represent a minority population in the space Israel controls, but rather the Jewish and Palestinian populations are nearly equal in that space, with roughly 7 million Jews and 7 million Palestinians between the river and the sea and 14 million each worldwide.

In 2022, Israel amended the Family Reunification Law that prevents Palestinians who do not hold Israeli citizenship who marry Palestinians with Israeli citizenship from being granted residency in Israel, much less citizenship. This policy is said to prevent a 'creeping Palestinian return' as noted by then Interior Minister of Israel Ayelet Shaked. See "Family Unification Bill Meant to Stop Palestinian 'Creeping Right of Return,' Israel's Shaked Says," *Haaretz*, February 9, 2022, https://www.haaretz.com/israel-news/2022-02-09/ty-article/shaked-family-unification-bill-meant-to-stop-palestinian-creeping-right-of-return/0000017f-e4f1-df2c-a1ff-fef118710000.

On the flip side, this same concept has been applied to Israel's 'creeping annexation' of the rest of Palestine. See "Creeping Annexation: A Pillar of the Zionist-Israeli Colonization of Mandatory Palestine," BADIL, December 2020, https://badil.org/cached_uploads/view/2021/04/19/wp25-creepingannexation-1618823962.pdf.

Chapter 52: Time to Go

156 The literal translation from the Arabic رب أخ لم تلده أمك is "God (gives you) a brother not born by your mother."

Chapter 53: Living in Palestine

157 This map first appeared in: Jennifer Williams and Javier Zarracina, "The Growth of Israeli Settlements, Explained in 5 Charts," Vox, December 30, 2016, https://www.vox.com/world/2016/12/30/14088842/israeli-settlements-explained-in-5-charts.

158 Cecilie Rohwedder, "Deep in the Forest, Bambi Remains the Cold War's Last Prisoner," *The Wall Street Journal,* November 4, 2009, https://www.wsj.com/articles/SB125729481234926717.

159 Nikola Budanovic, "Are you lost deer? The deer that still won't cross the German border," *The Vintage News,* June 8, 2018, https://www.thevintagenews.com/2018/06/08/iron-curtain-fence/.

Chapter 54: New Year's in Aqaba

160 Before Israel declared statehood in 1948, Eilat was known as Um Rashrash and was the final area to fall under Israeli control in 1949 during the War of Independence.

Epilogue

161 Palestinians commemorate the Nakba on May 15 since Israeli statehood became official at midnight on May 14, 1948.

162 Salman Abu Sitta has devoted his life's work to documenting the feasibility of the return of Palestinian refugees to their lands and homes. See Palestine Land Society, https://www.plands.org/en/home.

About the Author

Christa Bruhn is an American author, photographer, and culinary artist with a lifelong passion for peace and justice. She is the daughter of a German immigrant raised under Nazi Germany who spent his post-war life befriending those his fatherland sought to destroy. Through her father's own curiosity to explore his divided homeland as a professor of German, Christa was able to spend time on both sides of the Iron Curtain to witness the dual narrative of one nation.

Growing up in the city of Detroit following the rebellion of 1967, which left the city in economic and social disparity, Christa witnessed the hypocrisy of the American national narrative for indigenous peoples and people of color in the *Land of the Free and the Home of the Brave*. Over her lifetime, Christa has witnessed hopeful change with the fall of the Berlin Wall, reconciliation in South Africa and Northern Ireland, and increased awareness and understanding of racial injustice and inequality in the US.

Christa's journey to Israel and Palestine at the height of the Cold War sparked her passion for making a difference in the lives of the Palestinian people fragmented across the globe due to the dispossession of their homeland through the Zionist movement's reconfiguration of Palestine into the State of Israel. As the mother of three Palestinian Americans, Christa's hope is that Jewish Israelis and Palestinians can create a common narrative that honors the tragedies and transgressions of their unique historical experiences so that both peoples can live a life of dignity in a place they call home.

Christa holds a bachelor's degree in International Studies from the University of Michigan–Dearborn, a master's degree from the Center for Middle Eastern & North African Studies at the University of Michigan–Ann Arbor, and a doctorate in Educational Leadership & Policy Analysis from the University of Wisconsin–Madison. She has studied Spanish, French, Russian, Hebrew, and Arabic. Christa has published academic work on Palestine, peace education, and diversity and led and participated in roundtables on the future of Israel and Palestine. She splits her time between her home in Madison, Wisconsin, and among her extended family in the farming village of Jalameh, Palestine.

See https://christabruhn.com/ for more information.

Also by Christa Bruhn

"Yalo." *Creative Wisconsin Anthology,* Wisconsin Writer's Association. October 2021.

"Encounter." *Write City Magazine*. September 27, 2015.

Canaan Fair Trade Impact Study: 2005-2011. Lead Investigator. Burqin, Palestine: Canaan Fair Trade, 2012.

Transforming Education for Peace: A Volume in Peace Education. Jing Lin, Edward J. Brantmeier, and Christa Bruhn, eds, Charlotte, SC: Information Age Publishing, Inc, 2008.

"Higher Education as Empowerment: The Case of Palestinian Universities." *American Behavioral Scientist 49, 8.* April 2006.

"Higher Education as Empowerment: The Case of Palestinian Universities," in *Education, Social Development, and Empowerment among Indigenous Peoples and Minorities: International Perspectives.* Conference Proceedings edited by D. Champagne and I. Abu-Saad. Beer-Sheva, Israel: The Negev Center for Regional Development, Ben-Gurion University of the Negev, 2005 (also available in Arabic).

The Power of the University: Palestinian Universities as Vehicles of Social and Political Change. Doctoral dissertation. Madison: University of Wisconsin, 2004.

"Beyond the Headlines: Building Bridges Through Education." Guest Columnist. *The Badger Herald.* March 6, 2003.

"Higher Education in Transition: Current Realities in Palestinian Universities," in Palestinian American Research Center (PARC) Newsletter. Spring 2001.

The Palestinian Dialect of Al-Jalama: A Phonemic Study. Master's thesis. Ann Arbor: University of Michigan, 1993.

Printed in the USA
CPSIA information can be obtained
at www.ICGtesting.com
BVHW032046280823
668952BV00003B/4